MW00720947

RESTAURANTS

Editor-in-Chief
Alain Gayot

Editor
Alexandra Greeley

Editorial Director
Mary Lu Abbott

Managing Editor
Lisa Messinger

Contributing Editors
Michael Birchenall, Louis Charles,
Judith H. Cleary, Leslie Cotterman,
Sylvie Greil, Thomas Head, Roland Leiser,
Dennis Schaefer, Susan Kovach Shuman,
Christi Solomon, Alexander Sreiem,
Marsha Weiner

e-Editor
Sophie Gayot

Directed by
André Gayot

www.gayot.com

digitalcity.com

GAYOT

The Best of Beverly Hills
The Best of Chicago
The Best of Florida
The Best of France
The Best of Germany
The Best of Hawaii
The Best of Hong Kong
The Best of Italy
The Best of Las Vegas
The Best of London
The Best of Los Angeles
The Best of New England
The Best of New Orleans
The Best of New York
The Best of Paris
Paris, Ile-de-France & The Loire Valley
Paris & Provence
The Best of San Francisco
The Best of Thailand
The Best of Toronto
The Best of Washington, DC
The Best Wineries of North America

Atlanta Restaurants
Miami Restaurants
San Francisco Restaurants
Los Angeles Restaurants
New York City Restaurants
Washington, DC Restaurants

Tastes Newsletter, The Food Paper

GAYOT.com

Published by GaultMillau, Inc.
5900 Wilshire Blvd.
Los Angeles, CA 90036

Please address all comments regarding
WASHINGTON, DC RESTAURANTS to:
GaultMillau, Inc.
P.O. Box 361144
Los Angeles, CA 90036
E-mail: gayots@aol.com

Production: Susan Cranston
Page Layout & Design: Enrique C. Guizar
Operations: Harriet Callier
Washington, DC, map: Scott Lockheed

ISSN 1526-6532
ISBN 1-881066-57-6
Printed in the United States of America

Contents

INTRODUCTION   4

MAP OF AREAS COVERED 4
THE FLAVOR AND THE POWER 5
ABOUT THE RESTAURANTS 7
USING OUR RATING SYSTEM 7
OUR PRICING SYSTEM 8
ADVICE & COMMENTS 9
SAMPLE REVIEW 11
RESTAURANT SYMBOLS 11
TOQUE TALLY
    TOP RESTAURANTS: FOOD RATING 12

WASHINGTON, DC   15

MAP 16
INTRODUCTION 18
RESTAURANTS 18
QUICK BITES 81
GOURMET SHOPS & MARKETS 95

VIRGINIA SUBURBS   105

INTRODUCTION 106
RESTAURANTS 106
QUICK BITES 162
GOURMET SHOPS & MARKETS 190

MARYLAND SUBURBS   203

INTRODUCTION 204
RESTAURANTS 204
QUICK BITES 235
GOURMET SHOPS & MARKETS 256

GLOSSARIES   265

WINE SAVVY 266
GUIDE TO REGION 266
WINE TOURING 266
VINTAGE WINE CHART 270
GLOSSARY OF TASTING TERMS 271
GLOSSARY OF GRAPES 272
FOOD & WINE PAIRINGS 277
FOOD & WINE EVENTS 281
WATER SAVVY 285

RESTAURANT INDEXES   289

RESTAURANTS BY AREAS 290
RESTAURANTS BY CUISINES 298
RESTAURANTS BY FEATURES 304

INDEX   309

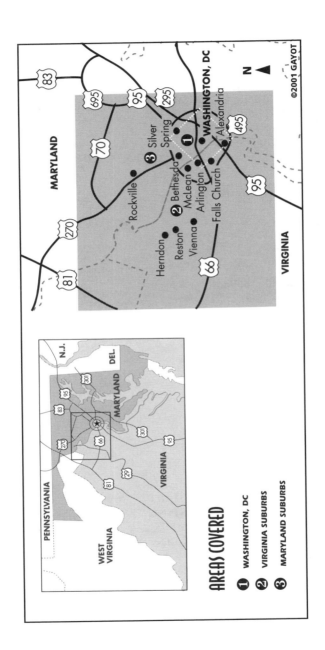

©2001 GAYOT

AREAS COVERED

1 WASHINGTON, DC

2 VIRGINIA SUBURBS

3 MARYLAND SUBURBS

THE FLAVOR AND THE POWER

No doubt, Washington, DC, has become a major restaurant scene. The capital and its surroundings today are home to top-flight restaurants, such as **Michel Richard Citronelle, 1789 Restaurant** and **The Inn at Little Washington**. Virtually every cuisine under the sun is represented here. Ethiopian, Lebanese, Burmese, Malaysian, Peruvian—name a place and you likely will find a restaurant serving dishes distinctive to that region. The mixture of embassies and consulates accounts for the wealth of ethnic eats in the area, and the capital's political and social prestige challenges chefs to excel. After all, this is both the nation's capital *and* a major tourist destination.

Chefs are responding to what customers want, and in today's market that seems to be flavor, flavor, flavor. Hence, we see the explosion of both Thai and Mediterranean restaurants since the foods from those parts of the globe are famous for assertive seasonings. Some of the trendiest places, such as Jeff Tunks' **TenPenh,** are serving fusion food, taking the best from different cuisines to create new taste sensations. We also see restaurants taking new pride in offering the best of traditional flavors undiluted by mass-market cooking. Consider the old-timer **Bangkok Garden** for decidedly flavor-packed Thai cooking.

Washingtonians also are looking for status and prestige, often rubbing elbows with Cabinet members, Senators and embassy staff at restaurants. Politicos are likely to be seen at upper-end restaurants such as the hot power spots, **West 24**, owned by headliners James Carville and Mary Matalin, and **The Caucus Room**, the venture of Haley Barbour and Tom Boggs.

In the suburbs, the dot.coms are reshaping social life. To the west of the District, the Dulles Corridor in Northern Virginia has become the Silicon Valley of the East Coast. With this influx of big business, name restaurants, such as the **Palm, The Capital Grille** and **eciti Café & Bar,** are heading to locations where the e-businesspeople can congregate over sandwiches, steaks, lobsters and pad Thai. Look for an expanded culinary scene where there's a building boom.

The capital and its environs are home to a broad spectrum of families, who enjoy the comfort foods from an earlier American era and dishes indigenous to all regions of America. Thus, you will see diners with home-style cooking at budget prices and cafés serving Cajun, Tex-Mex and Southern specialties.

Whether you're seeking an exceptional dining experience, a savory trip through the world's gastronomies or a plain family dinner with the kids, Washington, DC, has it for you. The following pages will help you make the best choice.

Bon Appétit,

André Gayot

WASHINGTON, DC
RESTAURANTS

RIGHTS

DISCLAIMER

We thank you for your interest in Gayot guides, and we welcome your remarks and recommendations about restaurants, shops, services, etc. Please direct your questions or comments to:

GaultMillau, Inc.
P.O. Box 361144
Los Angeles, CA 90036
E-mail: gayots@aol.com

ABOUT THE RESTAURANTS

Washington, DC, and the surrounding suburbs in Virginia and Maryland have literally thousands of places to dine, from elegant temples of fine cuisine to small stands where you can grab a quick bite and save a buck. Our team of professional restaurant critics has canvassed restaurants all over the area.

We have taken care to present a wide range of dining options from special places for memorable evenings to family-friendly cafés that don't dent the wallet. Throughout our listings, you will find big-name restaurants with star-studded clientele and plenty of spots that are hip, hot or just plain fun neighborhood hangouts.

Restaurant Updates

For the latest on restaurants in the Washington, DC, area: On the Internet, visit gayot.com/restaurants/washingtondc.html for the *Restaurant News* and digitalcity.com/washington/dining, where you will find our current *10 Hot Spots* and *reviews* for hundreds of restaurants.

Using Our Rating System

What decides the rating of a restaurant? What is on the plate is by far the most important factor. The quality of produce is among the most telling signs of a restaurant's culinary status. It requires a great deal of commitment and money to stock the finest grades and cuts of meat and the finest quality of fish. Ask any sushi chef if there's a difference in tuna, and with the flash of his knife he will tell you there certainly is. One extra-virgin olive oil is not the same as another. Ditto for chocolates, pastas, spices and one thousand other ingredients. Quality restaurants also attune themselves to seasonal produce, whether it is local berries or truffles from France. Freshness is all-important, too, and a telling indication of quality. This means not only using fresh rather than frozen fish, for example, but also preparing everything from scratch at the last possible moment, from appetizers through desserts.

What else do we look for in rating restaurants? Details are telling: If sauces are homogeneous, you know that the kitchen is taking shortcuts. The bread on the table is always a tip-off; similarly, the house wine can speak volumes about the culinary attitude and level of an establishment. Wine complements food, and wine lists and offerings can be revelatory. A list doesn't have to be long or expensive to show a commitment to quality.

Finally, among the very finest restaurants, creativity and innovation are often determining factors. These qualities, however, are relatively unimportant for simple, good restaurants, where the quality and consistency of what appears on the plates is the central factor. A restaurant that serves grilled chicken well is to be admired more than a restaurant that attempts some failed marriage of chicken and exotic produce, or some complicated chicken preparation that requires a larger and more talented kitchen brigade than is on hand. Don't be taken in by attempted fireworks that are really feeble sideshows.

Our rating system works as follows, with the highest possible score being twenty, based on the system of grading students in France.

The rankings reflect only our opinion of the food. The décor, service, ambience and wine list are commented upon within each review.

Restaurants that are ranked 13/20 and above are distinguished with toques (chef's hats) according to the table below. Renowned for worldwide guidebooks, Gayot ranks restaurants in major destinations, including Paris, London and New York. Thus, in our rankings here we are comparing the restaurants in this book to others in major cities. Also, our rankings are relative. A 13/20 (one toque) may not be a superlative ranking for a highly acclaimed (and very expensive) restaurant, but it is quite complimentary for a small place without much culinary pretension.

Note: When a restaurant is undergoing changes, we may give *No Rating*. Also, we rank only those places in the Restaurants chapters, not the choices in Quick Bites.

Exceptional *(4 Toques)* (rating of 19/20)	♟♟♟♟
Excellent *(3 Toques)* (ratings of 17/20 & 18/20)	♟♟♟
Very good *(2 Toques)* (ratings of 15/20 & 16/20)	♟♟
Good *(1 Toque)* (ratings of 13/20 & 14/20)	♟

Quick Bites

Sometimes you're not in the mood for a "dining experience." You want quick bites, and that's the title we've given our selection of the best fun food, such as a particularly good taco stand, a great burger joint or a cozy breakfast spot. You'll also find most of our Quick Bites are economical, with meals usually priced under $20 a person—and often much less.

Our Pricing System

In our reviews, we code restaurant prices using one to five dollar signs. Prices reflect the average cost of dinner for one person including appetizer, entrée, dessert, coffee, tax and tip. We've not included wine or other beverages, which vary greatly in price. Those who like to eat lightly, sharing appetizers and desserts, will spend less. Though the popularity of reasonably priced restaurants has forced many eateries to try to keep prices down, not all succeed. Forgive us if a restaurant has become more expensive by the time you visit it.

$	= under $20
$$	= under $35
$$$	= under $50
$$$$	= under $75
$$$$$	= $75 and up

Advice & Comments

Cuisine: Before Nouvelle Cuisine was introduced in the United States in the '70s, followed by California cuisine in the '80s and New American, Fusion, Pan-Asian, Mediterranean and Pacific Rim cuisine in the '90s, it was easy to classify restaurants by their cuisine—there was American, French, Italian, Continental, Chinese, Japanese, Greek etc., period. Today, the lines between the cuisines have blurred. New American and even Fusion have evolved into what is now called Contemporary. Furthermore, chefs create their own style of cooking, which might combine elements of some or all of the above.

We find it difficult to put a label on the type of cuisine a restaurant serves, yet we must for the sake of indexing—and so that readers will have a sense of what they'll be served when they dine there. In most cases, we have labeled a restaurant's cuisine according to what its owners and chefs call it. But that does not always make things easier. For we've found that though one restaurant may describe its cuisine as American, another as Contemporary and another as Eclectic, the dishes are quite similar—innovative takes on new and old themes, concocted of fresh regional ingredients and using a combination of elements from various ethnic cooking styles.

In the long run, who cares what a restaurant's cuisine is called? After all, it's not what type of cuisine you're eating that's important—it's how it tastes. And we hope it tastes great!

Dress code: Dressing up is relative in Washington. Generally, if you're off to one of the city's better restaurants, business suits for men and chic pants outfits are suitable for women. For the best restaurants, women don't have to dress up further, but will fit right in if they do. At some locations, say in Chinatown, Cleveland Park or Chevy Chase, dressy attire isn't usually the norm, but feel free to get spiffed up to some degree—sweats and T-shirts generally won't do. In the Virginia and Maryland suburbs, follow the same advice for top restaurants. Things get much more casual, though, at family-style eateries.

Menus: Most restaurants change their menus regularly, sometimes as often as daily, sometimes seasonally. In our reviews, we've identified both the dishes we enjoyed and others we found lacking. We can't, however, guarantee you'll find the same exact dishes when you go, given the constant menu restructuring.

Chefs: When you make reservations in a place with a famous chef, check to be sure he or she will be there, not traveling across the country demonstrating his or her skills. Also, all chefs have good days and bad, so don't be too put off if your experience is less stellar than was ours; with luck it will be better.

Parking: In Washington, do as most do—take the Metro or a cab to and from your destination. If you are driving, many restaurants offer valet service and in the evenings, street parking is much more readily available. In the Virginia suburbs, most restaurants offer ample free street parking, or at least, are situated with public lots nearby. In the Maryland suburbs, many restaurants offer ample free parking in adjacent lots.

Smoking (or not): Laws governing smoking in restaurants vary in the metro area. In general there's designated seating for smoking and nonsmoking, and you're given a choice upon entering.

Outdoor dining: It seems as though more and more restaurants of all stripes in Washington and the Virginia suburbs are setting up outdoor cafés or opening gardens out back. Given the climate, however, access is limited, usually from late May to September. For some reason, al fresco dining isn't very popular in the Maryland suburbs.

Tipping: Only a small number of restaurants handle tipping European-style by adding 15 percent directly on your bill. Aside from those few, a gratuity is automatically added only for large groups. Otherwise, keep in mind that tipping 15 percent of your pretax bill (including drinks) is customary. The quickest way to figure your tip is to double the tax. If you're with a large party, or you feel the service was above and beyond the call of duty, you may wish to leave 20 percent.

THE TOQUE, CIRCA 1700

Have you ever wondered about the origin of that towering, billowy (and slightly ridiculous) white hat worn by chefs all over the world? Chefs have played an important role in society since the fifth century B.C., but the hats didn't begin to appear in kitchens until around the eighteenth century A.D. The toque is said to be of Greek origin; many famous Greek cooks, to escape persecution, sought refuge in monasteries and continued to practice their art. The chefs donned the tall hats traditionally worn by Orthodox priests, but to distinguish themselves from their fellows, they wore white hats instead of black. The custom eventually was adopted by chefs from Paris to Peking.

Sample Review

The following key explains the information provided in our reviews.

LOCATION:
STREET ADDRESS, (CROSS STREET)
AREA OF TOWN, CITY

CUISINE TYPE
FOOD RATING
TOQUE AWARD

ESTABLISHMENT NAME

Michel Richard Citronelle   French   **19/20**

The Latham Hotel
3000 M St. NW (30th St. NW), Georgetown, Washington 20007
202-625-2150, Fax 202-339-6326
Breakfast, Lunch & Dinner daily, $$$$, Casual dressy

It's Washington's gain that chef Michel Richard has made Citronelle—and we are weighing our words carefully—one of the best restaurants in America. We are more than happy to herald this news, which is already well-known by DC hedonists who may prefer to keep it to themselves. Michel Richard Citronelle is not only a restaurant but also a theater. From the multitiered room, animated by a changing "mood wall," it's worthwhile watching the show that unravels on the brightly lit "stage"—an exhibition kitchen sparkling with immaculate glass, steel and copper props. The ebullient Richard orchestrates a symphony of fragrances and with steady gestures directs a seasoned cast, adding his own touch of genius: perhaps a pinch of spice, a dot of sauce, in a...

REVIEW

RESTAURANT FEATURES (SEE SYMBOLS BELOW)
PHONE & FAX NUMBERS, DAYS OPEN
PRICE CATEGORY & DRESS CODE

RESTAURANT SYMBOLS

A	Major credit cards taken	♥	Heart-healthy dishes
☎	Reservations suggested	👫	Kid-Friendly
🚗	Valet parking	🦉	Serves past midnight
P	Parking	🎷	Entertainment
🏃	Romantic setting	▼	Full bar
🍽	Outdoor dining	🍾	Great wine list
📷	View	🚃	Private room(s)

TOQUE TALLY
TOP RESTAURANTS: FOOD RATING

19/20 ♕♕♕♕

The Inn at Little Washington (VA)
Michel Richard Citronelle (DC)

17/20 ♕♕♕

Galileo (DC)

16/20 ♕♕

Gérard's Place (DC)
Makoto Restaurant (DC)
Marcel's (DC)
1789 Restaurant (DC)
Timothy Dean Restaurant & Bar (DC)
Yanÿu (DC)

15/20 ♕♕

Asia Nora (DC)	Kinkead's (DC)
Blackie's (DC)	La Colline (DC)
The Caucus Room (DC)	Nora (DC)
Chez Marc (VA)	Obelisk (DC)
Equinox (DC)	Palena (DC)
Gabriel (DC)	Sushi-Ko (DC)
Heritage India (DC)	TenPenh (DC)

14/20 ♕

Addie's (MD)	Bombay Bistro (MD)
Aranella Grill (DC)	Bombay Club (DC)
Ardeo (DC)	Bombay Tandoor (VA)
Bangkok Garden (MD)	Butterfield 9 (DC)
Big Bowl (VA)	Café Atlántico (DC)
Bistro 123 (VA)	Cashion's Eat Place (DC)
Bistrot Lepic (DC)	Cesco Trattoria (MD)
Black's Bar	Corduroy (DC)
& Kitchen (MD)	DC Coast (DC)
Black Coffee Bistro (VA)	eciti Café & Bar (VA)
Bombay Bistro (VA)	Entotto (DC)

Etrusco Trattoria (DC)
Hermitage Inn (VA)
I Ricchi (DC)
The Inn at
  Brookeville Farms (MD)
The Islander Caribbean
  Restaurant & Bar (DC)
Jaleo (DC)
Kaz Sushi Bistro (DC)
La Bergerie (VA)
La Côte d'Or Café (VA)
La Provence (VA)
Lafayette (DC)
Lansdowne Grille (VA)
L'Auberge
  Chez François (VA)
Le Jardin (DC)
Le Relais Restaurant
  & Bar à Vin (VA)
Lightfoot (VA)
Maestro (VA)
Matisse Café
  Restaurant (DC)
Melrose (DC)
Morton's
  of Chicago (DC, VA)
New Heights (DC)
Neyla (DC)
The Oceanaire
  Seafood Room (DC)
Old Angler's Inn (MD)

Osteria Goldoni (DC)
Persimmon, An
  American Bistro (MD)
Pesce (DC)
Primi Piatti
  Ristorante (DC, VA)
Red Sage (DC)
Red Tomato (DC)
Ristorante Geranio (VA)
Ristorante Il Borgo (VA)
Ruan Thai (MD)
Rupperts (DC)
Ruth's Chris Steak
  House (DC, VA, MD)
Saveur Restaurant (DC)
Sea Catch Restaurant
  & Raw Bar (DC)
Seasons (DC)
701 Pennsylvania Avenue
  Restaurant & Bar (DC)
Smith & Wollensky (DC)
Tabard Inn (DC)
Taberna del
  Alabardero (DC)
Tachibana (VA)
Teatro Goldoni (DC)
Thai Basil (VA)
Vidalia (DC)
The Vigorelli (DC)
West 24 (DC)

13/20 ♙

A Taste of Casablanca (VA)
Aditi (DC)
Al Tiramisu (DC)
Andalucia (MD)
Argia's (VA)
Austin Grill (DC, VA, MD)
B. Smith's (DC)
Bacchus (DC, MD)
Bamboo Joint Café (DC)
Bambulé (DC)
Bamyan Restaurant (VA)
Barolo Ristorante (DC)
Basil Thai Restaurant (DC)
The Bistro (DC)
Bistro Bis (DC)
Bistro Français (DC)
Bistrot du Coin (DC)
Blue Iguana (VA)
Blue Point Grill (VA)
Bobby Van's
  Steakhouse (DC)

Bombay Palace (DC)
Brasserie Les Halles (DC)
Cactus Cantina (DC)
Café Deluxe (DC, MD)
Café on M (DC)
Café Milano (DC)
Café Ole (DC)
Café Roval (MD)
Café Taj (VA)
The Capital
  Grille (DC, VA)
Carlyle Grand Café (VA)
Caspian Café (MD)
Centro Italian Grill (MD)
CF Folks (DC)
The Cheesecake
  Factory (DC, MD)
Christopher Marks (DC)
Clyde's of Chevy Chase (MD)
Clyde's of Georgetown (DC)
Clyde's of Tysons (VA)

Crisfield Seafood
Restaurant (MD)
Cuban Corner (MD)
Duangrat's (VA)
Elysium (VA)
Fairmont Bar
& Dining (MD)
FlatTop Grill (VA)
Flavors Soul Food (VA)
Fortune of Seven
Corners (VA)
Georgia Brown's (DC)
Grapeseed (MD)
Green Papaya (MD)
Hollywood East Café (MD)
Hope Key (VA)
Hunan Chinatown (DC)
I Matti (DC)
Inn at Glen Echo (MD)
Iron Gate Inn
Restaurant (DC)
J. Gilbert's Wood-Fired
Steaks (VA)
Japan Inn Restaurant (DC)
Jasmine Café (VA)
Johnny's Half Shell (DC)
La Chaumière (DC)
Lauriol Plaza (DC)
Lavandou Restaurant (DC)
Le Gaulois (VA)
Legal Sea Foods (DC, VA)
McCormick
& Schmick's (DC, VA)
Maggiano's Little Italy (VA)
Mandalay Restaurant
& Café (MD)
The Mark (DC)
Market Street
Bar & Grill (VA)
Marrakesh (DC)
Matuba (VA, MD)
Mes Amis Restaurant (DC)
Mezza 9 (VA)
Mike's American Grill (VA)
Mr. K's (DC)
Morrison-Clark
Restaurant (DC)
Mrs. Simpson's (DC)
Myanmar Restaurant (VA)
Nam's of Bethesda (MD)
Nick & Stef's
Steakhouse (DC)
The NM Café at
Neiman Marcus (VA)

Old Ebbitt Grill (DC)
Olives (DC)
The Oriental Regency (VA)
The Oval Room (DC)
Palm (DC, VA)
Palomino (DC)
Pasha Café (VA)
Peacock Café (DC)
Peking Gourmet Inn (VA)
Perry's (DC)
Petits Plats (DC)
Planet Wayside (VA)
The Prime Rib (DC)
Pulcinella Ristorante (VA)
Rhodeside Grill (VA)
Rio Grande
Café (VA, MD)
Sabang (MD)
Saint Basil Brick
Oven Grill (VA)
Sam & Harry's (DC, VA)
Sam Woo (MD)
Santa Fe East (VA)
Sen5es Bakery
& Restaurant (DC)
Sesto Senso (DC)
Shula's Steak House (DC)
South Austin Grill (VA)
South Beach Café (MD)
Spices (DC)
Suporn's Thai
Restaurant (MD)
Sweet Basil (MD)
Tahoga (DC)
Tako Grill (MD)
Tara Thai (VA, MD)
Tel-Aviv Café (MD)
Thai Square
Restaurant (VA)
Thanh Thanh (MD)
Tiffin, The Indian
Kitchen (MD)
Timpano Italian
Chophouse (MD)
Turning Point Inn (MD)
Tuscarora Mill (VA)
Two Quail (DC)
Udupi Palace (MD)
Wurzburg Haus
Restaurant (MD)
Zuki Moon (DC)

WASHINGTON, DC

MAP	**16**
INTRODUCTION	**18**
RESTAURANTS	**18**
QUICK BITES	**81**
AMERICAN	81
BAKERIES/CAFÉS	84
BARBECUE	86
CAFÉS & COFFEE SHOPS	87
COFFEEHOUSES & TEAROOMS	88
DELIS & BAGEL SHOPS	89
ETHNIC FLAIR	90
(Chinese, Indian, Japanese, Mexican,	
Middle Eastern, Pan-Asian, Salvadoran)	
PIZZA	93
GOURMET SHOPS & MARKETS	**95**
BAKERIES	95
CANDY & CHOCOLATES	95
CHEESE	96
COFFEE & TEA	96
ETHNIC MARKETS	97
(African/Middle Eastern, Asian, German,	
Italian, Latin American)	
FARMERS MARKETS	98
FISH, MEAT & POULTRY	99
GOURMET MARKETS & GOURMET TO-GO	99
WINE & SPIRITS	102

WASHINGTON, DC

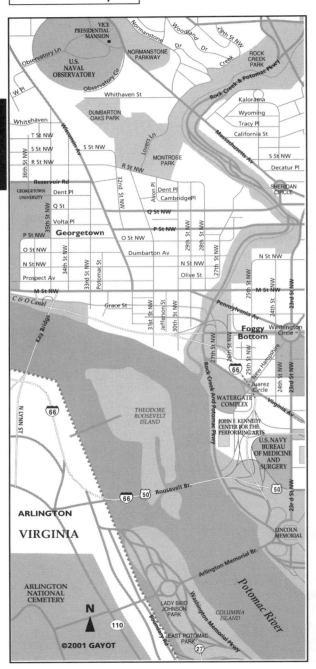

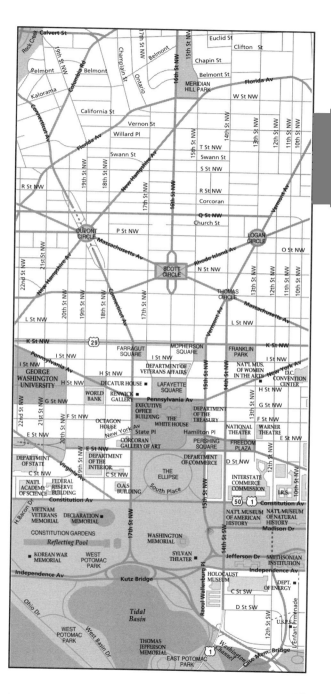

INTRODUCTION

The city bustles with hungry residents and commuters who haunt its neighborhoods and byways for every kind of cooking style and setting, from upscale to family-style restaurants. The nation's capital is also a capital destination for gourmets: Some of the best steaks, lobsters, noodles, ribs and burgers emerge from the kitchens in **Georgetown, Cleveland Park, Downtown, Adams Morgan, Chinatown** and along the **U Street corridor.** Name virtually any area of the city and you'll find terrific food.

RESTAURANTS

Aditi   Indian   13/20

3299 M St. NW (33rd St. NW), Georgetown, Washington 20007
202-625-6825, *Lunch & Dinner daily, $$, Casual*

One of the most popular Indian restaurants in DC, this modest little spot has the same limited menu as most local Indian restaurants, but the cooking is consistently good. The Indian feast is a real bargain, but if your appetite is smaller, you may order à la carte and still enjoy the moist tandoori chicken, the complexly spiced curries, the beautifully cooked pilafs and the superb breads. We like the vinegar-zested lamb vindaloo, too. Its sister restaurant—Aarathi in Vienna, VA—enjoys almost the same popularity.

Al Tiramisu   Italian   13/20

2014 P St. NW (20th St. NW), Dupont Circle, Washington 20036
202-467-4466, Fax 202-467-4468
Lunch Mon.-Fri., Dinner nightly, $$$, Casual dressy

Chef Luigi Diotaiuti exudes personality and charm, as well he might. He presides over an immensely hip restaurant that serves stylized Italian food. Start off with the grilled portobello mushrooms with goat cheese, and, at dinner, skip right on to the duck breast, rare tuna or beef tenderloin. You'll find inspired pasta dishes, and some of the pasta is made fresh on the premises. Although the kitchen offers other choices, such as gelato and crème caramel, the obvious dessert here is tiramisu. It's a cozy and neighborly restaurant with a mock fireplace, wine racks built into the walls and sun-bright colors. If you celebrity watch, you might catch sight of such locally based stars as Placido Domingo.

Anatolia Turkish Café   Turkish   12/20

633 Pennsylvania Ave. SE (Sixth St. SE), Capitol Hill, Washington 20003
202-544-4753, Fax 202-544-4753, *Lunch & Dinner Mon.-Sat., $, Casual*

One of Capitol Hill's answers to exotic cooking, Anatolia attracts eager lunchtime crowds from nearby government offices to its dark and mysterious interior, accented with just enough Turkish tidbits for authenticity. Anatolia offers a good introduction to Turkish cuisine, turning out simple and uncomplicated dishes with subdued flavors. Start with the lah-macun, a Turkish-style pizza of finely ground lamb and savory seasonings sprinkled on oil-brushed pita. Move on to kebabs (lamb, chicken, beef or combinations) or a house special, such as the izgara kofte, a platter of ground lamb patties as small as eggs and as familiar as hamburgers. Sleepy? Small cups of intense Turkish coffee will jolt you awake. Conclude with Turkish flan or baklava.

Aranella Grill   Italian/Grill   14/20

3421 Connecticut Ave. NW
(Ordway St. NW), Cleveland Park, Washington 20008
202-244-7155, Fax 202-244-9304, *Dinner nightly, $$, Casual*

Chef Elizabeth Bright-Mattia, owner of The Vigorelli (see review in this chapter), has expanded—upstairs. Her all-grill outdoor restaurant brings guests some rather luscious and rus-tic Italian cooking hot off the fire. At first, the rooftop setting was open to the elements, including wind, rain, and shine—and anything flying by. By weatherproofing the place, though, Bright has assured that people can sit and eat in comfort in even the most inclement weather. The menu undergoes some seasonal changes, but keep an eye out for the smashing grilled corn brightened with drizzles of lemon juice and the sausage wrapped in dough and then grilled. Main-course recommenda-tions include the Piedmontese rib-eye or the mixed grill. For a finish, pamper your sweet tooth with the special Salame di Cioccolato (chocolate "salami" surrounded by a mound of whipped cream).

Ardeo   Contemporary   14/20

3311 Connecticut Ave. NW
(Macomb St. NW), Cleveland Park, Washington 20008
202-244-6750, Fax 202-244-8960, *Dinner nightly, Brunch Sun., $$, Casual*

Local restaurant mogul Ashok Bajaj, who brought Washingtonians the Bombay Club and The Oval Room (see reviews in this chapter), opened this comfortable and stylish Cleveland Park spot. It quickly became a hangout for the many media types who live in the area, as well as thirtysomethings who trek across town to eat in funky style. The cooking is con-temporary and generally well conceived and executed, using such fashionable ingredients as baby greens, diver scallops (individually selected and scooped up by divers) and portobello mushrooms, which end up in such dishes as a spinach salad with strawberries and Stilton cheese dressed with a red onion mixture. Follow up your salad with pan-roasted red grouper or veal scaloppini with buttermilk mashed potatoes. Desserts tend to be homey and American, and you may delight in an apple-pecan crunch with rum sauce and vanilla ice cream. The short wine list is well priced.

Asia Nora   Pan-Asian   15/20

2213 M St. NW (22nd St. NW), West End, Washington 20037
202-797-4860, Fax 202-797-1300, *Dinner Mon.-Sat., $$$, Casual*

Chef Nora Pouillon takes us into uncharted culinary territo-ry with her serenely beautiful Asian restaurant, decorated in Thai colors and accented with Asian artifacts. The restaurant features interpretive Asian cooking—you'll find a smattering of flavors from most of Asia—using all-organic ingredients. Of course, the menu undergoes seasonal variations. After a bumpy beginning, Pouillon and her staff have hit their stride, and you can count on enjoying her many creative dishes, from dumplings rich with gingery flavors to tuna tartare. Other dishes worth savoring are the Thai seafood stew and the sesame-crusted ahi with a wasabi potato purée. If available, select the jasmine tea and cardamom crème brûlée for dessert, although anything you pick will be unusual. If you blanch at the final bill, keep in mind that you're paying for high-quality (all organic) ingredients and recipes from one of America's outstanding chefs. Pouillon's Nora restaurant in Dupont Circle became the nation's first certified all-organic restaurant (see review in this chapter).

Austin Grill   Tex-Mex   13/20

750 E St. NW (Seventh St. NW), Downtown, Washington 20004
202-393-3776, Fax 202-393-3005
Lunch & Dinner daily, Brunch Sat.-Sun., $$, Casual

Texans know a thing or two about good chili, and chefs at the Austin Grill have learned the secrets. Their bowls of simmered, shredded beef with ground chiles (anchos and chipotles) are just short of heavenly. It's a rugged dish, with enough fire-breathing potential to stand your hair on end. Fortunately, it comes with four small, warm flour tortillas you can dunk or use for wrapping. The tortillas help tame the flames. Terrific chili is only one of many delights on this funky restaurant's menu: fajitas, enchiladas, burritos, carnitas and quesadillas are all good choices. Check the menu's new seasonal specialties section, too, where you might find lamb chops with pineapple-chipotle glaze. If you need to quench your thirst with all this hot, spicy food, select a cooling tequila drink—there are several interesting margaritas like the signature lime-strawberry one—or a chilled brew. **Other locations.**

B. Smith's   Southern/Soul Food   13/20

50 Massachusetts Ave. NE
(N. Capitol St. NE), Capitol Hill, Washington 20002
202-289-6188, Fax 202-289-6199
Lunch & Dinner daily, Brunch Sat.-Sun., $$, Casual

If you haven't stopped in for a splendid Southern meal at this colossal Union Station eatery, you've missed one of Capitol Hill's major power-lunch scenes. At other times, expect to rub shoulders with suburbanites, tourists or city folk enjoying a rollicking time. Start big with jambalaya, deep-fried catfish sticks or the Southern classic, fried green tomatoes. For more of the South, tackle a catfish sandwich, a shrimp po' boy or even the Tennessee-style ribs. Size is a big feature here. Slightly smaller dishes include a hearty seafood gumbo or the "Swamp Thing," a dish of mixed seafood over Southern-style greens. End with a huge portion of strawberry shortcake that even two people can't finish. This is the same Ms. B. Smith from TV, books and the Web who offers advice on everything from gardening and home decorating to cooking. She also owns several restaurants in New York.

Bacchus   Lebanese   **13/20**

1827 Jefferson Pl. NW
(Connecticut Ave. NW), Dupont Circle, Washington 20036
202-785-0734, *Lunch Mon.-Fri., Dinner Mon.-Sat., $$, Casual*

Whether you dine in this original comfortable little dining room near Dupont Circle or under the tented ceiling of the two-tiered pavilion at the Bethesda branch, you're in for the best Lebanese cuisine in town. The menu is long, and it's best to come with a group and share. Start with baba ghanouj or hummus, or make an entire meal of mezze, a selection of Middle Eastern appetizers that might include stuffed grape leaves, pickled turnips, stuffed baby eggplant with pomegranate sauce, and miniature fried meat turnovers. Main course recommendations include kebabs, stuffed cabbage with pomegranate sauce or pilafs topped with slices of lamb or chicken. **Also located at** 7945 Norfolk Ave., Bethesda, MD, 301-657-1722.

Bamboo Joint Café   Jamaican   **13/20**

2062 Rhode Island Ave. NE (South Dakota Ave. NE), Washington 20018
202-526-7410, Fax 202-526-7548, *Lunch & Dinner daily, $, Casual*

"What kind of Chinese food do you serve?" The manager laughed at our question and replied, "Chinese food? This is a Jamaican restaurant." And so it is, a real sit-down place with table service and a menu that features such Jamaican favorites as escoveitched chicken, jerk chicken (of course), coco bread, peppered shrimp and a sensational goat curry, rich with turmeric and meat juices. Served with rice and peas, plus a side of fried plantains, the curry is dreamy, the sort of dish you could eat several times a week—and we'd bet a number of repeat guests do. No desserts were available on our visit, so we may never know what Jamaican black cake is. Resounding to the sounds of Jamaican music and the cheery patois of islanders, Bamboo Joint Café may become the restaurant hit of the budget-minded.

Bambulé   Mediterranean   **13/20**

5225 Wisconsin Ave. NW
(Jenifer St. NW), Friendship Heights, Washington 20015
202-966-0300, Fax 202-966-9020
Lunch & Dinner daily, Brunch Sun., $$, Casual dressy

Pegging itself as a Mediterranean-style (both French and Italian) restaurant, this uptown eatery is a small, tony place in Chevy Chase with handsome dining rooms, a stylish bar and a front terrace that exudes charm. With enough wrought iron and hanging greenery to evoke sunnier climes, it aims toward sophisticated diners who appreciate dishes like sautéed shrimp and scallops over black linguine. You may find such starters as the tempting grilled portobello mushroom packed with tiny shrimp and melting Fontina cheese. Equally commendable is the salade Niçoise, a warm-weather must when garden-fresh vegetables are best. Heartier dishes include sautéed chicken breast or veal scaloppine in a lemon-butter sauce, plus a range of pasta, seafood and steak offerings.

Bangkok One   Thai   11/20

1411 K St. NW (14th St. NW), Downtown, Washington 20005
202-393-6277, Fax 202-393-6271, *Lunch & Dinner daily, $$, Casual*

This downtown eatery has the same sleek look as the trendier Thai places around and offers much the same fare: In other words, no surprises here. Small and compact, Bangkok One does well at lunchtime, but due to its location where there are fancy trendsetters as neighbors, it faces stiff competition. Will the menu woo patrons with such standard dishes as pad Thai, vegetable- and chili-garnished drunken noodles and a very sweet panang chicken? Time will tell if this place can meet and beat the competition. To get repeat customers, the owners might be well advised to lengthen the menu and whip up more traditional Thai dishes to pique appetites and curiosity.

Barolo Ristorante   Italian   13/20

223 Pennsylvania Ave. SE
(Second St. SE), Capitol Hill, Washington 20003
202-547-5011, Fax 202-547-4390
Lunch Mon.-Fri, Dinner Mon.-Sat., $$$, Business casual

Under the very talented eye of chef/owner Enzo Fargione, lush Italian meals unfold in this small upstairs restaurant. Close to Capitol Hill, it has become a favorite of politicos, and it's not unlikely that you'll spot the Secret Service scoping out the place. Partners with DC superchef Roberto Donna, Fargione puts a twist on authentic Piedmontese dishes. Although the menu changes daily to keep up with market freshness, you may find such delicacies as these triumphs: roasted artichoke hearts with basil sauce or arugula and radicchio salad dressed with goat cheese. Entrées include a stunning pappardelle pasta with Gorgonzola cheese sauce or grilled rack of veal with port wine. Ask about desserts—such as a strudel, Piedmontese style or a raspberry panna cotta—and splurge, if you still have room.

Basil Thai Restaurant   Thai   13/20

1608 Wisconsin Ave. NW
(Q St. NW), Georgetown, Washington 20007
202-944-8660, Fax 202-944-8665
Lunch Mon.-Sat., Dinner nightly, $, Casual

This compact, bright-colored Thai restaurant attracts a young crowd, who love the hard-edged colors and for-sale artwork decorating the walls. They also come for the Thai cooking, although it doesn't fully explore the great cuisine. Still, what comes from the kitchen is sound and true to its origins. On the menu, the management marks the hot dishes with a bomb. Start with tod mun (fishcakes) marked with a bomb, but they're really not that hot. Other good dishes: kanom jeeb (steamed dumplings with a smashing tamarind dipping sauce); crispy tofu (hard to go wrong here); red duck curry; and drunken noodles. If you drop in for lunch, you'll find several specials that include crispy won ton or fried bean curd with pad Thai, a curry or a stir-fry entrée.

The Bistro — American — 13/20

The Monarch Hotel
2401 M St. NW (24th St. NW), West End, Washington 20037
202-457-5020, Fax 202-457-5010
Breakfast, Lunch & Dinner daily, $$$, Casual

Located in The Monarch Hotel, this casual eatery makes a perfect destination for business lunches or after-work meals when you don't want to get dressed up but want somewhat dressy food. Chef Alex Velasquez has devised a dinner menu that includes such starters as a casual black bean soup or something more upscale, such as seared diver scallops (selected and scooped up by divers) with an herb crust. Dinner entrées mean seared peppered rare ahi and grilled marinated boneless rib-eye lamb. At lunchtime, look for fancy sandwiches, such as a Maryland crab cake on brioche or a juicy grilled hamburger with fries and your choice of cheese. As you might expect from such a menu, desserts are imaginative and caloric.

Bistro Bis — French — 13/20

Hotel George
15 E St. NW (N. Capitol St. NW), Capitol Hill, Washington 20001
202-661-2700, Fax 202-661-2747
Breakfast, Lunch & Dinner daily, $$$, Business casual

A stylish French bistro with an American accent, Bis is the second restaurant of chef Jeffrey Buben, who also owns the Southern-inspired Vidalia (see review in this chapter). Set in the Hotel George on Capitol Hill, the three-level space features a zinc bar, a dining area with spacious leather booths and a glass-enclosed kitchen. Updated bistro classics, like a first-course ragoût of snails with artichokes and potatoes, coexist comfortably with such contemporary standards as grilled swordfish and tuna. The seared sea scallops Provençale, served in a sauce of garlic, tomato and olives and accompanied by a timbale of roasted eggplant, is a winner. We find that the food is best when Buben himself is in the kitchen, so if you care more about the cuisine than being seen, call ahead to ask if he is scheduled to be cooking when you plan to dine.

Bistro Français — French — 13/20

3124 M St. NW (Wisconsin Ave.), Georgetown, Washington 20007
202-338-3830, Fax 202-338-1421
Lunch & Dinner daily, Brunch Sat.-Sun., $$$, Casual

Around midnight, when most restaurants have closed, this very French Georgetown institution is likely to be full of chefs eating a midnight dinner of steak frites or rotisserie chicken. In fact, if you pop in around then, there's a good chance you'll spot celebrity chef Michel Richard, whose own highly rated Michel Richard Citronelle is nearby. Settle into one of the two dining rooms: pressed-tin ceilings and plenty of etched glass set against dark wood and further enhanced by French posters from the '30s. Choose from a set menu that offers all the bistro standards, from onion soup to a salad garnished with a warm confit of duck gizzards. Daily specials might include roasted duck leg confit with garlic potatoes, roast pork with a potato gratin, pot-au-feu or Moroccan-style couscous.

Bistro Med — Mediterranean — 11/20

3288 M St. NW (33rd St. NW), Georgetown, Washington 20007
202-333-2333, Fax 202-337-3569
Breakfast Thurs.-Sun., Lunch & Dinner daily, Brunch Sat.-Sun., $$, Casual

🅰 ☎ 🅿 🐱 😺 ⚗ 🍸 🍴 ⟳

No predicting the crowds here: You may eat in solitary splendor at lunch or find it crowded during typical off-hours. It's possible that Bistro Med is still finding its footing in the DC market, offering as it does yet another take on the Turkish-Greek-Mediterranean foods that have hit the metro area with such force over the past few years. Consider starting with the favorite, Imam Bayildi, a roasted eggplant dish that could use some flavor boosting here, and continue on to one of the numerous kebabs of lamb, beef, chicken or combinations thereof. Because the prices are reasonable, you can eat generously, even greedily, especially if you want to combine sandwiches, salads and Turkish-style pizzas at one sitting. Service may be slow.

Bistrot du Coin — French — 13/20 👨‍🍳

1738 Connecticut Ave. NW
(Florida Ave. NW), Dupont Circle, Washington 20009
202-234-6969, Fax 202-234-6965
Lunch Tues.-Sat., Dinner nightly, $$, Casual

🅰 ☎ 🐱 😺 ⚗ 🍸 🍴 ⟳

Come at night, says the voice on the phone. "It's really buzzy then, like, jammed and boisterous." We liked the daytime—midafternoon was crowded and buzzy enough. At other times, you'd best make reservations so you can rub elbows with the In Crowd; otherwise, you may have to wait. Start with the flavorful onion soup, which comes with plenty of melted cheese. Want something light? How about a tartine, which here is a slice of focaccialike bread with assorted toppings, such as vegetables or ham and cheese. Or go whole hog with the grilled steak (at lunch this becomes a steak sandwich), sliced duck breast or rabbit stew. It's all very French and very fun. Desserts include a custard tart, an apple tart and a crème brûlée. The acoustics aren't terrific, but you'll probably be having so much fun you won't care.

Bistrot Lepic — French — 14/20 👨‍🍳

1736 Wisconsin Ave. NW (S St. NW), Georgetown, Washington 20007
202-333-0111, Fax 202-333-2209, *Lunch & Dinner Tues.-Sun., $$$, Casual*

🅰 ☎ 🍸 🍴 ⟳

This cheerful French restaurant has won the hearts of those lucky enough to live in the neighborhood. If you want to make sure that you can occupy one of the 40-odd seats, it's best to call in advance, for the place fills up fast with faithful regulars. Chef-owner Bruno Fortin has constructed a menu that is short, direct and depends on seasonal fruits and vegetables. He prepares such interesting basics as onion tart or trout salad to start and follows with salmon in a potato crust and sautéed sea scallops. At lunchtime, we've thoroughly enjoyed the spring garden salad with grilled shrimp.

We're always interested to hear about **your discoveries and to receive your comments on ours.** Please let us know what you liked or disliked; e-mail us at gayots@aol.com.

Blackie's   American   15/20

1217 22nd St. NW
(M St., NW), West End, Washington 20037
202-333-1100, Fax 202-331-7850, *Dinner nightly, $$$, Business casual*

Shedding its burly red-meat image and part of its name, Blackie's (formerly Blackie's House of Beef) has landed squarely in the 21st century adding an improved interior, French executive chef Claude Rodier, upscale steak-and-more menu and seamless service. New image or not, four beef dishes still lead off the menu, from prime rib of beef to a butter-tender 18-ounce porterhouse steak. But Rodier also tempts patrons with such dishes as a rotisserie-roasted duck, gleaming with its lemon-ginger glaze and its delicately darkened skin, a bacon-wrapped pork medallion, sautéed scallops with lobster ravioli, and, another of our favorites, crab cakes fashioned from lump crab meat. Almost a cliché in this town, crab cakes can vary in appeal, but these, though small, are superior: quick seared and no bread crumbs. The result? Pure, tender, sweet crab meat, enhanced by grilled vegetables and a dollop of a rich lime-ginger cream sauce. As for desserts, consider one of the two soufflés. We are also partial to the chocolate and pineapple cheesecake which has pineapple bits layering the crust and a slick of chocolate on top.

Bobby Van's Steakhouse   Steakhouse   13/20

809 15th St. NW (H St. NW), Downtown, Washington 20005
202-589-0060, Fax 202-589-0062
Lunch Mon.-Fri., Dinner nightly, Brunch Sat.-Sun., $$$$, Casual

DC welcomes yet another steakhouse, this time starring local chef Will Biscoe, formerly of Indigo in Great Falls, VA. Filet, porterhouse, sirloin and rib-eye—plus selected seafood (Maine lobster, scallops, pepper shrimp and crab cakes)—are the stars here. If you drop by for lunch, try the Caesar salad with filet strips, although the huge hamburger nestled among fries and onion curls is also a draw. The restaurant's interior suggests a men's club, with dark leather upholstery. Check the daily specials before ordering—the clam chowder is a big success—and save room for the house-clams desserts, including a terrific chocolate truffle cake.

Bombay Club   Indian   14/20

815 Connecticut Ave. NW (I St. NW), Downtown, Washington 20006
202-659-3727, Fax 202-659-5012
Lunch Mon.-Fri., Dinner Mon.-Sun., Brunch Sun., $$$, Jackets suggested

One of the prettiest and most comfortable restaurants in Washington, the cool and chic Bombay Club, with its potted palms, rattan furniture, deeply cushioned chairs, ceiling fans and luxurious decorative details, re-creates the atmosphere of the British raj. So does the solicitous service. Not surprisingly, this has been one of the favorites of residents of the White House, just across Lafayette Square. You may come for the atmosphere, but the food will delight you, too: tandoori seafood is a specialty, and salmon and scallops emerge from the white-hot heat of the tandoor nicely crusted and with a moist interior. Other recommended dishes are lamb curry with apricots and fried fish with poppy seeds. Bombay Club is the product of local restaurant mogul Ashok Bajaj, who also brought Washingtonians Ardeo and the Oval Room (see reviews in this chapter).

Bombay Palace   Indian   **13/20**

2020 K St. NW (20th St. NW), Downtown, Washington 20006
202-331-4200, Fax 202-331-1505, *Lunch & Dinner daily, $$$, Casual dressy*

One of the grande dames of local Indian luxury restaurants, the Bombay Palace sets a standard that others have imitated but few have surpassed. The attentive service will make you feel like a maharajah, yet the prices are reasonable. Expect consistently good versions of all the Indian standards. The spicy lamb vindaloo has an outstanding depth of flavor under the heat. Chicken, first cooked in the tandoor, is then finished in a butter-enriched tomato sauce. Don't miss the breads, one of the glories of Indian cookery, which are done exceptionally well here.

Brasserie Les Halles   French   **13/20**

1201 Pennsylvania Ave. NW
(12th St. NW), Downtown, Washington 20004
202-347-6848, Fax 202-347-6911
Lunch & Dinner daily, $$, Casual dressy

The Washington branch of this French steakhouse and brasserie, which also has locations in New York, Miami and Tokyo, is lively and lots of fun. On warm days, the umbrella-shaded tables make the large front terrace a prime location. In inclement weather, we like the comfort of the turn-of-the-century Paris brasserie setting with its pressed-tin ceiling and mismatched lighting fixtures. Les Halles is the kind of place where you soon discover things you like so much that you never order anything else, such as the hanger steak served with the best pommes frites in town or the homemade shredded pork confit. If you want a real dinner bargain, the steak frites-salade platter is excellent. Desserts include splendid gâteau Basque and crêpes Suzettes.

Bua Thai   Thai   **11/20**

1635 P St. NW (17th St. NW), Dupont Circle, Washington 20009
202-265-0828, Fax 202-387-5820, *Lunch & Dinner daily, $$, Casual*

Bua Thai is one of the original "trendy Thai" restaurants in Washington. With its stark brick walls, the décor is unconventional and the cooking inventive. Pad woon sen is an interesting spin on the traditional pad Thai noodles, and the coco bouillabaisse is a Thai-influenced takeoff on the French seafood soup. The papaya salad and sautéed squid are favorites. If you can overlook some flavor hits and misses, you can relax and join in with the hip young crowd that frequents this restaurant. The wooden deck overlooking P St. is a popular spot in good weather.

Chefs are creative people. Therefore, of course, menus are subject to change. The dishes we describe should give you a good idea of the chef's range and style.

Burma Restaurant   Burmese   12/20

740 Sixth St. NW (H St. NW), Chinatown, Washington 20001
202-638-1280, *Lunch Mon.-Fri., Dinner nightly, $, Casual*

A ☎ **P** 🏠 ⟡

Up a flight of stairs in a weathered Chinatown building, Burma Restaurant is a rarity. Now that the nearby MCI Center is open, both tourists and conventioneers flock here, and the once-quiet restaurant is abuzz with patrons crowding in to sample one of Asia's least-known cuisines. For authentic flavors, start with gold fingers—batter-dipped and deep-fried pieces of squash. For a main course, try ohno kauswe, a coconut-milk-based sauce poured over egg noodles, or mohingar, the Burmese breakfast of fish soup. (Both are virtually the national dishes.) Add to this the typical Burmese snack: green tea leaf salad with garlic, sesame seeds and dried shrimp. Not every flavor or dish hits the mark, but you'll find enough from this exotic country to celebrate this no-frill restaurant's economical cuisine.

Busara   Thai   12/20

2340 Wisconsin Ave. NW
(Calvert St. NW), Georgetown, Washington 20007
202-337-2340, Fax 202-333-1364, *Lunch & Dinner daily, $$, Casual*

A ☎ 🍽 🍴 🍷 ⟡

With a menu geared to corral a devoted Western following, Busara welcomes all to a modern setting outfitted with Thai trappings. It's contemporary food and that means some of the dishes don't sound particularly Thai, especially the lamb curry and the starter soup called Bangkok bouillabaisse. Otherwise, look for the ubiquitous pad Thai, soft-shell crabs and honey roast duck. Diners have made Busara a hit that has warranted expansion from DC to Tysons Corner. Mealtimes may be busy, but you won't feel pressured to eat fast and clear out. **Also located at** 8148 Watson St., McLean, VA, 703-356-2288

Butterfield 9   American   14/20

Garfinkle's, 600 14th St. NW
(F St. NW), Downtown, Washington 20005
202-BU9-8810, Fax 202-BU9-6602
Lunch Mon.-Fri., Dinner nightly, $$$, Business casual

A ☎ **P** 🔔 🍷 ▲ ⟡

Butterfield 9 (the name was inspired by a New York City telephone exchange in a *Thin Man* movie) is a shining example of how owner, chef and designer have pooled their talents for one hot retro-cool place. It's in subtle shades of palest salmon and cozy gray and, amidst its minimalist décor, features almost-large-as-life black-and-white photographs of chic models. The setting aside, what counts here is executive chef Martin Saylor's menu, an amalgam of retro and ultramodern. Saylor plays culinary games to match the seasons, changing the menu frequently. Among our favorite appetizers are his generous crab cake with warmed garlic butter and crispy squid with chorizo. Entrées are either classic—roasted rack of lamb—or modern—stuffed trout with crab mousse or braised short ribs of bison. Lunches offer the same level of culinary diversion. Rita Garruba's desserts take the traditional track, such as a baked Alaska (for two) and a warm chocolate soufflé.

Cactus Cantina   Tex-Mex   13/20

3300 Wisconsin Ave. NW (Macomb St. NW)
Cleveland Park, Washington 20016
202-686-7222, Fax 202-362-5649
Lunch & Dinner daily, $$, Casual

Cactus Cantina is a colorful and always-crowded spot to take the family for lusty Tex-Mex in Cleveland Park. Tortillas are made in an elaborate glassed-in machine that may interest the kids while they're waiting for a table. Once seated, don't limit yourself to the combination platters. Some of the best offerings come from the mesquite grill—barbecued quail, grilled shrimp, crusty spareribs and the inevitable fajitas. Start your meal with a tamale, soft and flavorful inside its cornhusk wrapping and stuffed with smoky shreds of pork. Portions are generous: Expect enough food for a doggie bag. The margaritas here, made from a mix, are a disappointment. Have Mexican beer instead.

Café Asia   Pan-Asian   12/20

1134 19th St. NW (M St. NW), Downtown, Washington 20036
202-659-2696, Fax 202-659-2984
Lunch Mon.-Sat., Dinner nightly, $$, Casual

Easily one of the most popular downtown lunchtime and after-work destinations for casual eats, this Pan-Asian place has it all: great sushi, sparkling stir-fries, searing noodle dishes and soups and terrific curries, all executed and delivered with finesse. The food is so good and the prices so reasonable that you probably will return often to eat your way across Asia. We love the ultra-fresh sushi. Five sushi chefs may be wielding knives at any given time. The blistering-hot Malaysian curry laksa is also a standout. Nothing disappoints here, which is why you'll be lucky to find a seat in the downstairs dining area, at the sushi bar or upstairs in the loft. **Also located at** 1550 Wilson Blvd., Arlington, VA, 703-741-0870

Café Atlántico   Latin American/Contemporary   14/20

405 Eighth St. NW (D St. NW), Downtown, Washington 20004
202-393-0812, Fax 202-393-0555
Lunch Mon.-Sat., Dinner nightly, Brunch Sat., $$$, Casual dressy

The Nuevo Latino cooking of chef Christy Velie has made this dramatic three-level restaurant, installed in a former power plant, a destination for those who want to eat as well as those who want to be seen. The two bars are known for colorful, powerful Latin American cocktails. Start with a caipirinha (made with a Brazilian sugar cane liquor), a mojito (a mint-and lime-flavored rum drink) or a pisco sour (immature Peruvian grape brandy and bitters, frosted with a spoonful of beaten egg white). The cuisine features updated versions of Latin American classics, such as bean stew, ceviche, guacamole, a pork chop stuffed with dried apricots and bacon, duck leg confit and a terrific chocolate-banana bread pudding with ice cream. For the ultimate in self-indulgence, don't miss the Saturday brunch (called a Latino dim sum), a nonstop eating fest. It includes small portions of menu items selected by the chef and comes in several courses; you get to select more helpings of your favorites at the end of the meal.

Café Citron   Latin American/Caribbean   11/20

1343 Connecticut Ave. NW (N St. NW)
Dupont Circle, Washington 20036
202-530-8844, Fax 202-530-8846
Brunch, Lunch & Dinner daily, $, Casual

In Dupont Circle territory, this Latino bistro looks as beck-oning as a strawberry margarita, but its kitchen falters. The menu is ambitious enough, but its narrow spectrum focuses on an assortment of dishes that sound suspiciously like Tex-Mex cooking, with one or two Caribbean things thrown in for fun. We lunched on the daylong brunch menu offering of huevos rancheros, and the salsa poured over the eggs tasted more like canned than homemade. The Peruvian chupe de camarones, a thin broth with bits of seafood and vegetables thrown in for good measure, was fine. Escabeche de Pescado had a vinegar sauce that was too strong. We ended with a sautéed banana in a pool of a disappointing caramel/orange sauce.

Café Deluxe   American   13/20

3228 Wisconsin Ave. NW (Macomb St. NW)
Cleveland Park, Washington 20016
202-686-2233, Fax 202-686-1901, *Lunch & Dinner daily, $$$, Casual*

There are not a lot of places to eat in the restaurant-poor area around the National Cathedral, so Café Deluxe has been a hit from the day it opened. Its classy Art-Deco atmosphere and down-home American cooking seem to be exactly to the taste of the boomer generation, whose members often wait an hour for one of chef Ian Crandall's applewood-smoked pork chops with mashed potatoes or grilled meatloaf with Creole sauce. **Also located at** 4910 Elm St., Bethesda, MD, 301-656-3131.

Café La Ruche   French   11/20

1039 31st St. NW (M St. NW), Georgetown, Washington 20007
202-965-2684, Fax 202-337-8852
Lunch & Dinner daily, Brunch Sat.-Sun., $$, Casual

This French-inspired old favorite in Georgetown may still be a local tradition, but it's starting to feel timeworn, and the menu needs some revivifying. It offers a mix of soups, entrée salads, sandwiches and light and regular entrées such as paella and beef bourguignon with pasta (which doesn't seem particu-larly French). Considering the French background music, we opted for a classic meal, starting with potato leek soup (too thin) and onion soup (too little flavor), then moved on to the house special, the croque monsieur. Ideally, this sandwich should be crispy yet "eggy," flavorful yet subtle. It was neither. The high point of the meal was the crème caramel, as rich and firm as made in any haute kitchen in the city.

Going to Hawaii, Chicago, San Francisco, Las Vegas, Los Angeles or London? Look for Gayot's "The Best of" guidebooks to destinations worldwide. Also for hotel and travel information from our books and the latest updates, visit us on the Internet at gayot.com.

Café on M — Contemporary — 13/20

The Westin Grand, Washington
2350 M St. NW (24th St. NW), West End, Washington 20037
202-955-4488, Fax 202-429-9759
Breakfast, Lunch & Dinner daily, $$$, Casual

Blink your eyes twice and you may think you've landed at an intimate New York nightclub, with a chummy bar, Art-Deco light fixtures and subdued music. All that's missing is a live piano and the fox trot. Sounds dated, but, in fact, the menu is anything but stodgy. The Chesapeake crab soup (light, without cream) is a mildly peppery broth loaded with shreds of crab meat. The rack of lamb, generously portioned and wisely seasoned, is outstanding: It's got a crisp exterior, rare interior and is bathed in a mustardy-garlicky sauce. We were also delighted with the treatment of the pan-seared sea bass nestled in scoops of a delicate bouillabaisse sauce. Worthy desserts include chocolate mousse and lemon tart. This is one terrific hotel coffee shop.

Café Midi Cuisine — French/Mediterranean — 12/20

1635 Connecticut Ave. NW (S. St. NW)
Dupont Circle, Washington 20009
202-234-3090, Fax 202-234-8972
Breakfast, Lunch & Dinner daily, $, Casual

A neighborhood place serving the Dupont Circle area, this casual eatery stars a selection of dishes with French, Spanish and Mediterranean influences: Vegetable rösti, croque monsieur and chilled Andalusian gazpacho are just a smattering of what you'll find. There is also straightforward American fare such as roasted chicken, barbecued pork ribs and smoked turkey sandwiches. And the vegetarian is not forgotten since vegan dishes, pastas and all-vegetable entrées amplify this otherwise meaty menu. If you want to start your day here, you'll find a Provençal breakfast with eggs, bacon, croissant and potato rösti; muffins; croissants; and scrambled eggs with a refreshing lemon accent.

Café Milano — Italian — 13/20

3251 Prospect St. NW (Wisconsin Ave. NW)
Georgetown, Washington 20007
202-333-6183, Fax 202-333-6594
Lunch & Dinner daily, $$$$, Casual dressy

We rather fancy the couturier-inspired interior of this Georgetown Italian restaurant, its walls decorated with framed ties and scarves from Milan's top designers. Georgetown café society seems to like it, too, for they've made this a favorite gathering place. The fact that it's open until 1 a.m. Thursdays through Saturdays—late for DC—is a plus. There's usually a wait for a table, but the food is generally worth it, and you can order either a pasta and a glass of wine or a four-course meal. We've enjoyed the enormous veal chop, delicate angel hair with basil and tomatoes, the fettuccine Bolognese, various risotti and grilled fish.

Café Ole
Mediterranean/Tapas   **13/20**

4000 Wisconsin Ave. NW (Upton St. NW)
Cleveland Park, Washington 20016
202-244-1330, Fax 202-244-0330
Lunch & Dinner daily, Brunch Sun., $$, Casual

Many folks in the neighborhood declare that this is their
very favorite restaurant, a *Cheers* kind of place with a decidedly
Mediterranean flair. Count us among the fans of the Ole and
other fare. We've lounged here after the movies (a theater is
around the corner) and dipped into the Ole's bread basket of
pita chips, focaccia and lavash. Since tapas portions are small,
you probably will move quickly on to heftier fare. We've loved
the Moroccan lamb stew, but wished for more substantial por-
tions, and doted on a wonderful combination of grilled
Merguez sausage, mashed potatoes and tomatoes. And we've
thoroughly enjoyed the Lebanese Celebration (marinated and
grilled chicken with bulgur). Problem is, you end up ordering
many little plates and paying one big bill. What may also be on
that bill: wine. There are lots of good ones by the glass.

Café Soleil
French/Mediterranean   **12/20**

839 17th St. NW (I St. NW), Downtown, Washington 20006
202-974-4260, Fax 202-463-6262
Lunch & Dinner Mon.-Sat., $$$, Casual dressy

Café Soleil looks as if it wants to mimic a Parisian bistro
upgraded to a small chic brasserie. The ambience works with
the shining tableware on a pristine white cloth contrasting with
a well-polished dark wood bar, Art-Deco mirror and pseudo
Toulouse Lautrec Moulin Rouge frescos. In this French environment, Café Soleil cannot decently escape the French
bistro's usual fare, such as escargots, onion soup, vichyssoise,
tournedos and bavette—all authentic and worthy of trying. But
the restaurant has other ambitions such as offering a choice of
eclectic tapas like hummus and smoked salmon. Italian? That's
here, too, with a risotto navigateur, grilled veal scaloppine and
a choice of pasta dishes. You might stay on neutral ground with
a breast of chicken or a tuna au poivre (au poivre is so much
more chic than pepper-crusted), guaranteed by the menu to
be seared to perfection, although that does not always seem to
be the case.

The Capital Grille
Steakhouse   **13/20**

601 Pennsylvania Ave. NW (Sixth St. NW)
Downtown, Washington 20004
202-737-6200, Fax 202-637-8821
Lunch Mon.-Fri., Dinner nightly, $$$$, Business casual

Shortly after opening, this clubby steakhouse on the Capitol
end of Pennsylvania Avenue established itself as the power
restaurant of choice for congressional Republicans. The menu
at this upscale national chain is much like that of any other
such steakhouse—massive cuts of aged beef, giant lobsters, cottage fries and creamed spinach. We must admit, though, that
we haven't found the beef (which is displayed in the windowed
walk-in refrigerator near the entrance) to be up to the quality
of that at such other power steakhouses as Morton's and

Ruth's Chris. The wine list has a good selection of French and California bottles. **Also located at** 1861 International Dr., McLean, VA 703-448-3900

Caravan Grill   Persian   **12/20**

1825 18th St. NW (S St. NW), Adams Morgan, Washington 20009
202-518-0444, *Lunch & Dinner daily, $, Casual*

Situated along the trendy 18th Street restaurant strip, this Persian eatery has a loyal following, especially among older folks and the Persian community. There's good reason for that—the food is glorious. Chef Esmail Dehi watches proudly as people feast at his lunch or dinner buffet. It's easy to overeat here. Who can pass up seconds on the chicken or the succulent lamb shanks? Don't ignore the full menu, though, especially the assorted kebab choices. The cubed chicken is delicious and authentically seasoned, as are the ground-meat kebabs. The atmosphere has Middle Eastern charm and the staff is attentive.

Cashion's Eat Place   Contemporary   **14/20**

1819 Columbia Rd. NW (18th St. NW)
Adams Morgan, Washington 20009
202-797-1819, Fax 202-797-0048
Dinner Tues.-Sun., Brunch Sun., $$, Casual

It's Sunday morning, and it looks as though everyone in Washington has turned up for brunch at Cashion's. It's usually a hip and friendly crowd sharing boisterous laughter, although solo patrons also seem to feel at ease as they enjoy their morning paper and coffee. The small dining room and bar fill up fast except in warm weather, when large French doors are thrown open to the fenced-in front patio. The Sunday attraction is chef Ann Cashion's robust brunch menu, featuring the usual eggs and omelets, plus the less usual croque monsieur sandwich, grilled rainbow trout and a grilled pork chop with grits. At dinner, the menu offers truly trendy dishes: roasted quail stuffed with fennel and pine nuts or buffalo hanger steak with Yukon gold mashed potatoes. The menu changes daily, so don't fall too much in love with the spit-roasted leg of lamb—it might not be there next time. Cool jazz, great food and a neighborhood atmosphere make Cashion's a must.

The Caucus Room   American   **15/20**

401 Ninth St. NW (D St. NW), Downtown, Washington 20004
202-393-1300, Fax 202-393-6066
Lunch Mon.-Fri., Dinner Mon.-Sat., $$$, Business casual

Billing itself as a nonpartisan restaurant—two of the principals are Democrat Tom Boggs and former RNC chairman Haley Barbour—The Caucus Room proves yet again that Washington can accommodate another high-brow destination for the kind of folks whose faces turn up regularly on C-SPAN and the nightly news. It's like an old-time Washington restaurant: dark woods and dark leather-covered banquettes provide a suitable backdrop for the kind of menu where even the simplest sandwich—we liked the blackened grouper on brioche with a peppery coating on the fish—will set you back a fair amount of change. Portions are generous, though. The seafood timbale with lobster and lump crab meat and Maryland crab cakes are good starters. The Caesar salad is ambitious with loads of cheese and buttered toast for croutons. Entrées include herb-crusted Chilean sea bass, filet mignon medallions, Dover sole, Kansas City strip steak on the bone, lobster and coq au vin. Desserts are standard: chocolate cake, ice cream and bread pudding. If you like rubbing elbows with power brokers, this is a must restaurant.

CF Folks   American   13/20

1225 19th St. NW (Jefferson St. NW), Downtown, Washington 20036
202-293-0182, Fax 202-457-9078, *Lunch Mon.-Fri., $, Casual*
No credit cards.

Why wait in line for one of the few barstools or tables that are premium commodities at this lunch spot? The food is reasonably priced, which for downtown DC is remarkable. The jocular bantering of the staff puts a light-hearted spin on things. The food is both wholesome and delicious, and even slightly quirky, as in such specials as catfish with Cajun rémoulade or acorn squash stuffed with shrimp and béchamel. Specials change daily, but you can always count on good sandwiches such as a Reuben with pastrami rather than corned beef and almond-chicken salad sandwich. There are brownies and chocolate chip cookies for dessert, plus a daily special. Sitting outside may be an almost year long choice because of the overhead heating, but indoors or out, you'll get a kick out of listening to the DC gossip at neighboring tables.

The Cheesecake Factory   American   13/20

Chevy Chase Pavilion, 5345 Wisconsin Ave.
NW (Western Ave. NW), Chevy Chase, Washington 20015
202-364-0500, Fax 202-364-0338, *Lunch & Dinner daily, $$, Casual*

If you don't want to wait forever for a table, plan to visit during the off-hours. Everyone loves the hip atmosphere, mammoth portions of funky foods and outstanding cheesecakes at this upscale national chain. You'll face two dilemmas: what to choose from the multipage menu and how to avoid overeating. Choices include everything from zany pizzas to overstuffed sandwiches to overflowing salad bowls. We've enjoyed the Santa Fe and Thai noodle salads, all of the burgers and the mix of Tex-Mex eats. Whatever you do, pace yourself so you can enjoy one of more than 30 varieties of cheesecake. Or pack up a whole cappuccino-white chocolate cheesecake or other gem to go? **Also located at** White Flint Mall, 11301 Rockville Pike, N. Bethesda, MD, 20891, 301-770-0999.

Chef Geoff's   American   12/20

Sutton Plaza, 3201 New Mexico Ave. NW (Lowell St. NW)
Washington 20016
202-237-7800, Fax 202-237-3565
Lunch Mon.-Sat., Dinner nightly, Brunch Sun., $$, Casual

Situated next to Sutton Place Gourmet, this uptown eatery probably will become a favorite neighborhood haunt. It's got an enticing menu, about 25 percent of which changes regularly. Fall in love with something simple like the charcoal-grilled burger with a tumble of fries and crispy bacon or more sophisticated like the roasted butternut squash soup, gently textured and delicately seasoned, and brightened with a swirl of heavy cream. Lunches linger on here, especially for folks who can idle on the large brick patio out front. It's a magnet for families with youngsters since here the kiddies can run wild. Dinners includes entrées such as grilled New York strip with blue cheese mashed potatoes or spicy black bean-goat cheese ravioli. Homey desserts by pastry chef Jennifer Blakesley will send nostalgic shivers down your back: milk and cookies and root beer floats lead the list. Chef Geoff is Geoffrey Tracy, who is a presence in more than name only; he heads the kitchen staff.

Christopher Marks   Contemporary   13/20

1301 Pennsylvania Ave. NW (E St. NW)
Downtown, Washington 20004
202-628-5939, Fax 202-737-0072
Lunch Mon.-Fri., Dinner nightly, $$$, Business casual

Replacing the Sporting News Grille, this newer, more somber version of a downtown power spot offers a sterling menu with many amply portioned good-old-American favorites and a selection of Italian-inspired dishes. Starters feature fried calamari, bruschetta, a crab cake club sandwich and a signature chopped salad that liberally mixes Gorgonzola and olives in a fresh vegetable and chickpea foundation. Entrées include pastas, an outstanding roasted chicken that's crusted with herbs and served with dreamy garlicky mashed potatoes, steaks and chops. Dessert selections are worthy, especially the rich molten chocolate cake.

City Lights of China   Chinese   12/20

1731 Connecticut Ave. NW (S. St. NW), Dupont Circle, Washington 20009
202-265-6688, Fax 202-265-1369, *Lunch & Dinner daily, $$, Casual*

This dependable, basement-level Chinese restaurant is always filled with a neighborhood crowd who put up with the brisk, impersonal service because they know they'll get good, spicy Hunan and Szechuan cooking. The noodle dishes are inexpensive, tasty and filling. Specialties include a good Peking duck, fresh squid country-style and a beautifully steamed whole sea bass on rock salt. We appreciate the pretty and serene setting, the soft lighting and the sophisticated appointments, but mostly we appreciate the consistently good food.

Clyde's of Georgetown   Contemporary   13/20

3236 M St. NW (Wisconsin Ave. NW), Georgetown, Washington 20007
202-333-9180, Fax 202-625-7429
Lunch & Dinner daily, Brunch Sat.-Sun., $$, Casual

Despite the enlargement of the kitchen and the sprucing up of its three dining areas, this Clyde's location remains as comfy and familiar as an old sneaker. Washingtonians owe thanks to this place for popularizing pub food and making chili and burgers glamorous fare. From this original location, Clyde's has expanded to become a major local restaurant group. Its many attractions include the convivial setting and design and seasonal-fresh dishes on a menu that changes daily, except for a few core items. At Georgetown, chef Jeff Eng produces sizzling flavors, such as spicy fried shrimp drizzled with pepper sauce and served on a bed of celery slaw. Pair this with the Buffalo chicken sandwich and its pepper sauce, and you'll exit blazing. Many desserts here come from Clyde's upscale 1789 Restaurant (see review in this chapter)—if the lemon chess pie shows up, order two or three slices. It's that good. **Other locations.**

Coco Loco   Brazilian   12/20

810 Seventh St. NW (H St. NW), Chinatown, Washington 20001
202-289-2626, Fax 202-289-4349, Lunch & Dinner Mon.-Sat., $$, Casual

🅰 ☎ 🅿 ⬚ 🍴 😷 🎭 & 🍷 🛆 💱

To inspire some Latino energy, Coco Loco offers patrons a wide range of fun and feasting options. Try the Brazilian churrascaria (a steakhouse with grilled and skewered meats—nights only), a contemporary Mexican menu, a bar that serves up rum-based tropical drinks and a nightclub with salsa and merengue lessons. If that isn't enough, you can drop by at lunchtime for lighter Latino fare, such as fresh corn soup, a Cuban frita (pork burger, chorizo, onion and garlic), quesadillas with spinach and sea scallops ceviche. Stopping in is a little like setting foot in a carnival—maybe it's the general atmosphere, maybe it's the snappy colors, maybe it's the flower- and fruit-decorated tabletops— or maybe it's the total experience.

Confucius Café   Chinese   12/20

1721 Wisconsin Ave. NW (R St. NW), Georgetown, Washington 20007
202-342-3200, Fax 202-342-3854, Lunch & Dinner daily, $, Casual

🅰 ☎ 🍴 🍷 🛆 💱

Rave reviews keep this place hopping with after-work drop-ins who love the stylish and serene Chinese-influenced décor. The food, however, does not always get down to business. Instead, it seems to be all about splashy fare and quick impressions. The pretty appetizer dumplings can be tender or tough, and the non-Chinese chicken satay may turn up fried, not grilled. We did like the shrimp in shells, with their sprinkling of pepper and sesame seeds—this dish was the best part of the meal. You might also have good luck with the Peking duck. You'll find an extensive menu, but mostly it's the same food you'll find at any local Chinese eatery.

Corduroy   American   14/20   🍴

Four Points Hotel
1201 K St. NW (12th St. NW), Downtown, Washington 20005
202-589-0699, Fax 202-589-0688, Lunch & Dinner daily, $$, Casual dressy

🅰 🅿 🍴 🍷 🛆

Corduroy stars chef Tom Power, who has worked at Michel Richard Citronelle. His compact menu sets forth beautifully staged meals composed of the freshest and best ingredients prepared and served simply. If you drop in at lunch, the menu is less imposing than at dinnertime, with such dishes as lobster omelet, penne pasta with garlic and sausage and mussels marinière. More robust dinner entrées include Rhode Island rockfish, roast baby chicken or a tenderloin of beef. Power also offers a good, if expensive, wine list, and puts out a bar menu for diners on the run. For dessert, the best, though not only, choice is chocolate hazelnut bars. Alas, much of the menu changes daily, or we'd make a habit of ordering the silken root vegetable soup and the Manhattan steak with bistro fries—a perfect pairing. Corduroy is small, unhurried, and, as yet, somewhat undiscovered. Wait until more foodies find this place—but without much signage at street level, it may be awhile.

Daily Grill   American   12/20

The Georgetown Inn
1310 Wisconsin Ave. NW (N St. NW), Georgetown, Washington 20007
202-337-4900, Fax 202-337-3702
Breakfast, Lunch & Dinner daily, $$, Casual

The food at this chain seems to depend on the chef—quality and consistency have varied between locations. Scanning the eclectic menu, you'll see that this restaurant group specializes in a certain kind of American food that seems to touch on the diversity of the culture at large: quesadillas to start, lusty pastas, meatloaf, pork chop and chicken potpie entrées. We've enjoyed the cheeseburger, but found the overwhelming Cobb salad, served chopped in small pieces and mounded on the plate, lacking in flavor. Desserts are a good bet—they include fresh fruit cobbler and New York cheesecake. **Also located at** 1200 18th Street NW, Washington, DC, 202-822-5282, and 2001 International Dr., McLean, VA, 703-288-5100.

DC Coast   American   14/20

3000 M St. NW (30th St. NW), Downtown, Washington 20007
202-216-5988, Fax 202-371-2221
Lunch Mon.-Fri., Dinner Mon.-Sat., $$$, Casual

In the '80s, chef Jeff Tunks did fusion cooking at the River Club and in the early '90s, Cal-Italian at DC's jazzy Notte Luna. Now, after a stint in California, he's back. This time it is at his own restaurant, a beautifully restored Art-Deco space that was formerly a bank in the lobby of the Tower Building. Soaring ceilings, a bustling bar scene and Tunks' way with seafood—inspired by the West Coast, Gulf Coast and Chesapeake Bay—made DC Coast a hot spot from the day it opened. Asian influences give nuance, and Cajun and Southwestern influences give guts to Tunks' cooking. His double-cut pork chops with puréed sweet potatoes are breathtaking, by themselves reason enough to come here. Among other excellent dishes, which change from time to time, are a Chinese-style smoked lobster, Moroccan-style free-range chicken and a Hong Kong-style striped sea bass.

The Diner   American   12/20

2453 18th St. NW (Columbia Rd. NW)
Adams Morgan, Washington 20009
202-232-8800, Fax 202-232-8807, *Open 24 hours, $, Casual*

It's called a diner, but with its comfy booths and full bar (with stools) in the back, this place could pass for a more upscale restaurant. The menu, too, suggests something more elitist than your local neighborhood eatery. How often do diners serve haricots verts, grilled salmon fillets with herb butter or Parisian carrots? There is also a lovely rosemary roasted chicken with darkly crisped skin and loads of herb flavor. You also will find casual fare from burgers and hot dogs to meatloaf and macaroni and cheese, from hand-cut onion rings and chili to grilled cheese and BLT sandwiches. An intensely rich and moist chocolate cake is an ideal dessert. Since The Diner is always open, breakfasts are big deals here, and are as eclectic as the rest of the menu. There are eggs plain or as omelets, jumbo pancakes and croque monsieur with ham, béchamel sauce and melted cheese and croque madame with a fried egg.

District ChopHouse & Brewery   12/20

American/Brewpub
509 Seventh St. NW (E St. NW), Downtown, Washington 20004
202-347-3434, Fax 202-347-3388
Lunch Mon.-Sat., Dinner nightly, $$, Casual

Everything in the ChopHouse is large: the booths, the portions, even the forks. But the food isn't just big, it's good. The onion rings are fabulous; the planked salmon is excellent; if you like thin crust on your pizza, you will love ChopHouse's version; the meats are cooked to suit your order; and, should you ever tire of these menu items, the daily specials offer surprises. A variety of outstanding beers are brewed upstairs. This is a great place for a date, before the theater, for a business meal or to meet someone for the first time.

Entotto   Ethiopian   14/20

1609 Foxhall Rd. NW (Reservoir Rd. NW)
Georgetown, Washington 20007
202-333-1200, Fax 202-333-1207
Lunch Mon.-Sat., Dinner nightly, $$, Casual

Don't make the mistake of thinking that Ethiopian food is too hot, too humble or perhaps too foreign to tackle. Instead, head for this Georgetown restaurant run by an Ethiopian-French couple, who are the owner-chefs. Chic patrons don't mind eating with their fingers, although knives and forks are available. The refined dishes include an exquisite tuna appetizer stirred with mild and piquant seasonings. Entrée choices are excellent, too: You can't go wrong with any dish served on the tangy, flat, spongy injera bread. The doro watt, a piquant chicken stew, is a favorite, but you can enjoy a broader introduction to the cuisine by selecting the combo of assorted stews and vegetables. For dessert, select fresh seasonal mangos, sorbets, French cake or fruit salad.

Equinox   Contemporary   15/20

818 Connecticut Ave. NW (I St. NW), Downtown, Washington 20006
202-331-8118, Fax 202-331-0809
Lunch Mon.-Fri., Dinner Mon.-Sat., $$$, Casual dressy

The spare good taste evident in the décor of chef Todd Gray's contemporary restaurant reflects the style of his cooking: He takes the best available ingredients and lets them speak for themselves. Formerly the chef at Galileo, Gray modifies his menu frequently and changes its seasonally. Indicative of his offerings are the sweet Maine crab salad with Gala apples and the roasted boneless quail with fig cornbread stuffing. Among the main courses, we've been impressed with the Cervena venison and the lamb loin, which appear with varying accompaniments. A good choice when available is the "cowboy chop," Angus beef for two with potato latkes and baby spinach. The five-course dégustation menu is available with paired wines for an additional charge.

Etrusco Trattoria — Italian — 14/20

1606 20th St. NW (Q St. NW), Dupont Circle, Washington 20009
202-667-0047, Fax 202-319-0035, *Dinner Mon.-Sat., $$$, Casual dressy*

The décor glows with warm, earthy, Etruscan colors, and flamboyant stands of fresh flowers accent the pale mustard-colored walls and terra-cotta tiled floor. Chef-owner Francesco Ricchi's food is simply outstanding: a thick and hearty classic vegetable soup, roasted portobello mushrooms or warm baby octopus to start, followed by good pastas and entrées. You might opt for a grilled strip steak cooked Piedmontese-style and served with mashed potatoes or choose the sliced roast pork. For pasta fans, the pappardelle with duck sauce stands out. The Italian desserts are classic, elegant and delectable. Try the lavish Grandpa's Cake, more accurately a chocolate cream pie with almonds. The clientele is chic, the service courteous and friendly, and sitting under the glass roof makes for a certain kind of drama. It's apt to be crowded, so make reservations. And, unless you have nerves of steel, take the Metro or a cab from somewhere else—parking is difficult.

Faccia Luna Trattoria — Italian — 12/20

2400 Wisconsin Ave. NW (Calvert St. NW)
Glover Park, Washington 20007
202-337-3132, Fax 703-841-0467, *Lunch & Dinner daily, $$, Casual*

This almost-pub has some of the trendiest casual foods around. There are meat- and vegetable-filled sandwiches that come as king-sized grinders, a heaping antipasto platter, hand-made pastas with unusual toppings and distinctive pizzas. We love the Florentine pizza crowned with spinach and ricotta cheese but can always be tempted by the Portofino pizza with anchovies and pesto or the stromboli (a Margherita pizza turnover). Portions are not overly generous, but most diners won't walk away hungry. The crowd is young and hip, and the place is always full at mealtimes. **Other locations.**

Fadó Irish Pub — Irish — 12/20

808 Seventh St. NW (H St. NW), Chinatown, Washington 20001
202-789-0066, Fax 202-789-4310
Lunch & Dinner daily, Brunch Sun., $$, Casual

You don't have to be Irish and you don't have to drink stout to fall in love with this Chinatown Irish pub. The floors are rough-hewn stone befitting a medieval castle, and the wooden tables and benches are reminiscent of a farmer's cottage. It can be so busy at lunchtime that reservations are in order. For a truly Irish repast, consider the signature dish, the boxty, a potato pancake stuffed and rolled with a filling. The chef has created four versions of the dish, all sounding rather Americanized: grilled vegetable; barbecue chicken, shrimp and Andouille sausage; seafood; and steak and portobello mushroom. All day you can order the Irish breakfast: two eggs, Irish sausages, rashers, black-and-white puddings, baked beans and homemade brown bread. Desserts include rhubarb custard pie and a harvest bread pudding. The main draw here is the wooden bar with its convivial crowds.

Famous Luigi's   Italian   **12/20**

1132 19th St. NW (M St. NW), Downtown, Washington 20036
202-331-7574, Fax 202-429-9334
Lunch Mon.-Fri., Dinner nightly, $$, Casual

This is one DC restaurant that attracts young and old alike
with its comfortable surroundings and abundant foods.
Excellent pizza is a big part of the draw. There are 42 choices
of toppings. Even so, the plain pizza with Italian sausage is just
about as good as it gets, but check out the regular menu, too.
It's a madhouse at lunchtimes.

Florida Avenue Grill   Southern   **12/20**

1100 Florida Ave. NW (11th St. NW)
Columbia Heights, Washington 20009
202-265-1586, Fax 202-332-4655
Breakfast, Lunch & Dinner Tues.-Sat., $, Casual

The busiest hours at this Washington old-timer mean a
patient wait for one of the few booths or bar stool seats.
Although good Southern food has been served here since
1944, breakfasts may be the most popular meal. Fortunately for
late-risers, breakfast is served until 1 p.m. Heady aromas of
sausage and scrapple, country ham and bacon, eggs and home
fries, pancakes and maple syrup can weaken a dieter's will.
Everything here is made from scratch—if the cooking seems a
bit slow, it's just that the crowds never thin out. Lunch items
include hefty sandwiches such as Cajun catfish or pork chops,
and dinners are homey meals starring baked turkey, sautéed
chicken livers over rice and short ribs with collard greens and
candied sweet potatoes. Save room for dessert: bread pudding,
peach cobbler or banana pudding. And, best of all, eating here
is a budgeter's dream.

Full Kee Restaurant   Chinese   **12/20**

509 H St. NW (Sixth St. NW), Chinatown, Washington 20001
202-371-2233, *Lunch & Dinner daily, $, Casual*
No credit cards.

A no-frills restaurant that consistently rates good marks and
draws large crowds, this Chinatown establishment serves up
the ultimate in bargain fare. Portions are generous and flavors
authentic. Basically Cantonese, the menu features loads of
noodle dishes in many guises, from stir-fried chow foons to
rich soups. We love the shrimp dumplings and noodle soup
but are not so crazy about the beef brisket and noodle dish.
On the other hand, we'd return often for some of the congee
offerings and the Chao Zhou-style marinated duck.

Gabriel   Spanish/Latin American   **15/20**

Radisson-Barcelo Washington Hotel
2121 P St. NW (21st St. NW), Dupont Circle, Washington 20037
202-956-6690, Fax 202-956-6641
Breakfast & Dinner daily, Lunch Mon.-Fri., Brunch Sun., $$$, Business casual

Luxury restaurants are common in hotels, but it's unusual to
find a good moderately priced restaurant—and a Latin one at
that—in any hotel. Gabriel is popular with the after-work
crowd for its reasonably priced selection of sherries, which go

well with such tapas as the roast pork and cheese tamale, pupusas crowned with grilled sea scallops and chorizo and braised, duck-filled quesadillas. It's not surprising that the food has captured a happy audience since chef Greggory Hill is outstanding. Dinners may include seared sea scallops, a pork tenderloin, and pan-seared crab cakes. For desserts, look for the Mexican chocolate flan and and an almond cake. Some of his best dishes appear at the popular Sunday brunch. You can enjoy all the usual breakfast items, along with a variety of hot and cold Mediterranean vegetable dishes, but the pièce de résistance is a whole roast suckling pig. With all the Spanish sparkling wine you can drink, Sunday brunch is a treat.

Galileo   Italian   17/20   🍴🍴🍴

1110 21st St. NW (L St. NW), Downtown, Washington 20036
202-293-7191, Fax 202-331-9364
Lunch Mon.-Fri., Dinner nightly, $$$$, Casual dressy

Chef Roberto Donna's flagship restaurant has undergone some changes. He's remodeled it to install a restaurant within a restaurant—Laboratorio del Galileo—where he cooks an 8-to 12-course prix-fixe menu several evenings each week for a maximum of seven tables. Guests can watch their meal being prepared and even wander around the self-contained kitchen. The main dining room at Galileo remains intact, serving Donna's frequently changing menu. Keep an eye out for the remarkably light pastas, the stuffed pastas with beautifully thin wrappers, fresh scampi with morel mushrooms, truffled rabbit loin and whole grilled fish. Desserts tend to be lush and extravagant and may include chocolate espresso cake. Donna's wine cellar is distinctive, consisting of hand-picked wines from Italy, France and the United States. Not feeling quite so upscale? Head over to Donna's more casual I Matti or Il Radicchio locations (see reviews in this chapter)

Georgia Brown's   Southern   13/20   🍴

950 15th St. NW (K St. NW), Downtown, Washington 20005
202-393-4499, Fax 202-393-7134
Lunch Mon.-Fri., Dinner nightly, Brunch Sun., $$, Business casual

Southern cooking appeals to the child in us who loves crunchy fried chicken and mashed potatoes splashed with a rich brown gravy. Of course, Georgia Brown's—a downtown Southern-food mecca—is really for sophisticated adults, with its upscale décor, bar area and menu; just check the place during cocktail hour or at lunch. But the warm country biscuits and cornbread sticks, the crispy catfish fingers and the cherry pepper vinegar are lush reminders of traditional Southern (that is, South Carolinian) home cooking. Other treats? Charleston she-crab soup, fried green tomatoes, Carolina gumbo and jumbo lump crab cakes. For dessert, servers tempt with a tray displaying Key lime pie, sweet potato cheesecake, peach cobbler and bourbon pecan pie—all served with a scoop of Jack Daniels ice cream.

Find the name you are looking for, quickly and easily, in **the index**.

Gérard's Place   French   16/20

915 15th St. NW (I St. NW), Downtown, Washington 20005
202-737-4445, Fax 202-737-5555
Lunch Mon.-Fri., Dinner Mon.-Sat., $$$, Casual dressy

Before his move to the U.S., Gérard Pangaud earned accolades at his restaurant in Paris. In its early years, Gérard's Place did not impress us with its décor, but recent improvements have made it more elegant. But whatever we thought about the dining room or the stemware, Pangaud's cooking has rarely disappointed. His cuisine is daringly simple yet dazzling; he has a talent for taking the best ingredients and doing just enough to them to bring out their natural flavors. Many of his dishes, of course, are available only seasonally. If these are on the menu, consider the medallion of rabbit, accompanied by chanterelles and fresh peas or the roasted rockfish. His signature poached lobster sparkles with a sauce of ginger, lime and Sauternes. A tempting tasting menu is available and must be ordered by everyone at the table.

Gordon Biersch Brewery Restaurant   12/20

American/Brewpub
Courtyard by Marriott
900 F St. NW (9th St. NW), Downtown, Washington 20004
202-783-5454, Fax 202-783-0404
Lunch & Dinner daily, Brunch Sun., $$, Casual

Located a scant block from the MCI Center, this stagey modern-day pub occupies a turn-of-the-century bank building, where elegant marble columns and floors, wrought-iron window gratings and carved ceilings add charm. Although the service may straggle a bit, the staff is friendly and helpful, making the wait for the popular Southwest chicken sandwich with the intensely garlicky side of fries worthwhile. Starters include soups, pot stickers, crispy artichoke hearts and beer-battered onion rings. Main dishes encompass classic salads, brick-oven baked pizzas (how about a Thai chicken pizza with Asian barbecue sauce?), pastas, stir-fries and homey favorites like meatloaf with mashed potatoes. If you are a fan of banana splits, conclude your meal with a whipped cream-topped wedge of the banana split cheesecake nestled in a chocolate cookie crust. Like German lagers? You can get your fill here, a brew restaurant that is a cut above most other pubs and a great place to fuel up before or after the big games at MCI Center.

Grill from Ipanema   Brazilian   12/20

1858 Columbia Rd. NW (18th St. NW)
Adams Morgan, Washington 20009
202-986-0757, Fax 202-265-4229
Dinner nightly, Brunch Sat.-Sun., $$, Casual dressy

The restaurant's pulsating, authentic Brazilian mood and food are drawing crowds of hip customers. It's a lively place that will undoubtedly make you feel as though you are at a party. If you can't read or pronounce the Portuguese, it's all explained in menu blurbs. It's a toss-up whether to order lightly breaded alligator or crab meat to start. For the entrée, we heartily recommend the feijoada, the Brazilian national dish best suited to a frigid night. Filled with chunks of beef, pork and sausage, this rich and spicy stew is spectacular. Other choices are garlicky chicken, assorted seafood stews and hearty beef, sausage and pork dinners that will stir your heart to do the tango. This is a must destination, but be warned, nearby nighttime parking is almost impossible to find

Heritage India   Indian   15/20

2400 Wisconsin Ave. NW (Calvert St. NW)
Glover Park, Washington 20007
202-333-3120, Fax 202-333-3106, *Lunch & Dinner daily, $$$, Casual dressy*

You may feel as if you've stumbled into a mogul's palace, especially if you study the Indian photos and prints on the walls. And you'll feel as pampered as a maharaja when you sit down at a table set with fancy cutlery and dinnerware. The food is just as rarified, for New Delhi-trained chef Sudhir Seth draws his inspiration from such Indian classical styles as dum cooking (slow-steamed dishes cooked in clay vessels). Tandoori dishes are outstanding, especially the peppery prawns, the butter-tender lamb kebabs and the breads, light as clouds. His superlative desserts include shahi tukra, an Indian bread pudding laced with a sweet, scented syrup. The dinner crowds tend to be as dressy as the restaurant, and if you want to do the restaurant justice, you should come with friends so you can try more dishes.

Hogate's   Seafood   12/20

800 Water St. SW (Maine Ave. SW), Waterfront, Washington 20024
202-484-6300, Fax 202-488-3840
Lunch & Dinner daily, Brunch Sun., $, Casual

Thronged at lunchtime, this enormous 60-year-old waterfront restaurant attracts tourists by the busload and plenty of locals, too. If you're part of the crowd in line, keep your fingers crossed for a water-view table. Despite the elegant ship's-interior motif, landlubbers will find that the food and ambience are casual. And whatever your seafood cravings, Hogate's probably has the answer, from tuna kebabs to crab cakes and a New England clambake, plus much more. Sunday brunch also features fish on the raw bar, but more customary breakfast fare includes waffles and eggs, all enjoyed with live jazz. Take home a pack of the restaurant's famous rum buns—enormous slabs are served when you're seated—available packed to go at the front shop.

Houston's   American   12/20

1065 Wisconsin Ave. NW (M St. NW), Georgetown, Washington 20007
202-338-7760, Fax 202-338-2213, *Lunch & Dinner daily, $$, Casual*

Want good casual food that's reliable, if not trendy? That's the hallmark of Houston's, an old favorite locally for its predictably good salads, burgers (including a vegetable burger made with oat bran) and fries, steaks and barbecued ribs. Check under the "This and That" section, where you'll find such add-ons as cheddar Parmesan toast and couscous, plus a grilled artichoke medley that's sensational. **Also located at** 12256 Rockville Pike, Rockville, MD, 301-468-3535, and 7715 Woodmont Ave., Bethesda, MD, 301-656-9755.

Hunan Chinatown   Chinese   13/20

624 H St. NW (Seventh St. NW), Chinatown, Washington 20001
202-783-5858, Fax 202-393-1375, *Lunch & Dinner daily, $$, Casual*

🅰 ☎ ♥ ⚒ 🍸 ▲

This is a long-standing Chinatown institution, slightly worn but still attractive. Its dependable menu has a mix of Hunan and Szechuan dishes, but our favorites have always been the parchment prawns and quite good orange beef. Look for other classics such as pan-fried dumplings, boiled dumplings in spicy peanut sauce, tea-smoked duck, spicy eggplant and crispy whole fish. It may be crowded after MCI Center events or when conventions are in town, so you may want to reserve a table if you have a group of four or more people.

Hunan Peking   Chinese   12/20

Georgetown Court, 3251 Prospect St. NW, 2/F
(Wisconsin Ave. NW), Georgetown, Washington 20007
202-337-8888, Fax 202-337-9346, *Lunch & Dinner daily, $, Casual*

🅰 P 📷 ♥ ⚒

From its second-story location, this Georgetown eatery offers patrons a bird's-eye view of the passing scene, which makes for great entertainment during meals. You'll run into plenty of local college students, who use the place as a kind of second dining room. And why not? The menu offers plenty of typical Chinese choices, from Peking duck and General Tso's chicken to fried rice and pork in plum sauce. We like the Hunan-style string beans, chicken with shrimp and scallops, and the tender and flavorful dumplings.

I Matti   Italian   13/20

2436 18th St. NW (Columbia Rd. NW)
Adams Morgan, Washington 20009
202-462-8844, Fax 202-462-1008
Lunch Wed.-Sat., Dinner nightly, $$$, Casual

🅰 ☎ P 🍸 ▲ ⟲

Even though the food is generally very good at I Matti, Roberto Donna's casual Adams Morgan trattoria, it's best to avoid it on weekends when waits are long, reservations are often meaningless and the staff is overworked. This could be said of most of hot restaurateur Donna's places, whether it's upscale Galileo or the casual Il Radicchio locations (see reviews in this chapter). But on a quiet weeknight, you'll be well served with a delicious pizza ortolana, a mixed grilled-vegetable pie; pasta dishes like gnocchi tossed in pesto; grilled filet of beef; and seasonal game specials. Ask about wine dinners, which are staged in the upstairs dining room.

I Ricchi   Italian   14/20

1220 19th St. NW (N St. NW), Dupont Circle, Washington 20036
202-835-0459, Fax 202-872-1220
Lunch Mon.-Fri., Dinner Mon.-Sat., $$$$, Jackets suggested

🅰 ☎ P 🍸 ▲

This has been one of Washington's favorite upscale Italian restaurants since it opened in 1989. The only thing that's changed over the years is the addition of greenery to the clean-lined dining room. The specialty of the house is hearty Tuscan food, simply and deliciously cooked on a wood-fired grill or oven. Game and meat dishes are the thing to order here, and pastas are good, too. Spectacular breads are made in-house. The wines can be pricey, but you're sure to find one that you might order if you were dining at the original I Ricchi near Florence.

Il Radicchio — Italian — 12/20

223 Pennsylvania Ave. SE (Second St. SE)
Capitol Hill, Washington 20003
202-547-5114, Fax 202-547-5799, *Lunch & Dinner daily, $$, Casual*

The name Roberto Donna has become synonymous in this town with Italian restaurants that run the gamut from the ultra-chic Galileo to the modest and casual I Matti and Il Radicchio locations (see other reviews in this chapter). The emphasis here is on hearty, peasant-style fare that features pizzas (with loads of funky toppings, including radicchio), pasta dishes with homemade sauces and spit-roasted chicken with roasted potatoes (a great take-home dish, for those on the run). Appetizers include bruschetta and antipasti. A winner is the roasted peppers in anchovy sauce; it's loaded with garlic, so be advised. It's tempting to hang out here sipping wine and forking into a wedge of ricotta cheesecake, but at mealtimes, expect crowds and a bustle. **Also located at** 1801 Clarendon Blvd., Arlington, VA, 703-276-2627.

Iron Gate Inn Restaurant — 13/20

Mediterranean/Contemporary
1734 N St. NW (18th St. NW), Downtown, Washington 20036
202-737-1370, Fax 202-223-4045
Lunch Mon.-Fri., Dinner Mon.-Sat., $$, Casual

The white-washed stone entrance, grapevine-covered patio complete with lion's head fountain, and cozy dining rooms give this downtown establishment a distinct European air. It makes an ideal setting for intimate trysts as well as group meetings. Contemporary American flavors with a big addition of Mediterranean accents are combined here with great success. Lamb shines in a number of preparations, especially the shank with orzo. Another good choice is the boned roast chicken served with garlicky mashed potatoes and raisin chutney. Dessert lovers will marvel at the rich chocolate truffle pie, but if calories matter, consider the leaner sorbet or lemon mousse instead.

The Islander Caribbean Restaurant & Bar 14/20

Trinidadian/Caribbean
1201 U St. NW (12th St. NW), U St. Corridor, Washington 20009
202-234-4955, Fax 202-232-7745, *Lunch & Dinner daily, $, Casual*

Trinidadian Addie Green rules in this island kingdom, and she should: She's undoubtedly the best Caribbean cook in Washington. You'll hear an island beat in the background and some native patois, but people of every persuasion adore her cooking, because it is honest and true. If you know little about Trinidadian food, let Addie's menu teach you. We'd walk a mile or two just for her curried goat rotis with feather-light bread and her puffy island-inspired crab cakes. Green is famous for her fish dishes and her side dishes from peleau (rice with pigeon peas) to cabbage are good, too. Sip an island drink, like the sweet and spicy sorrell, and you may just want to limbo.

Jaleo   Spanish   14/20

480 Seventh St. NW (E St. NW), Downtown, Washington 20004
202-628-7949, Fax 202-628-7952
Lunch & Dinner daily, $$$, Casual dressy

This lively tapas restaurant is around the corner from the Shakespeare Theater and a block from the MCI Center. No surprise that it's always busy, but tables turn over quickly, so the wait usually isn't as long as it looks. Besides, the fun doesn't really start until later in the evening, when the place is full of jaleo (Spanish slang for commotion). There are lots of entrées, but ordering a table full of small plates and washing them down with a bottle of sherry or a pitcher of sangría is what's fun about this place. The selection changes seasonally but usually includes sausage with white beans, grilled portobello mushrooms, Spanish cold cuts and poached octopus in olive oil.

Japan Inn Restaurant   Japanese   13/20

1715 Wisconsin Ave. NW (R St. NW), Georgetown, Washington 20007
202-337-3400, Fax 202-337-9229
Lunch Mon.-Fri., Dinner Mon.-Sat., $$$, Casual

One of Washington's oldest Japanese restaurants, this place attracts local Japanese businessmen and folks from the Japanese Embassy. But plenty of others head here for the solid Japanese cooking and for the drama of the teppanyaki grill upstairs, where the energetic chef heats up the central grill, oils it well, then cooks orders in stages—meats first, vegetables last—seasoning and stirring all the while. He's all business: He doesn't toss his cleaver, ingredients or raw eggs into the air in comic antics. Try one of the combination grill dinners for a good sampling of flavors. The extensive menu offers plenty of classic Japanese dishes served in other dining areas, too. In any case, don't miss out on the ginger ice cream for dessert.

Jockey Club   Fusion   11/20

The Westin Fairfax Hotel, 2100 Massachusetts Ave. NW (21st St. NW) Dupont Circle, Washington 20008
202-835-2100, Fax 202-293-0641
Breakfast, Lunch & Dinner daily, $$$, Jackets & ties required

For many years, the Jockey Club was the place where political and social Washington met. The clubby dining room opened on the eve of John F. Kennedy's inauguration and was a favorite of both Democratic doyenne Pamela Harriman and Republican First Lady Nancy Reagan, whose favorite chicken salad is still on the menu. Since the departure of longtime chef Hidemasa Yamamoto, however, the food has been in serious decline, although it's still a favorite lunch spot for Georgetown matrons. Dinner means traditional fare like New York steaks, crab cakes, Dover sole and rack of lamb.

Johnny's Half Shell   Seafood/Contemporary   13/20

2002 P St. NW (20th St. NW), Dupont Circle, Washington 20036
202-296-2021, Fax 202-296-5952, *Lunch & Dinner Mon.-Sat., $$, Casual*

Diners indulge their seafood fantasies at Johnny's Half Shell. It's a splashy, must-go restaurant, long on ambience and big on showy groups gathering for dinner, drinks and a round of '40s jazz. Its appropriate motto? "Seafood Specialties, Strong Drink." We recommend starting with oysters or clams on the half shell. For an entrée, try the sautéed soft-shells or a wood-grilled wild rockfish filet. The Chesapeake seafood stew is also good and very reasonably priced. Meat-eaters can select the wood-grilled Piedmontese beef rib-eye or a farm-raised chicken. Linger on at the bar after dinner to enjoy the lively scene.

Kaz Sushi Bistro   Japanese/Sushi   **14/20**   🍳

1915 I St. NW (19th St. NW), Downtown, Washington 20006
202-530-5500, Fax 202-530-5501
Lunch Mon.-Fri., Dinner Mon.-Sat., $$, Casual

Kazuhiro (Kaz) Okochi defined the art of sushi in DC when he was at Sushi-Ko, and it's easy to see why: His knife cuts are clean and his fish pieces look like sculptures. Now that Kaz has set up his own sushi bar, patrons can dig into a variety of classics, offbeat rolls and assorted sushi bar and kitchen specialties. Check the daily list for whimsical creations such as the shrimp with salsa. For sheer refreshment, end dinner with the three tiny scoops of green tea ice cream. If you sit at the sushi bar, you can chat with Kaz; otherwise, the bamboo-toned dining room offers a tranquil Asian setting.

Kinkead's   Seafood   **15/20**   🍳🍳

2000 Pennsylvania Ave. NW (20th St. NW)
Foggy Bottom, Washington 20006
202-296-7700, Fax 202-296-7688
Lunch Mon.-Sat., Dinner nightly, Brunch Sun., $$$$, Business casual

Chef Robert Kinkead's eclectic seafood menu centers on pristinely fresh fish and shellfish prepared in a variety of ways, from simply grilled to elaborately prepared Thai or Scandinavian stews. Kinkead's spectacular shellfish platter may seem like an expensive treat with its big price tag, but it serves six easily. Standards include crusty fried clams, grilled squid with creamy polenta, crab cakes and pepita-crusted salmon with a corn-chile ragoût. The menu changes daily to feature the very best of the catch-of-the-day. In the mood for casual? Sit at the downstairs bar or at the raw bar. The upstairs dining room, with its open kitchen, has the charm of yesterday's brasseries.

La Chaumière   French   **13/20**   🍳

2813 M St. NW (28th St. NW), Georgetown, Washington 20007
202-338-1784, Fax 202-965-4597
Lunch Mon.-Fri., Dinner Mon.-Sat., $$$, Casual

The country-inn atmosphere and the reliable cooking at this Georgetown institution have made it a favorite neighborhood gathering spot for more than three decades. Lunchtime is especially busy. The menu consists of basic bistro fare—dishes like onion soup, mussels in garlic butter and sole meunière. Specialties include tripes à la mode de Caën and quenelles de brochette Lyonnaise, but you can also get more up-to-date dishes such as duck foie gras with cassis sauce. Check with your server for the daily specials, which have included crab-filled crêpes, couscous and cassoulet.

La Colline — French — 15/20

Hall of States
400 N. Capitol St. NW (D St. NW), Capitol Hill, Washington 20001
202-737-0400, Fax 202-737-3026
Breakfast & Lunch Mon.-Fri., Dinner Mon.-Sat., $$$, Ties suggested

Executive chef Robert Greault's Senate-side French restaurant is certainly the best restaurant on Capitol Hill and one of the best dining values in the city. Greault was one of the early super-star chefs in the city's most expensive restaurants, and here he prepares food that is no less sublime—maybe even more so—at reasonable prices. Located inside a sterile modern office building, the dining room is crisp and handsome and the service is friendly but correct. The menu changes daily, but be on the lookout for the terrine of foie gras, crayfish gratin, Louisiana shrimp Creole and a stew of baby lamb shanks. Friday's special is bouillabaisse, and it's worth a special trip.

Lafayette — American — 14/20

The Hay-Adams Hotel
800 16th St. NW (H St. NW), Downtown, Washington 20006
202-638-2570, Fax 202-638-3803
Breakfast, Lunch & Dinner daily, $$$$, Jackets & ties required

The venerable Hay-Adams Hotel is one of Washington's pre-eminent destinations, and it follows that its high-profile restaurant, the Lafayette, should be the scene of some elegant meals. Under the direction of executive chef Frederic Lange, the kitchen pulls out the stops, and guests may wonder, "Do I dare eat all the bread first?" It's that good. Even if you have your heart set on the grilled yellowfin tuna, let the waiter tell you about the day's specials. Then consider the choices from the menu: two Cobb salads, one traditional and one made with assorted seafood. Standouts include: crab cakes served and a mixed grill of petit filet mignon, lamb chop with lobster mashed potatoes and quail. Whatever you select, save some room for dessert. The chocolate truffle cake warrants a chocolate splurge.

Lauriol Plaza — Latin American/Caribbean — 13/20

1835 18th St. NW (T St. NW), Adams Morgan, Washington 20009
202-387-0035, Fax 202-387-8311
Lunch Mon.-Sat., Dinner nightly, Brunch Sun., $$, Casual

This popular Adams Morgan eatery often overflows at happy hour and attracts a hip, young crowd enlivened by the Latino atmosphere and pitchers of margaritas. The bar also offers tequila shots for the strong of heart. Crowds seem to adore the Latino flavors, including a range of Mex and Tex-Mex dishes, from ceviche and tostones (Puerto Rican) to quesadillas, enchiladas, fajitas, chiles rellenos and tacos, plus more serious platters. This place is also a serious Sunday brunch hangout for the locals, who dig the meet-and-greet scene. The brunch menu includes some Yankee favorites, such as eggs Benedict and french toast, plus some south-of-the-border dishes. If you like your eggs over easy, try the huevos rancheros served with a layer of black beans, tortillas and salsa.

Lavandou Restaurant   French   **13/20**

3321 Connecticut Ave. NW (Ordway St. NW)
Cleveland Park, Washington 20008
202-966-3002, Fax 202-966-0982
Lunch Mon.-Fri., Dinner nightly, $$, Casual

As sunny, bright and inviting as a beach cabana on the Riviera, this uptown restaurant is a real find, an underpublicized place that locals obviously treasure. To embrace warm weather, staff members throw open the front windows, making a window seat imperative; you sit inches from passersby, with the sun splashing across the table. That's at lunchtime, of course, when the menu is less imposing: You'll find duck liver terrine or a house salad to start, a handful of soups, several unusual sandwiches (such as the fancy grilled tuna with Niçoise olives and drizzles of olive oil on rye bread studded with olives), composed salads and assorted heartier fare such as grilled flank steak or carbonnade. Even if you think you're sated, ask to see the dessert plate with its colorful array of calorie-laden pastries and tarts.

Le Jardin   French   **14/20**

1027 19th St. NW (M St. NW), Downtown, Washington 20036
202-833-4800, Fax 202-833-4761
Lunch Mon.-Fri., Dinner Mon.-Sat., $$, Business casual

What may impress you most here is the intimacy of the room and its slightly posh décor. The brick and wood walls, plank floors, lace-curtained windows and fireplace of this townhouse suggest gentility, and the front bricked patio is a decorous place to alight for an al fresco meal. Problem is, the room feels cramped, and we wonder how the staff navigate without tripping over chair legs. The menu offers an affordable though not inexpensive array of dishes, among which the crab-cake sandwich with fresh, hot frites makes an outstanding midday repast. You might start with the classic French onion soup, which has citrus undertones and plenty of smooth, rich melted cheese swirled through it. Dinners star rack of lamb, a veal chop and pepper-crusted tuna or a bouillabaisse. The impressive wedge of chocolate mousse cake elicits ohs and ahs, so save room for it. Overall, there's a satisfying mix of French and American flavors; however, there's talk of a move toward an all Provençal-style cuisine.

Lebanese Taverna   Lebanese   **12/20**

2641 Connecticut Ave. NW (Woodley Rd.)
Woodley Park, Washington 20008
202-265-8681, Fax 202-483-3007
Lunch Mon.-Sat., Dinner nightly, $$, Casual

This lively and attractive Middle Eastern restaurant is a gathering place for the young and hungry who live in the many moderately priced apartment buildings along Connecticut Avenue in Woodley Park. You can create a satisfying meal out of the mezze, appetizer-sized dishes that are the Middle Eastern equivalent of tapas, such as grilled spicy sausages with tomato sauce, spinach-stuffed turnovers or a layered dish of eggplant and chickpeas. You'll find some of the best dishes,

It must be the water.

de Ladoucette Pouilly-Fumé: "Subtle green plum, mineral and herb with notes that carry through from start to the long, mouthwatering finish. Appealing for its subtlety and grace." - *Wine Spectator*

SETTING THE STANDARD FOR THE WORLD'S WHITE WINES.

de Ladoucette

Pouilly-Fumé
France

however, among the main courses, such as the rotisserie chicken enveloped in a thin Lebanese pancake, the kebabs and the pilafs. **Also located at** 5900 Washington Blvd., Arlington, VA, 703-241-8681.

Legal Sea Foods Seafood 13/20

2020 K St. NW (20th St. NW), Downtown, Washington 20006
202-496-1111, Fax 202-496-1611
Lunch Mon.-Fri., Dinner nightly, $$$, Casual

Boston's much-loved Legal Sea Foods, part of a leviathan whose holdings include numerous restaurants, retail markets, a mail-order business and a frozen seafood division, has not made an easy transition to the nation's capital. The clubby 240-seat downtown restaurant seems to have everything it needs to attract a power lunch clientele, but indifferent service and long waits have marred its reputation. We've been disappointed with their signature clam chowder and steamed lobster, although we've enjoyed the fresh oysters and fried clams. The best bet here is to sit at the bar and order the great lobster roll or the simply prepared grilled fish. The wine list has an intelligent selection and fair prices, with a leaning toward California whites. **Other locations.**

Levante's Turkish/Middle Eastern 12/20

1330 19th St. NW (P St. NW), Dupont Circle, Washington 20036
202-293-6301, Fax 202-293-3732
Lunch & Dinner daily, Brunch Sun., $, Casual

With its bold blues and yellows, this Middle Eastern restaurant has taken DC by storm. Drop in at lunch or dinner and scan around for a vacant table. It seems everyone has stopped by for a glass of wine, a loaf or two of the restaurant's superb hot bread dunked in golden olive oil and one of the oversized Turkish pides—a "pizza boat" loaded with your choice of toppings. We are addicted to the red lentil soup to start and always end up with an order of garlicky hummus and the lamb pide. Bigger appetites will enjoy the moussaka, kebab or veal and lamb chop entrées. The staff is very friendly and helpful, and that attitude is contagious: Everyone seems to have a good time. **Also located at** 7262 Woodmont Ave., Bethesda, MD, 301-657-2441.

Luigino Italian 12/20

1100 New York Ave. NW (12th St. NW)
Downtown, Washington 20005
202-371-0595, Fax 202-371-6482
Lunch Mon.-Fri., Dinner nightly, $$$, Casual

The excitement in this spare, high-ceilinged, modern trattoria is in the open kitchen. In fact, if you sit up close to the action at the dining counter in front, you'll enjoy both the aroma and the sight of Carmine Marzano's cooking. Marzano turns out Italian dishes more characteristic of his grandmother's generation than his own. His specialties include splendid slow-cooked, old-fashioned stews such as stufatino of baby goat and rabbit with black olives and potatoes. Start with half an order of pasta, then proceed directly to one of these—unless his rotisserie grilled boneless suckling pig is on the menu. If it is, you don't even need to read the menu to choose your main course.

M & S Grill — American — 12/20

600 13th St. NW (F St. NW), Downtown, Washington 20005
202-347-1500, Fax 202-347-0234
Lunch Mon.-Fri., Dinner nightly, $$, Casual

In the spirit of New York's old-time grills, M & S has a soft-edged saloon feel. But the menu is modern American all the way since it's hard to imagine some dapper gent from the 1800s diving into a plate of fried calamari with cocktail sauce, a bowl of lusty tortilla and chicken soup or a succulent meatloaf-cheddar sandwich with a spread of horseradish mayonnaise. The extensive menu is studded with more of the same—offerings that include some of the best of America's bar food and restaurant dishes. Whatever else you order, make sure you close with Jake's Famous Chocolate Truffle Cake, the signature dessert. An offspring of the successful upscale McCormick & Schmick's chain, this eatery sports heavy, dark woods.

McCormick & Schmick's — Seafood — 13/20

1652 K St. NW (17th St. NW), Downtown, Washington 20006
202-861-2233, Fax 202-822-4679
Lunch Mon.-Sat., Dinner nightly, Brunch Sun, $$$, Ties suggested

The downtown branch of this upscale national seafood chain has one of the liveliest after-work bar scenes in town. Its velvet-curtained private booths make it a popular spot for business lunches and evening assignations. The seafood is top quality, and there are usually about 30 varieties of fresh fish and shellfish available. Look for some unusual fish varieties, like South African swordfish or Louisiana black drum, plus succulent oysters and clams. We advise ordering the simplest preparations: oysters and clams on the half shell, Dungeness crab when it's available, or grilled fish with lemon butter. For lunch, you can't beat the smoked salmon club sandwich. Close any meal with Jake's Famous Chocolate Truffle Cake, the restaurant's signature dessert. **Other locations**.

Makoto Restaurant — Japanese — 16/20

4822 MacArthur Blvd. NW (U St. NW)
West Georgetown, Washington 20007
202-298-6866, Fax 202-625-6602
Lunch Tues.-Sat., Dinner Tues.-Sun., $$$, Business casual

Makoto is one of those unique Japanese restaurants where the food is so sophisticated and elegant that you may be tempted to frame it as wall art. Constructed like a Japanese country inn, with a wooden entrance door leading downstairs to a small wood-paneled dining room, Makoto requires its guests to take off their shoes and wear special slippers. You may want the comfort of sitting at one of the discreet wall tables, but one pleasure here is to lean over the partition of the sushi bar and watch the experts at work. It's all a symphony of flowing movement and precision techniques for a meal that transcends the ordinary. The menu suggests a complete dinner with specific categories: sushi, yakimono, nabe, nimono, kobachi—about eight in all, composed of the freshest ingredients. Otherwise,

order elements of this meal à la carte, and follow this advice:
Select lots of sushi, which is some of the best this side of Tokyo.
The perfect beverages? Warmed saké or green tea.

Malaysia Kopitiam   Malaysian   12/20

1827 M St. NW (18th St. NW), Downtown, Washington 20036
202-833-6233, Fax 202-833-6232, *Lunch & Dinner daily, $$, Casual*

An arrival on M Street in downtown DC, this Malaysian
eatery has moved in from Wheaton and renamed itself.
Kopitiam means coffeehouse, a term that doesn't adequately
describe the full range of food. Most dishes are traditional,
although some, such as the stuffed lotus root, are the chef-
owner's invention. We can highly recommend the various dish-
es and swear by the roti canai and roti wrap, both starring an
unusual Indian-style bread. If you like heat, add the beef ren-
dang to your meal. Sample one of the restaurant's native
desserts, from tapioca cake to kuih lapis. The kitchen may
stumble on a few flavors, but the lively menu reads like the
country's travel log.

Mama Ayesha's   Middle Eastern   12/20

1967 Calvert St. NW (Connecticut Ave. NW)
Adams Morgan, Washington 20009
202-232-5431, Fax 202-232-1231, *Lunch & Dinner daily, $, Casual*

Looking as mysterious as a sultan's den, this Calvert Street
restaurant resonates with exotic music and laughter. The latter
emanates from the families and large groups gathered around
the tables. Despite all the bazaar-like charm, the food does not
measure up, and the service, although friendly, moves at a
snail's pace. Most of the dishes mirror what other area Middle
Eastern restaurants serve, but the appetizer hummus with meat
stands out. The lamb kebab is predictable, although the meat
cubes are both large and tender. Heftier dishes include a baked
lamb shank and broiled chicken. Vegetarians will find plenty of
fuel—stuffed grape leaves, couscous or yellow squash. Still hun-
gry? Conclude with sweet Arabian coffee and flaky baklava.

Marcel's   Continental   16/20

2401 Pennsylvania Ave. NW (24th St. NW)
West End, Washington 20037
202-296-1166, Fax 202-296-6466
Lunch Mon.-Fri., Dinner Mon.-Sat., $$$$, Casual

The warm stone-walled décor hasn't changed much at the
former Provence, but in its incarnation as Marcel's, inspired
and inventive chef Robert Wiedmaier cooks in the French style
but with Flemish accents. This style means lots of shellfish and
stacks of crisp, twice-fried Belgian frites. Problem is, the menu
undergoes seasonal changes, and you may not find your
favorites always listed. Roasted diver scallops (the succulent
catches hand-selected by divers) and the coquilles St. Jacques
make great beginnings. For entrées, the rack of lamb or the
pepper-crusted entrecôte with a Stilton flan are outstanding.
Hearty stews such as the Belgian classic carbonnade à la fla-
mande or game meals such as a fork-tender venison hit the
spot on cold nights. Don't skip desserts, particularly, if avail-
able, Wiedmaier's chocolate biscuit with praline ice cream and

chocolate and caramel sauces or most especially his pastry-wrapped poached pear with a caramel sauce. The bar is lively and a great place to hang out with friends. Popular and often crowded, Marcel's demands respect and attention from DC's gastronomes. Ask about his tasting menu.

The Mark   Contemporary   **13/20**

401 Seventh St. NW (D St. NW), Downtown, Washington 20004
202-783-3133, Fax 202-783-0197, *Lunch & Dinner Mon.-Sat., $$, Casual*

The trendy contemporary menu at this handsome, glass-walled restaurant in the downtown arts-and-theater district ranges from Asia to Italy and the American Southwest. The ingredients are good, and chef Alison Swope's way with them is highly creative. If you can squeeze in at lunchtime, try the outstanding chopped salad with grilled vegetables and chicken or beef. At dinner, look for dishes such as braised lamb shank, cinnamon-smoked duck breast and miso-glazed Norwegian salmon. Save room for her signature white chocolate cheesecake for dessert.

Marrakesh   Moroccan   **13/20**

617 New York Ave. NW
(Sixth St. NW), Chinatown, Washington 20001
202-393-9393, Dinner nightly, $$$, Casual dressy
No credit cards.

Dining here may be one of Washington's biggest surprises to those not forewarned. First, you really need to make reservations. Next, although the food is abundant, coming here is more about soaking up the exotic atmosphere and applauding the very talented belly dancer than about eating. Third, you'll leave this sumptuous place in a state of sensory overload: The ambience—with colorful tiles, splashing fountain, lush carpets, painted ceiling, pulsating music and general ebullience—probably will inspire your wanderlust for distant ports. There's no written menu, and as the server washes your hands in a stylish ceremony, you may hear that you'll feast on the following courses: salad (carrots, tomatoes, cucumbers and eggplant) with bread, bastila (Moroccan meat-filled pastry), half a roast chicken with lemon sauce, lamb with honey and almonds, couscous with steamed vegetables, fruits, and at the end, minted tea with honey-soaked baklava.

Matisse Café Restaurant   **14/20**

French/Mediterranean/Contemporary
4934 Wisconsin Ave. NW (Fessenden St. NW)
Friendship Heights, Washington 20016
202-244-5222, Fax 202-244-1039
Lunch Tues.-Fri., Dinner Tues.-Sun., Brunch Sun., $$$, Casual dressy

Like a French stage setting, Matisse makes a surreal statement with its spacious dining rooms, curvilinear graphics and flowing designs. Even the flowers mimic the curlicues and sweeping lines of the interior. It's a three-level setting, but the basement is really the open kitchen, all functional and shiny. This makes a suitable backdrop for the exquisite foods prepared by chef-owner Fritz Siegfried, who is Swiss by birth, training and temperament. Look for such fine details as reduced veal stock that requires no unnecessary thickeners, overnight-marinated frogs' legs, twice-fried pommes frites, and an intense crème brûlée sandwiched between layers of sculpted tuilles cookies. If it's available, order the special chocolate "brick" with layered dark chocolate and caramel. The menu changes seasonally, and Siegfried moves from sizzling rib-eye steaks in fair weather to hearty cassoulets for chilly nights. Matisse caters to sedate matrons at lunchtime, power Washington at night—and anyone who appreciates haute settings and food.

Meiwah   Chinese   12/20

1200 New Hampshire Ave.
NW (M St. NW), West End, Washington 20036
202-833-2888, Fax 202-833-2828, *Lunch & Dinner daily, $$$, Casual*

🅰 ☎ 🅿 🍴 🎵 🍸 🍶 ➰

Meiwah isn't as popular yet as City Lights of China in Dupont Circle, which at one time had the same ownership. Although the menu features dishes from all over China, the best one may be a simple vegetable stir-fry of baby Shanghai bok choy and black mushrooms. The Mongolian lamb and the appetizer crispy Cornish hen also merit a few golden chopsticks, but you may find that many of the other dishes sound too familiar to tempt you if you're seeking an exciting Chinese culinary adventure.

Melrose   Contemporary   14/20 ♟

Park Hyatt Washington
1201 24th St. NW (M St. NW), West End, Washington 20037
202-955-3899, Fax 202-408-6118
Breakfast & Dinner daily, Lunch Mon.-Sat., Brunch Sun., $$$$, Business casual

🅰 ☎ 🅿 🍴 ❤ 🎵 🐾 🍸 🍶

Melrose is at its prettiest during the day, when its corner location admits light from two sides and its pleasant plant-filled patio offers outdoor dining beside a refreshing fountain. The Sunday brunch is one of the best in town. It begins with an appetizer buffet, complete with a lavish selection of fresh shellfish, and the main course is served at the table. At other times, customers celebrate executive chef Brian McBride's upscale dishes, which may turn up as an appetizer of crab meat-stuffed prawns or an entrée of pumpkin ravioli with truffled sunchoke purée. The crab cakes, available at brunch and dinner, are model versions of this regional dish. And you can count on the rack of lamb to be near perfection. The homey desserts might include a warm chocolate bread pudding or a fruit crisp. Melrose is close to the Kennedy Center, so it's a good choice for pre-theater dining.

Mendocino Grille & Wine Bar   American   12/20

2917 M St. NW (29th St. NW), Georgetown, Washington 20007
202-333-2912, Fax 202-625-7888
Lunch Mon.-Sat., Dinner nightly, $$$, Business casual

🅰 ☎ 🅿 🍸 🍶

It's not just the name: The wood-and-stone simplicity of this American-style restaurant, designed by Adamstein and Demetriou, who also did the lovely Bis, Catalan West and Coco Loco, can almost make you believe you're in one of the most beautiful spots in California rather than Georgetown. The spare, flower-bedecked dining room is a good place for an intimate lunch. Try the tart of spinach and crab meat or one of many salads, pizzas and sandwiches. The crowd gets lively after 8 p.m., when there's more variety and greater heft in chef Michael Chmar's dinner menu that includes Asian-influenced seafood dishes, lamb, chicken and steak entrées. The wine bar features mostly California wines, with at least 20 by the glass, available in two- or five-ounce tasting flights.

Mes Amis Restaurant   French   13/20   ♨

2809 M St. NW (28th St. NW), Georgetown, Washington 20007
202-333-0234, Fax 202-333-1174
Lunch Tues.-Fri., Dinner Tues.-Sun., $$$, Casual dressy

🅰 ☎ 🥢 🍴 🍷 🍶 ⟳

Squeezed into a tiny space on M Street, this French restaurant may be small, but its menu encompasses much more than just the usual French offerings of cheese-encrusted onion soup, snails and beef bourguignon. Of course, there is onion soup, but it contains five varieties of onions. There are even several versions of Caesar salad. Though not French, it is especially good garnished with broiled fresh fish and accompanied by crusty baguettes to mop up the excellent dressing. Entrées include lamb sausage and osso buco with couscous, rack of lamb with truffled potatoes and filet mignon with shallot confit. Desserts are worth trying, too: profiteroles, chocolate mousse cake and three kinds of crème brûlée.

Meskerem Ethiopian   Ethiopian   12/20

2434 18th St. NW (Columbia Rd. NW)
Adams Morgan, Washington 20009
202-462-4100, Fax 202-362-5812, *Lunch & Dinner daily, $, Casual*

🅰 🍴 🍷 🍶 ⟳

You can never go wrong with the yedor watt (known elsewhere as doro watt), the richly seasoned chicken stew plus hard-cooked egg served traditionally on injera bread. We also favor the kik alitcha, a purée of yellow split peas, gently seasoned with herbs and spices and served with a mound of injera. Ask about house specialties. The décor is bright and cheery with a splashy sun motif.

Michel Richard Citronelle   19/20

French/Contemporary
The Latham Hotel
3000 M St. NW (30th St. NW), Georgetown, Washington 20007
202-625-2150, Fax 202-339-6326
Breakfast, Lunch & Dinner daily, $$$$, Casual dressy

🅰 ☎ P 🥢 🍴 🍷 🍶 ⟳

It's Washington's gain that chef Michel Richard has made Citronelle—and we are weighing our words carefully—one of the best restaurants in America. We are more than happy to herald this news, which is already well-known by DC hedonists who may prefer to keep it to themselves. Michel Richard Citronelle is not only a restaurant but also a theater. From the multitiered room, animated by a changing "mood wall," it's worthwhile watching the show that unravels on the brightly lit "stage"—an exhibition kitchen sparkling with immaculate glass, steel and copper props. The ebullient Richard orchestrates a symphony of fragrances and with steady gestures directs a seasoned cast, adding his own touch of genius: perhaps a pinch of spice, a dot of sauce, in a precise movement that indicates clearly his role as the master du grand art. Prepare yourself to savor his ever-changing and evolving creations: perhaps the caviar Penguin, a voluptuous combination of caviar and potato purée, or the rouget with endive and calamari sauce, or the Maine razor clams with cauliflower tabbouleh and ahi tuna—all so simple and natural, a virgin bouquet of flavors approaching perfection. We acclaim the latest creation, the squab four ways. Different parts of the squab are prepared in four manners and presented on four different square plates—a clockwork art. The cheeses—a dozen or so—are stored and served at exactly the right temperature. The final bouquet of desserts brings an explosion of colors, textures and tastes, reminding us of Richard's beginnings as a superb pastry chef. Don't miss the unexpected refinement of a tomato, basil and pineapple concassé in a lime, wine, olive oil pesto sauce. Yes! There is no better way to sample Richard's inspired modern French cooking than by ordering his pricey seven-course dégustation menu. The wine cellar, managed by Mark Slater, lives up to the high quality of Richard's cooking. Don't be shy about asking the master to custom-design a meal for you. Richard is an artist, and his palette will please your palate, although not necessarily your wallet. Still, the experience will be worth every penny, as his is some of the best cooking in America.

Miss Saigon   Vietnamese   11/20

3057 M St. NW (31st St. NW), Georgetown, Washington 20007
202-333-5545, Fax 202-333-6459, Lunch & Dinner daily, $$, Casual

🅰 ☎ 🍴 ▲

Miss Saigon is one of the few DC-based Vietnamese restaurants that is worthy competition for the fine Vietnamese restaurants clustered around the Clarendon Metro station or those at the Vietnamese shopping complex, Eden Center—where people flock for great Vietnamese cooking. In fact, in the past, we've considered it among the city's very best Vietnamese food. But lately, we've been disappointed with some inconsistent dishes. Still, we recommend the crisp spring rolls; the garden rolls stuffed with shrimp, pork, and vegetables; shrimp in lemon grass and chili; and mixed seafood marinated in oyster sauce.

Mr. K's   Chinese   13/20   🍲

2121 K St. NW (21st St. NW), Downtown, Washington 20037
202-331-8868, Fax 202-223-4484, Lunch & Dinner daily, $$, Casual dressy

🅰 ☎ P 🍴 🍷 ▲ 🍽

Mr. K's has a sherbet palate cleanser between courses, fine china, linen tablecloths and classical music—not your typical Chinese restaurant. Further adding to that fact is that Mr. K's doesn't even offer carryout food. The menu, too, has many Western overtones: Lobster Grand Marnier and filet of sole Sauvignon, for example. Firecracker Lobster, Pecan Shrimp, Empress Beef and Pork Loquat, though, do strike more of a Far Eastern note. Surprisingly, the Lamb Marengo, which we thought might well come with the typical brandy and tomatoes of a Marengo dish, is actually accented by chilies and consists of lamb slices tossed with scallions, garlic and ginger—no one flavor predominates, not even the chili heat. Just because Mr. K's is different doesn't mean it's not popular. It is, attracting a well-heeled crowd. There's an affiliated branch in Manhattan.

Some establishments change **days of operation** without warning. It is always wise to check in advance.

Mrs. Simpson's   American   13/20

2915 Connecticut Ave. NW
(Cathedral Ave.), National Zoo, Washington 20008
202-332-8700, Fax 202-332-1306
Dinner Tues.-Sun., Brunch Sun., $$, Casual dressy

Anglophiles will adore this tiny restaurant with its comprehensive collection of Mrs. Simpson memorabilia—yes, that Mrs. Simpson, who won the heart and hand of a British monarch. As charming as a lady's tearoom with its fresh flowers, this Mrs. Simpson makes a big fuss over food. We have thoroughly enjoyed the restful brunch whipped up by executive chef Aimé Adompo, including the Duchess Brunch with scrambled eggs and smoked salmon, the Mrs. Simpson's single crab cake, and the french toast with berries and maple syrup. Our favorite: the Belgian waffle with melted butter and maple syrup. We suggest starting with the worthy onion soup, though you may prefer the lighter garden salad. Dinners encompass pasta, risotto, a magret of duck and a dish called "An English Tradition" with calf's liver. The coffee is strongly bracing, and if you have room finish with a slice of carrot cake or cheesecake.

Mixtec   Tex-Mex/Mexican   12/20

1792 Columbia Rd. NW (18th St. NW)
Adams Morgan, Washington 20009
202-332-1011, *Lunch & Dinner daily, $, Casual*

Sometimes gruff and unfriendly, the staff are the least of the reasons you come to this budget-priced place, where the Tex-Mex fare is the real draw. The scene is set by the strains of Mexican music that filter out from somewhere and the color food photos on the wall. Start with their queso fundido, accompanied by a mug of hot Mexican chocolate, then opt for the Mexican submarine sandwiches served on French bread or one of the hearty platos of typical food such as the chiles rellenos, the burrito norteño and the chicken mole. Otherwise, the menu holds few temptations, although you can eat yourself silly here and still keep a pocketful of change.

The Monocle   American   12/20

107 D St. NE (First St. NE), Capitol Hill, Washington 20002
202-546-4488, Fax 202-546-7235
Lunch & Dinner Mon.-Fri., $$$, Business casual

At the Monocle, the closest restaurant to the Senate side of the Capitol, you can almost always count on seeing political celebrities. Its private rooms upstairs is the location for countless political fundraisers. But although it's known mainly as a power place, the food is better than one might think. The kitchen turns out fine versions of Mid-Atlantic regional favorites: crab cakes, grilled and fried fresh fish, homey pot roast, and, of course, steaks and chops.

Prices are based on a complete dinner for one, including appetizer, entrée, dessert, coffee, tax and tip—but excluding wine or other beverages.

Morrison-Clark Restaurant 13/20

Contemporary
The Morrison-Clark Inn
1015 L St. NW (11th St. NW), Downtown, Washington 20001
202-898-1200, Fax 202-289-8567
Breakfast & Dinner daily, Lunch Mon.-Fri., Brunch Sun., $$$, Ties suggested

In this downtown inn, crafted from two adjoining Victorian townhouses, chef Bob Beaudry has redesigned the menu to offer a spread of sophisticated American dishes with some significant Asian and Southwestern accents. Like many DC restaurants, the menu changes seasonally, so expect some surprises from time to time. You may feast on a grits soufflé with crayfish and étouffée sauce appetizer followed by a Cuban pork sandwich entrée for lunch, or choose something more conventional. Dinner offerings tend to be more elaborate such as the seared Muscovy duck breast. Two longtime signature dishes remain on the menu: the Romaine-Roquefort Salad and the beloved lemon chess pie. We enjoy dining in the tall-windowed dining room, with its voluptuous floral arrangement, but in nice weather, we grab a table outside on the brick courtyard.

Morton's of Chicago Steakhouse 14/20

1050 Connecticut Ave. NW (L St. NW), Downtown, Washington 20036
202-955-5997, Fax 202-955-5889
Lunch Mon.-Fri., Dinner nightly, $$$, Business casual

Morton's steaks are even bigger than its reputation as watering holes for political bigwigs or a spot where Monica Lewinsky dined with her attorney. The real reason to come is for one of the aged, top-quality porterhouses, available in one-and-a-half- or three-pound cuts. To avoid ruining your appetite, go easy on the starters—perhaps a house salad or a plate of sliced beefsteak tomatoes with red onion and blue cheese. As a side, one of the football-sized baked potatoes does nicely. The service is excellent, as is the wine list, and, if you are not in the mood for beef, you can secure a good chop or a fresh piece of salmon. **Also located at** 3251 Prospect St. NW, Washington, DC 202-342-6258; and 8075 Leesburg Pike, Vienna, VA, 703-883-0800.

Nathan's American 12/20

3150 M St. NW (Wisconsin Ave. NW), Georgetown, Washington 20007
202-338-2000, Fax: 202-333-2509
Lunch & Dinner daily, Brunch Sun., $, Casual

Chefs come and go and its menu changes seasonally, but Nathan's retains a firm hold on its popularity as an after-hours destination because of its friendly staff and cozy, lean-on-the-bar atmosphere. Located at the main Georgetown intersection of Wisconsin and M, it attracts tourists as well as locals, who'll drop in for burgers, sandwiches and heavier fare. But its main reason for being is its bar—figure on crowds from late afternoon on.

New Heights — Contemporary — 14/20

2317 Calvert St. NW (Connecticut Ave. NW)
Woodley Park, Washington, DC 20008
202-234-4110, Fax 202-234-0789
Dinner nightly, Brunch Sun., $$$, Business casual

Considered a good proving ground of DC chefs, the kitchen at New Heights is now under the direction of executive chef Scott Ostander, a Culinary Institute of America graduate. He brings to his cooking American flavors accompanied by international flair, taking classic dishes and introducing new, sometimes offbeat, ingredients. His menu includes a braised lamb shank and Indian vindaloo masala; seared Big Island Kajiki marlin; and guajillo-glazed steelhead salmon with crispy onion rings and a black bean-huitlacoche relish. Look for fresh local produce in season from organic growers in Pennsylvania. You may also recognize many old favorites on the menu, including the famed black bean pâté.

Neyla — Mediterranean — 14/20

3206 N. St. NW (Wisconsin Ave. NW), Washington 20007
202-333-6353, Fax 202-333-6636, *Dinner nightly, $$$, Casual*

With its pale sun-yellow walls, wood-framed mirrors, sparkling candles and burgundy swags, Neyla looks a little like an Arabian sheik's tent, minus the stamping horses and gazelle platters. Promising Mediterranean cooking with many Lebanese and some Western overtones, Neyla puts on a food show that demonstrates how well some cross-cultural cooking can work. Grill cooks skewer tender beef cubes for a turn over the fire while others lift great puffs of fresh pita, like giant floury pillows, from the heat. Meanwhile, you're scooping up the slightly salty labne, or thickened yogurt, drizzled with olive oil. Instead of kebabs, however, you may have chosen something more Westernized, such as a filet of Atlantic salmon or roasted tamarind-lacquered duck or even a New York strip steak seasoned with Lebanese spices. Or you may, as we did, decide that for this meal, the last should really come first. To begin, throw away convention and order the rosewater crème brûlée, a dessert that will forever change the way you view this sweet. Perched on a pool of swirled chocolate and custard sauces, little mounds of creamy custard are layered with crispy shreds of phyllo dough, a tantalizing combination. With this, you may want to sip some Turkish coffee. Then pampered and well-fed, you will exit into the anything-but desert of Georgetown.

Nick & Stef's Steakhouse — Steakhouse — 13/20

MCI Center
601 F St. NW (6th St. NW), Downtown, Washington 20004
202-661-5040, Fax 202-347-1233
Lunch Mon.-Fri., Dinner nightly, $$$, Casual

Despite sharing the same space with the MCI Center, management has sagely retained a starkly sophisticated look here and hasn't succumbed to an all-sports venue. Thus, it's dressy enough to wine and dine VIPs. Yet, after games upstairs you can bet that fans come to this steakhouse dressed in their sweats and sport togs, ready to dig into lusty steak dinners. The kitchen, under the direction of executive chef Joseph Gillard, takes its meats seriously; just check out the glassed-in dry-aging room opposite the front door. Menu items are grouped by the dozen and are categorized by starters, vegetables, meat entrées, sauces and potatoes. There are also daily specials such as the bone-in 20-ounce Kansas City strip steak. Dry-rubbed with a salt and pepper mix pressed into the meat, this steak comes with a charred and crusty exterior that seals in all meat juices and flavors. Everything on the menu is à la carte. Appealing potato sides include a crispy blue cheese potato cake, two variations of mashed potatoes and sweet potato fries. Lemon meringue pie and a classic American chocolate cake are good desserts.

Nora | Contemporary | 15/20 ♙♙

2132 Florida Ave. NW (R St. NW), Dupont Circle, Washington 20008
202-462-5143, Fax 202-234-6232
Lunch & Dinner Mon.-Sat., $$$$, Casual dressy

Nora Pouillon's lovely restaurant, decorated with museum-quality Amish crib quilts, was certified as the first all-organic restaurant in the country. But long before that honor, chef-owner Pouillon steadfastly selected only the finest organic ingredients—many locally raised—and even fish from certified waters for this and her other restaurant, Asia Nora, in the West End (see review in this chapter). At Nora, organic ingredients run the gamut from greens to peppercorns to coffee. This approach appeals to many more than just vegetarians or granola types. A fashionable cross-section of Washingtonians show up for Pouillon's greens, classy wines and such showy dishes as rack of lamb with Mission figs. The menu changes often and seasonally, but some of the favorites are the smoked trout tower as an appetizer, and signature entrées like rockfish and duck breast prepared a number of ways. A popular dessert is the soufflé cake with cappuccino ice cream—cranked on the premises, of course. Nora is a restaurant that celebrates the beauty of honest, seasonal ingredients prepared with passion and verve.

Obelisk | Italian | 15/20 ♙♙

2029 P St. NW (21st St. NW), Dupont Circle, Washington 20036
202-872-1180, *Dinner Tues.-Sat., $$$$, Casual*

In the modest dining room with about a dozen tables, chef-owner Peter Pastan serves some of the most authentic and delicious Italian cooking in the city. His inspiration comes from those tiny off-the-beaten-path restaurants in Italy, where the proprietor cooks what he feels like on a particular day, depending on what's good in the market. Pastan's four-course, fixed-price meal costs from $50 to $55, depending on what he's found in the market, and it's one of the great bargains of Washington dining. A meal might start with a delicious veal terrine, go on to a delicate pasta course such as beet-stuffed ravioli with chive-butter sauce and then a mixed grill of game. Before the good desserts, don't miss the optional cheese course, as it may consist of any number of excellent Italian cheeses that are best with a drizzle of fruity olive oil.

The Oceanaire Seafood Room Seafood **14/20**

1201 F St. NW (12th St. NW), Downtown, Washington 20004
202-347-BASS, Fax 202-347-9858
Lunch Mon.-Fri., Dinner nightly, $$$, Casual dressy

A ☎ P Y ⓘ ↻

Reminiscent of a '30s restaurant, this 9,000-square-foot place with plush cherry-wood paneling promises and delivers especially fresh seafood in a variety of ways. Check the top of the menu for the catches of the day—about two dozen fish varieties—and listen to your server's specials before you make any decisions. The menu includes big shrimp cocktails and crab-cake appetizers, clams casino, oysters Rockefeller (plus a splendid assortment of fresh oysters—at the oyster bar or at your table) and soups (a Maryland blue crab soup leads the list). Menus are drawn up twice daily so that chef Jason Tepper can present the freshly arrived catch, popularly served simply grilled or broiled and brushed with olive oil and lemon. The crab Louie salad might be a lighter choice than the cioppino, but we adored the latter, a seafood stew that is a mix of fish and shellfish in a peppery broth—sensational. Desserts are wickedly outsized; you'll wish for an elastic-waisted outfit if you plan to finish off the for-two portions of cheesecake or Key lime pie. Smaller old-fashioned desserts like Toll House cookies with milk or a root beer float may become all the rage in this town where looking back is as much fun as peering into the future. Service here is courteous and diligent.

Old Ebbitt Grill American **13/20**

675 15th St. NW (F St. NW), Downtown, Washington 20005
202-347-4800, Fax 202-347-6136
Breakfast & Lunch Mon.-Fri., Dinner nightly, Brunch Sat.-Sun., $$, Casual

A ☎ P 🍴 👓 Y ⓘ ↻

A celebrity hangout in downtown Washington, the Old Ebbitt Grill, part of the Clyde's restaurant group, captures the city's be-there spirit in an exuberant, Old-World setting. Lawyers rub elbows with politicos, secretaries with salesmen. Everyone eats well here. The place is known for its big portions. The restaurant's oyster bar is a mecca, and its annual oyster bash draws big crowds. Many diners swear by the crab cakes, but in a restaurant that touts a partially revised menu daily, there's always something to intrigue and amuse. Best bets: the grilled lamb steak with mashed sweet potatoes and the raspberry bread pudding with its swirl of crème anglaise. Weekend brunches are bounteous, bustling affairs where you'll find mighty good pancakes.

Old Europe German **12/20**

2434 Wisconsin Ave. NW (Calvert St. NW)
Glover Park, Washington 20007
202-333-7600, Fax 202-625-0553
Lunch Mon.-Sat., Dinner nightly, $$, Casual

A ☎ 🍴 🍷 Y ⓘ ↻

More than 50 years old, Old Europe is one of the few German restaurants in the Washington area. You can always find large portions of satisfying würsts and schnitzels, but the real draw at Old Europe is its succession of festivals throughout the year: Oktoberfest; a winter game festival, when black radishes, butcher's platters and steins of beer are served; a spring asparagus festival, when you can get one-pound servings of green or rare white asparagus; and a May wine festival, when dinner is accompanied by goblets of Riesling steeped with woodruff.

Olives Contemporary 13/20

1600 K St. NW (16th St. NW), Downtown, Washington 20006
202-452-1866, Fax 202-452-8245
Lunch Mon.-Fri., Dinner Mon.-Sat., $$$, Casual dressy

A spin-off of acclaimed chef Todd English's famous Charlestown, Mass., restaurant (which now also has branches in New York and Las Vegas), Olives attracts well-heeled crowds who pack into its clubby, well-appointed dining areas. Taken singly, items are praiseworthy, even elegant. A number of dishes have become our favorites. Unfortunately, however, the menu undergoes regular face-lifts, so don't get too attached to any one thing. We loved the fork-tender beef brisket with blue cheese and onion jam layered on an English muffin, but it has vanished. However, the grilled rib-eye of beef with Parmesan frites is also a good choice. If your mouth is watering, don't jump in the car too quickly. Call first: Don't show up without reservations or you may wait for hours for one of the seats in this extremely hot spot.

Osteria Goldoni Italian 14/20

1120 20th St. NW (M St. NW), Downtown, Washington 20036
202-293-1511, Fax 202-452-0875
Lunch Mon.-Fri., Dinner nightly, $$$$, Casual dressy

Chef-owner Fabrizio Aielli was a sous chef under Roberto Donna at nearby Galileo until he began cooking at his own excellent restaurant with its more formal upstairs dining room and livelier downstairs space. Aielli specializes in traditional Italian dishes and his own outstanding version of contemporary Venetian cooking. His pastas are simultaneously light and complex in flavor, and he prepares a creamy, olive-oil-enriched polenta. On the daily-changing menu, dinner may begin with an antipasto of robiola cheese topped with slices of delicate eggplant along with rustic salami. If they're available, order the fettuccine with rabbit ragoût or the whole fish baked in parchment paper with artichokes. For dessert, choose the turban of chocolate, if it's available. Check out the crowd: You may see some major political players. Also check out Aielli's other excellent restaurant, Teatro Goldoni, another downtown location. There the focus is on Venetian cuisine and the dramatic setting its name implies (see review in this chapter).

The Oval Room Contemporary 13/20

800 Connecticut Ave. NW (I St. NW)
Downtown, Washington 20006
202-463-8700, Fax 202-785-9863
Lunch Mon.-Fri., Dinner Mon.-Sat., $$$, Business casual

The name suggests its proximity to the Oval Office just across Lafayette Square. No surprise, then, that the handsome eatery has been a restaurant of choice for executive branch power dining. Chef George Vetsch's contemporary menu realizes the virtues of simplicity—a creamy asparagus soup enriched with country ham, a perfect roast chicken with a pile of crisp fries, seared halibut with artichokes. Expect to see famous faces—or the faces behind the famous faces—lunching here. The restaurant is an offspring of local restaurateur Ashok Bajaj, who owns the popular Bombay Club and Ardeo (see reviews in this chapter).

Palena — Italian/American — 15/20 🍴🍴

3529 Connecticut Ave. NW (Porter St.)
Cleveland Park, Washington 20008
202-537-9250, Fax 202-537-9375, *Dinner Mon.-Sat., $$$, Casual dressy*

🅰 📷 ⚡ 🍸 ▲ 🍸

As Ann Amernick and Frank Ruta promised when they joined forces to cook, they are delivering authentic, Italianesque main dishes with American undertones—all followed by Amernick's exquisite desserts. The pair cooked together at the White House before their career paths diverged years ago, and have met up again to feed sophisticated Washingtonians well, starting with the fresh made-on-the-premises sturdy whole-grain breads with a decidedly rustic quality. You may find that Ruta's tasting menu, with a set price that seems to vary from one time to the next, may give you the best sense of what his cooking is about. Otherwise, select from à la carte dishes that change frequently, some even daily. Starters have included goat cheese canederli with mushrooms or sea scallops with chestnut purée. Grilled duck breast or a veal chop stuffed with peppers are excellent main courses. A dry-aged sirloin with wine sauce was richly flavored. But dinner cannot really be concluded until you have dealt with Amernick's treats, the best of which is her chocolate-toffee torte in a pool of mocha crème anglaise. It's a small and stylish restaurant warmed by pale-yellow colors, fresh-cut flowers and floral prints on the wall.

Palm — Steakhouse — 13/20 🍴

1225 19th St. NW (N St. NW), Dupont Circle, Washington 20036
202-293-9091, Fax 202-775-1468
Lunch Mon.-Fri., Dinner nightly, $$$$, Casual

🅰 📷 🅿 ⚡ 🍸 ▲ ↻

If The Capital Grille is the power lunch spot of choice for Republicans, the Palm is the preferred Democratic hangout. Lunch and dinner are equally busy. The lunch menu features the Palm's signature beef salad over sliced tomatoes and a list of surprisingly good Italian and Cajun-inspired dishes. In the evening, go for the New York strip or one of the gigantic lobsters that they're famous for, accompanied by an order of cottage fries and creamed spinach. Instead of dessert, opt for a Cognac and an expensive cigar—it's that kind of place. **Also located at** 1750 Tysons Blvd., Vienna, VA, 703-917-0200

Palomino — Mediterranean — 13/20 🍴

Ronald Reagan International Trade Center
1300 Pennsylvania Ave. NW (13th St. NW)
Downtown, Washington 20004
202-842-9800, Fax 202-842-9803
Lunch Mon.-Fri., Dinner nightly, $$$, Casual dressy

🅰 📷 🅿 ⚡ 🍴 ♥ 🍴 🍸 ▲ ↻

Palomino is both chic and slightly avant-garde, but foodies know the real score: They come for its sizzling grilled meats and seafood and hearty-lusty pastas, all inspired by

Mediterranean tastes and techniques but with an American spin. We've loved the specials—grilled salmon resting on a bed of greens and wild African spicy chicken soup—but are just as content with the potent Caesar salad with sheets of fresh Parmesan. If your taste runs to oddball pizzas, consider the hearth-baked pies (only at lunch) for a change of pace. The smoked leg of lamb the size of a football is a showstopper. If you crave desserts, you may want to forgo everything except several servings of the tiramisu, which, depending on the season, may be chocolate-dense or brimming with berries in its pool of custard sauce. Palomino, part of an upscale Seattle-based national chain, makes a perfect pre-theater destination. Or come back after the show and enjoy its signature drinks—with another portion of tiramisu.

Paolo's — Italian — 12/20

1303 Wisconsin Ave. NW (N St. NW), Georgetown, Washington 20007
202-333-7353, Fax 202-342-2846, *Lunch & Dinner daily, $$, Casual*

It's easy to fall in love with a place like Paolo's. Its Georgetown location is right in the heart of things, and patrons often drift in from the sidewalk. The passing pedestrians are part of the entertainment; the other part is the snappy and trendy Italian food. It's not classical, but somewhat Americanized, with such offerings as duck confit pizza with apple butter coulis and a pulled roasted chicken salad. There is a succulent filet mignon with an asparagus side made with Gorgonzola and walnuts. The restaurant is so popular that you'll probably wait but, in fine weather, enhanced seating means eating outdoors, an ideal option for people-watching. At one time Paolo's had a higher profile locally, but now it has only two locations—a pity for those of us who love its lusty and unconventional fare and laid-back ambience. **Also located at** 11898 Market St., Reston, VA, 703-318-8920.

Peacock Café — American — 13/20

3251 Prospect St. NW (Wisconsin Ave. NW)
Georgetown, Washington 20007
202-625-2740, Fax 202-625-1402
Lunch & Dinner daily, Brunch Sat.-Sun., $$, Casual dressy

The brothers Farivar have created a Georgetown spot that solves all your dining-out problems—at least on weekends. Brunch here on a Belgian waffle, lunch on the Gorgonzola-rich bistro burger and dine on the fancy shellfish bowl of mussels, crayfish and scallops on a tangle of pasta. One brother seats customers, chats with old-timers (this has become a neighborhood meeting place) and keeps service flowing. The other brother creates his simple, elegant fare from market-fresh produce, meats and fish. The restaurant's clean, straight lines and mirrored walls look sophisticated yet casual. Late night, the bar turns into a singles hangout. Expect crowds from lunchtime on—many are regulars who love to linger over coffee or drinks.

For **guidebooks to other cities worldwide,**
visit: gayot.com

Perry's
Contemporary　　**13/20**

1811 Columbia Rd. NW (18th St. NW)
Adams Morgan, Washington 20009
202-234-6218, Fax 202-934-9453
Dinner nightly, Brunch Sun., $$, Casual

The young and the restless—and plenty of others, too—have turned Perry's into an Adams Morgan event. Climbing the stone staircase to its second-story address, you might think you've slipped into a period piece: It's decorated in burgundy and red and lit by a funky and improbable chandelier. The long bar and the rooftop dining annex are lively places that attract a young and worldly set. The menu is surprising, pairing unusual Japanese sushi with an eclectic assortment of American regional main dishes that change seasonally. We swooned over the chicken breast stuffed with an arugula mousse and perched atop mashed potatoes, the pan-seared Chilean sea bass and the marinated pork tenderloin. There is a huge roll of lobster, tuna, avocado and cucumber wrapped in rice. Perry's may put on a nightlong party, but its most outrageous event is the Sunday morning brunch—you have to see it to believe it. Perry's does not take reservations, and if you hanker for rooftop seating, plan to arrive early or you probably will have to wait.

Pesce
Seafood　　**14/20**

2016 P St. NW (20th St. NW), Dupont Circle, Washington 20036
202-466-3474, Fax 202-466-8302,
Lunch Mon.-Sat., Dinner nightly, $$, Casual

This simple café on P Street, with its menu written on a blackboard, features some of the best seafood cooking in the city. The menu generally includes a number of first courses and soups, a pasta dish or two, and about 10 fish entrées. You get the best and freshest of what's available—fresh Carolina shrimp with garlic butter, shad roe, soft-shell crabs, diver scallops (hand-gathered by divers), Maine clams and plump oysters. There's seldom a misstep. Pesce's reputation is outstanding, making it a popular destination for the many foodies who flock here.

Petits Plats
French　　**13/20**

2653 Connecticut Ave. NW (Calvert St. NW)
Woodley Park, Washington 20008
202-518-0018, Fax 202-518-0045
Lunch Tues.-Sat., Dinner, Tues.-Sun., $$, Casual

Petits Plats offers a nicely served and streamlined assortment of mainly French fare. We recommend the deftly seasoned and arranged plate of asparagus with tapenade to start, followed by the grilled trout—usually served with bok choy and lemon butter, but as a special the fish may turn up as a salad with balsamic-dressed greens. The boneless quail confit with truffles and calf's liver prepared with pearl onions and caperberries was outstanding. As the restaurant's name suggests, servings are small; that is, discreet portions that won't surfeit but will satisfy.

Phillips Flagship Seafood Restaurant   Seafood **12/20**

900 Water St. SW (Maine Ave. SW), Waterfront, Washington 20024
202-488-8515, Fax 202-484-8161
Lunch & Dinner daily, Brunch Sun., $$$, Casual

Phillips Flagship is much less an impress-the-client kind of restaurant than a seafood free-for-all. Sunday brunches are meant for the whole family to indulge in a never-ending display of foods. On sunny days, head for the terrace, a pretty setting overlooking docked boats and the Potomac beyond. This serious seafood restaurant serves great crab cakes, stuffed jumbo shrimp, lobster and a clambake for two. **Also located at** 8330 Boone Blvd., Vienna, VA, 703-442-0400.

The Prime Rib   Steakhouse   **13/20**

2020 K St. NW (20th St. NW), Downtown, Washington 20006
202-466-8811, Fax 202-466-2010
Lunch Mon.-Fri., Dinner Mon.-Sat., $$$$, Ties suggested

The ambience of the Prime Rib evokes that of an elegant supper club of the '40s—gold-trimmed black walls, black-tie-clad waiters and a Lucite-topped grand piano that's played during lunch and dinner. The name reveals the specialty: the best roast beef in town. You also can get that rib cut as a steak. If you choose not to eat red meat, the best alternatives are two superb regional seafood dishes: crab imperial (lump crab meat lightly bound with mayonnaise) and baked shrimp stuffed with crab meat. This is one of those rare "in" restaurants where you can actually carry on a conversation and be heard no matter how many people are waiting for a table in the bar.

Primi Piatti Ristorante   Italian   **14/20**

2013 I (Eye) St. NW (20th St. NW), Downtown, Washington 20006
202-223-3600, Fax 202-296-3725
Lunch Mon.-Fri., Dinner Mon.-Sat., $$$, Casual dressy

Dressier and pricier than most local Italian eateries, Primi Piatti has staked out its reputation on quality ingredients that are thoughtfully and well prepared. Always popular here—besides the dense, peasant-style breads and crunchy breadsticks—are the antipasto platters and the robustly sophisticated pastas and lunchtime designer pizzas. This is one restaurant that appeals to yuppie and seniors alike. Its sister restaurant at Tysons Corner has an almost-identical menu, lofty atmosphere and upscale location. **Also located at** 8045 Leesburg Pike, Vienna, VA, 703-893-0300

Red Sage   Southwestern   **14/20**

605 14th St. NW (F St. NW), Downtown, Washington 20005
202-638-4444, Fax 202-928-8430
Lunch Mon.-Fri., Dinner nightly, $$$, Business casual

Chef Morou Ouattara and his staff have shaken things up a bit at this classy Southwestern eatery, with its very costly décor and price-driven image. Many, of course, think his food is worth it. Entrées might include charcoaled ostrich filet or fire-roasted quail. The chili is a signature dish. There are three versions. We adore the steak and black bean mix. If you're price-conscious, sit upstairs in the Border Café. Food there is a treat, too. The roasted tortilla soup with chicken, queso and avocado is a thick, hot and altogether outstanding rendition of this Southwestern classic. Just as good is the chipotle barbecue brisket quesadilla. It's an addictive entrée. Desserts like bittersweet chocolate brownie, warm cobbler and a three-nut caramel bar satisfy whether you are sitting upstairs or downstairs.

Red Tomato — Italian — 14/20

2030 M St. NW (21st St. NW), Downtown, Washington 20036
202-463-9030, Fax 202-463-9034
Lunch Mon.-Fri., Dinner Mon.-Sat., $$$, Casual dressy

The divine Italian food prepared by executive chef Enzo Febbraro is just hitting center stage, although this restaurant remains somewhat underappreciated. With its tomato-colored walls and snappy décor, the Red Tomato makes its own statement and it's a positive one. We've loved the sautéed foie gras on toast splashed with balsamic vinegar to start; and the veal chop served with whipped potatoes and a carrot casserole to follow. Other standouts: the grilled tuna steak and the roasted rack of lamb with an olive-mustard crust. For a refreshing conclusion, try the lemon custard tart. But don't get too attached to anything, because if you become a repeat customer, this is the kind of place where you want to sample everything.

Roof Terrace Restaurant — American — 12/20

The John F. Kennedy Center for the Performing Arts
2700 F St. NW (Potomac Pkwy. NW), Foggy Bottom, Washington 20566
202-416-8555, Fax 202-416-8551
Lunch (matinee days), Dinner nightly, Brunch Sun., $$$, Casual dressy

As a destination restaurant for culture buffs, the Roof Terrace has no equal in DC. Within moments, patrons can descend to a concert, theater or other event in the Kennedy Center after dining. The dinner menu may feature such interesting entrées as succulent crab cakes, grilled tuna, pan-seared duck breast, braised lamb shanks and an onion-crusted salmon. Dessert choices include a caramel toffee cheesecake. Brunches are popular and entail a buffet tour of the kitchen, where the food is set out in big displays; the dessert table is usually laid out in the restaurant proper.

Ruppers — Contemporary — 14/20

1017 Seventh St. NW (New York Ave. NW
Chinatown, Washington 20001
202-783-0699, *Dinner Wed.-Sat., $$$, Casual*

Its location on the edge of Chinatown may look iffy, but Ruppers is one of DC's hippest restaurants, with its spare yet trendy décor. It's as popular with DC suits as with suburbanites. It's useless to tell you what to expect on the menu, because the chef's cooking is always driven by what is freshest at the market. At one meal, your appetizer may be air-dried paper-thin slices of venison about the size of a silver dollar; at another, foie gras with luscious dates. You may fall madly in love with the Angus steak on a bed of turnip greens with mashed potatoes, but at your next visit the menu may star sliced buffalo tenderloins paired with sweet roasted turnips. The food is unique.

So, too, are the breads, which are baked several times during the day. You'll want to smuggle some home. Desserts are deliciously unpredictable: The selection may include an apple and pear brioche or maple ice cream on a waffle.

Ruth's Chris Steak House   Steakhouse   14/20

1801 Connecticut Ave. NW (S St. NW)
Dupont Circle, Washington 20009
202-797-0033, Fax 202-667-4257, *Dinner nightly, $$$, Business casual*

The Connecticut Avenue branch of an upscale international steakhouse chain that started in New Orleans, Ruth's Chris is often filled with conventioneers from the Washington Hilton up the street. The big attraction is the steak, USDA Prime, cut in large portions, cooked to order and dripping in butter, New Orleans-style. But you'll find assorted other dishes, too, such as lobster, veal, chicken and select seafood. There are plenty of vegetable and potato dishes and desserts on the menu, but the appetizers and salads tend to be forgettable. **Other locations.**

Sala Thai   Thai   12/20

2016 P St. NW (20th St. NW), Dupont Circle, Washington 20036
202-872-1144, Fax 202-872-0073, *Lunch & Dinner daily, $$, Casual*

Everyone seems to love this restaurant. Just look at the crowds on a weekend night. Folks from the neighborhood descend the stairs for one of the cramped tables (try fitting three or four dishes on the tiny table for two!) Its minimalist décor and trendy menu are both appealing. Cute names like Pinky in the Blanket (deep-fried shrimp in egg roll wrappers) and Wild Pork (stir-fried pork in red curry) don't mean the food isn't highly distinguished. We loved the soft-shell crabs, grilled chicken with sticky rice. **Also located at** 2900 N. Tenth St., Arlington, VA, 703-465-2900.

Sam & Harry's   Steakhouse   13/20

1200 19th St. NW (M St. NW), Dupont Circle, Washington 20036
202-296-4333, Fax 202-785-1070
Lunch Mon.-Fri., Dinner Mon.-Sat., $$$$, Business casual

Most steakhouses look like men's clubs. Sam & Harry's, with its two-tiered dining room, French doors and jazz-themed art, looks like a sophisticated downtown restaurant. The specialty steak here is a porterhouse, custom-cut for Sam & Harry's by a Chicago packer. If you want something other than steak, alternatives are lamb or veal chops, large lobsters and grilled fish. The wine list is long and impressive. **Also located at** 8240 Leesburg Pike, Vienna, VA, 703-448-0088.

San Marzano   Italian   12/20

3282 M St. NW (Prospect St. NW), Georgetown, Washington 20007
202-965-7007, Fax 202-965-3341, *Lunch & Dinner daily, $$, Casual*

It's slick and sleek and ultra-modern, a testimony to how well the Italian pizza-bar concept can go upscale. Its wide-open interior allows patrons to gaze out the front windows or, from almost any seat, watch the kitchen staff prepping the thin-crust pizzas and assorted salads and pastas. Sample the salade Niçoise for an authentic Mediterranean flavor and conclude the meal with a wedge of cheesecake or a piece of tiramisu. You can opt to sit at the front bar or select a table instead for an easy drop-in meal. It's also ultra-casual, so bring along the kids.

Saveur Restaurant   French/Contemporary   14/20

2218 Wisconsin Ave. NW (W St. NW), Glover Park, Washington 20007
202-333-5885, Fax 202-333-1104
Lunch Sun.-Fri., Dinner nightly, Brunch Sun., $$$, Casual

Although chef Keo Koumtakoun has moved from Virginia's La Provence restaurant to the stoves at Saveur Restaurant, at times, you'll still be feasting on Provençal flavors. However, there are lots of imaginative dishes that can't be categorized. Hope to find such fare as the fettuccine with a ragoût of beef sirloin, the roasted eggplant appetizer topped with slowly melting Roquefort cheese and a roasted rosemary chicken with homemade mashed potatoes—heavenly. Other dinner choices may include rack of lamb or pan-seared duck breast. Desserts seem less inspired, but for calorie watchers, the kitchen has created Coco Saveur, a mock crème brûlée with egg whites and a shot of coconut flavor. It's definitely a be-seen-in kind of place, with distinct uptown cachet.

Sea Catch Restaurant & Raw Bar   Seafood   14/20

1054 31st St. NW (M St. NW), Georgetown, Washington 20007
202-337-8855, Fax 202-337-7159, *Lunch & Dinner Mon.-Sat., $$, Casual*

In an idyllic setting by the C&O canal, this Georgetown spot is super chic yet casual. It's a place to relax at the raw bar over oysters and chilled wine or to dine seriously on the terrace on seafood. Although it receives little press, it may be one of the area's best seafood destinations. Chef Jeff Shively is a Louisianan who's proud to serve the day's best catch—the restaurant never uses frozen food. If it's available, select the seafood gumbo, which is superb. If you adore crab cakes, you probably will find Shively's—made from jumbo lump crab meat without fillers—among the best in town. For dessert, try his special white chocolate mousse cake with chocolate curls. In agreeable weather, sit outside overlooking the rippling waters, fishermen and strollers. Otherwise, enjoy the vast and elegant interior dining room and the long marble bar.

Seasons   Contemporary   14/20

Four Seasons Hotel
2800 Pennsylvania Ave. NW (29th St. NW)
Georgetown, Washington 20007
202-342-0810, Fax 202-342-1673\
Breakfast & Dinner daily, Lunch Mon.-Fri., $$$, Casual

This serene restaurant manages to maintain a harmonious balance between classic and contemporary, making it a perfect place for an intimate tête-à-tête or a serious business dinner. Elegant and intimate, it offers well-spaced tables and lovely views of the gardens. The ingredients used in the cuisine are always of high quality and are prepared to bring out the impeccable, intense natural flavors. Health-conscious diners appreciate the alternative cuisine, which offers such appetizers as crunchy vegetable vermicelli with seared ahi, and such entrées as sea bass, salmon or mahi mahi simply grilled with fresh vegetables. More sophisticated dishes include the glazed oysters with Smithfield ham or the timbale of crab, salmon, avocado and tomato. Follow with roast veal steak accompanied by ginger and apples or oriental sea bass with ginger sauce. Desserts include delicious homemade ice creams and a wonderful flourless chocolate cake. The wine list is impressive, and you can even find bargains, such as a very pleasant Saint Joseph.

Sen5es Bakery & Restaurant   French   13/20

3206 Grace St. NW (Wisconsin Ave. NW)
Georgetown, Washington 20007
202-342-9083, Fax 202-342-3807
Breakfast Tues.-Sun., Lunch & Dinner Tues.-Sat., Brunch Sun., $$$, Casual

As charming as a French country parlor, yet oozing big-city sophistication, Sen5es is Georgetown's bakery sensation. But it also has a postage stamp-sized dining room. Sen5es' offers rather imaginative lunch and dinner menus—the latter may include roasted scallops on Belgian endive coleslaw or warm goat cheese toast salad and entrées such as wild mushroom duck confit risotto or roasted rack of lamb with saffron rice pilaf and pomegranate sauce. If your sweet tooth rules or you stroll by for a snack, you may not get one step past the glass pastry counter. These are no ordinary desserts. As proof, sample the lemon meringue tart. Its towering meringue cloud dusted with powdered sugar hides a rich lemon cream curd in a short cookie crust. Prepare to share or else request a doggie bag—for most, it's too rich to eat at one sitting.

Sequoia   American   10/20

Washington Harbour Complex
3000 K St. NW (30th St. NW), Georgetown, Washington 20007
202-944-4200, Fax 202-944-4210
Lunch & Dinner daily, Brunch Sat.-Sun. $$$, Casual

This enormous restaurant, which resembles the dining room of a luxury liner docked on the Georgetown riverfront, is not particularly appealing for its food, but its deck is one of the few places you can eat outdoors in good weather and enjoy a view of the river. Even indoors, you get a decent bird's eye view of the Potomac. Service is negligent and the food is indifferent, but order a beer or a glass of wine and enjoy watching the crew teams practice on the river. If you do decide to eat, the cuisine is decidedly American: lots of steaks and seafood

Sesto Senso   Italian   13/20

1214 18th St. NW (Connecticut Ave. NW)
Dupont Circle, Washington 20036
202-785-9525, Fax 202-785-9522,
Lunch Mon.-Fri., Dinner Mon.-Sat., $$$, Business casual

At lunchtime, the two-story Sesto Senso, with its dark-wood bar, mustard-yellow walls and balcony, could be practically any downtown restaurant that caters to the business crowd. In the evenings, the atmosphere is quite different. The crowd is younger and more casually dressed, and after 11 p.m. on weekends, Sesto Senso becomes a nightclub, a lively part of the downtown singles scene. During serving times, you can enjoy chef Fabio Beggiato's rustic Italian cooking: sophisticated pasta dishes, creamless soups and creamy risottos, long-cooked stews and braised meats.

701　　　　American　　　14/20　♟

701 Pennsylvania Ave. NW (Seventh St. NW)
Downtown, Washington 20004
202-393-0701, Fax 202-393-0242
Lunch Mon.-Fri., Dinner nightly, $$$, Casual dressy

🄰 🕾 P 💻 🔌 🍸 🍴 ♡

The contemporary elegance and innovative menu at this downtown supper club have made it a favorite spot for dinner before or after a performance at one of the nearby theaters. Fish is particularly well done here—perhaps sea bass with a corn crust in a fresh tomato sauce or Virginia trout on a creamy bed of grits. It's also a good place for a after-theater drink and dessert, particularly in the spring and summer, when you can sit at one of the outdoor tables overlooking the Navy Memorial.

1789 Restaurant　　Contemporary　　16/20　♟♟

1226 36th St. NW (Prospect St. NW), Georgetown, Washington 20007
202-965-1789, Fax 202-337-1541, *Dinner nightly, $$$$, Jackets required*

🄰 🕾 P 🚶 🍸 🍴 ♡

This elegant Georgetown restaurant, set in a Federal-style townhouse with blazing fireplaces and historical prints, is Washington's favorite spot for Thanksgiving or Christmas dinners. Thanks to executive chef Ris Lacoste, it's also become one of the city's hottest restaurants year-round, so don't be surprised to find famous faces—from President Bush to Julia Child—dining in quiet splendor. Lacoste's cooking is inspired, generous and beautifully presented. Her menu changes with the seasons, but if you're lucky, you may find her Champagne oyster stew appetizer, an ultra-rich and decadent heavy-cream concoction textured with plump oysters and walnuts. The entrée selections are just as imaginative. Depending on the season, you may indulge in rack of lamb with creamy feta potatoes or a glazed roast pork chop with sweet potato bread pudding and a bourbon-laced applesauce. Desserts may include warm apple turnovers, a bittersweet chocolate terrine or a lemon chess pie. The wine list is distinguished and highly varied.

Sholl's Colonial Cafeteria　　American　　12/20

1990 Building
1990 K St. NW (20th St. NW), Downtown, Washington 20006
202-296-3065, Fax 202-296-0695
Breakfast & Lunch daily, Dinner Mon.-Sat., $, Casual
No credit cards. P 🍴

This is one Washington restaurant that stands alone. It has survived downtown rent hikes, the influx of high-profile restaurants, and the invasion of fast-food chains and eateries. It's the one place in Washington where everyone is welcome—the homeless and the highbrow, the downtrodden and the yuppie. The dishes resemble those cooked in homes a generation ago: comfort food, and plenty of it. Everything is served cafeteria-style. The menu changes frequently, but those who eat here don't care, because they come for the TLC and the rock-bottom prices. The roast chicken is tender and savory, the mashed potatoes creamy and the banana cream pie textured with banana slices—what more can anyone ask for? It's a Washington institution (it's been serving meals for more than 70 years) well deserving of its status.

Shula's Steak House   Steakhouse   13/20

Wyndham City Center Hotel
1143 New Hampshire Ave. NW (M St. NW)
West End, Washington 20037
202-828-7762, Fax 202-331-9781
Breakfast, Lunch & Dinner daily, $$$, Business casual

Football coaching great Don Shula has launched a successful group of steakhouses nationwide and these have now touched down in the Washington metro area. The big news here is big steaks, as in custom cuts of Angus beef, from a filet mignon to a 48-ounce porterhouse steak. For a double dose of beef, start off with the Shula's steak soup, which tastes a little like Hungarian goulash without the pepper. You'll find the requisite Caesar salads in many different guises. The menu boasts options besides steaks, including such entrées as salmon and a chicken and lobster Oscar or lighter dishes, such as the "knife and fork" sandwiches, which are too big to pick up easily. At least, the rare hamburger was a real handful and with the side of hot, crispy fries, enough to satisfy any yearning for steak and at a much lower price. For the finishing touch, cheesecake and Key lime pie are tempting. **Also located at** Tysons Corner Marriott, 8028 Leesburg Pike, Vienna, VA, 703-506-3256.

Smith & Wollensky   Steakhouse   14/20

1112 19th St. NW (L St. NW), Downtown, Washington 20036
202-466-1100, Fax 202-728-2020
Lunch & Dinner daily, $$$, Business casual

One of the city's most upscale steakhouses, Smith & Wollensky brings new meaning to the idea of power meals and extravagant steak cuts. Check out the crowds at lunch: execs and politicos, puffing cigars, swirling brandies and devouring huge wedges of beef. Most three-course meals here cost plenty, but with careful choices you can get away with a $30 tab at lunch. The service is impeccable, the décor is elegantly New York, the menu is short and sweet and the meat is steak. Or prime rib. We loved the steak sandwich with thick potato fries for lunch, because consuming a 28-ounce prime rib midday seems excessive. Sides, which are made for two, are extra. Whipped potatoes or hashed browns are de rigueur. Non-beefeaters can find solace in the crackling pork shank, which has its fans, or the assorted seafood presentations.

Spices   Pan-Asian   13/20

3333-A Connecticut Ave. NW (Ordway St., NW)
Cleveland Park, Washington 20008
202-686-3833, Fax: 202-686-0149
Lunch Mon.-Sat., Dinner nightly, $, Casual

With its expanded incarnation and funky all-Asian look, Spices is even more of a draw for its many regulars. Because it is related to the famed Yanÿu (see review in this chapter) and

Oodles Noodles (see review in *Quick Bites*), Spices makes for good Asian feasting that is consistently reliable and flavorful. Our favorite way to eat here is to launch the meal with sushi from the expanded sushi bar. Then head to a robust entrée, such as the Malaysian curry laksa, a souplike dish including coconut milk, vermicelli, sliced meat and squares of fried tofu. Noodles dishes are good, especially the chor koay teow, a Singaporean/Malaysian specialty made with flat rice noodles. Although noodle dishes are our favorites, the curries and grilled dishes are also notable.

Star of Siam   Thai   12/20

1136 19th St. NW (L St. NW), Downtown, Washington 20036
202-785-2839, Fax 202-785-2838
Lunch Mon.-Sat., Dinner nightly, $$, Casual

An old-timer, this downtown Thai restaurant is picture-perfect inside, with its serene Thai motif and the pretty front patio for outdoor eating. But the kitchen can't be counted on for always dishing up delicacies. We loved the red duck curry, but have found other dishes to be overseasoned and heavy. Lunch is a good time to stop by, and your best bets are the fried fish cakes and the steamed Thai spring roll with a crab meat stuffing. For entrées, specials include assorted classic noodle dishes, hard to find in these parts. The duck noodle soup is a sure bet, although the broth seemed forgotten with the Chiang Mai curry noodle soup. Office workers and shoppers fill the place quickly midday, so call ahead for a table. **Also located at** 2446 18th St. NW, Washington, DC, 202-986-4133.

Sushi-Ko   Japanese   15/20

2309 Wisconsin Ave. NW (Calvert St. NW)
Glover Park, Washington 20007
202-333-4187, Fax 202-333-7594
Lunch Tues.-Fri., Dinner nightly, $$, Casual

A recent remodeling took the décor from Japanese traditional to techno-trendy, but that's in keeping with the young crowd that seems to love this place. Actually, people of all stages and ages should come for the daring sushi creations, the exacting wine list (yes, French burgundies do go with sushi) and the clever yet straightforward entrée choices of teriyaki, roasted salmon and assorted tempuras. But you can't skip the sushi, which is fresh and succulent. Sushi-Ko remains the most popular sushi bar in the area, so don't be surprised if you face a long wait for a seat. It's a great star-gazing spot: Who knows whom you'll see coming up the stairs to the second-story dining area? We've noted plenty of bigwigs.

Szechuan Gallery Restaurant   Chinese   12/20

617 H St. NW (Sixth St. NW), Chinatown, Washington 20001
202-898-1180, *Lunch & Dinner daily, $$, Casual*

If you really want to savor some authentic Chinese food, ask the waiter for the Chinese menu, where the kitchen staff posts dishes not available on the more familiar-sounding list. It helps if you bring along a friend who speaks Chinese; that way, you can determine which fish is freshest and what specials the chef is willing to stir together. We recommend any of the clam or crab dishes in season, plus the beef with coriander and dried bean curd, and crisp-fried baby fish with peanuts. If you still have an appetite, add an order of Yu Ling duck and the salt and pepper shrimp. Located right in the middle of Chinatown, this has been a longtime favorite of locals and has managed to stand the test of time. Despite the competition, it's usually quite busy.

Tabard Inn — American — 14/20

Tabard Inn
1739 N St. NW (18th St. NW), Dupont Circle, Washington 20036
202-833-2668, Fax 202-785-6173
Breakfast & Lunch Mon.-Sat., Dinner nightly, Brunch Sat.-Sun., $$, Casual dressy

The living room of this Dupont Circle inn looks a bit like a showroom at an auction house, but there's more coherence in the dining room, where chef David Craig, who formerly operated the postage stamp-sized kitchen at Pesce, cooks a regularly changing menu reflecting contemporary tastes and his own Scottish background. Lunch offers several appetizing meat and vegetable sandwiches and light main dishes. If it's offered, try the lamb tenderloin with ricotta gnocchi. Successful dinner main courses have included roast Cornish game hen with pearl tapioca, duck confit with onions and a fig-cherry compote, and striped bass with braised cabbage. In fine weather, the garden is charming, a wonderful place to enjoy a meal in the sunshine.

Taberna del Alabardero — Spanish — 14/20

1776 I St. NW (18th St. NW), Downtown, Washington 20006
202-429-2200, Fax 202-775-3713
Lunch Mon.-Fri., Dinner Mon.-Sat., $$$$, Business casual

There's an old-fashioned elegance about this decade-old Spanish restaurant. One visit and you'll understand what many Americans may not be aware of—that there's a world of Spanish cooking beyond paella. Start with smoky peppers stuffed with codfish or almost-greaseless fried squid. Main courses might include roast pork with raisin sauce or beef with peppers and boiled potatoes. If you decide to have that paella, try the luxurious lobster version, and don't miss the crema catalana for dessert. Ask about dinners cooked by visiting chefs from Spain.

Tahoga — Contemporary — 13/20

2815 M St. NW (29th St. NW), Georgetown, Washington 20007
202-338-5380, Fax 202-338-5328
Lunch Mon.-Fri., Dinner nightly, $$$, Casual dressy

Named after the Indian tribe that once inhabited the land where Georgetown sits, Tahoga serves innovative contemporary American cooking in a spare and attractive modern setting. Light, refreshing starters have included yellow tomato gazpacho and a salad of white asparagus and feta. Pistachio-crusted perch, a bacon-wrapped rabbit loin with fava beans and a delicious herb-roasted chicken with collard greens and grits were excellent main courses. The garden is particularly pleasant in clement weather.

Teatro Goldoni — Italian/Venetian — 14/20

1909 K St., NW (19th St., NW), Downtown, Washington 20006
202-955-9494, Fax 202-955-5584
Lunch Mon.-Fri., Dinner Mon.-Sat, $$$, Casual dressy

In a brightly theatrical setting with harlequin patterns everywhere, this Venetian restaurant stars superchef Fabrizio Aielli of Osteria Goldoni fame. At this his second downtown restaurant, Aielli takes charge of the kitchen to create such dramatic fare as lobster risotto—if you haven't enjoyed one of his fabulous risottos, you have yet to experience a certain nirvana—baby cannelloni stuffed with rabbit and sautéed sea scallops with a ragù of pancetta, roasted fennel and served with purple potatoes. The lunch and dinner menus change every so often, so your favorite may disappear. However, the restaurant name "teatro" suggests what this experience is all about: Gather a group of friends for a party then ask for seating in the mezzanine dining area that overlooks the glassed-in kitchen. This gives you a front seat for Aielli's kitchen drama. Also inquire about the chef's table.

TenPenh — Pan-Asian/Contemporary — 15/20

1001 Pennsylvania Ave. NW (Tenth St. NW)
Downtown, Washington 20004
202-393-4500, Fax 202-393-4744
Lunch Mon.-Fri., Dinner Mon.-Sat., $$$, Casual dressy

Executive chef Jeff Tunks, owner of the excellent DC Coast, is trying his hand at this luxurious Asian/Pacific-inspired eatery, which showcases a sampling of classics. Of course, these haven't left the kitchen without some of Tunks' special touches, a softening of a curry sauce here and perhaps a pairing of Asian and Western ingredients there. As devoted Asian food fans, we were pleased with how the kitchen handled most dishes, especially the wok-seared spicy calamari salad to start—why not a toss of toasted cashews for crunch? Good, too, were the artfully arranged plump Filipino lumpia with assorted dipping sauces. As for entrées, we debated whether the red Thai curry prawns could stand more chili heat—probably so—and decided the classy steamed vegetable assortment served in a bamboo basket with a peanut dipping sauce may have been the meal's best bet. If available, try one of the fish perched on a bed of mashed potatoes spiked with Japanese wasabi. Pastry chef David Guas came up with a tempting trio of tropics-inspired crèmes brûlées and a five-spice chocolate cake. Perhaps the best of the lot, but only Asian by a stretch of the imagination: a chocolate "cup" cake with a warm and gooey center accompanied by a splash of aromatic passion fruit sauce and ice cream.

Thai Room — Thai — 12/20

5037 Connecticut Ave. NW (Nebraska Ave. NW)
Uptown, Washington 20008
202-244-5933, *Lunch & Dinner daily, $, Casual*

The first—and for a while the only—Thai restaurant in DC, Thai Room strides into a venerable old age. If you haven't eaten here in some time, you'll notice some changes; for one, the lunch buffet is gone. But mostly, Thai Room has retained its look and menu. Unlike its trendier competitors, it serves familiar Thai dishes, which are more predictable than glamorous. You can count on the roast duck to be flavorful and the tod mun (fried fish cakes) to be mild enough for most people to enjoy. We also like to order the chicken and basil, the shrimp green curry (not on the menu, but ask for it), and the crispy mee krob rice noodle dish. While you dine, enjoy the Thai décor and the neighborhood feel of the place.

Thai Town   Thai   12/20

2655 Connecticut Ave. NW (Calvert St. NW)
Woodley Park, Washington 20008
202-667-5115, *Lunch & Dinner daily, $$, Casual*

Surely part of the charm here is the friendly staff and the street scene, a lively drama passing by morning, noon and night. As for the food, in this highly competitive Thai restaurant market, this spot remains yards ahead of some of its challengers. We liked the fat soft-shell crabs and the plump cubes of fried tofu. One of the oldest Thai restaurants in the area, this place offers pretty outdoor seating on the front terrace, while the interior looks softly and colorfully Thai.

Thaiphoon   Thai   12/20

2011 S St., NW (Connecticut Ave. NW)
Dupont Circle, Washington 20009
202-667-3505, Fax 202-667-8018, *Lunch & Dinner daily, $$, Casual*

In a city saturated with Thai restaurants, is there room for more? Thaiphoon may truly make you wonder. Be warned that the flavors are slightly off kilter, so that true Thai aficionados may be disappointed in such dishes as the duck salad, composed of sliced roast duck nestled in a bed of field greens. (It would have been better if the greens were of the Thai variety.) A better appetizer choice is the fried tofu squares with a side of sweet/sour dipping sauce. As for entrées, the menu holds no surprises, offering not much more than tried-and-true variations. For some reason, the Thai iced coffee even seemed to be lacking much of the expected caffeine punch. If you are in the neighborhood and looking for a pleasant place to catch up with friends, this restaurant is as good as any. On the other hand, if you crave the punch of chilies, lemon grass and lime leaf, head elsewhere.

Timothy Dean Restaurant & Bar Southern 16/20

St. Regis Washington
923 16th St. NW (K St. NW), Downtown, Washington 20006
202-879-6900, Fax 202-879-6909
Breakfast daily, Lunch Mon.-Fri., Dinner Mon.-Sat., $$$$, Casual dressy

When native Marylander Timothy Dean came home, he returned with a splash: his own restaurant at the lofty St. Regis hotel. But Dean's dramatic return should not surprise. After all, he trained with super-chef Jean-Louis Palladin, once one of DC's hottest shots, and he has put in his time behind plenty of stoves, including a stint at DC's Hay Adams Hotel. As chic as always, the setting is less intimidating, however, and the décor, more inviting. Even such flourishes as serving soup from pitcher to bowl add elegance without pretension. And energetic Dean has learned his kitchen lessons well: Maximize flavor, minimize artifice. What he presents is food with character and hints of his Southern roots: Maryland she-crab soup with mirepoix; sautéed Maryland soft-shell crab with savoy cabbage; plus a snappy pan-seared diver scallops (hand-selected by divers) with a lobster-scented polenta cake. We loved the fragrant rosemary roast chicken and declared the Angus beef burger perfect. We swooned over the dense chocolate crème brûlée and the glazed cheesecake with a shard of dried pineapple. Dean features excellent wines from boutique vineyards in California.

The Tombs   American   12/20

1226 36th St. NW (Prospect St. NW), Georgetown, Washington 20007
202-337-6668, Fax 202-337-1541
Lunch & Dinner daily, Brunch Sun., $, Casual

Another one of the Clyde's Restaurant Group's famed restaurants, The Tombs is all about college crowds, sporting events (crew, in particular) and casual eats at almost any hour, even into the wee hours of the morning. Parents, professors, students (Georgetown U. is nearby) and area residents crowd into its brick-lined, cave-like rooms. In true college style, some patrons even have carved initials on tabletops. The sporty foods range from chicken finger appetizers to bowls of the famous chili. It's a safe bet that the Southwestern chicken salad will satisfy—it comes with all the yummy taco tastes and loads of salad topping and is served on a warm, squishy pizza crust.

Tony & Joe's Seafood   Seafood   12/20

Washington Harbour Complex
3000 K St. NW (30th St. NW), Georgetown, Washington 20007
202-944-4545, Fax 202-944-4587
Lunch & Dinner daily, Brunch Sun., $$$, Casual dressy

It's hard to imagine a better view in all Washington, especially for al fresco dining. Right on the river's edge, this harbor spot lends itself to tropical reveries. Sit outdoors for a close look at the live steel band and great crowd-watching. It seems as if every giddy young Washingtonian shows up here for after-work drinks and seafood. Hot crab dip served with crisp French bread croutons makes for a good start. Smaller appetites will like the deep-fried alligator or tender catfish fingers. The grilled big-eye tuna steak is luscious, the crab-stuffed flounder rather plain. Meat-eaters will find some good choices, too: chicken, ribs and several cuts of steak. The desserts are uninspired, so splurge on other courses.

Two Quail   American   13/20

320 Massachusetts Ave. NE (3rd St. NE)
Capitol Hill, Washington 20002
202-543-8030, Fax 202-543-8035
Lunch Mon.-Fri., Dinner nightly, Brunch Sun., $$, Casual dressy

New arrivals to Washington will soon hear about this Capitol Hill favorite, a place that has made its reputation as much for its zany Victorian décor as for its interesting menu. Indeed, the interior is almost unbelievable, for every nook and cranny has been filled to overflowing—you probably will have a sense that you've just entered a collectibles store. Problem is, there's little room left over to spread out or to find privacy, so you and your neighbors may become best friends. Even so, due to its soft lighting and cozy décor, this is often mentioned as one of Washington's most romantic restaurants. Specialties have included spicy seafood pasta in macadamia cream sauce, roasted chipotle Cornish hens and fish salad topped with mango salsa. Desserts, not made on the premises, vary by day, and include assorted tarts, cheesecake and carrot cake.

Vidalia   Southern   14/20   ♔

1990 M St. NW (20th St. NW), Downtown, Washington 20036
202-659-1990, Fax 202-223-8572
Lunch Mon.-Fri., Dinner nightly, $$$$, Business casual

A ☎ P ✕ ♙ ⌷ ▲ ↻

Both the quality of the cooking and the service seem to have suffered a bit since chef Jeffrey Buben spends less time here after opening Bistro Bis (see review in this chapter) on Capitol Hill. This sophisticated, Southern-style restaurant is still popular, though, and chef Peter Smith works hard to turn out notable dishes. We love the setting—sponged-yellow walls, cabinets displaying heirloom china—as cheerful as the dining room in the best hotel in a small Southern town. Buben's menu is Southern-inspired: In season, the roasted Vidalia onion is a signature starter, as is the shrimp and grits. Main courses consist of improvisations on traditional Southern favorites—chicken and dumplings, chicken and dressing, soft-shell crabs, pork chops. The lemon chess pie makes for a spectacular ending.

The Vigorelli   Italian   14/20   ♔

3421 Connecticut Ave. NW (Ordway St. NW)
Cleveland Park, Washington 20008
202-244-6437, Fax 202-244-9304
Lunch Mon.-Fri., Dinner nightly, $$$, Casual

A ☎ ⊟ ♙ ⌷ ▲

Chef Elizabeth Bright-Mattia specializes in the cooking of Liguria from the Italian Riviera. You may notice wonderful smoky aromas since much Ligurian food is cooked over and with wood fires, which do terrific things for pizzas, the specialties here. One of the cook's best creations is the pizza topped with spicy lamb sausage with ricotta and feta cheeses, though you'll also find less complex pies such as the simpler pizza margherita with fresh tomatoes and fresh mozzarella. We've also enjoyed some of the full entrées, such as the Ligurian fish stew, that mark the outstanding Vigorelli cooking. For meat dishes, try the baby lamb chops with pistachio brittle and mint. Bright-Mattia makes her pastas fresh daily and uses only Italian olive oil in her cooking. The menu undergoes seasonal alterations, so dishes do change. Check out the wine list for the Italian imports to complement these Ligurian meals.

Vivo! Ristorante   Italian   12/20

1509 17th St., NW (P St. NW), Dupont Circle, Washington 20036
202-986-2627, Fax 202-986-4019
Lunch Mon.-Sat., Dinner nightly, $$, Casual

A ♙ ▲

With Roberto Donna's remake of this location of his Il Raddichio into Vivo! Ristorante, customers can expect more of the same but with slightly higher prices and more trattoria-styled dishes. Pizzas, too, still reign, but there is also grilled lamb steak, stuffed veal shoulder and a cotoletta of veal, Milanese style. Specials might include roasted half duckling or seared salmon. The hearty pasta dishes are good options, including fresh Napoli-style pappardelle with a ragù of pork rib and sweet onions. You'll find the atmosphere much like before, with plenty of conviviality and crowds hunkered down for a full meal and plenty of conversation over wine.

West 24   American   14/20

1250 24th St. NW (M St. NW), West End, Washington 20037
202-331-1100, Fax 202-331-0202
Lunch Mon.-Fri., Dinner Mon.-Sat., $$$, Casual

Can anyone be so blasé that he or she does not know about the owners? They are James Carville and Mary Matalin, the Ragin' Cajun and wife, who gained national prominence during the Clinton years for politics not as usual. They are as much in the spotlight with this Washington power spot, a glam restaurant for DC's elite. Intimate and clubby in a dark-wood kind of way, this sprawling place pipes out R&B tunes and cool jazz as a backdrop for the kind of upscale Midwestern and Southern foods the couple likes most. It helps that chef James Rippuhn and pastry chef Andrea Kirkley can re-create this fare so faultlessly. Trouble is, everything appeals, so narrowing down choices can be problematic. We opted for the potato pierogi with truffles and the chilled yellow tomato soup, which frankly tastes like a superior gazpacho with lots of gingery overtones. The grilled pork chop with sides of creamy andouille grits and fried okra is a winning main course. Lunch causes a decision struggle: fried green tomatoes, that Southern classic, are tart and crunchy under a tangy buttermilk dressing. And the entrée-sized cornmeal-crusted catfish or beef short ribs are heavenly, but who can pass up a fried oyster po' boy sandwich with fresh Cajun-spiced potato chips on the side? For dessert, be tempted by a chocolate cheesecake flan or a passion fruit crème brûlée.

The White Tiger   Indian   12/20

301 Massachusetts Ave. NE (Third St. NE), Capitol Hill, Washington 20002
202-546-5900, Fax 202-544-7444, *Lunch & Dinner daily, $$, Casual*

We love the Capitol Hill location, which has about it an air of the Raj, a kind of Indian mystique with its hushed service, elegant tableware and outstanding Indian cooking. Every dish, from the luscious freshly baked breads (the Kashmiri naan is outstanding) to the curries (especially the lamb vindaloo), shines on its own. The total effect is a memorable meal. The Virginia branch of the restaurant has not transplanted to the suburbs so easily and can't compete with its downtown cousin, at least not yet. So if you want top Indian food, head to Capitol Hill. **Also located at** 146 E. Maple Ave., Vienna, VA, 703-242-0500.

Going to Hawaii, Chicago, San Francisco, Las Vegas, Los Angeles or London? Look for Gayot's "The Best of" guidebooks to destinations worldwide. Also for hotel and travel information from our books and the latest updates, visit us on the Internet at gayot.com.

The Willard Room American 12/20

Willard Inter-Continental Washington
1401 Pennsylvania Ave. NW (14th St. NW)
Downtown, Washington 20004
202-637-7440, Fax 202-637-7326
Breakfast, Lunch & Dinner Mon.-Sat., $$$$, Casual

One of the grandest dining rooms in Washington, The Willard Room has a soaring ceiling supported by faux-marble columns, dark-wood paneling and richly upholstered furniture. It's hard to think of a luxury food item, from foie gras to truffles to caviar, that doesn't appear on this menu, but the conception may not always be cutting edge. Steaks and chops are the best choices—a very good filet of Black Angus beef or a pan-fried venison chop. The service is as smooth and sophisticated as the setting and the patrons. This is a magnet for power brokers and deal makers, and it would not be surprising that many DC visitors make this dining room a "must" destination.

Yanÿu Chinese/Asian/Fusion 16/20

3435 Connecticut Ave. NW (Ordway St. NW)
Cleveland Park, Washington 20008
202-686-6968, Fax 202-686-2966
Dinner nightly, $$$, Casual dressy

After much hard work, talented chef Jessie Yan opened her upscale Chinese restaurant offering classic Chinese cooking to showcase her own particular polish. Unlike her more casual restaurants—Spices (see review in this chapter) and the two Oodles Noodles (see reviews in *Washington, DC/Quick Bites* and *Maryland/Quick Bites*)—Yanÿu brims with elegance, from the lacquered, gold-tipped chopsticks to the fine ceramic tea service and the portraits of the Chinese emperor and empress. The customers take it all seriously and expect a particular kind of Chinese feast. So don't expect egg foo yung: It's not that kind of restaurant. Instead, savor the fresh abalone poached in superior stock and the jumbo prawns glazed with a crunchy exterior and spiked with shredded garlic. Don't skip the superb Big Duck with its crackling, fat-free skin and succulent flavors. Wind up your meal with the jasmine tea and the gingery crème brûlée. Memorable food.

Zanzibar on the Waterfront Caribbean/American 11/20

700 Water St. SW (Seventh St. SW), Waterfront, Washington 20024
202-554-9100, Fax 202-554-9103
Dinner Tues.-Sun., $$, Casual dressy

This place has a waterfront view, but it's just about invisible at night. Fortunately, big flavors are on view, too. Mapping your way through the menu may be a challenge—it's hard to say whether a Smoked Tuna Ina appetizer has much in common with a tropical fruit plate topped with cottage cheese. The dinner menu is a real mix and match: The kitchen pairs a ground-nut-vegetable ragoût (peanut stew) with an entrecôte of beef. A restaurant part of the time, Zanzibar turns into a nightclub and entertainment spot after dinner.

Zed's Ethiopian Restaurant   Ethiopian   12/20

1201 28th St. NW (M St.), Georgetown, Washington 20007
202-333-4710, Fax 202-333-1085, *Lunch & Dinner daily, $$, Casual*

This Ethiopian eatery has long played to Washington crowds, and its white-tablecloth setting in a fancy corner location on M Street is as stylish as any French restaurant. But somehow Ethiopian cooking loses something when it's moved away from the colorful basketry tables; large, humble serving dishes; and casual settings, where eating with one's fingers seems perfectly acceptable. Most dishes offered here are rich stews, some fiery and all intended to serve one. Coming here with friends means ordering several dishes, served on a large wheel of injera, the traditional Ethiopian flatbread. We love doro watt (chicken stewed in a peppery sauce) and yebeg kaey watt (lamb stewed in a similar sauce). Two people might consider the combination dish with four choices. The best accompaniment is chilled African beer, followed by a piece or two of pastry for dessert.

Zorba's Café   Greek   12/20

1612 20th St. NW
(Connecticut Ave. NW), Dupont Circle, Washington 20009
202-387-8555, Fax 202-387-7070, *Lunch & Dinner daily, $, Casual*

A smiling Anthony Quinn beams out from many different angles—he is, after all, Zorba the Greek, and so makes a fitting photograph for this all-Greek and very casual eatery. His photos only add to the Greek atmosphere in this family-run café: copper cookware, hanging plants, Greek music and food turn eating into a homespun affair where the entire family can relax and enjoy. In good weather, the best place to be is on Zorba's outdoor patio trimmed with pretty plants. Indoors, you can sit upstairs or down after you've placed your order at the back counter (don't wait to be seated because there's no hostess.) The menu includes familiar shish kebabs and moussaka plus yéro (also known as gyro), falafel, subs, salads and specialty pizzas. We found the falafel in pita bread a bit salty, but adored the heaping yéro plate with its sliced mixture of well-seasoned ground beef and lamb served with a Greek salad and fries. Dessert selections are limited to rice pudding, apple pie, cheesecake, kataífi and an absolutely dazzling honey-drenched baklava.

Zuki Moon   Japanese/American   13/20

George Washington University Inn
824 New Hampshire Ave. NW (I St. NW)
Foggy Bottom, Washington 20037
202-333-3312, *Lunch Mon.-Fri., Dinner nightly, $$, Casual*

Chef Mary Richter, who was once the chef at Cities restaurant, has a flair for taking ethnic cuisines and stamping them with her own imagination and creativity. At this tiny Japanese gem, with its soothing Asian colors and décor, she has polished up various Japanese classics and turns out a clean and clear assortment of noodle dishes, grills and tempuras. The kitchen may be best known for such noodle offerings as the udon, soba and ramen bowls, some with seafood toppings, others with meats. But you can happily make a satisfying meal with assorted starters—we love the short ribs and gyoza. Double your orders and call it dinner, but don't leave without a scoop or two of her house-made ice creams that are delicate and tempting.

QUICK BITES

AMERICAN

American City Diner of Washington

5532 Connecticut Ave. NW (Morrison St. NW)
Chevy Chase, Washington 20015
202-244-1949, *Breakfast, Lunch & Dinner daily, $, Casual*

A P 🍴 👁

Want a soda? Need a hot dog? Crave liver and onions with mashed potatoes? Then this homey, folksy eatery will fill the bill, especially as it's open 24 hours a day on Friday and Saturday. You can expect courteous service, but the food isn't any great shakes. Our hot dog was warm, the sauerkraut cold and the bun squishy. However, the prices here are so low that you may not care. Besides, it's got a certain nostalgic charm: a Wurlitzer jukebox plays and a model train runs around overhead. Check out the specials, and there's plenty on the regular menu. In the end, you may want to eat breakfast and drink milk shakes all day long.

Ben's Chili Bowl

1213 U St. NW (12th St. NW), U St. Corridor, Washington 20009
202-667-0909, Fax 202-667-0058
Breakfast & Lunch Mon.-Sat., Dinner nightly, $, Casual
No credit cards. 🍴 👁

Ben's is a true neighborhood fixture along the U Street corridor. Opened in 1958, it has always attracted plenty of local fans and big-name entertainers (we hear this is one of Bill Cosby's favorites), not for its looks, which are free of frills, but for its chili, the dish that made it famous. Composed of ground meat and kidney beans, the chili is served with crackers and, if you want, a scoop of shredded cheese that melts down through the mixture. Mildly hot and aromatic, this is one chili that will stick to your ribs. Also famous: the chili dog. Ben's is apt to be crowded, even mid-afternoon, so plan to double-park like others do and wait for your chili. Or park, eat in, and order up a whole meal of country-home cooking, with a bowl of chili as the centerpiece.

Booeymongers

3265 Prospect St. NW (32nd St. NW)
Georgetown, Washington 20007
202-333-4810, Fax 202-333-8309
Breakfast, Lunch & Dinner daily, $, Casual

A 🍱 🍴 🍸

This deli/sandwich shop with the strange name will brighten anyone's day with its snazzy selection of specialty sandwiches, such as the Gatsby Arrow and the Scheherazade. Or you can create your own with basic meat, egg, tuna or chicken salad fillings topped with fixings of your choice. Salads, soup and quiches round out the menu. You can start your morning with a bang: Breakfast on pastries, big egg specials, bagels and a cup of hot coffee. **Also located at** 5252 Wisconsin Ave. NW, Washington, DC, 202-686-5805; and 4600 East-West Hwy., Bethesda, MD, 301-718-9550.

Bullfeathers of Capitol Hill

410 First St. SE (D St. SE), Capitol Hill, Washington 20003
202-543-5005, Fax 202-488-7160, *Lunch & Dinner daily, $, Casual*

When Teddy Roosevelt was hungry he'd grumble, "Oh, bullfeathers!" Hence the theme and name of this well-frequented eatery on Capitol Hill. Lobbyists, senators, representatives, and lifetime civil servants can be seen chowing down on great burgers while the televisions at the bar stay tuned to CNN and C-Span for the latest-breaking news. If burgers don't interest, you'll find plenty of salads, fish, soups and other offerings to satisfy your appetite as you eavesdrop on some of the most well-informed conversation in the country.

Chadwicks

5247 Wisconsin Ave. NW (Jennifer St. NW)
Friendship Heights, Washington 20015
202-362-8040, Fax 202-237-7818, *Lunch & Dinner daily, $, Casual*

Chadwicks isn't a power dining spot. It set out to be a neighborhood hangout, and it succeeded. Although the bar isn't horseshoe-shaped like the one in *Cheers*, this is a place where inside-the-Beltway heavyweights come, not to be seen, but to get a good meal, at a good value, with the kids. Aside from the burgers, which have lots of fans, the menu has a range of meats, poultry, fish, soups, salads, sandwiches and terrific Buffalo wings. Save room for desserts like mud pie and Key lime pie. **Also located at** 3205 K St. NW, Washington, DC, 202-333-2565; and 203 S. Strand St., Alexandria, VA, 703-836-4442.

Chicken Out Rotisserie

4866 Massachusetts Ave. NW (Tilden St.)
Spring Valley, Washington 20016
202-364-8646, Fax 202-364-0633, *Lunch & Dinner daily, $*

This chicken eatery is a local success story, the kind of "to riches" tale that makes an entrepreneur out of many. From a single location in Maryland, the owners took that simple idea—cook wholesome food from scratch and charge reasonable prices—and spun it into a local empire. Locations are squeaky clean, service is prompt and courteous, and the food, generally as good as (or maybe better than) homemade. Choose this chain for an all-out chicken or turkey feast, or at least a sandwich or salad. We recommend the half-chicken meal with mashed potatoes and fresh vegetables and an apple crisp for dessert. Everything is available for takeout. **Other locations.**

ESPN Zone

555 12th St. NW (E St. NW), Downtown, Washington 20004
202-783-ESPN, Fax 202-737-7404, *Lunch & Dinner daily, $, Casual*

Billing itself as the "ultimate sports dining and entertainment venue," ESPN Zone exists solely to entertain. Yes, there's a menu featuring all-American fare, from Maryland crab soup to cheeseburger pizzas, baby-back ribs and meatloaf, but the steady stream of visitors filing through the front door to whoop it up may be more interested in playing games than eating. You can stick with low-price fare with the pastas and sandwiches or splurge on something pricier. With about 200 television sets simultaneously broadcasting sporting events and with the general hullabaloo, the decibel level is deafening—this is not the place for conversation, unless you know someone well or don't want to know someone well. Laid out on three levels, ESPN Zone offers a sporting outlet for everyone, particularly if you want to try your hand at something downstairs in the gaming room.

Hawk 'n' Dove

329 Pennsylvania Ave. SE (Fourth St. SE), Capitol Hill, Washington 20003
202-543-3300, Fax 202-543-2529
Lunch & Dinner daily, Brunch Sun., $, Casual

Because of its clear view of the Capitol, the Hawk 'n' Dove feels a bit like a company commissary—and the company is the U.S. government. A favorite of employees of the Library of Congress, it offers a certain comfort level for regulars, who can come in and order "the usual." The intelligent and well-read crowd brings dignity to the two-martini lunch, which is affordably priced here. But eating here is more about the conversation than the food, although the burgers are decent enough for any gourmand. After hours, interns and students working on the Hill make good use of the pool table in the back room, guaranteeing a change in the atmosphere.

J Paul's

3218 M St. NW (Wisconsin Ave. NW)
Georgetown, Washington 20007
202-333-3450, Fax 202-342-6721, *Lunch & Dinner daily, $, Casual*

Always filled with an enthusiastic crowd of tourists and locals, J Paul's somehow never feels crowded and always feels inviting. While you're waiting for a table at this saloon, the bar is accommodating, and windows offer a delightful opportunity to people-watch. Excellent sandwiches, large salads and seasonal seafood offerings are favorites, as are the terrific burgers.

Johnny Rockets

3131 M St. NW (Wisconsin Ave. NW)
Georgetown, Washington 20007
202-333-7994, Fax 202-333-7995, *Lunch & Dinner daily, $, Casual*

If you could turn the clock back a few decades, you'd be eating at a place like Johnny Rockets. You'd listen to the jukebox, eat underdone fries and overdone burgers and sip Cokes or milk shakes. And that's just what today's twenty- and thirtysomethings are doing. This is really a glorified soda fountain, offering a big dose of nostalgia plus casual eats for every generation. You'll find more than just burgers: club sandwiches, BLTs, hot dogs, chili dogs and grilled cheese sandwiches are also on the menu. Service may be disjointed and slow; on the other hand, the place is not about haute cuisine. A good destination for a slow trip down memory lane. **Also located at** Union Station Food Court, 50 Massachusetts Ave. NW, Washington, DC, 202-289-6969; and 11000 S. Hayes St., Pentagon City Mall, Arlington, VA, 703-415-3510.

Lindy's Bon Appétit

2040 I St. NW (Pennsylvania Ave. NW)
Foggy Bottom, Washington 20006
202-452-0055, Fax 202-463-5113
Breakfast, Lunch & Dinner daily, $, Casual

Some of the best burgers in DC are at Lundy's Bon Appétit. Best of all, you can pick one of 23 toppings, and if you don't like beef, you can opt for vegetarian or turkey instead. Don't skip the fries—they come hot and salty right from the deep fryer. Other fare is available and, if you like, you can head upstairs to the "dressier" part of the restaurant for indoor seating (same menu) at Lindy's Red Lion, a favorite pub/hangout. But there's something so attractively grubby about ordering in the hash-house setting downstairs—you become part of a 25-year-old tradition among GWU students who've called this a second home.

Luna Grill & Diner

1301 Connecticut Ave. NW (N St. NW)
Dupont Circle, Washington 20036
202-835-2280, Fax 202-835-2281
Breakfast, Lunch & Dinner daily, $, Casual

It seems silly to think that one diner (which does not even resemble a diner) could cause such a stir, but this place merits raves and return visits, not only for its outrageous décor but also for its rather funky menu, which includes several surprising dishes: spicy bourbon barbecue chicken breast, grilled New York steak and a Pittsburgh-style barbecue sandwich with coleslaw. We particularly like the hamburger with a side of their fries, but are just as happy with the Reuben sandwich. If you'd rather, you can order breakfast (like strawberries and cream or cinnamon raisin french toast) all day. **Also located at** 4024 28th St., Arlington, VA, 703-379-7173.

Philadelphia Cheesesteak Factory

3347 M St. NW (33rd St. NW), Georgetown, Washington 20007
202-333-8040, Fax 202-333-8036, *Lunch & Dinner daily, $, Casual*

Philadelphia Cheesesteak Factory serves trademark cheesesteaks until well past midnight, and that means plenty of happy nearby college students. Join the crowd if you want the real thing (ingredients are imported daily from Philadelphia), plus good fries and onion rings. Other choices: assorted hoagies, burgers, fish cutlets and salads. Once located in a nearby shack, the restaurant has expanded to fit its bigger setting. **Also located at** 7413 Baltimore Ave., College Park, MD, 301-864-8040.

BAKERIES/CAFÉS

Bread & Chocolate

2301 M St. NW (23rd St. NW), West End, Washington 20037
202-833-8360, *Lunch & Dinner daily, $, Casual*

The idea of combining a wedge of freshly baked, buttered and cinnamon-sprinkled bread with a mug of hot chocolate probably is enough to tempt even the most stubborn dieter. Those are the kind of combinations available at Bread & Chocolate. Consider the special morning eye-opener, the french toast, which has chocolate added to the batter mix. You'll find plenty more chocolate options—try the chocolate cake—but you can also sample such savory dishes as a chicken, mozzarella and pasta salad, French onion soup and Hungarian goulash in cup or bowl. This is a comfort-food mecca. **Other locations.**

Bread Line

1751 Pennsylvania Ave. NW (18th St. NW)
Downtown, Washington 20006
202-822-8900, Fax 202-822-8256, *Breakfast & Lunch Mon.-Fri., $, Casual*

A P 🍴 🛍

Mark Furstenberg, of Marvelous Market fame (see *Gourmet Shops & Markets*), started the bread craze in DC, and he makes the best baguette in town here. Don't come expecting to have a relaxing lunch, though, for this bare-bones shop near the White House is usually crowded and a bit chaotic, even after the main lunch hour. You'll find scones and muffins for breakfast; soups, salads and sandwiches (don't miss the BLT on brioche during tomato season) for lunch; and a platter of English farmhouse cheeses and a small selection of wines and beers for an after-work or pre-theater snack. Sadly, it's closed for dinner and on weekends, so order a platter of knishes, empanadas, samosas—and a baguette—to take home.

Corner Bakery

529 14th St. NW (F St. NW), Downtown, Washington 20045
202-662-7400, Fax 202-662-7401
Breakfast, Lunch & Dinner daily, $

A 🛍

It seems no matter how early we get to Corner Bakery, the big, fat, squishy cinnamon rolls are gone. Fortunately, there is a lot more on the menu. Start with breakfast: coffee, fruits, and a bowl of granola, bagels, muffins, and yogurt. Later, the kitchen is turning out heartier goods: ample bowls of soups, sandwiches, pizzas and salads, to eat in or take out. The sweets still beckon, but now they're transformed into brownies, cookies and cakes. Fresh baked loaves of bread are also a staple here. **Other locations.**

Firehook Bakery & Coffee House

1909 Q St. NW (Connecticut Ave.), Dupont Circle, Washington 20009
202-588-9296, *Breakfast, Lunch & Dinner daily, $*

A 🛍

What a pity that baker Kate Jansen can't clone herself and/or her restaurant so that every town and byway in the metro area would have a Firehook Bakery. Stunningly successful, these bakeries have grown from one to many locations, each with its share of pastries, pies, tarts, breads and casual sandwiches to eat in or take out. Many folks drop in for morning coffee and a sweet roll, but sandwiches are just as much of a lure. An overstuffed tuna salad sandwich on one of the designer breads, hot coffee and a pastry make for a great midday meal. **Other locations.**

Heller's Bakery

4220 Fessenden St. NW (Connecticut Ave. NW)
Friendship Heights, Washington 20016
202-265-1190, *Breakfast & Lunch daily, Dinner Mon.-Sat.*, *$*, *Casual*

A 🏃

This appealing bakery can accommodate people grabbing a quick breakfast sweet, taking a coffee break or stopping by for a fast lunch of empanadas or chicken salad. But chances are that most patrons come to indulge in the store's tempting array of baked goods, from fritters and chocolate chip cookies to napoleons, layer cakes and fruit pies. This is also one of only a handful of places that often sells Mexican pan dulce, pastries worth the trip. **Also located at** 3221 Mt. Pleasant St., NW, Washington, DC. 202-265-1190; and 7000 Commerce St., Springfield, VA 703-644-9555.

Reeves Restaurant & Bakery

1306 G St. NW (13th St. NW), Downtown, Washington 20005
202-628-6350, *Breakfast, Lunch & Dinner Mon.-Sat.*, *$*, *Casual*

A 🏃

Native Washingtonians know Reeves as a city landmark—a favorite destination since 1886. It offers an array of savory dishes, from serious breakfast platters, deli sandwiches and hefty burgers to crunchy fried chicken and veal Parmigiana (all available to eat downstairs in the dining room or to-go). But it's probably best known for its baked goods, especially its pies. The strawberry pie lives up to its standout reputation. The cherry, blueberry and lemon pies are also scrumptious. Cakes are certainly not chopped liver—everything from cheesecake to old-fashioned devil's food is made with extreme care and precision.

BARBECUE

Capital Q

707 H St. NW (Seventh St. NW), Chinatown, Washington 20001
202-347-8396, Fax 202-347-8397, *Lunch & Dinner Mon.-Sat.*, *$*, *Casual*

A **P** 🍴 🏃

This Chinatown barbeque joint has lots of fans who adore Texas-style grub. And since the opening of the MCI Center, expect to find tourists and locals alike hunkering down at the eating counter for some ribs. Revel in the smoky Texas sausages and pulled chicken or even the offbeat chopped beef and black bean tacos or giant smoked baked potato. But whatever you do, don't skip the ribs—they are glorious, meaty and super-smoky, with enough bottled heat to sear your mouth. Sides include skins-on chunky mashed potatoes, collard greens, pork and beans, home fries and coleslaw. Don't miss the creamy banana pudding for dessert—take some home for a midnight snack.

Old Glory All-American Bar-B-Que

3139 M St. NW (Wisconsin Ave. NW)
Georgetown, Washington 20007
202-337-3406, Fax 202-342-1819, *Lunch & Dinner daily*, *$*, *Casual*

A **P** 🍴 🐄 **Y**

This rollicking, noisy barbecue spot is always full of people, lounging at the downstairs bar or eating ribs fast and furiously at one of the tables upstairs or down. Featuring all-American barbecue, Old Glory specializes in St. Louis-style spareribs and baby-back ribs, but you can also pick up beef brisket, pulled chicken, steak or lamb, as well as lesser dishes, like burgers and salads. Any meal you select can be heated up with sprinkles of one of six barbecue sauces, from Carolina- to Memphis-style. Wind up with a satisfying dessert, either the apple crisp or a rich brownie sundae.

Rockland's Barbeque & Grilling Company

2418 Wisconsin Ave. NW (Calvert St. NW)
Glover Park, Washington 20007
202-333-2558, Fax 202-333-1931, *Lunch & Dinner daily, $, Casual*

This original location of Rockland's looks dingy from the outside, but inside you'll find a crowd gnawing on its crunchy ribs and awesome casual grub. Seating is very limited, so expect to wait unless you drop by at an off hour. The menu offers smoky ribs in whole, half or quarter slabs and several interesting sides. We think the quarter slab of ribs with the Texas corn pudding is a perfect lunch, but for a change of pace, you may prefer chicken, fish or vegetables grilled to order or even a grilled leg of lamb sandwich. There aren't many desserts—but there are plenty of bottled hot sauces you can purchase. **Also located at** 4000 Fairfax Dr., Arlington, VA, 703-528-9663.

CAFÉS & COFFEE SHOPS

Donna's

St. Gregory Hotel
2033 M St. NW (20th St. NW), Downtown, Washington 20036
202-223-2981, Fax 202-223-2983, *Breakfast, Lunch & Dinner daily, $, Casual*

What can you say about a coffee shop—actually, coffeehouse or maybe trendy café—that serves a honeydew martini, chocolate mousse cake and a four-cheese pizza? You can say this is no ordinary coffee shop. The St. Gregory is not your run-of-the-mill hotel, either: Standing over a faux vent is a Marilyn Monroe statue in her famous billowing-skirt pose. This coffee shop makes a sophisticated statement about good food, good drink and good times. If it all sounds too adult, you'll be pleased to hear that kids aren't forgotten: Donna's offers PB&J sandwiches, cheese-and-tomato pizzas and toasted cheese. (Or maybe this is just what you'd like for a quick comfort-food snack.)

Wrap Works

1079 Wisconsin Ave. NW (M St. NW), Georgetown, Washington 20007
202-333-0220, Fax 202-333-0594, *Lunch & Dinner daily, $, Casual*

These little sandwich shops show how creative cooks can turn bread and filling into magic. Wraps have become something of a cliché, but not when you bite into something like the Coat & Thai chicken (spicy peanut chicken with fresh spinach plus extras) in a red chile tortilla or Kung Pao-Wow chicken in a sesame wheat tortilla. You can also create your own wrap from a selection of ingredients. Another good bet: the silken, chilly smoothies. **Other locations.**

COFFEEHOUSES & TEAROOMS

Ching Ching Cha, a Chinese Tea House

1063 Wisconsin Ave. NW (M St. NW), Georgetown, Washington 20007
202-333-8288, Lunch & Dinner Tues.-Sun., $, Casual dressy

Seeking serenity in a jaded world? The Chinese offer the tea-house, where uplifting and satisfying hot tea, served with a carefully wrought snack (dim sum), soothes and comforts. In Washington, that means Ching Ching Cha, a hassle-free setting where patrons can choose to sit Asian-style on the floor or at a Western-style table. The teas here are outstanding, freshly brewed (try the jasmine tea, which tastes like an infusion of flowery perfume) and served with flourish. Snacks include dumplings (like the excellent Mongolian lamb), chicken rolls, marbled tea eggs, sweet tartlets and cookies and more substantial dishes, including curried chicken, mustard miso salmon and steamed tofu.

Politics & Prose

5015 Connecticut Ave. NW (Nebraska Ave. NW)
Uptown, Washington 20008
202-364-1919, Breakfast, Lunch & Dinner daily, $, Casual
No credit cards.

Book lovers have the best of both worlds here: fantastic reads and good coffee and snacks. Indeed, they are encouraged to sit, read and sip in the downstairs eating area with its comfortable furniture. You could spend the day here, with almost all the comforts of home at your fingertips. Try a tuna melt, turkey melt or grilled cheese or a hearty soup and salad. There is a wide selection of coffees and teas.

Teaism

2009 R St. NW (Connecticut Ave. NW)
Dupont Circle, Washington 20009
202-667-3827, Breakfast, Lunch & Dinner daily, $, Casual

Teaism is not just about drinking tea (although there are plenty of varieties)—the restaurant group also offers fruit juices, beer, wine, saké and assorted lunch and dinner edibles. You'll find a mostly Asian menu that includes soups (including the Japanese tea soup, ochazuke), sandwiches, bento boxes (Japanese small meals in pretty boxes), hearty entrées (including Thai chicken curry) and sides of Indian bread or sticky rice. Morning meals include sourdough waffles and Irish oatmeal with mango and raisins. Take home your favorite tea (how about pu-erh Camel Breath?) and pick up teapots, scoops and books on brewing. Sit upstairs, downstairs or outside. **Other locations.** Also see review in *Gourmet Shops & Markets/ Cofffee & Tea.*

Xando

1647 20th St. NW (R St.), Dupont Circle, Washington 20009
202-332-6364, Breakfast, Lunch & Dinner daily, $, Casual

Relax at a terrace table or sit inside and sip coffee or tea any way you like them. The menu spans the casual food scene, from grilled "xandwiches" to wraps to gooey desserts. Finish your visit with s'mores (the marshmallow-graham cracker treat many of us remember from childhood camping adventures) and a mug of hot caramel apple cider. Hear jazz guitar music playing in the background and the whoosh of espresso makers while you lounge on mismatched furniture. Read books and newspapers, eat a tuna-cranberry wrap, eye for-sale artwork and chat with folks from the neighborhood—this is a major meeting place and is often crowded. **Other locations.**

DELIS & BAGEL SHOPS

a.k.a. Friscos

4115 Wisconsin Ave. NW (Van Ness St. NW)
Tenleytown, Washington 20016
202-244-7847, Fax 202-686-9668, *Lunch Mon.-Sat., $, Casual*
🅰 ♥ 👬

Think Berkeley and Birkenstocks, and you've pretty much got the idea of Friscos, a throwback to the '60s, when many devotees ate sprouts and big sandwiches bursting with wholesome ingredients. You'll find plenty of creative reminders here. Friscos also produces salads chock-full of crunchy, healthful ingredients and interesting sides, such as a spicy chili. **Also located at** 4632 Wedgewood Blvd., Frederick, MD, 301-698-0018.

Einstein Bros Bagels

1815 Wisconsin Ave. NW (S St. NW), Georgetown, Washington 20007
202-333-4436, *reakfast, Lunch & Dinner daily, $, Casual*
🅰 P ♥ 👬

If you're a New Yorker and mad for bagels, you'll appreciate this group of bagel restaurants that sells classic bagels and good toppings. We love the onion bagel with salmon "shmear" (salmon cream cheese). Even if you're not a New Yorker, how can you go wrong with a wild blueberry bagel and some fruit shmear? Einstein Bros isn't just about bagels: In the tradition of sensible eateries, it offers a little something for everyone, including wraps, muffins, yogurts, iced and hot coffee, salads and, naturally, bagel sandwiches—try the hot BBQ chicken. Remember, if you want to eat bagels for dinner, most stores close in the early evening. **Other locations.**

Georgetown Bagelry

3245 M St. NW (31st St. NW), Georgetown, Washington 20007
202-965-1011, *Breakfast & Lunch daily, Dinner Mon.-Sat., $, Casual*
No credit cards. 👬

You've got to love a place that looks as used as an old shoe but is still jammed with customers even in the mid-afternoon. It's a tribute to the store's bakers that people flock here for the thick, yeasty bagels that come in almost every imaginable flavor with assorted generous spreads. You can dine even more grandly on interesting bagel sandwiches; BLT, burger, cheeseburger and pastrami. But the store's biggest draw might be its homemade pizza, sold by the slice, just like in New York. Try the white pizza, loaded with garlic. **Also located at** 5227 River Rd., Bethesda, MD, 301-657-4442.

Some establishments change **days of operation** without warning. It is always wise to check in advance.

Krupin's

4620 Wisconsin Ave. NW (Chesapeake St. NW)
Tenleytown, Washington 20016
202-686-1989, *Breakfast, Lunch & Dinner daily, $$, Casual*

A 🖐 P 🍴

Washington's favorite deli boasts terrific corned beef, smoked fish that is brought in from Brooklyn and a beef-in-the-pot that is a generous combination of chicken soup, matzoh balls, and boned short ribs of beef that would do any Jewish mother proud. The main attraction (other than the food) is Morty and Mel, the Krupin brothers themselves, who are often wise-cracking with the customers and one another. Some people go just for the show.

Wagshal's Delicatessen

4855 Massachusetts Ave. NW (49th St. NW)
Spring Valley, Washington 20016
202-363-5698, *Breakfast, Lunch & Dinner daily, $, Casual*

A P 🍽 🍸

This small deli in the shadow of American University serves excellent sandwiches. The turkey is freshly roasted (always the telling sign of a good deli) and the corned beef is good. Since opening its doors in 1925, Wagshal's has kept up with the shifting tastes and lifestyles of its upscale suburban neighborhood and now offers full-menu catering throughout the week, complete with gourmet breads, desserts and salads. Also see review in *Gourmet Shops & Markets/Gourmet Markets & Gourmet To-Go.*

ETHNIC FLAIR

Chinese

China Boy

817 6th St. NW (H St. NW), Chinatown, Washington 20001
202-371-1661, Fax 202-371-8139, *Lunch daily, $, Casual*
No credit cards. P 🍴

Probably the least dressy, least frilly eatery in Washington is this tiny Chinatown spot, where elderly Chinese gather all day. There's no printed menu, just a board listing a few dishes. But you can count on the noodles being fresh: They're made right out back and upstairs. The chow foon with beef is excellent. Food can be eaten there or prepared for takeout. Surprisingly, China Boy has been a well-kept secret.

Indian

Amma Indian Vegetarian Kitchen

3291-A M St. NW (33rd St. NW), Georgetown, Washington 20007
202-625-6625, *Lunch & Dinner daily, $, Casual*

A ♥ 🍴

This is an excellent spot for vegetarian Indian food. Packed with flavor (the mango lassi is sweetly intense) and served speedily, the food wows with its diversity and, well, healthfulness. You can't help feeling like you're bursting with energy after a punchy meal of idli sambar and mysore masala dosa, a potato wrap that comes in a paper-thin folder. **Also located at** 344 E. Maple Ave., Vienna, VA, 703-938-5328.

Japanese

Hibachi Brothers Japanese Restaurant

4441-B Wisconsin Ave. NW (Albemarle St. NW)
Tenleytown, Washington 20016
202-537-3717, Fax 202-362-6757, *Lunch & Dinner daily, $, Casual*
🅰 P 🍴 ⬭

Outfitted in wood panels, delicately colorful paper lanterns and Japanese prints, this is a serene spot for a reasonably priced Japanese meal. Seating is available at wooden booths, the sushi bar and even in a small tatami room that you can rent for a private get-together. The menu is more extensive than many of its sushi competitors and delves into the world of hibachi grilling for beef, chicken and vegetable entrées. It also features tempura, teriyaki and agemono dishes. The sushi is also excellent: tightly rolled and precisely cut. You can't go wrong with such popular sushi as tuna, salmon and California rolls.

Mexican

Burrito Brothers

1815 M St. NW (Connecticut Ave. NW)
Georgetown, Washington 20007
202-785-3309, Fax 202-785-3316, *Lunch & Dinner daily, $, Casual*
🅰 🍴

One of the granddaddies of the burrito-and-wrap restaurants in the city, this spot was opened by a man passionate about burritos. The formula is simple: Take a flour tortilla, add a meat or bean (and rice) filling, drizzle it with toppings and/or cheese and chilies, wrap it and eat. The short menu includes fajitas, quesadillas and tacos, but burritos star. The offerings include vegetarian chili, meatless tacos and burritos and kiddie's quesadillas, tacos and nachitos. Prices are so low that impoverished students can fill up for less than $10. **Other locations.**

The Burro

2000 Pennsylvania Ave. NW (20th St. NW)
Foggy Bottom, Washington 20006
202-293-9449, Fax 202-293-9472, *Lunch daily, Dinner Mon.-Sat., $, Casual*
🅰 P 💻 🍴

Referring to itself as DC's cocina fresca, or fresh kitchen, The Burro declares that burritos can be healthful and fashionable. They (and tacos) are also delicious. We recommend the Bean Grande burrito and the chicken soft taco. Although the menu is not extensive, it does wrap itself around the favorites—beans, beef and chicken—plus a little something extra for the trendy: fish tacos. If you eat here on a hot day, ask for a bone-chilling smoothie. **Also located at** 1621 Connecticut Ave. NW, Washington, DC, 202-483-6861.

The Well Dressed Burrito

1220 19th St. NW (Jefferson Pl. NW), Downtown, Washington 20036
202-293-0515, Fax 202-293-0546, *Lunch Mon.-Fri., $, Casual*
No credit cards.

You can't go at night or on weekends. Don't expect to be able to use your credit cards or even tables and chairs. But, when this tiny place is open, do find superb Tex-Mex grub at this pocket-sized takeout joint, especially the burritos, which are overstuffed with flavorful meat, bean or chicken fillings. Our favorite: the plain burrito packed with chunky shreds of savory beef and melted cheese. A close runner-up: El Gordo, a super-sized flour tortilla oozing chicken (or beef, or vegetables) and refried beans. There's plenty more, including chicken or beef fajitas, grilled nachos, grilled quesadillas, grilled burritos, and a selection of salads filled with spicy flavors.

Middle Eastern

Fast Fettoosh

3277 M St. NW (32nd St. NW), Georgetown, Washington 20007
202-342-1199, Fax 202-342-1190, *Lunch & Dinner daily, $, Casual*

A somewhat worn but charming addition to the main Fettosh restaurant, this takeout area offers some stretches of tiled counter and a few stools, ready to accommodate anyone who wants a Middle-Eastern snack without all the fuss and frenzy of a full-service restaurant. In fact, you can order pretty much the same fare as you'll see on the restaurant menu. We especially recommend the beef sandwich and the delicious desserts.

Moby Dick House of Kabob

1070 31st St. NW (M St. NW), Georgetown, Washington 20007
202-333-4400, *Lunch & Dinner daily, $, Casual*
No credit cards.

Moby Dick has made its name serving kebabs and fresh breads. The first location was in Bethesda. Now all Washington is in on the secret, because the chain has expanded. Depending on the hour, getting a table may be a challenge. Plan to order ahead, otherwise you may join a line waiting for the terrific kebabs wrapped in fresh-baked breads. We're addicted to the kubideh kebab in hot bread with its side of tangy yogurt. Add a shirazi salad and you've got a meal. Always check out the specials Monday through Friday; these are full-blown Persian entrées that are more substantial than a sandwich. **Other locations.**

Pan-Asian

Oodles Noodles

1120 19th St. NW (L St. NW), Downtown, Washington 20036
202-293-3138, Fax 202-467-0558, *Lunch & Dinner Mon.-Sat., $, Casual*

It's rare for a pan-Asian restaurant to excel in several cooking styles, but Oodles Noodles manages to do so. The menu offers Thai, Vietnamese, Japanese and Chinese noodle dishes, all in serving pieces authentic to the country of origin. Any of these dishes make for a satisfying lunch or a light dinner: Thai drunken noodles, spicy Japanese seafood ramen, or rice-noodle soups in a Chinese clay pot. If you're on a budget, you can have a noodle dish plus an appetizer or salad for far less than what pasta would cost at one of the nearby upscale Italian restaurants. There's a reason for the distinguished feats here: The owner is Jessie Yan, who also owns DC's hot spots Spices and Yanÿu (see reviews in *Restaurants*). **Also located at** 4907 Cordell Ave., Bethesda, MD, 301-986-8833.

Pan-Asian Restaurant

2020 P St. NW (21st. St. NM), Dupont Circle, Washington 20036
202-872-8889, Fax 202-872-8886, *Lunch & Dinner daily, $, Casual*

Not to be confused with the other Pan-Asian noodle shop by the same name, this Dupont Circle eatery makes for casual noodle noshing at its best. But noodles are only part of its menu, which takes you on a gastronomic tour of much of Asia. Look for soft-shell crabs in season, Cantonese roast duck, grilled Filipino and Thai chicken and assorted Thai-style curries. Since noodles are a mainstay, though, turn to the extensive selection, from Thai drunken noodles to chilled Japanese soba noodles. We love the Cozy Noodles, a Chinese-inspired sesame noodle dish with a spicy peanut sauce, but we've also been tempted by kway tway mee, the popular Singaporean dish with a variety of noodles and toppings.

Sticks & Bowls

1300 Connecticut Ave. NW (N St. NW), Downtown, Washington 20036
202-296-4001, *Breakfast, Lunch & Dinner Mon.-Fri., $, Casual*
No credit cards.

Although it's somewhat of a copycat of other pan-Asian noodle places around town, food here is flavorful and served in very generous portions. Order up front; start with either a rice or noodle base, then pick your toppings and await your order. We liked the crispy chicken noodles with a hot Szechuan topping. Breakfast? Not noodles, but pancakes or bagels with plenty of topping choices.

Salvadoran

Julia's Empanadas

2452 18th St. NW (Columbia Rd. NW)
Adams Morgan, Washington 20009
202-328-6232, *Lunch & Dinner daily, $, Casual*
No credit cards.

Yes, there really is a Julia: a kind, hard-working woman who still gets into her kitchen every day to help make all the tender-crusted empanadas for which she is famous. There are eight tasty choices, including chorizo, Chilean-style beef, and satlenas. There's little else on the menu, unless you want soup and some fruit-filled empanadas for dessert. The secrets to Julia's success are that she keeps the formula simple and insists on high-quality, made-from-scratch food. **Also located at** 1000 Vermont Ave. NW, Washington, DC, 202-789-1878; and 1221 Connecticut Ave. NW, Washington, DC, 202-861-8828. Also see review in *Gourmet Shops & Markets/Gourmet Markets & Markets To-Go.*

PIZZA

California Pizza Kitchen

1260 Connecticut Ave. NW (N St. NW)
Downtown, Washington 20036
202-331-4020, Fax 202-331-4101, *Lunch & Dinner daily, $$*

You have to have a sense of humor to enjoy CPK's outrageous pizza toppings. They are innovative, offbeat and likely to raise eyebrows among traditionalists. That's probably a quick and then forgotten reaction, though, since this is one of the country's most popular chains. We enjoy the rosemary-chicken-potato pizza, the tandoori chicken and the Thai chicken pies. Not everything is so ingenous: Sticklers for the conventional will find pepperoni; vegetarian; and five-cheese-and-fresh-tomato pies. Hungry for more? Check out the menu for soups, salads, sandwiches and pasta dishes. This tiled, shiny-clean restaurant is casual, fun and often crowded. **Other locations.**

Ledo Pizza

4400 Connecticut Ave., NW (Van Ness), Washington 20008
202-244-8109, Fax 202-237-5825
Lunch & Dinner daily, $, Casual

A P ☰

A restaurant group that started with its first store in College Park, Md., these popular pizza restaurants have a devoted following among students, families and anyone who likes hearty Italian-style meals. The menu offers salads, pasta entrées, over-stuffed subs, sandwiches, and burgers. Its pizzas, however, have made its name and fame: The dough and sauce are prepared fresh daily; toppings are high-quality ingredients. Expect to find clean, busy restaurants for sit-down meals. **Other locations.**

Pizzeria Paradiso

2029 P St. NW (21st. St. NM), Dupont Circle, Washington 20036
202-223-1245, *Lunch & Dinner daily, $, Casual*

A ☰

This cheerful and always-crowded pizza parlor, with its faux ruins stenciled on the ceiling, stylized pies painted on the walls and a wood-burning pizza oven, serves some of the best pizza this side of Naples. At peak times, we guarantee a wait for one of the dozen or so tables and handful of bar stools, but stick it out. Try one of the house combinations—the classic margherita, the rich quattro formaggi or the bottarga with its captivating topping of an egg, chopped parsley and freshly grated salted fish roe. The Atomica, as the name suggests, is nuclear-hot and outstanding. If you'd prefer, there's also a short sandwich list—house-baked rolls filled with cold cuts, pork or lamb.

Prospect Pizza & Pastries

3203 Prospect St. NW (32nd St. NW), Georgetown, Washington 20007
202-298-6800, Fax 202-298-3251
Lunch & Dinner Tues.-Sat., $$, Casual

A ☰

Forget the sausage and cheese pies when you visit this charming spot, the cook indulges your pizza fantasies with such wonderfully eclectic toppings as prosciutto, smoked mozzarella, fresh arugula and truffle oil; artichoke hearts, baby spinach, fennel, cherry tomatoes and herbed oil; and, finally, lamb sausage, plum tomatoes, button mushrooms and shallots. But if your tastes run to something less complicated, consider the rather divine white pizza studded with whole roasted garlic cloves and plenty of melting cheeses. Crusts are fork-tender, delicate and completely irresistible. Speaking of irresistible, for dessert, try the Mocha Pizza, a brown sugar crust topped with coffee gelato and chocolate sauce.

GOURMET SHOPS & MARKETS

BAKERIES

Firehook Bakery & Coffee House

1909 Q St. NW (19th St. NW), Dupont Circle, Washington 20009
202-588-9296, Fax 703-519-7681, *Open daily*

A

The Firehook Bakery still makes its breads in a 17-foot-diameter wood-burning oven, assembled by a master baker at its original location in Alexandria. The bakery uses organic flours, and the breads are pulled from the oven when the baker determines they're ready. The result is a bread that has a thicker European crust and a chewy center. The bakery has the traditional selection of bread styles and flavors, but the pistachio stick is guaranteed to sell out early on the days it's baked. The pastries are impeccable and as outstandingly cutting-edge as the breads. This is a baker's bakery. **Other locations.** Also see review in *Quick Bites*.

Marvelous Market

1511 Connecticut Ave. NW
(Q St. NW), Dupont Circle, Washington 20036
202-332-3690, *Open daily*

A

The original owner and master bread maker, Mark Furstenberg, has left, but his recipes and style remain. The baguette is still a staple, and the bakery still makes the Palladin, a very light bread that was originally created for DC chef Jean-Louis Palladin, when he was the toast of Washington culinary circles. The market always has been known for its sandwiches. This is among the "bread houses" with a raisin-pecan bread leading the lineup—here with essence of orange peel to create the twist of flavor that draws people back for more. **Other locations.**

CANDY & CHOCOLATES

Chocolate Chocolate

1050 Connecticut Ave. NW (L St. NW)
Downtown, Washington 20036
202-466-2190, Fax 202-466-2191, *Open Mon.-Fri.*

A

The store offers a fine selection of chocolate candies from around the world. The truffles will dazzle you with a chocolate rush. One of the highlighted brands is that of Joseph Schmidt, the San Francisco chocolatier who has been making his signature Belgian chocolate egg-shaped truffles since 1983. This is a small place, but it packs a mighty chocolate punch.

Find the name you are looking for, quickly and easily,
in **the index**.

Les Délices d'Isabelle

1531 Wisconsin Ave. NW
(P & Q Sts. NW), Georgetown, Washington 20007
202-944-1898, Fax 202-944-1899, *Open daily*

A

This small store carries the Belgian Leonidas chocolates exclusively. You will find scores of the different filled chocolates in varying shapes, and there are seasonal specialties for holidays.

Pâtisserie Poupon

1645 Wisconsin Ave. NW (Q St. NW), Georgetown, Washington 20007
202-342-3248, Fax 202-342-7703, *Open Tues.-Sun.*

A

This chic French pastry and candy shop in Georgetown is perfectly suited to its upscale location. The kitchen specializes in handmade candies concocted with the finest of French chocolates. The shop is a particular must at any holiday time, for the busy candy makers churn out fantasy confections that may look like anything from Christmas trees to windmills. This store ranks high on the chocoholic's investment list for serious shopping.

CHEESE

Bowers Fancy Dairy Products

Eastern Market, 225 Seventh St. SE
(Pennsylvania Ave. SE), Capitol Hill, Washington 20003
202-544-7877, *Open Tues.-Sun.*
No credit cards.

An Eastern Market institution, Bowers has been selling quality cheeses since 1963. Its selection includes hundreds of varieties of both domestic and imported cheeses flown in from around the world. You will find the familiar, the lesser-known and the hard-to-get, including a large selection of French, Dutch and English soft and hard cheeses. Raclette, used in the Swiss fondue dish, also is stocked. The attitude is down-home friendly, and domestic cheeses are treated with the same care as the imported ones.

COFFEE & TEA

Teaism

400 8th St. NW
(Pennsylvania Ave. NW), Downtown, Washington, DC, 20004
202-638-6010, *Open daily*

A

A favorite among tea lovers, the three Teaism shops in Washington have the area's best selection and the most knowledgeable staff. Each market is complemented by a small restaurant. Visitors will find black tea from India, green tea from Japan, oolongs from Taiwan, white tea from China and other teas from Korea, Kenya, Sri Lanka and Vietnam. Usually about 40 choices are available. Teaism also carries the caffeine-free herbal infusions. **Also located at** 800 Connecticut Ave. NW, Washington, DC, 202-835-2233; and 2009 R St. NW, Washington, DC, 202-667-3827. Also see review in *Quick Bites*.

Your Local Guide To:

Restaurant Guides

Entertainment

Weekend Plans

City Visitor's Guides

Travel Plans

Live Music

Arts & Culture

Shopping

Sports & Recreation

digitalcity.com

a division of America Online, Inc.

When it comes to
creating wealth,
decision makers
know where they can find
a capital idea

Forbes
CAPITALIST TOOL *Never settle*

ETHNIC MARKETS

African/Middle Eastern

Addisu Gebeya

2202 18th St. NW
(Wyoming St. NW), Adams Morgan, Washington 20009
202-986-6013, Fax 202-986-1190, *Open daily*

A

The foods and utensils of Ethiopia fill this store in Adams Morgan, a neighborhood populated with many ethnic shops and restaurants. Considering the growing popularity of Ethiopian food, serious aficionados can pick up an authentic small clay sheklas stove for the home that can be used to make the vegetarian or meat wats (stews) of the country. You also can buy the spices used in Ethiopian dishes, such as cardamom, ginger, coriander and the little brown seeds of fenugreek, which are ground to become a key ingredient. The store is informal and the staff helpful, if you are understanding in appreciating English is not the first language spoken here.

Merkato Market

2116 18th St. NW
(Wyoming Ave. NW), Adams Morgan, Washington 20009
202-483-9499, Fax 202-483-9497, *Open daily*

A

For Ethiopian food lovers, Merkato is a major food source. Here you can find the basis of all Ethiopian cuisine, the spongy tangy injera bread. For the adventurous cook, the ancient ground grain teff that makes injera can be purchased also. Coffee connoisseurs will appreciate the Ethiopian coffees from Sidamo and Harar. The basis for much of the fiery heat in the cuisine can be found here in the berbere, the thick red paste of ginger, cardamom, coriander, fenugreek, nutmeg, cloves, cinnamon and allspice ground with oil and water. The shelves also are stocked with lentils.

Asian

Da Hua Market

623 H St. NW (Seventh St. NW), Chinatown, Washington 20001
202-371-8888, *Open daily*

A

This long-time cornerstone of Chinatown is a giant market with everything Asian that you need for preparing its varied cuisines. Beyond the fresh produce, you can browse shelves filled with soy sauces, hot sauces and all kinds of canned and dried items.

We're always interested to hear about **your discoveries and to receive your comments on ours.** Please let us know what you liked or disliked; e-mail us at gayots@aol.com.

German

German Deli

1331 H St. NW (13th St. NW), Downtown, Washington 20005
202-347-5732, Fax 202-347-4958, *Open daily*

A

The German Deli has been serving Washingtonians for more than 60 years. Along with its sister location, Café Mozart, it has provided a rare local outlet for home-style German cooking and products. The store has an extensive selection of domestic and imported German sausages and deli meats. You won't find any better bratwurst, knackwurst and weisswurst in the area. Don't forget the sauerkraut and German potato salad. Breads and pastries are abundant if that's where your taste buds want to go.

Italian

A. Litteri

517 Morse St. NE
(Florida Ave. NE), Capital City Market, Washington 20002
202-544-0183, Fax 202-543-4409, *Open Tues.-Sat.*

A

This is "the" Insider Washington Italian grocery, probably the oldest in the city. Located in a warehouse district, it's a busy place. Families flock to this old-fashioned store, where olive oils are sold by the gallon (although the trendier designer brands are lined up on the shelves). Freezers are loaded with pastas and gnocchi, and shelves are stocked with popular brands of dried pastas. Cheeses and deli items abound, but pay particular attention to the sausages, which are authentic, and either hot or mild.

Latin American

Casa Pena

1636 17th St. NW (R St. NW), Dupont Circle, Washington 20009
202-462-2222, Fax 202-462-2445, *Open daily*

A

The friendly scene at Casa Pena creates a lively atmosphere as the neighborhood's residents search for a wide variety of Latino foods. If you're interested in the latest craze in teas, the exotic yerba mate, you can find five different ones as well as the gourd itself. Among other items are spicy chorizo sausages, fruit paste in guava, mango and papaya, tubers like yuca, boniato and yautia and grains like quinoa. The mood is friendly and welcoming.

FARMERS MARKETS

Neighborhood Farmers Street Markets

TUESDAY
Downtown—USDA Farmers Market, U.S. Department of Transportation, 400 Seventh St. SW, 10 a.m.-2 p.m. (May-Nov.), 202-366-0674.

THURSDAY
Downtown—USDA Farmers Market, U.S. Department of Labor, 200 Constitution Ave. NW, 10 a.m.-2 p.m. (June-Nov.), 800-384-8704 or 202-219-5710, ext. 163.

FRIDAY
Downtown—USDA Farmers Market, USDA parking lot, 12th St. & Independence Ave., 10 a.m.-2 p.m. (June-Nov.), 800-384-8704.

SATURDAY
Capitol Hill—225 Seventh St. SE, sunrise-sellout, 202-546-2698.

SUNDAY
Dupont Circle—20th St. NW (between Q St. & Massachusetts Ave.), 9 a.m.-1 p.m. (Apr.-Dec.), 202-331-7300.

FISH, MEAT & POULTRY

Cannon's Seafood

1065 31st St. NW (M St. NW), Georgetown, Washington 20007
202-337-8366, Fax 202-337-0360, *Open Mon.-Sat.*
A **P**

   Going strong for 60 years in Washington, Cannon's is the source for any cook looking for ultrafresh seafood. The market has a large selection of lobsters, crabs and jumbo lump crab meat, spiced shrimp and smoked fish. You can buy your fish—from Chilean sea bass to the local favorite, rockfish—whole or fileted. There's always a good selection of favorites such as tuna, halibut and salmon. If you want something you don't see, ask the fishmonger; he'll do his best to find it on the market—even that six-pound lobster you crave. **Also located at** 762-A Walker Rd., Great Falls, VA, 703-759-4950.

Pruitt's Seafood

Maine Avenue Wharf
1100 Maine Ave. SW (Ninth St. SW), Waterfront, Washington 20024
202-554-2669, Fax 202-554-0126, *Open daily*
A **P**

   One of the best of the Maine Avenue harbor fish stands, Pruitt's has built a reputation that brings many local chefs to this spot on the river. The lobster are lively and fresh, and you may even find West Coast Dungeness crab on ice. Many people shop for the croakers, halibut, the local favorite rockfish, red snapper and, of course, Maryland blue crabs. The waterfront scene can be hectic with all the stands vying for sales, but take your time checking the catch.

GOURMET MARKETS & GOURMET TO-GO

Dean & DeLuca

3276 M St. NE (Wisconsin Ave. NW), Georgetown, Washington 20007
202-342-2500, Fax 202-342-2525, *Open daily*
A

   The DC transplant of the quintessential New York gourmet food store bustles with a brisk trade of Georgetown locals, tourists and foodies from Virginia, the District and Maryland, all shopping for the unusual and the desirable. Dean & DeLuca delights in carrying the trendiest produce, often available nowhere else. The cheese counter has more than 100 different cheese varieties, many imported, plus a complete line of American cheeses. In the downstairs housewares section, an impressive collection of tools and pans invites a gourmet gadget shopping binge. The fine chocolate counter includes an exclusive selection from the Belgian house of Manon, known for its quality and antique molds. The store tour reveals assorted fine charcuterie, wines, coffee and tea, and, of course, a smorgasbord of vinegars and oils. Service can be slow, uninterested and even surly—and without the New York staff's efficiency. Shoppers come back, though, because Dean & DeLuca has what you can't find anywhere else.

Fresh Fields

2323 Wisconsin Ave. NW (Calvert St.), Georgetown, Washington 20007
202-333-5393, Fax 202-333-5392, *Open daily*

A P

Fresh Fields is part of Whole Foods Market, which claims to be the world's biggest retailer of natural and organic foods. Here you will find a large, creatively merchandised produce department, an in-house bakery, extensive prepared-foods counters and large wine and cheese departments. Most stores have a wide-open feel and a welcoming ambience. Home of the best grocery salad bar—with couscous, bean and tofu salads for the health-conscious—Fresh Fields also has one of the area's finest butcher shops, featuring naturally raised beef, lamb and pork. Shoppers can find the favorite chicken brands of local chefs: Eberly and Bell and Evans. Some locations have coffee and juice bars, the latter run by Jamba Juice, featuring its California-created power smoothies. **Other locations.**

Julia's Empanadas

2452 18th St. NW
(Columbia Rd.), Adams Morgan, Washington 20009
202-328-6232, Fax 202-789-1641, *Open daily*
No credit cards.

Julia's has made these simple Latino pastries into a gourmet dream, with flaky half-moon crusts and numerous fillings, from spicy beef, chicken and pork to vegetables. Dessert empanadas have generous fillings of cooked fruit. Regulars love the hand-held eat-on-the-run treats that make this fast food with flavor. Side orders are available and the rice pudding is luscious. **Also located at** 1000 Vermont Ave. NW, Washington, DC, 202-789-1878; and 1221 Connecticut Ave. NW, Washington, DC, 202-861-8828. Also see review in *Quick Bites*.

Lawsons

1350 Connecticut Ave. NW
(New Hampshire Ave. NW), Dupont Circle, Washington 20036
202-775-0400, Fax 202-529-7667, *Open Mon.-Sat.*

A

This classy upscale deli caters to the lunch crowd during the day and to urban dwellers in the evening. Prepared foods to go include pastas, quesadillas, roasted chicken and a generous selection of vegetables and salads. In the specialty food section, look for the good olive oils and pastas.

Magruder's Grocery

3527 Connecticut Ave. NW
(Porter St. NW), Cleveland Park, Washington 20008
202-237-2531, Fax 202-237-2572, *Open daily*

A P

Owned by a Washington family since opening in 1875, Magruder's stores have maintained a neighborhood feel, while moving into the 21st century. Locally the stores have built their reputation in their produce departments. Serving the multicultural needs of the Washington area, the produce in this store extends beyond the expected to include fresh broccoli rapini, malanga roots, black radishes, daikon radishes, yuca, taro and boniato. Yellow tomatoes and Key limes are available all year. We have found maridol papayas as big as footballs. The store has over 50 cheeses including the popular triple cream St. André, Blarney from Ireland and Manchego from Spain. **Other locations.**

The Markette

401 Seventh St. NW (D St. NW), Downtown, Washington 20004
202-783-3133, Fax 202-783-0197, *Open Mon.-Fri.*

A

Here The Mark (see review in *Restaurants*) has addressed a major public-policy issue: How can customers of the popular DC restaurant have their favorite Mark food at home? By shopping at The Markette, which occupies the space next to the restaurant and each weekday prepares a selection of appetizers, soups, salads and dinners to go. The food is fully cooked and directions for microwaving at home are given with the orders. The entrées range from three-cheese ravioli with andouille sausage and shrimp to spring vegetable fettuccine or an entrée salad of Black Angus tenderloin.

Sutton Place Gourmet

3201 New Mexico Ave. NW
(Cathedral Ave. NW), American University, Washington 20016
202-363-5800, Fax 202-363-7060, *Open daily*

A P

Sutton Place Gourmet was one of the first specialty gourmet markets in the Washington metro area. An expansion has added components of Hay Day Markets and Balducci's, the ultimate snazzy gourmet market from New York City. Special Balducci's selections include lentils from Castelluccio in Umbria and Arborio rice, grown in the Po Valley of northeastern Italy. Hay Day has brought open-produce sections to the center of the stores. Shoppers also will find a good wine selection here. Only Dean & DeLuca competes at this price level—this is no place to shop if you're looking for a bargain. **Other locations.**

We're always interested to hear about **your discoveries and to receive your comments on ours.** Please let us know what you liked or disliked; e-mail us at gayots@aol.com.

Wagshal's Delicatessen

4855 Massachusetts Ave. NW
(49th St. NW), Spring Valley, Washington 20016
202-363-5698, Fax 202-363-6607, *Open daily*

A **P**

Next door to its companion meat market, Wagshal's Delicatessen is stocked with an inventory of outstanding pastas, knishes, chicken breasts (including stuffed birds) and savory meat pot pies. You can preorder any number of meals to be picked up on the way home; Wagshal's makes a wonderful beef brisket that has become a neighborhood classic. Service can be more abrupt than in the butcher shop, but the food is worth a cross word or two. Salads are standard but well-made. Also see review in *Quick Bites*.

Washington Park Gourmet

2331 Calvert St. NW (24th St. NW), Woodley Park, Washington 20008
202-462-5566, Fax 202-667-7418, *Open daily*

A

This Woodley Park market is an excellent source for easy-to-finish dishes that wanna-be cooks can heat at home. Check out the rice-filled grape leaves and the house meatloaf. Pizzas are available for carryout. The frozen ravioli and spaghetti sell out fast, so call ahead to avoid disappointment. The market has a small produce department, and the baking is done on the premises. Fruit tarts are always a good buy.

WINE & SPIRITS

Bell Wine Shoppe

1821 M St. NW (18th St. NW), Downtown, Washington 20036
202-223-4727, Fax 202-466-8070, *Open Mon.-Sat.*

A

Fred and Bob Luskin of Bell Wine Shoppe are known for the breadth of their expertise in wines, and they share it in regular local seminars. Supporters of East Coast and Virginia wines, Bob and Fred carry one of the best inventories from regional wineries. The staff can guide both new and experienced buyers to the wines that match their menus and palates.

Calvert Woodley

4339 Connecticut Ave. (Van Ness St. NW), Van Ness, Washington 20008
202-966-4400, Fax 202-537-5086, *Open Mon.-Sat.*

A

Staples here are Bordeaux, Burgundy and Rhone varietals, but aficionados of South Africa, Chile or New Zealand wines also will find gems amid the more than 3,000 bottles from all over the world. Owner Ed Sands directly imports many of these himself. A selection of 300 cheeses, 50 coffees and many deli meats complement the spirits. Occasional wine dinners and tastings are held.

For **updated Gayot Washington, DC restaurant reviews,**
visit: digitalcity.com/washington/dining

Chevy Chase Wine & Spirits

5544 Connecticut Ave. NW
(S. Chevy Chase Circle), Chevy Chase, Washington 20015
202-363-4000, Fax 202-537-6067, *Open Mon.-Sat.*

A P

   Owner Buddy Weitzman carries about 3,500 international labels with focus on France, Italy and California. While 75 percent of the core business is devoted to the grape, the store is known nationally for its excellent beer selection of over 1,000 kinds. You'll also find a full range of other spirits.

Grape Finds

1643 Connecticut Ave. NW
(R St. NW), Dupont Circle, Washington 20009
202-387-3146, Fax 202-387-7874, *Open Mon.-Sat.*

A

   Grape Finds represents the new breed of wine store, with light woods in a contemporary design and ultramodern retail lighting. The traditional wine lingo has been replaced as well; instead, you'll find wines that are inventoried as "bold," "bubbly" and "sweet." The idea is to take away the intimidation—and the big surprise comes when you realize that most of the wines cost less than $15.

MacArthur Beverages

4877 MacArthur Blvd. NW
(48th Pl. NW), Upper Georgetown, Washington 20007
202-338-1433, Fax 202-333-0806, *Open Mon.-Sat.*

A

   Established in 1957, MacArthur Beverages has in-house specialists in all the major wine regions of the world. It's especially strong in estate Burgundies and Italian and California wines. Its staff has been expanded to include people who can answer food-and-wine-pairing questions from the perspective of a chef. With floor space increased by about 50 percent, there are many more selections showcased.

Rodman's Gourmet Foods

5100 Wisconsin Ave. NW (Garrison St. NW), Chevy Chase, Washington 20016
202-363-3466, *Open Mon.-Sat.*

A P

   Among the biggest sellers in the area, Rodman's has an excellent selection of wines for all tastes and budgets, especially for those who simply want an inexpensive bottle to enjoy now. Its selection of more than 3,000 bottles includes many table wines priced at $8-$25. You can also choose from among 200 kinds of beer. **Other locations**.

Schneider's of Capitol Hill

300 Massachusetts Ave. NE
(Third St. NE), Capitol Hill, Washington 20002
202-543-9300, Fax 202-546-6289, *Open Mon.-Sat.*

A P

   Run by two brothers, this Capitol Hill store has a national and international clientele and reputation. The brothers pride themselves on their ability to locate hard-to-find older wines and are strongest in French and California selections.

Gourmets, gourmands, globetrotters and wine lovers—get the latest news, updates and tips at GAYOT.com. Now, thousands of dining reviews in 60 U.S. cities at your fingertips!

VIRGINIA SUBURBS

INTRODUCTION   **106**

RESTAURANTS   **106**

QUICK BITES   **162**

     AMERICAN   162

     BAKERIES/CAFÉS   165

     BARBECUE   167

     BREWPUBS   171

     COFFEE SHOPS & DINERS   172

     DELIS & BAGEL SHOPS   174

     ETHNIC FLAIR   175

       (Afghan, Armenian, Chinese, Cuban, French,
       Indian/Pakistani, Italian, Japanese, Mediterranean,
       Mexican, Middle Eastern, Peruvian, Vietnamese)

     HEALTHY/VEGETARIAN   186

     ICE CREAM & MORE   186

     PIZZA   188

GOURMET SHOPS & MARKETS   **190**

     BAKERIES   190

     CANDY & CHOCOLATES   192

     COFFEE & TEA   192

     ETHNIC MARKETS   192

       (Asian, German, Indian, Italian,
       Latin American, Middle Eastern, Russian)

     FARMERS MARKETS   197

     FISH, MEAT & POULTRY   197

     GOURMET MARKETS & GOURMET TO-GO   198

     KITCHEN EQUIPMENT   200

     WINE & SPIRITS   200

INTRODUCTION

Northern Virginia goes from the banks of the Potomac, running along the shoreline of **Rosslyn** and **Alexandria** and points a bit south, then expanding to **Falls Church**, **Arlington**, **McLean**, **Herndon**, **Reston**, **Vienna**, **Fairfax** and west to **Chantilly**, **Centreville** and **Manassas**. For restaurant lovers, it's also easy to include **Leesburg** and **Middleburg** into that geographical mix—for dedicated foodies are often not averse to driving a distance for an excellent meal.

RESTAURANTS

A Taste of Casablanca Moroccan **13/20**

3211 N. Washington Blvd. (Wilson Blvd.)
Clarendon, Arlington 22201
703-527-7468, Fax 703-527-2618, *Lunch & Dinner daily, $$, Casual dressy*

A Taste of Casablanca is a hangout for embassy and Peace Corps types, plus anyone who wants a bit of culinary excitement over tea. Overstuffed cushions in bold floral prints; Moroccan collectibles, paintings, and prints; and Arab-bazaar music are appealing. The sensual aromas and flavors of the food alone will transport you to distant lands. Depending on the size of your group, start with a bastila, the classic Moroccan pastry dish, packed with chicken (or seafood), almonds, parsley and eggs and then scented with cinnamon. Those from this part of the world, of course, often cook fruit with meat, and one outstanding example here is the lamb with raisins and almonds accompanied by a big mound of turmeric-tinted rice. For another exotic experience order a pot of Moroccan tea, which tastes like liquid fragrant roses splashed with sugar and mint. Desserts include fruit or Moroccan pastry, but another pot of tea may suffice.

A Taste of the World Asian/Latin American **12/20**

Sunset Business Park
283 Sunset Park Dr. (Spring St.), Herndon 20170
703-471-2017, *Lunch Mon.-Fri., Dinner Mon.-Sat., $, Casual*

Chef-owner Shirley Roth has taught cooking locally and runs two restaurants showcasing global cuisines. At A Taste of the World she has pulled together an ambitious menu with Latino, Caribbean and Asian foods. The South Indian rava idlis, or steamed rice cakes, have a nice sour bite and come with flavored sambars; the Trinidadian chicken curry and roti seemed more North Indian than Caribbean. Check out her Filipino fare: This is her native cooking and some of her best.

Going to Hawaii, Chicago, San Francisco, Las Vegas, Los Angeles or London? Look for Gayot's "The Best of" guidebooks to destinations worldwide. Also for hotel and travel information from our books and the latest updates, visit us on the Internet at gayot.com.

Aegean Taverna Restaurant   Greek   12/20

2950 Clarendon Blvd. (Garfield St.), Clarendon, Arlington 22201
703-841-9494, Fax 703-841-4783
Lunch Mon.-Fri., Dinner nightly, Brunch Sun., $$, Casual

🅰 🖥 📷 ⛛ 🍷 🍸 🖊 ⬭

Although it is no great culinary adventure, this Greek eatery does offer an attractive Mediterranean atmosphere, loads of fun and good Greek wine. There are also plenty of zesty Greek flavors piled on your plate, starting with the tzadziki (yogurt, cucumber and garlic sauce), delicious with crusty bread or the stuffed grape leaves. The lamb shank in tomato sauce is slightly bland, but the moussaka was good. It's best to come in a group—that way, you can swap flavors for a full-fledged Greek banquet.

Alpine Restaurant   Italian   12/20

4770 Lee Hwy. (Glebe Rd.), Arlington 22207
703-528-7600, Fax 703-528-7625, *Lunch & Dinner daily, $, Casual*

🅰 🔔 P 🖊 🍴 🖊 🍷 🍸 🍶 ⬭

In business for about 30 years, this has been one of Virginia's most enduring restaurant institutions, a stop-in place for every kind of local celebrity from sports figures to politicos: Just look at the photos smiling out from the front walls. Customers love this old-timer because intimate dining rooms suggest "country cottage" or "mountain hideaway," and each has its own charm. If there's a table free, ask for one in the room with the fireplace—it's a cozy setting to enjoy the chef's solid Italian cooking and a good place to listen to the quiet piano music or the strolling guitarist. Try some homemade pastas—the gnocchi with Gorgonzola is outstanding. And for something more substantial, the osso buco makes a fine main course with a side of garlicky mashed potatoes. If you've left room, tiramisu is a suitable dessert.

Argia's   Italian   13/20   👨‍🍳

124 N. Washington St. (Rte. 7), Falls Church 22046
703-534-1033, Fax 703-534-5858, *Lunch & Dinner daily, $$, Casual*

🅰 P 🖥 🍴 🍸 🍶

Several words apply here: charming, rustic, welcoming. The menu is welcoming, too. We started with the beef carpaccio. We found the salami, provolone, and caramelized onion combination sandwich a particular delight. Pastas are distinguished, and you might want to splurge on the homemade gnocchi with fresh tomatoes and green olives, with smoked mozzarella. Also good: chicken breast stuffed with sun-dried tomatoes and beef tenderloin with truffled mashed potatoes. Take heed of the waiter's warning when you order: Leave room for dessert. The ricotta cheesecake, a rarity in these parts and seemingly best done in New York's Little Italy, is memorable.

Austin Grill   Tex-Mex   13/20   👨‍🍳

8430-A Old Keene Mill Rd. (Rolling Rd.), W. Springfield 22152
703-644-3111, Fax 703-644-3199
Lunch & Dinner daily, Brunch Sat.-Sun., $$, Casual

🅰 P 🍴 🍸 🍶

Texans know a thing or two about good chili, and chefs at the Austin Grill have learned the secrets. Their bowls of simmered, shredded beef with ground chiles (anchos and chipotles) are just short of heavenly. It's a rugged dish, with enough fire-breathing potential to stand your hair on end. Fortunately, it comes with four small, warm flour tortillas you can dunk or use for wrapping. The tortillas help tame the flames. Terrific chili is only one of many delights on this funky restaurant's menu: fajitas, enchiladas, burritos, carnitas and quesadillas are all good choices. Check the menu's new seasonal specialties section, too, where you might find lamb chops with pineapple-chipotle glaze. If you need to quench your thirst with all this hot, spicy food, select a cooling tequila drink—there are several interesting margaritas like the signature lime one—or a chilled brew. **Other locations.**

Bamyan Restaurant Afghan   13/20

Super K-Mart Centre, 458 Elden St. (Jonquil Ln.), Herndon 20170
703-471-8376, Fax 703-471-8372
Lunch Mon.-Sat., Dinner nightly, $, Casual

If you remember Bamyan from Old Town Alexandria, you'll be happy to find it again at this Herndon relocation, where parking is easier and the setting is infused with Afghan charm. You'll find plenty of memorabilia from its exotic routes, suggesting to guests that Afghanistan is both beautiful and extremely remote. If you know about Indian and Persian cooking, you'll find this cuisine a familiar blend of the two. We enjoy the sombosa, a fried turnover filled with pleasantly seasoned chickpeas and ground beef, but the muntoo, or steamed dumplings, also makes a good meal beginning. The aush soup is a hearty meal-in-the-bowl dish of flavorful broth, pasta, ground beef, and a swirl of homemade yogurt. As for entrées, the most outstanding come from the grills, and of these the combination kebab with chunks of lamb, beef and chicken is outstanding. Stew-like dishes such as the kadu palow provide stout and filling meals. The best dessert is the plain firni, a cornstarch puddinglike dish that is soothing and comforting. The only minus here: ultra-slow service.

Bella Luna   Italian   11/20

19 S. King St. (Rte. 7), Historic District, Leesburg 20175
703-777-5000, *Lunch & Dinner daily, $$, Casual dressy*

Fronting on King Street and decorated to look like a charming parlor in shades of lime and lemon, with fresh flowers, candles and wooden floors, this small Italian restaurant offers standard Italian fare with a few dishes that stand out. Of these, the peanut soup rates thumbs up as does the fettuccine Alfredo. On the other hand, our most favorite of Italian appetizers, the antipasto platter, could use a little kitchen reconstruction to make it less of a salad, more of an assortment of goodies. The chef offers a fairly extensive though not unusual menu, and you'll find various pastas, veal and chicken dishes.

Big Bowl   Pan-Asian   14/20

Reston Town Center, 11915 Democracy Dr. (Library St.), Reston 20190
703-787-8852, Fax 703-787-8559, *Lunch & Dinner daily, $$, Casual*

Cookbook author and Asian food expert Bruce Cost has brought to the area one of his immensely popular Big Bowl restaurants. Featuring primarily dishes from China, Thailand and Vietnam, with plenty of noodle-based entrées, Big Bowl's recipes combine the freshest raw ingredients in the market and the best staples that Cost can locate. He even has looked for special noodle makers. Everything, even the house ginger ale, is made from scratch. While we would wish for some flavor changes, most dishes are true to their roots. Such entrées as the blazing flat noodles and the Szechuan garlic chicken with hand-cut noodles absolutely sparkle. Patrons also can select their own veggies and meat for a stir-fry, letting the kitchen crew then cook their personal dishes. For dessert, the lively ginger cake with ice cream is excellent. Bring friends so you can explore more dishes here, but be warned: lines may be long

Bistro 123   French   14/20

246 Maple Ave. E (Glyndon St.), Vienna 22180
703-938-4379, Fax 703-255-9042
Lunch & Dinner Mon.-Fri., Dinner Sat., $$, Casual dressy

When you need an infusion of French charm and culture, to say nothing of terrific cooking, select Bistro 123. The customers are chic, the décor very upscale French, and the food, a mix of French, Italian, and American influences. Thanks to the genius of chef-owner Raoul Jean-Richard, the menu sparkles with many unusual dishes. Look for such stars as his confit of duck leg with a truffle sauce, or if available, the veal sweetbreads. The elegant desserts are just as dazzling, including his silken crème brûlée. He has also selected a fine assortment of wines that pair well with his food.

Black Coffee Bistro   American   14/20

101 S. Madison St. (Federal St.), Middleburg 20118
540-687-3632, Fax 540-687-4692
Lunch Tues.-Sat., Dinner Tues.-Sun., Brunch Sun., $$$, Casual

Owner-chef Bryan Kimmett grows his own herbs out back and keeps a steady hand on the cook-pot. It's a charming place, an old home fixed up downstairs for guests (Kimmet, wife and baby live upstairs) and as pretty as a country cottage, which it probably once was. The menu is inventive and includes such dishes at lunch as a three-cheese ravioli to start and a pancetta and blue cheese burger sandwich. Heartier fare might include lemon-basil fried chicken. This is a classy hometown spot that brings sophisticated big-city cooking out to horse country.

Blue Iguana   Contemporary   13/20

Fair Lakes Shopping Center
12727 Shops Lane (Fair Lakes Pkwy.), Fair Lakes, Fairfax 22033
703-502-8108, Fax 703-222-2969
Lunch & Dinner daily, Brunch Sun., $$, Casual

This quirky little restaurant with its successfully inventive and ambitious menu brings city-style food to the 'burbs. We recommend the appetizer that offers three air-light corn cakes bathed with a chipotle cream and topped with several large shrimp. You can follow this up at lunch with assorted salads or offbeat sandwiches and small entrées, such as oven-roasted salmon or smoked lamb enchiladas. The dinner menu charts a slightly more expensive and daring course with roasted apricot chicken, pan-seared scallops and roasted pork loin on a bed of braised fennel with peas. For a delicious dessert, splurge on the chocolate truffle cake. Despite the dressy menu, the emphasis here is on casual dining.

Blue Point Grill   Seafood   13/20

600 Franklin St. (S. Washington St.), Old Town, Alexandria 22314
703-739-0404, Fax 703-684-1853
Lunch Mon.-Sat., Dinner nightly, Brunch Sun, $$$$, Casual dressy

This sophisticated seafood restaurant just south of Old Town Alexandria has some nice touches. There is a terrace for summer dining, and an attractive raw bar has a rotating selection of a dozen or so kinds of oysters. We like the clean good looks and ambience of the place established by wide swathes of glass and sparkling white tablecloths—even when it starts to get loud as the evening wears on. The best dishes are the simplest, when the excellent ingredients are allowed to speak for themselves—grilled swordfish served with garlic mashed potatoes, pepper-crusted tuna with white beans, cedar-planked salmon cooked in the wood-fired oven. For dessert, zero in on the gooey fudge cake.

Bombay Bistro   Indian   14/20

3570 Chain Bridge Rd. (Lee Hwy.), Fairfax 22030
703-359-5810, Fax 703-359-5811, *Lunch & Dinner daily, $$, Casual*

The dressier of the two Bombay Bistros, this location shows off some colorful Indian trappings in serene surroundings. Less crowded than its sister restaurant, it nevertheless does big business at lunchtime. We like the consistently good lamb vindaloo, which here is appropriately hot and sour (and in generous portions), the outstanding smoky-flavored dal makhani, the South Indian masala dosa (potato-stuffed pancake) and swear by the delicious tandoori-baked breads. The famed buffets make a good excuse for overeating. Whatever you do, save room for the mango ice cream. **Also located at** 98 W. Montgomery Ave., Rockville, MD, 301-762-8798.

Bombay Tandoor   Indian   14/20

Westwood Center Bldg.
8603 Westwood Center Dr. (Rte. 7), Tysons Corner, Vienna 22182
703-734-2202, Fax 703-734-2457, *Lunch & Dinner daily, $$, Casual*

An elegant Indian restaurant, pretty as a Mogul's chamber, now graces the Route 7 corridor between Falls Church and Leesburg and it offers outstanding dishes with a certain Raj-like elegance. Best of all, the menu explores dishes that don't often turn up on local menus: Start with fish koliwada, then continue to lamb tikke peshawari, lobster tail masala and an achari of chicken pieces marinated overnight in Indian pickle spices. Breads are exquisite. Desserts, too, are special so be sure to save some room for the gulab jamun and gajer hulwa.

Busara   Thai   12/20

8142 Watson St. (Leesburg Pike), McLean 22102
703-356-2288, Fax 703-356-0056, *Lunch & Dinner daily, $, Casual*

With a menu geared to corral a devoted Western following, Busara welcomes all to a modern setting outfitted with Thai trappings. It's contemporary food and that means some of the dishes don't sound particularly Thai, especially the lamb curry and the starter soup called Bangkok bouillabaisse. Otherwise, look for the ubiquitous pad Thai, soft-shell crabs and honey roast duck. Diners have made Busara a hit that has warranted this expansion from DC to Tysons Corner. Mealtimes may be busy, but you won't feel pressured to eat fast and clear out. **Also located at** 2340 Wisconsin Ave. NW, Washington 20007, 202-337-2340.

Café Asia — Pan-Asian — 12/20

1550 Wilson Blvd. (N. Pierce St.), Rosslyn, Arlington 22209
703-741-0870, Fax 703-741-0960, *Lunch & Dinner daily, $$, Casual*

If you adore the food at DC's Café Asia, you'll find the same fare in Arlington, but served forth in an entirely different way. Imagine a high-tech, hard-edge setting, and you've got the picture. In fact, "bar" is the key word here because Café Asia offers three: a sushi bar, a coffee bar and a liquor bar...a little something for every mood and every palate. We still love the lusty Asian dishes the kitchen puts out, especially the spicy Chinese ravioli and the Malaysian curry laksa. **Also located at** 1134 19th St. NW, Washington, DC, 202-659-2696.

Café Monti — Italian/Austrian — 12/20

3250 Duke St. (S. Quaker Lane), Alexandria 22314
703-370-3632, *Lunch Mon.-Fri., Dinner Mon.-Sat., $, Casual*

Alexandria's big culinary secret, Café Monti, looks about as appealing as a used-car lot, but don't let looks deceive you. Inside its humble exterior lies a kitchen worthy of its Austro-Hungarian roots and a chef who can create fabulous strudels and goulashes (both soup and stew) and do all this at cut-rate prices. You won't believe your eyes when you assess the refrigerator case crammed with elegant pastries such as profiteroles, tiramisu, and apple strudel; you also won't believe the rather zany menu that spans two European countries and includes pizza, pasta, wienerschnitzel and Italian subs.

Café Montmartre — French/Bistro — 12/20

1625 Washington Plaza (N. Shore Dr.), Reston 20190
703-904-8080, Fax 703-904-0328, *Lunch & Dinner daily, $, Casual*

This very casual French bistro with its enviable lake view has caught on in a big way—a phenomenon that may be attributed as much to the scenery, the sidewalk-café ambience and cool-weather weekend jazz as to the food. We liked the lamb roast, an occasional evening special, but the luncheon steak sandwich of too-thin beef was a major disappointment. A better choice would be the salade Niçoise, which boasts a healthy portion of tuna and greens. You may be happier with desserts, from fruit tarts and chocolate mousse to crème caramel and cheesecake. Martini aficionados will appreciate the special martini menu.

Café Parisien Express — French — 12/20

4520 Lee Hwy. (Woodrow St.), Arlington 22207
703-525-3332, Fax 703-525-3340
Breakfast, Lunch & Dinner Mon.-Sat., Brunch Sun., $, Casual
No credit cards.

To people in the neighborhood, this French fast-food eatery has become something of a tradition. Open for breakfast with

111

coffee, croissants, quiches, and omelets, it carries its fans throughout the day in a casual setting that recalls a French boulevard café. Don't expect a gourmet menu or flawless wait service, however. What you will find is a congenial staff at the order counter, a pastry case filled with buttery delicacies (try the hazelnut cake with its rich buttercream icing) and a menu that draws upon such French classics as croque monsieur, escargots and French onion soup (here topped with a piece of puff pastry and a wedge of melted cheese). We like the Gourmet Burger, an elongated hamburger served on a section of baguette with a side of mushroom sauce.

Café Rose — Persian — 12/20

Stratford Motor Lodge
300 W. Broad St. (Little Falls St.), Falls Church 22046
703-532-1700, Fax 703-532-1748
Lunch & Dinner daily, $$, Casual

This delightful little restaurant, which looks forlorn situated in the motel parking lot, has been a magnet for the local Persian community for years. Once upon a time you might have found a famous Persian poet seated here with his cup of Persian tea. Hence, Persian music makes the perfect background for a meal of home-made stuffed grape leaves, the delightful aush reshdeh (a Persian vegetable and noodle soup) and one of the many kabob choices. As always, we love the kubideh kabob, but we also applaud the cook's gormeh sabzi, or beef stew, and the eggplant bademjan was topnotch, as too, are the rice platters with various meat toppings. Small and unpretentious, Café Rose remains a favorite with Persians and Westerners alike.

Café Taj — Indian — 13/20

Marketplace
1379 Beverly Rd. (Old Dominion Dr.), McLean 22101
703-827-0444, Fax 703-827-2707
Lunch & Dinner daily, $$, Casual

Years may pass, but time does not diminish the luster of this tiny Indian eatery. Its soothing décor and on-target dishes appeal to its large suburban fan club. The restaurant is especially busy at lunchtime, when local businesspeople line up for the lavish buffet. Plan to start any meal with an appetizer of vegetable pakoras or samosas. Any of the breads are special, but the house naan stuffed with nuts and dried fruits is sensational. If you fear spicy heat, stick to mild classic curries such as the butter chicken or the chicken tikka masala. If you like it hot, then opt for the lamb vindaloo which is some of the best in town. Chill down with a just-sweet-enough mango lassi (the yogurt beverage), plus an order of kulfi (ice cream).

The Capital Grille — Steakhouse — 13/20

1861 International Dr. (Leesburg Pike), Tysons Corner, McLean 22102
703-448-3900, Fax 703-448-8344
Lunch Mon.-Fri., Dinner nightly, $$$, Business casual

This elegant location sports the dark woods, handsome bar and upholstery that suggest an exclusive men's club, except that everyone is welcome. Near the front door, pause to consider the refrigerated cuts of dry-aged beef behind glass—this should work up your appetite for the restaurant's famous, hefty cuts of steak, from the 20-ounce sirloin to the 24-ounce porter-house. Starters include smoked Norwegian salmon and fresh lobster and crab cakes, and sides round up such favorites as Sam's mashed potatoes and fresh asparagus with hollandaise. For lunch, there are sandwiches, entrée salads and a selection of steaks, seafood and roast chicken. Desserts include a home-made Key Lime pie and cheesecake with strawberries. **Also located at** 601 Pennsylvania Ave. NW, Washington, DC, 202-737-6200.

Carlyle Grand Café   American   13/20

4000 S. 28th St. (S. Quincy St.), Shirlington, Arlington 22206
703-931-0777, Fax 703-931-9420
Lunch & Dinner daily, Brunch Sun., $$, Casual

This impressive Shirlington Village restaurant under the direction of chef Jeffrey Potter has a lively downstairs bar-restaurant, and a more sedate upstairs dining room with an attractive Art-Deco ambience. The eclectic contemporary menu manages to be both imaginative and sensible and stars an interesting array of contemporary dishes. Start with the lob-ster pot stickers or an order of house-made potato chips with melted blue cheese—in fact, we dare you not to finish every last one of them. Main-course recommendations include expertly grilled steaks and chops, usually accompanied by deliberately lumpy mashed potatoes; fresh seafood; and a good selection of salads and lighter fare, including sliced sesame-crusted rare tuna over baby lettuce. For dessert, there's no waf-fling: Go straight for the flourless warm chocolate waffle with macadamia-brittle ice cream.

Carmello's & Little Portugal   Italian/Portuguese   12/20

9108 Center St. (Battle St.), Old Town, Manassas 20110
703-368-5522, Fax 703-398-9874
Lunch Mon.-Fri., Dinner nightly, $$, Casual dressy

One of the few restaurants in the DC area that serves Portuguese food, Carmello's & Little Portugal offers a dual menu that includes a short but sweet list of Portuguese eats as well as Italian specialities. Try the Mexilhao a Espanhola or Tapas Mistas appetizers, then move to Frango a Marniheiro (sautéed chicken breast with shrimp and bacon), Lombo de Vaca a Porto (grilled filet mignon in an espresso and port wine sauce) or the lusty and aromatic seafood stew, the Carne de Porco a Alentejana, a heady mixture of pork, clams, and cubed potatoes with garlic and white wine. Have an Italian dessert—there are no Portuguese ones generally well-heeled and well-dressed, so you may not want to drop by in shorts and a T-shirt.

Casa Gonzalez   Tex-Mex   11/20

37 Catoctin Circle SE (King St.), Leesburg 20175
703-779-8620, Fax 703-779-8620, *Lunch & Dinner daily, $, Casual*

With Mexican trappings adorning the walls, Casa Gonzalez sets the stage for a Tex-Mex food fest way north of the border. Basically geared for family tastes, it offers food that even tots can handle, though adults may miss some of the more heated Mexican seasonings. The nachos with beans and cheese were adequate; the cheese-stuffed chiles rellenos not as pleasing;

and the enchilada supreme, an abundant dish with chicken, bean, beef, and cheese enchiladas, just fine. Kids may prefer something from the children's menu, such as chicken nuggets and fries, but Mexican-inspired choices include burritos, tacos and quesadillas.

Chao Pra Ya   Thai   12/20

2465 J-1 Centreville Rd. (Foxmill Dr.), Herndon 20171
703-713-0103, Fax 703-713-0599, *Lunch & Dinner daily, $$, Casual*

A P 🍽 👬 Y ˙

Named for the river that flows through Bangkok, this small but elegant suburban Thai restaurant falls right in with the mainstream: It looks sleek and modern, with its Thainess coming not from Thai trinkets but from the swirling water patterns on the tables and walls. Very popular at lunch—dinners are less crowded—this restaurant offers the standard Thai menu, but the dishes are cooked with panache. Start with the combo sampler, a bargain method to taste the satay, spring rolls, shrimp balls, fried tofu and stuffed chicken wings. Then if you like to breathe fire, order the "wild pork," a stir-fry of pork with red curry paste, green peppercorns and chilies. It's sublime. We also recommend the crispy duck with basil and the above-average pad Thai. The kitchen will make up specials for you: We asked for stir-fried tofu and bean sprouts, something to cool the palate after the wild chilies.

Chez Marc   French   15/20 👨‍🍳👨‍🍳

7067 Centreville Rd. (Rugby Rd.), Manassas 20111
703-369-6526, Fax 703-369-0185
Lunch Thurs.-Fri., Dinner Mon.-Sat., $$$, Casual

A 📷 P 👨 Y 🍷

If you are lucky, Chef Marc Fusilier will greet you at the door of his charming Old-World French restaurant while Edith Piaf music is playing in the background. This hidden gem, which dedicated foodies appreciate, offers really sensational French food at more or less American prices. Fusilier is a man with great culinary skills: Although the special set menu offers soup, salad and entrée choices, focus on the main menu which features some sublime dishes. For a real splurge, start with coquilles St.-Jacques Provençales or escargots. The intensely flavorful lobster bisque is a signature dish. For entrées, concentrate on the French dishes, some with an American spin, such as the duckling with a berry sauce. If available, order the sensational sliced pork filets with slivered apples. For drama at dessert, order the flamboyant Grand Marnier soufflé ahead of time; the low-keyed crème caramel is also dazzling, both rich and silky.

China Garden   Chinese   12/20

USA Today Bldg., 1100 Wilson Blvd. (Lynn St.), Rosslyn 22209
703-525-5317, Fax 703-525-5568, *Lunch & Dinner daily, $$, Casual*

A P 👬 Y ↻

Perhaps best known for its all-out, highly charged dim sum meals on Sunday, the restaurant is equally known for lunch and dinner during the week, when Cantonese-style cooking reigns. Check out the seafood dishes. Fresh crabs and lobster Cantonese-style are particular favorites, but you won't go wrong with any of the dishes, especially the chef's recommendations. We recommend the stuffed bean curd, deep-fried then braised in crab sauce and served on seasonal greens. If you plan for a Sunday dim sum splurge, better arrive early; shortly after noontime the place gets packed.

The Cincinnati Café   American   12/20

Hunters Woods Center
2260 Hunters Woods Center (S. Lakes Dr.), Reston 20191
703-715-2500, Fax 703-715-2640
Breakfast Sat.-Sun., Lunch & Dinner daily, $, Casual

A P ♥ ♟ 👓 Ｙ ♦

This funky and fun café, calling itself "an American bistro," is going places, maybe even cloning nationwide. Clean and friendly, with an energetic staff who pay attention to details, the café specializes in such basics as hamburgers, nachos, spa dishes for lighter appetites, pastas, crêpes, salads, soups and a hot-hotter-hottest Cincinnati chili, the dish that may have inspired the name. This chili is so good it should be required eating, and it comes with or without beans, spaghetti, cheese and onions. Desserts and breads are made in the nearby bakery, and all sound gooey and caloric.

Clyde's of Tysons   Contemporary   13/20   🍽

8332 Leesburg Pike (Rte. 123), Tysons Corner, Vienna 22182
703-734-1901, Fax 703-790-1422
Lunch & Dinner daily; Brunch Sun., $, Casual

A P ♟ Ｙ ♦ ⟷

The first major downtown restaurant to open at Tysons Corner, this Clyde's holds a special spot in many Virginians' hearts: It's one of the best local places to take mom on Mother's Day. Year round, though, it attracts regular patrons. Lunch draws a business crowd; after work locals head here for a lusty meal and a stop at the bar; Sunday brunch captures the whole family, who oogle the lush greenery and murals. As with all Clyde's restaurants, the menu offers certain core items (chili and hamburgers, for sure), but menus change daily, and also feature seasonal favorites, from Maine lobsters in the fall, to Copper River salmon and fresh asparagus in the spring, to local farm-fresh produce come summer. Favorites include their crispy Thai spring rolls, stuffed with shredded cabbage and pork and the sausage and chard rigatoni, an ample pasta dish suited to a farmer's country meal. Few dishes though surpass the soft-shell crab sandwich or the blackberry pie, both available only in season. Among other Clyde's in the metro area, the ones at Reston Town Center and Alexandria's Mark Center also are popular with Virginia diners. **Other locations.**

Copeland's of New Orleans   Southern   12/20

Old Centreville Crossing
13810 E. Braddock Rd. (Rte. 29), Centreville 20121
703-222-0089, Fax 703-222-1350, *Lunch & Dinner daily, Brunch Sun., $$, Casual*

A P 🍽 ♟ Ｙ

Let the good times roll at Copeland's of New Orleans, a Southern-style restaurant with a mighty big menu. Starring such New Orleans flavors as the Creole andouille sausage, red beans and rice, shrimp etoufée and blackened chicken and red fish. Most of the main courses have a Louisiana lilt, but you can find mainstream dishes like burgers, prime rib and Caesar salad. The menu rotates dishes several times a year, but one mainstay seems to be the Cajun Gumbo Ya Ya, a stew with shrimp, scallops and seasonings. It's a lusty combo of zingy flavors, and if you want an inkling of what New Orleans cooking is all about, you might want to start here. Like to begin your Sundays with a bang? Drop in for brunch and load up on some beignets, eggs Sardou and french toast stuffed with a bananas Foster-style mixture. **Also located at** 4300 King St., Alexandria, VA, 703-671-7997; and 1584 Rockville Pike, Rockville, MD, 301-230-0968.

Corkie's Grill   American   12/20

Chesterfield Shopping Center
6238 Old Dominion Dr. (Kirby Rd.), McLean 22101
703-533-5880, *Breakfast, Lunch & Dinner daily, $, Casual*

Although it will never be called chic or even "in," Corkie's Grill is as comforting and homey a restaurant as you're likely to find in the DC area. In fact, in this and a previous location, Corkie's has been a destination for many who want home-style food at those times when cooking seems just too much work. Cook/owner Corkie (aka Joan Kirkham) sees to it that you get what you want, and offers theme meals that change monthly plus nightly dinner specials. You might find dishes from Vietnam or another overseas destination served certain nights of the week. And come the holidays, hers is a popular destination for everyone who wants the taste of tradition without all the bother. Her breakfasts are special, too. How about a stack of blueberry pancakes with sausages on your way to work?

Costa Verde Restaurant   Peruvian   11/20

946 N. Jackson St. (Wilson Blvd.), Arlington 22201
703-522-6976, Fax 703-522-4523, *Lunch & Dinner daily, $, Casual*

Tucked into a building adjacent to an auto garage, this seems like an unlikely site for a large, family-sized Peruvian restaurant that serves up gigantic portions and has a staff that patiently deals with toddlers on the run. With its friendly bar and circulars announcing a Latino pop group, Costa Verde gives out vibes that it turns into an after-hours nightclub. But for those who come to eat, eat well they will, with a large and tempting array of dishes at their fingertips. We turned to our favorite appetizer, the papa rellena (mashed potatoes stuffed with a savory ground-meat filling). This succulent bundle is deep-fried for a crunchy potato exterior. The extensive entrée selections include seafood dishes like sautéed octopus and squid to the more traditional steaks and chicken dishes done Peruvian style. We tried the costilla de chancho, or baby short ribs in garlic sauce, but found no bones for gnawing.

Don Pablo's, The Real Enchilada   Tex-Mex   12/20

13050 Fair Lakes Shopping Ctr. (Fair Lakes Dr.), Fairfax 22033
703-222-9770, Fax 703-222-0946, *Lunch & Dinner daily, $$, Casual*

Suggestive of ranchos and rancheros, bandidos and tacos, this small group of Tex-Mex eateries is as much about cheery ambience as about food. You'll find that plenty of the dishes are more north than south of the border, but as the menu states, this was grub cooked for Texas cowhands. It's plain and simple fare—with some notations about fat grams—that won't win gold medals, but it obviously appeals to a mass crowd of the young and hungry and those in between. We can recommend the chiles rellenos, the refried beans and the freshly made tortillas. There's plenty more here to whet your whistle and curb your appetite, from freshly made lemonade to iron-skillet pie. Prices are reasonable, flavors fine, atmosphere fun: That equals a good night out. **Other locations**.

Duangrat's   Thai   13/20

5878 Leesburg Pike (Columbia Pike), Falls Church 22041
703-820-5775, Fax 703-820-6206, *Lunch & Dinner daily, $$$, Casual*

There's a Thai restaurant on almost every corner in the Washington area, but Duangrat's has a particular reputation in town. We appreciate the handsome setting: The walls are hung with Thai icons and art objects, the servers are dressed in traditional Thai costumes, and the tables are covered in silky cloths. Our favorites include moist chicken bhram with peanut sauce, gingery chicken over crispy noodles, sweet-spicy pork and trout grilled in banana leaves with tamarind. Even if you don't usually order dessert in Asian restaurants, order it here: Both the black sticky rice pudding with coconut cream sauce and the baked mungbean mousse, like a rich bread pudding, are delicious. The restaurant owns a Thai market around the corner. Also see review in *Gourmet Shops & Markets/Ethnic Markets*.

eciti Café & Bar   American   14/20

8500 Tyco Rd. (Springhill Rd.), Tysons Corner, Vienna 22102
703-760-9000, Fax 703-556-3200, *Dinner Mon.-Sat., $$$, Business casual*

It's a scene, a techie paradise where all the e-folks hang out after work. Chef Jamie Stachowski, former acolyte of Jean-Louis Palladin and former chef at DC's Pesce, has turned the restaurant section of this immense adult playpen into a formidable dining destination, challenging DC's big-name restaurants. Indeed, Stachowski can persuade the after-hours crowds that there's some other purpose besides drinking, dancing and schmoozing for coming to this Tysons smash hit—it's to eat!! Why not, when the menu offers such daring dishes as the veal meatballs, wrapped with basil leaves, sauced with a lavender-accented veal juice and accompanied by fresh pappardelle noodles? We enjoyed the roasted rack of lamb, too, a tribute to flavor with its slick of plum malt vinegar reduction. The lobster strudel, BBQO (barbecued ostrich cutlet) and the Havana pork chop marinated in chili oil are all popular. The e-crab cake comes with a scallop mousse on top. Pastry chef David Collier punctuates the meal's end with several sweet temptations, including a show-stopper, the Gianduja marjolaine, two layers of rich buttercream with meringue between them

Eiffel Tower Café   French   12/20

107 Loudoun St. SW (Wirt St. SW), Historic Downtown, Leesburg 20175
703-777-5142, Fax 703-777-5143
Lunch & Dinner Tues.-Sun., $$$, Casual

This pretty French restaurant set on the ground floor of one of Leesburg's old homes looks like a cross between a Victorian tearoom and a private dining room. The kitchen serves classic French fare: tender lamb stew with baby carrots, sweet peas and blanched radishes. You can start with a vegetable and goat cheese salad or fresh marinated salmon, move on to sea scallops with a purée of celeriac or poached chicken breast with a vegetable medley, then conclude with house-made pastries or a very smooth crème brûlée. The kitchen offers a "quick" lunch menu that includes the lamb stew. The restaurant charms, a perfect special-occasion destination.

Elysium American 13/20 🍽

Morrison House Hotel
116 S. Alfred St. (King St.), Old Town, Alexandria 22314
703-838-8000, Fax 703-684-6283
Breakfast daily, Dinner Tues.-Sat., Brunch Sun., $$$, Business casual

🅰 ☎ 🅿 🎄 🍸 🍴 ⟳

Located in the elegant Morrison House Hotel, this equally elegant restaurant is presided over by executive chef Gian Piero Mazzi. Breakfasts may include Parisienne crêpes with fresh berries, banana and hazelnut cream, pancakes with Valrhona chocolate chips, bananas or Maine blueberries and a basket of homemade breakfast pastries. Dinners have featured goat cheese terrine with beluga caviar followed by a confit of duck, venison sausage and Hudson Valley foie gras with white bean cassoulet.

Euro Bistro German/Italian/Asian 11/20

F & M Bank Centre, 114 Elden St. (Herndon Pkwy.), Herndon 20170
703-481-8158, Fax 703-481-5164
Lunch Mon.-Fri., Dinner Mon.-Sat., $$, Casual

🅰 🅿 🎄

How one wants a little place like this to succeed, where chef-owner Raimund Stieger takes his time to construct an offbeat menu. But the menu might well be too far out, for it combines classic Austro-Hungarian dishes with a couple of Thai transplants, and the effect is a bit confusing. Much better is the wienerschnitzel, properly breaded and lightly fried, than the rather bland and unmemorable rice noodles with curry, which promises fire and delivers ice. The classic desserts include a nice crème brûlée and a rich chocolate mousse cake with a grainy texture. Despite our misgivings, we would certainly return, but stick to the European fare. It's obviously a favorite with locals, who pack in during main meal hours.

Faccia Luna Trattoria Italian 12/20

2909 Wilson Blvd. (Fillmore St.), Clarendon, Arlington 22201
703-276-3099, Fax 703-841-0467, *Lunch & Dinner daily, $, Casual*

🅰 🅿 🍽 🎄 🍸 🍴

This almost-pub has some of the trendiest casual foods around, with meat- or vegetable-filled sandwiches that come as king-sized grinders, a heaping antipasti platter, handmade pastas with offbeat toppings and unusual pizzas. We recommend the Florentine pizza topped with spinach and ricotta cheese, but can always be tempted by the Portofino pizza with anchovies and pesto or the stromboli, a Margherita pizza turnover. You can add on toppings to suit your taste, for an extra charge, of course. Portions are not overly generous, but you certainly will not walk away hungry. This place attracts a young, hip crowd, and the place is always hopping at main meal times. **Other locations.**

We're always interested to hear about **your discoveries and to receive your comments on ours.** Please let us know what you liked or disliked; e-mail us at gayots@aol.com.

FlatTop Grill   Pan-Asian/Contemporary   13/20

4245 N. Fairfax Dr. (Taylor St.), Ballston, Arlington 22203
703-528-0078, Fax 703-528-0310, *Lunch & Dinner daily, $$, Casual*

This Arlington eatery, featuring stir-fries of the customer's own creation, has won a big following in a short time. It's all about mixing and matching ingredients (including pineapple cubes and shredded cheese) and 40 sauces for a unique creation. Newcomers may be mystified by the drill, but once you catch on, it's simple. Head to the fixings bar with your numbered stick, which you use to skewer the raw ingredients you desire. With bowl (too small, by our standards) in hand, you walk along the line, picking and choosing from among noodles, rice, vegetables, tofu and eggs, all of which you heap into the bowl (meats go in a separate bowl) and cover with sauces of your choice. Once the cooks work their magic, you decide if you want this served as a soup, salad or moo shu pancake. Because the serving is smallish, you'll surely return for seconds. While you wait, you can try one of the Asian beers and one of the atypical appetizers (for example, the Thai fish cakes don't contain fish but crab meat) and hold onto enough appetite for one of the over-the-top desserts. The lemon-ginger cheesecake makes sense after this mix-and-match meal. **Also located at** 3714 Macomb St. NW, Washington, DC, 202-244-0075.

Flavors Soul Food   Southern   13/20

3420 Carlyn Hill Dr. (Columbia Pike), Falls Church 22041
703-379-4411, Fax 703-379-4473, *Lunch & Dinner Tues.-Sun., $, Casual*

Not exactly on Main Street, this little soul-food eatery takes some effort to find from way out in the 'burbs, but once there, you probably will thrill to its home-style cooking. We recommend the hickory-smoked BBQ ribs with sides of greens and mashed potatoes, but if experimenting with other dishes becomes mandatory, the second choice would be the battered and fried fish, either white or sea trout, with the same sides. We might consider the smoked pork shoulder heaped in a tall stack, but at that rate, why not just settle for the ribs and end the meal with a serving of fresh apple cobbler? There are probably enough calories on the menu to feed an army, but why not enjoy a genuine feast?

Fleming's Prime Steakhouse & Wine Bar   12/20

Steakhouse
Courtyard by Marriott
1960-A Chain Bridge Rd. (Rte. 7), Tysons Corner, McLean 22102
703-442-8384, Fax 703-442-3828, *Dinner nightly, $$, Casual dressy*

Part of a growing national steakhouse chain, Fleming's is carving out its niche among several other big-muscle beef places in its Tysons' neighborhood. Appealing to families and offering a rather casual, after-work atmosphere, Fleming's presents a menu limited to five different cuts of steak, and the requisite lamb, veal, and pork chops, plus chicken and several seafood dishes. Indeed, its wine list is lengthier than its menu. It's also a strictly à la carte menu, so if you want a few vegetables, better look to the pricey sides of potatoes several ways, spinach, broccoli or mushrooms. We loved the mashed skin-on potatoes with roasted garlic, which come in a very generous portion, probably enough to feed two. You also have several appetizer choices, from onion rings to Caesar salad, though this version lacked the requisite garlic and anchovy punch. Dessert choices are also limited to the expected cheesecake, Key lime pie, crème brûlée and chocolate cake selections, though the after-dinner cordials and gourmet coffee drinks are notable.

Food Factory   Indian/Pakistani/Middle Eastern   12/20

Ballston Commons
4221 N. Fairfax Dr. (Stewart St.), Arlington 22203
703-527-2279, Fax 703-465-9377, *Lunch & Dinner daily, $, Casual*

A P ⛩ ♨

We challenge anyone to find better kebabs or more fiery curries at these bargain prices. But just as pleasing are the chilied chapli kebab cooked over charcoal and wrapped in fresh-baked tandoor bread. Also terrific: the restaurant's various curries and dals. It's generally crowded, especially on weekends when Washington's hip vie for the weekend specials: haleem, nehari, and paya (spicy pig's trotters). **Also located at** 8145 #G, Baltimore Ave., College Park, MD, 301-345-8888.

Fortune of Reston Chinese Seafood Restaurant
Chinese   12/20

North Point Village
1428 North Point Village Center (Baron Cameron Ave.), Reston 20194
703-318-8898, Fax 703-318-8990, *Lunch & Dinner daily, $$, Casual*

A P ⛩ ♨ Y

A Reston favorite ever since its opening day, this mostly Cantonese restaurant offers a standard Chinese menu, plus something extra: daily dim sum. We love to stop here for the selection of nearly 70 varieties of dumplings, and appreciate that dim sum has seemingly gone mainstream. Well, it's in the 'burbs in this conservatively decorated and pleasant shopping-mall Chinese restaurant, a distant relative of the Fortune restaurant in Falls Church. Don't want dim sum? Plenty of diners enjoy the subdued Cantonese fare, especially the seafood: scallops, conch, squid, cuttlefish, abalone and sea cucumber. Of course, if you prefer things hot, the cook stirs up several Szechuan and Hunan specialties.

Fortune of Seven Corners   Chinese   13/20   👨‍🍳

Seven Corners Shopping Center, 6249 Arlington Blvd.
(Patrick Henry Dr.), Seven Corners, Falls Church 22044
703-538-3333, Fax 703-538-3335, *Lunch & Dinner daily, $$, Casual*

A P ⛩ Y ♻

Relocated several miles down the road from its original digs, Fortune continues to specialize in its hectic dim sum feast, served daily, and in its excellent Cantonese cooking, especially seafood dishes. Indeed, the kitchen tackles everything from conch and cuttlefish to live lobster, abalone, and sea cucumber. If you instead crave orange beef or General Tso's chicken, you won't be disappointed. But perhaps most of us keep coming back for the rattling dim sum carts carrying the steamed pork, shrimp, or shark's fin dumplings, turnip cakes, spring rolls, pork buns and the rich egg custard tarts. This is what—justifiably—made the restaurant's reputation.

Galaxy Restaurant   Vietnamese   11/20

Square Towers, 155 Hillwood Ave. (Annandale Rd.), Falls Church 22046
703-534-5450, *Lunch & Dinner Wed.-Mon., $$, Casual*

A P ♨ ⚓ ℉

Although this rather large and stagy Vietnamese restaurant apparently has quite a following, many diners serious about Vietnamese food still head to Eden Center for ethnic goodies. But you can certainly find several pleasant dishes here, from the soft shrimp and pork rolls (goi cuon) to the tasty stuffed grape leaves. Disappointing, however, are the caramel fish and the sweet 'n' sour fish soup, which had many vegetables, little fish and a forgettable broth. You might have more luck with the rice vermicelli and grilled meat dishes and any of the rice noodle soups.

Ghin Na Rhee Restaurant   Thai   11/20

2509 Harrison St. (Lee Hwy.), Arlington 22207
703-536-1643, *Lunch Tues.-Sat., Dinner nightly, $, Casual*

A P ♨ ℉

Because this Arlington restaurant is so far off the beaten track, it has been largely undiscovered. Even so, it manages to attract enough of a following to continue serving pretty decent Thai fare. The luncheon buffet is a real bargain, and so are the appetizers and entrées on the regular menu. If it's available, try the chef's special Thai crêpe with its curiously sweet and crunchy filling of peanuts, coconut and large shrimp. The menu is short, but sticks to some good Thai basics without the frills. And at least at lunchtime, plenty of locals gather for trips to the buffet.

The Greek Taverna   Greek   12/20

Marketplace, 6828 Old Dominion Dr. (Beverly Rd.), McLean 22101
703-556-0788, Fax 703-442-9052
Lunch Mon.-Fri., Dinner nightly, $$, Casual

A ☎ P ♨

Soulful Greek folk music tinkles in the background, but it's the lusty Greek cooking that stamps this tiny restaurant with a Mediterranean spirit. You'll find both hot and cold appetizers—the skordalia (cold whipped potatoes) are for real potato lovers. For the main meal, there are plenty of traditional Greek dishes and grilled entrées, including moussaka, pastitsio, lamb kebabs and baby lamb chops. The arni stammas is a heavenly lamb lover's stew. For dessert, the orange crème caramel is velvety and intensely flavored. It can be crowded on weekends, so make reservations or plan to eat here early.

Haandi   Indian   12/20

Falls Plaza Shopping Center
1222 W. Broad St. (Haycock Rd.), Falls Church 22046
703-533-3501, Fax 703-533-3502, *Lunch & Dinner daily, $$, Casual*

A P ♨ ℉

Much acclaimed and well-established, the Haandi Indian restaurants have offered one of the first Indian dining experiences in the metro area, and continue to hold their own against a flood of Indian upstarts. The menu reads like a familiar guidebook to Indian eats and you won't find much that's unfamiliar or jolting. Note that all foods are mildly spiced and if you want to turn up the heat, you'll have to ask. Hence, it may appeal to diners who love temperate, familiar dishes. We enjoyed the unusual daal masala, a simmer of various lentils cooked in mild spices, and credit the tandoor for good bread But we love such dishes as fiery vindaloos lavished with chilies, and this one was too mild. **Also located at** 4904 Fairmont Ave., Bethesda, MD, 301-718-0121.

Hama Sushi & Grill Japanese Restaurant 12/20

Japanese/Sushi
2415-B2 Centreville Rd. (Fox Mill Rd.), Herndon 20171
703-713-0088, Fax 703-713-6677, *Lunch & Dinner daily, $$, Casual*

Most mealtimes are crowded, even though the space has been doubled to incorporate a sushi bar, regular dining tables and a special screened-off area for Japanese-style dining events: Patrons remove their shoes, pad across the tatami mats and sit on cushions. This Herndon eatery has gained its reputation because of its ultra-fresh sushi, but the kitchen turns out a fair array of other typical Japanese dishes, from several teriyakis and tempuras to the filling and satisfying donburi dishes, best for chilled winter eves. Especially good is the chirashi sushi, loaded with plenty of fresh fish and some crunchy pickled vegetables. The only drawback: As the restaurant has expanded, its service seems slower. Maybe management needs to hire another sushi chef or two.

Hamburger Hamlet   American   12/20

1601 Crystal Dr. (18th St. S.), Crystal City, Arlington 22202
703-413-0422, Fax 703-413-0429
Lunch & Dinner daily, Brunch Sun., $$, Casual

You have to hand it to a place that's built its reputation on hamburgers. From a plain burger to a sautéed mushroom burger to a Cajun-spiced burger, there are 15 burgers in all. The rest of each menu consists of an all-American assortment of dishes that caters to every taste. Salads include Chinese chicken, Santa Fe chicken and turkey pasta. Other good choices: chicken and seafood entrées, pasta and New York strip steak. Fresh fruit shakes are chilled and flavorful and a substitute for dessert. Otherwise, select among cheesecake, Key lime pie and a baked apple crisp. Don't overlook the Sunday brunch, with its interesting egg dishes. **Other locations.**

Hermitage Inn   American   14/20

7134 Main St. (Chapel Rd.), Historic Clifton, Fairfax 20214
703-266-1623, Fax 703-968-0259
Dinner Tues.-Sun., Brunch Sun., $$$, Business casual

Chef-owner Serge Barbe runs a pretty historic inn in the town of Clifton, as yet fairly untouched by the developers' shovel. May the town remain in this pristine state, with the inn as its focal point. Always a destination for a celebratory meal, the Hermitage Inn exudes both charm and history; on the site of the former Clifton Hotel, it was once the destination of some of America's VIPs, including Teddy Roosevelt. The menu runs to American cooking tinged with Mediterranean-French accents and dishes are always lavish. Consider a menu that stars escargots; a Mediterranean "beggar's purse" filled with pesto, sun-dried tomatoes and caramelized onions; pan-seared garlic prawns; and for the main course grilled New Zealand lamb with a pistachio crust. Lamb of any kind here is one of the kitchen's best efforts, so splurge, saving room for a dessert of chocolate terrine. Brunches are good, too.

Hope Key · Chinese · 13/20

3131 Wilson Blvd. (Highland St.), Clarendon, Arlington 22201
703-243-8388, Fax 703-243-3226, *Lunch & Dinner daily, $, Casual*

Read Chinese? You'll find many worthy dishes written about on the red menu strips stuck to the walls. If you don't have a translator, we'll provide some tips. Best bets among appetizers: fried stuffed bean curd and fried shrimp balls. For entrées, the endless menu offers such treats as steamed rockfish and sautéed snow pea tips (a real delicacy). Try the chicken hot pot which is filled with noodles, chicken pieces and a medicinal herb that's good for eyesight. With so many choices you'd better bring an appetite and a group of friends.

Hunan Number One · Chinese/Dim Sum · 12/20

3033 Wilson Blvd. (N. Garfield St.), Arlington 22201
703-528-1177, Fax 703-528-1185, *Lunch & Dinner daily, $$, Casual dressy*

In the heart of Arlington, this fancy-dress Chinese restaurant provides an array of daily dim sum plus predictable and solid standard Chinese cooking. In other words, it's safe to take visiting relatives who don't know much about flashy Chinese cooking. Although we are addicted to the dim sum, we enjoy several entrée items, from the shell-on baked jumbo shrimp with salt to the rice noodles, Singapore style, slightly hot and very good. Also good: the Peking duck and shredded pork in garlic sauce. This place may be as popular for its food as for its traditional Chinese décor. Expect to find Chinese lions guarding the door and several decorative screens and other items brightening the interior.

Huong Que (Four Sisters Restaurant) · 12/20

Vietnamese
Eden Center
6769 Wilson Blvd. (Roosevelt St.), Seven Corners, Falls Church 22044
703-538-6717, Fax 703-538-7080, *Lunch & Dinner daily, $$, Casual*

Grand in scale and more gentrified than other eateries in the center, this place is run by four sisters. That's not what Huong Que means, though—the Vietnamese words actually translate loosely to "home-style cooking," and that's what this restaurant features. We've come to love the spicy caramel fish with its balanced sweetness, the hot 'n' sour shrimp soup, the soft summer rolls packed with filling and the flavorful "shaky" beef cubes and crisp greens. The extensive menu provides something that even the pickiest eater probably will find pleasing.

For **guidebooks to other cities worldwide,**
visit: gayot.com

Huong Viet — Vietnamese — 11/20

Eden Center
6785 Wilson Blvd. (Roosevelt St.), Falls Church 22044
703-538-7110, *Lunch & Dinner daily, $, Casual*
No credit cards. P ☕

It looks dowdy and its menu is worn, but Huong Viet has an enduring appeal for many regulars. The menu features standard Vietnamese fare, from the soft spring rolls to the beloved shrimp on sugar cane. The food is not haute Vietnamese, but several dishes make the trip worth it: Try the caramel fish and the stir-fried watercress with garlic sauce. We can also recommend the grilled beef and lemon grass on skewers.

The Ice House Café — American — 12/20

760 Elden St. (Spring St.), Herndon 20170
703-437-4500, Fax 703-437-7738
Lunch Mon.-Fri., Dinner nightly, $$$, Casual dressy

It's the 'burbs answer to a classy family place that on the weekends turns into a jazz and bar destination in the later night hours. Lunches are casual and popular and hamburgers are the signature sandwich. Dinners are definitely dressier meals, featuring such entrées as a grilled pork loin with honey-rosemary glaze, hickory-smoked rack of lamb in wine sauce with sun-dried cranberries and an interesting grilled Norwegian salmon with a Thai chili-peanut sauce. The menu is interesting, eclectic, and shot through with Asian influences. Desserts stack up well to big-city creations. We enjoy the chocolate marble cheesecake with crème anglaise, perfect with an after-dinner drink.

Il Radicchio — Italian — 12/20

1801 Clarendon Blvd. (Rhodes St.), Arlington 22201
703-276-BOBS, Fax 703-276-0723, *Lunch & Dinner daily, $$, Casual*

The name Roberto Donna has become synonymous in the Washington metro area with Italian restaurants that run the gamut from the ultrachic Galileo to the modest and casual I Matti and Il Radicchio (see reviews in *Washington, DC /Restaurants*). The emphasis here is on hearty, peasant-style fare that features pizzas (with loads of funky toppings, including radicchio), pasta dishes with homemade sauces and spit-roasted chicken with roasted potatoes (a great take-home dish, for those on the run). Appetizers include bruschetta and antipasti. A winner is the roasted peppers in anchovy sauce; it's loaded with garlic, so be advised. It's tempting to hang out here sipping wine and forking into a wedge of ricotta cheesecake, but at mealtimes, expect crowds and a bustle. **Also located at** 223 Pennsylvania Ave. SE, Washington, DC, 202-547-5114.

Ratings are based solely on the restaurant's cuisine. We do not take into account the atmosphere, décor or service; these are commented on in the review.

The Inn at Little Washington   19/20

Contemporary

Intersection of Main & Middle Sts. (Main St.), Washington 22747
540-675-3800, Fax 540-675-3100
Dinner Wed.-Mon.; May & Oct. nightly, $$$$$, Jacket & ties suggested

The Inn's chef Patrick O'Connell is to American gastronomy what Winslow Homer is to American painting: He found his inspiration in the great French masters, but he created his own art in his own way. Located 67 miles from downtown Washington, the Inn is as American as it gets. At sunset you can imagine early American characters strolling in from the surrounding countryside in search of some good victuals. Because he's self-taught, O'Connell is not entangled in the stiff mold of great classical rules and techniques. No one has a stronger culinary personality and style in this country, which, of course, gives free rein to his fertile imagination. But his instinct rings a bell before he crosses the line with his exuberance. Every night there's a different seven-course tasting menu, with optional wine pairings. Appetizer choices might include chilled goose foie gras with rhubarb-Riesling sauce and pickled cherries, carpaccio of baby lamb with rosemary mustard and an improvisation on traditional Virginian fare like O'Connell's crab-cake "sandwich" with fried green tomatoes. After an interlude of a baby green bean salad with summer truffles or perhaps a lemon-rosemary sorbet, you might savor such main courses as local rabbit braised in apple cider with wild mushrooms, lobster with grapefruit, orzo and citrus-butter sauce or thrice-cooked duck with aromatic Asian spices and pineapple on wild rice-pecan pilaf. It's hard to choose from among the dozen or so desserts, but we stand by the roasted plum "pizza" (sometimes rhubarb is used) with buttermilk ice cream and any of the homemade ice creams. The wine list is probably thicker than the local phone book and filled with treasures. Service is impeccable. Be prepared to pay the price, a big one, for such a memorable experience

J. Gilbert's Wood-Fired Steaks American 13/20

6930 Old Dominion Dr. (Rte. 123), McLean 22101
703-893-1034, Fax 703-893-1036
Lunch Mon.-Fri, Dinner nightly, $$$, Business casual

If you measure popularity by a crowded parking lot, then J. Gilbert's must be one of Northern Virginia's most sought-after restaurants. It's a sleek makeover of Charley's Place, and locals evidently adore the change in venue and menu. With dim lighting, modern jazz in the background, a happening bar and intimate dining areas, the restaurant is an upscale, yet still casual, place. Its contemporary American menu has Southwestern influences in evidence in dishes like the crab cakes with Taos tumbleweed, a symphony of crab meat with Southwestern julienne vegetables and crispy tortilla straws. The grilled corn and smoked chicken tortilla soup with guacamole is a triumph of flavors and textures. Under the guidance of chef Frank Fernandez, good steaks star on the menu, as the restaurant's name attests. But if you prefer a meal without beef, the wood-fired chicken with mashed potatoes is a winner. When the dessert tray comes around, you'll find several good choices, but the hazelnut cheesecake with shavings of white chocolate is exceptional.

J. R.'s Stockyards Inn   Steakhouse   **12/20**

8130 Watson St. (International Dr.), Tysons Corner, McLean 22102
703-893-3390, Lunch Mon.-Fri., Dinner nightly, $$$, Casual dressy

Neither hip nor trendy, this staid, '50s-style restaurant looks like a ranch house that got swept up in a Texas tornado and resettled in suburban McLean. But it has a very up-to-date, upscale steak menu featuring first-rate cuts of beef. Although the kitchen prepares assorted non-beef dishes, passing up steak here makes little sense. So here's the beef: prime ribs, New York strips, porterhouses, marinated sirloin and others. You can't go wrong with any cut of beef here, as businessmen discover over lunch, couples and groups over dinner. Desserts come out on a tray for your selection: Try the cheesecake.

Jasmine Café   Contemporary   **13/20**

1633-A Washington Plaza (N. Shore Dr.), Lake Anne, Reston 20190
703-471-9114, Fax 703-471-9059
Lunch & Dinner daily, Brunch Sun., $$, Casual

One of Reston's little treasures, Jasmine Café is the pet project of owner and sometime cook Eduardo Faubert. It has survived the arrival of local mega restaurants, because the restaurant delivers solid American cooking, drop-in neighborliness and a splendid lakeside location. Most nights seem like old-home week at this flashy little place, and friends may stop by just for drinks and dessert. But a full meal is a good choice. Faubert is noted for his many specials, including the hot artichoke dip with pita chips and his cast-iron-seared tenderloin. He handles chocolate anything very well, although his strawberry-rhubarb cobbler is mighty fine, too.

Kazan Restaurant   Turkish   **12/20**

McLean Shopping Center
6813 Redmond Dr. (Chain Bridge Rd.), McLean 22101
703-734-1960, Fax 703-743-9636
Lunch Mon.-Fri., Dinner Mon.-Sat., $$$, Casual

Though the exotic décor fell victim to a splendid Westernization, the exotic food remains. The imam bayildi (eggplant dish), hummus, and dolma are outstanding, as is the bread, which is tender, supple, and warm. Doner kebab, served only on certain days of the week, is a signature dish; and if you miss that, order instead any of the lamb dishes, either as ground or sliced. Of course, beef, chicken, seafood, and vegetarian dishes are also available, but the lamb is the best bet. Sweets come as an orange baklava (worth waiting for), a thick and rather bland Turkish rice pudding, and the more Western crème caramel and chocolate mousse cake.

Konami Japanese Restaurant   Japanese   **12/20**

8221 Leesburg Pike (International Dr.), Tysons Corner, Vienna 22182
703-821-3400, Fax 703-821-9082, *Lunch & Dinner daily, $$, Casual*

Small and unpretentious, Konami takes the middle road with its pleasantly Asian décor and stylish lunch box specials. So pretty they're worth the trip in, these offerings differ in composition from chicken teriyaki, ebi shumai, and a California roll in one box to beef curry, a California roll, tekka maki, and tempura udon in another—nine different lunch box choices in all. But should you seek heartier fare, such as plates of sushi and sashimi to start before a bowl of noodle soup or a breaded pork chop, you have that choice. Dinners mean more options, including two chirashi selections. As always, you can finish up with a simple dessert of green tea ice cream or mango sherbet.

La Bergerie   French   14/20

218 N. Lee St. (Cameron St.), Old Town, Alexandria 22314
703-683-1007, Fax 703-519-6114
Lunch Mon.-Sat., Dinner nightly, $$$, Business casual

Brothers Jean and Bernard Campagne, natives of the Basque region of France, run this elegant Old Town restaurant with a near-perfect balance between comfort and style, tradition and innovation. The house specialty is the robust cooking of their native region—a Basque pipérade of vegetables, a filet of pork en confit, hearty bowls of garbure béarnaise—but there's much else to appreciate: beautifully cooked fish, flavorful rack of lamb, loin of venison. Before you order dinner, order dessert, for the heavenly soufflés—Grand Marnier, chocolate, raspberry or hazelnut—must be selected in advance.

La Côte d'Or Café   French   14/20

6876 Lee Hwy. (Rte. 66), Arlington 22213
703-538-3033, Fax 703-573-0409, *Lunch & Dinner daily, $$$, Casual*

Although its exterior resembles a seaside cabin, La Côte d'Or is pure upscale French inside. That may partially explain its appeal to affluent suburban diners, many of whom reserve tables a day or two in advance. Its glorious menu also accounts for its popularity, even though many dishes are priced at top dollar. But the cost counts for nothing when you can enjoy splendid, classic French food. Don't miss the trademark lobster bisque or the excellent garlicky fish soup. We also recommend the impressive veal chop in a rich blue cheese sauce. Desserts are wheeled up on a cart, and many, like the raspberry mousse cake, which layers raspberries and chocolate, are irresistible. The main rooms look small, but there is also a large enclosed patio for large groups and for overflow crowds.

La Provence   French   14/20

144 Maple Ave. W (Anita St.), Vienna 22180
703-242-3777, Fax 703-242-3983
Lunch & Dinner Mon.-Sat., $$$, Casual dressy

This popular restaurant has a sunny décor and a splendid menu to match. Clever chef Vone Xayavong takes a bold approach to his food, turning out bright Provençal cooking with an occasional unexpected Asian touch or two. The menu has evolved slowly, and you can still find his roasted eggplant cake with Roquefort cheese, a flavorful winner. The bouillabaisse is an intense seafood broth laced with scallops, shrimp, and chunks of boneless fish. We also recommend filet of monkfish with an eggplant mousse. Chocolate desserts get good treatment here, but the chef's cheesecake is sublime.

Lunchtime, when it's easier to secure a table, draws an affluent mix of retirees and local business people. Dinner reservations are probably essential.

Lakeside Inn   American   12/20

11150 South Lakes Dr. (Sunrise Valley Dr.), Reston 20191
703-264-0781, Fax 703-715-0180
Lunch & Dinner daily, Brunch Sun., $$, Casual

Popular for its lakeside location, this Reston watering hole has an active bar scene and an all-American menu. Old favorites include crab-cake sandwiches, prime rib (a house special), steaks, French onion soup, salads, baby back ribs and sandwiches. In other words, typical American fare. We recommend the excellent hamburger and the big club sandwich. Desserts are predictable.

Lansdowne Grille   Contemporary   14/20

Lansdowne Resort
44050 Woodridge Pkwy. (Rte. 7), Leesburg 20176
703-729-4073, Fax 703-729-4096
Lunch daily, Dinner Mon.-Sat., $$$, Resort casual

All that guests at Lansdowne Resort need to do is slip downstairs to the refurbished Lansdowne Grille with its panoramic golf course views and its distinguished menu to enjoy chef Konrad Meier's sublime cooking. Outsiders must make this a destination restaurant. The menu has always made for an interesting culinary experience: We recommend the Caesar salad, with a luscious saltiness from the requisite anchovies. Free of clever devices, the menu offers a straightforward look at steaks, veal chops, barbecued pork chops and roasted free-range chicken. We ordered sides—garlic mashed potatoes, creamed spinach, and sugar snap peas—only to find that sides serve two, maybe three people each. But don't let that deter you from dessert. There is also a well-chosen wine list.

Las Tapas   Spanish   12/20

710 King St. (Washington St.), Old Town, Alexandria 22314
703-836-4000, Fax 703-836-4668, *Lunch & Dinner daily, $$, Casual*

What this restaurant offers is a festive Spanish atmosphere that complements the rich, garlicky flavors of the very authentic tapas food the kitchen serves. Whether your dishes between the hot and cold, the seafood and meat, you can't go wrong. We loved the steamed octopus in vinaigrette, the chicken with garlic (and loads of it), the garlic potatoes and the fried calamari. With more than 40 tapas choices, plus several different variations of paella and noodle dishes—to say nothing of the dinner entrée selections that include meat and seafood dishes such as zarzuela de mariscos—you'll get plenty of Latino flavor here. Dessert: flan, of course. Note that the sangría is especially refreshing and only mildly sweet.

CLOSED

For **Gayot restaurant reviews in other U.S. cities,**
visit: digitalcity.com/dining

L'Auberge Chez François   French   14/20

332 Springvale Rd. (Georgetown Pike), Great Falls 22066
703-759-3800, *Dinner Tues.-Sun., $$$$, Business casual*

This sprawling, many-roomed country auberge has good Alsatian food. Hospitality overflows. It's family owned and the hosts treat customers like family. The price of your main course includes first course, salad and dessert. Specialties include house-made pâtés, veal kidneys with mustard sauce, giant choucroute platters and game in season. The plum tart is a homey and delicious dessert. The inn's romantic garden with gazebo and pretty plants is an ideal alfresco seating area in good weather. Good food plus cordial service means advance reservations are recommended.

Layalina   Middle Eastern   11/20

5216 Wilson Blvd. (George Mason Dr.), Arlington 22205
703-525-1170, Fax 703-525-6561, *Lunch & Dinner Tues.-Sun., $, Casual*

Much of the food here is bland and overcooked, although we can recommend the lamb shank, baked until the meat falls easily off the bone or the special eggplant stuffed with ground lamb. Ask to see the house-baked pastries, which are appealing and unusual. The main draw here is really the lush and exotic Middle Eastern décor: rich burgundy rugs, gilded archways and gorgeous artifacts.

Le Canard   French   11/20

Danor Plaza, 132 Branch Rd. (Maple Ave.), Vienna 22180
703-281-0070, Fax 703-255-3465
Lunch Mon.-Fri., Dinner nightly, $$$, Casual dressy

Tucked away in a suburban strip mall, this restaurant with a French name and a Moroccan-born chef offers its own take on French cooking. The menu encompasses five duck dishes, all worthy of trying. Less worthy was the salty onion soup (oh, for more cheese!) and sautéed shrimp in a lackluster wine sauce. The calves liver smothered with bacon was certainly tender and thick, although a bit mushy. Less interesting: the veal Français with a sprinkling of salty capers. The kitchen would do well to toss out its salt shaker. Since man cannot live by food alone, this is also a popular destination for its late-night bar scene and piano entertainment.

Le Gaulois   French   13/20

1106 King St. (Henry St.), Old Town, Alexandria 22314
703-739-9496, *Lunch & Dinner Mon.-Sat., $$$, Casual dressy*

We enjoy the food most here during winter, when you can settle into such classic dishes as pot-au-feu, the French family dinner of boiled beef and vegetables; cassoulet; and confit of duck served on a bed of lentils. Sometimes the kitchen offers low-cal cuisine minceur dishes, which—surprise, surprise—don't measure up in taste to everything else on the menu. We were disappointed by wilted lettuce in our salad. The wine list shows an effort to search out lesser French wines of good quality and good value. In its favor, the garden patio resembles a cloistered European courtyard and makes a charming setting for alfresco meals.

Le Petit Mistral   French   **12/20**

6710 Old Dominion Dr. (Chain Bridge Rd.), McLean 22101
703-748-4888, Fax 703-533-2498, *Lunch Mon.-Fri., Dinner nightly, $$$, Casual*

🅰 ☎ 🄿 🍸 ▮

A quick scan of the lunch crowd tells the tale: The restaurant's move from Capitol Hill to McLean, VA, has not diminished its popularity. The faces in the crowd though are definitely different. Instead of power brokers, there is a leisure crowd who can linger over dessert until mid-afternoon. No one seems bothered by a big-city tab, although the prix-fixe three-course lunch has many takers. The regular menu offers a fair assortment of dishes, from almond caraway crusted salmon steak to roasted duck breast with spiced bulgur. The higher-priced dinner menu resembles the lunch menu, with several additions, including mignonettes of pork and seared jumbo sea scallops.

Le Relais Restaurant & Bar à Vin   French **14/20** 🍴

Seneca Square, 1025 Seneca Rd. (Rte. 7), Great Falls 22066
703-444-4060, Fax 703-444-2562
Lunch & Dinner Tues.-Sun., Brunch Sun., $$$, Casual

🅰 ☎ 🄿 🖳 🍸 ▮ ⟳

Le Relais offers customers a variety of choices beyond what to order: an upfront takeout and catering section; a handsome wood-paneled bar; and a formal dining room with a fireplace. Its seasonal menu leans toward classic French with a definite emphasis on elegant presentation and attentive service. You can dine simply or lavishly. Whatever your tastes, you can't go wrong with the roasted free-range chicken with its glistening herb-stuffed skin and the accompanying piped potatoes. The kitchen also caters to vegetarians, with an elegant vegetable cake. The wine list is impressive. The excellent brunch provides an outlet for gourmands who want to put an exclamation point onto their weekend activities.

Lebanese Taverna   Lebanese   **12/20**

5900 Washington Blvd. (McKinley Rd.), Arlington 22205
703-241-8681, *Lunch Mon.-Sat., Dinner nightly, $, Casual*

🅰 ☎ 🄿 🍴 🍸 ▮

The original location of the area's Lebanese Taverna restaurants, this looks every bit like someone's living room, slightly expanded, and without the overstuffed furniture. You'll find the same good cooking that its more famous and newer DC restaurant provides, but without the glitz. It's definitely a family destination. The kitchen serves fare that even the kids will like, from the Lebanese pizzas and sausage sandwiches, to more sophisticated goodies for mom and dad: roasted half chicken, lamb with warmed yogurt, lamb shish kebab, and vine leaves encasing pieces of lamb, beef and rice. **Also located at** 2641 Connecticut Ave. NW, Washington, DC, 202-265-8681.

Legal Sea Foods   Seafood   **13/20** 🍴

Tysons Galleria
2001 International Dr. (Rte. 123), Tysons Corner, McLean 22102
703-827-8900, Fax 703-847-9750, *Lunch & Dinner daily, $$$, Casual*

🅰 🄿 ♥ 🍴 🍸 ▮

Boston's much-loved Legal Sea Foods, part of a leviathan whose holdings include numerous restaurants, retail markets, a mail-order business and a frozen seafood division, has not made an easy transition to the nation's capital and metro area. This hectic and often-crowded location, though, is obviously popular with upscale shoppers in the area. Its upstairs bar has formal dark woods, and downstairs is more casual. We've been disappointed with their signature clam chowder and steamed lobster, although we've enjoyed the fresh oysters and fried clams. The best bet here is to sit at the bar and order the great lobster roll or the simply prepared grilled fish. The wine list has an intelligent selection and fair prices, with a leaning toward California whites. **Other locations.**

Lightfoot   Contemporary   14/20

11 N. King St. (Market St.), Historic District, Leesburg 20176
703-771-4129, Fax 703-771-2285
Lunch & Dinner daily, Brunch Sun., $$$, Casual dressy

The bankers who built and founded Leesburg's People's National Bank in 1888 could never have imagined that their ornate offices would emerge in 1999 as a rather retro, upscale restaurant with food that is just short of glamorous. Owner-cook Ingrid Gustavson and her sister Carrie keep a close watch on the eclectic menu, offering their highbrow clientele such whimsies as an appetizer of a creamy tomato soup infused with basil. It's worth listening carefully to the day's specials, although the regular menu has its own treasures. We recommend the thick pork chop seasoned with a hoisin-style sauce. Also consider the filet mignon or seared duck. Definitely save room for dessert. If it appears, don't skip the luxurious quadruple-chocolate butter-dense tart for dessert, but if that's not offered, you can count on other options being outstanding, too. Visit the upstairs piano bar and on the way out, say farewell to the lifelike wax butler standing near the front door.

Little Saigon Vietnamese Restaurant   12/20

Vietnamese
6218-B Wilson Blvd. (Peyton Randolph Rd.), Falls Church 22044
703-536-2633, Fax 703-536-2633, *Lunch & Dinner daily, $, Casual*

Long a favorite in the local Vietnamese community, Little Saigon is a restaurant at which you can order the set dinner menu, but why not mix and match? We recommend the classic seafood soup with pineapple chunks, the deep-fried whole fish with ginger sauce, and the bowl of rice noodles topped with spring rolls and grilled pork. Have questions? Let the staff help with your choices.

Little Viet Garden   Vietnamese   12/20

3012 Wilson Blvd. (Highland St.), Clarendon, Arlington 22201
703-522-9686, Fax 703-524-9372, *Lunch & Dinner daily, $$, Casual*

The snappy pseudo-tropical décor with twinkling lights certainly makes this respected eatery stand out. The good food helps, too. Starters include the fresh and fried spring rolls and grilled beef on skewers. Other favorites include grilled shrimp on sugar cane and the caramel chicken, pork, fish, or shrimp. For a slightly different take on Vietnamese cooking, you might try the roasted quail and the crispy whole flounder with ginger sauce. You'll find plenty of noodle dishes. We recommend the bowl of rice vermicelli with spring rolls. Since the outdoor patio is charming, this is an alfresco favorite in warm weather.

Luciano Italian Restaurant & Pizzeria   12/20

Italian
Tysons Corner Center
7946 Tysons Corner Center (Rte. 7), Tysons Corner, McLean 22102
703-893-8488, Fax 703-938-3491, *Lunch & Dinner daily, $$, Casual*
No credit cards. P ♟ ▲

The earliest location of this popular family restaurant, Luciano has made its name locally by its good service and the quality of its Italian dishes, which are several notches above the usual Italian-American menu. Try the artichoke bruschetta or crusty mozzarella sticks as starters. Consider skipping meat and seafood entrées and moving directly the outstanding pizzas and calzones. **Also located at** 2946 G Chain Bridge Rd., Oakton, VA, 703-281-1748; and 1054 Elden St., Herndon, VA, 703-736-9830.

McCormick & Schmick's   Seafood   13/20

Reston Town Center
11920 Democracy Dr. (Dulles Toll Rd.), Reston 20190
703-481-6600, Fax 703-481-9533, *Lunch & Dinner daily, $$$, Casual*

🅰 ☎ P ♟ 🍸 ▲ ♡

One of Reston's hottest meet-and-greet spots, this upscale national seafood restaurant is rarely uncrowded. Even the very long oval bar with plenty of stools is usually packed, especially after work and on weekends. To solve the wait problem, the restaurant takes reservations in the main dining rooms. Seating includes private dining areas enclosed by velvet drapes, the ultimate in privacy. The restaurant's seafood menu changes twice daily—for lunch and dinner—and offerings depend on the freshest catch. Look for some unusual fish varieties, like South African swordfish or Louisiana black drum, plus succulent oysters and clams. Also on the lunch menu: pastas and entrée salads. Despite the menu changes, several core items remain, such as the cedar-planked salmon and the restaurant's signature dessert, a Jake's Famous Chocolate Truffle Cake. **Other locations.**

Maestro   Italian/Contemporary   14/20

The Ritz-Carlton, Tysons Corner
1700 Tysons Corner Blvd. (International Dr.), McLean 22102
703-917-5498, Fax 703-506-4305, *Open Breakfast & Dinner daily,
Lunch Mon.-Fri., Brunch Sun., $$$, Business casual*

🅰 ☎ 🚗 🍴🏠♟ ♪ 🍸 ▲ ♡

A new setting—in sunny gold, shades of rose and copper accents—with an open kitchen showcases the new menu, new orientation, new name (formerly The Restaurant) and new chef, Fabio Trabocchi, from London's Floriana. In our *The Best of London* guide, we noted that this young chef had created waves there with sensational cooking, a good introduction for his American career. The restaurant's new menu stars not only the Italian food of Trabocchi's childhood but also many contemporary dishes that he interprets in his own style. Hence, the bill of fare runs along two courses, the traditional (La Tradizione) and the modern (L'Evoluzione), and guests are invited to sample from both. From the latter, look for such inspirations as a trio of tartare featuring marinated wild salmon with chive cream and osetra caviar, scallop tartare with Ligurian olives and lemon con-fit tomato, and crab meat with langoustines and rouille. Other signature dishes are marubini pasta filled with potato purée, braised baby leeks and Swiss chard in black truffle sauce; and half a Maine lobster with lobster-filled ravioli and sautéed arti-choke with ginger in a citronette of crustacean and port jus. In addition, a special tasting menu featuring one seasonal ingredi-ent like truffles or asparagus also is available. Vincent Feraud, best known as the knowledgeable and charming sommelier at Jean-Louis at the Watergate and most recently at Lespinasse in Washington, DC, is the sommelier at Maestro. The wine cellar boasts an impressive selection of almost 500 wines from Italy, France and the U.S.

Maggiano's Little Italy   Italian   13/20

Tysons Galleria
1790 International Dr. (Chain Bridge Rd.), Tysons Corner, McLean 22102
703-356-9000, Fax 703-356-5190, Lunch & Dinner daily, $$, Casual

Hip Italian ambience in the New York manner and giant portions define Maggiano's. Both aspects attract standing-room-only crowds of every age making for a fun, frenzied atmosphere. It's no use stopping by unless you are hungry, for every dish easily serves two, maybe more—though you can order half portions. The bread basket with its wedges of focac-cia as well as the wine glasses overflow. We recommend the roasted red peppers with sheets of fresh Parmesan, the garlic mashed potatoes and the roast chicken with its sprinkling of garlic, rosemary, and olive oil. Best dessert? The dense choco-late zuccoto cake. Plan ahead and make reservations, or you'll have to wait with the hungry hordes. **Also located at** 5333 Wisconsin Ave., Washington, DC, 202-966-5500.

Malibu Grill   Brazilian   12/20

5715 Columbia Pike (King St.), Falls Church 22042
703-379-0587, Fax 703-379-1605, *Lunch & Dinner daily, $$, Casual*

A Brazilian twist on America's beloved eat-all-you-can buffet theme, Brazilian steakhouses open their doors to customers who go to the salad and entrée bars before, during, and after eating loads of meat. This steakhouse (churrascaria) is as snap-py as a samba and the ideal destination for real carnivores. The meat served here is primarily beef, along with sausages, turkey and game meats. The meats are carried from table to table by waiters holding a long meat-laden skewer in one hand and a sharp carving knife in the other. Each waiter carries a different meat selection; they'll slice off what you want before moving to the next table. Meat is cooked to a sizzling doneness over the huge grills in the open kitchen.

Mandarin Inn   Chinese/Malaysian   12/20

3045 Mount Vernon Ave. (Kennedy St.), Alexandria 22305
703-548-4052, Fax 703-548-4788, *Lunch & Dinner daily, $$, Casual*

It's a little-known fact that this primarily Chinese restaurant also serves Malaysian food. Both the owner and the cook (brother and sister) are from Malaysia, hence, the selections of rendang, satay, acar timun, Hokkien mee, and that dazzler, char koay teow, the stir-fried flat rice noodles with shrimp or chicken. The spicy dishes make a pleasant change of pace from the much more familiar lo meins, won ton soups and kung pao chickens.

Manila Café　　Philippine　　12/20

Lee Center, 6639 Backlick Rd. (Old Keene Mill Rd.), Springfield 22150
703-644-5825, Fax 703-451-8189, *Lunch & Dinner Wed.-Mon., $, Casual*

Ⓐ Ⓟ ♟

One of the area's few authentic Filipino restaurants, Manila Café is a humble destination with no frills but with cheery white walls plastered with color snapshots. It looks and feels like a family kitchen, and it's tempting to forego ordering from the menu to take advantage of the small, aromatic selection on the buffet display. However, if none of these dishes look familiar, ask for guidance from the staff. Simpler would be to scan the menu with its English translations and select the pork or chicken adobo (a rich vinegary stew that may well be a national favorite), pancit bihon (noodles sautéed with shrimp), and for dessert, the merienda favorite, halo halo with ice cream (crushed ice topped with sweetened fruits, milk and ice cream). Want to impress your friends at a dinner party? Serve (with one day advance notice) the lechon (whole roasted pig), plus some Filipino side dishes.

Marie's Restaurant　　Mediterranean/American　　12/20

South Lakes Village
11130 M South Lakes Dr. (Sunrise Valley Dr.), Reston 20191
703-620-6555, Fax 703-391-0545
Lunch & Dinner Mon.-Sat., $$, Casual

Ⓐ Ⓟ 💻 📷 ♟ Ⓨ

Located on a lake, this family eatery was one of the early establishments in Reston, opening up long before the major restaurant influx of the '90s. The menu is a mélange of Italian, Greek, Lebanese and American dishes. Start with the Lebanese kibbeh, a fried torpedo-shaped combination of ground beef and crushed wheat. Then move on to popular entrées such as the Greek kebabs and the souvlaki and gyro platters. Some of the American choices include crab cakes, stuffed flounder and rib-eye steak. Kids have their own mini menu. Key lime pie, caramel apple pie and specialty cheesecakes are good desserts.

Mark's Duck House　　Chinese/Dim Sum/Vietnamese　　12/20

Wilson Center
6184-A Arlington Blvd. (Patrick Henry Dr.), Falls Church 22044
703-532-2125, Fax 703-532-5095, *Lunch & Dinner daily, $, Casual*

Ⓐ Ⓟ ♟

Whether you are in the mood for Hong Kong-style congee for breakfast, dim sum served Cantonese-style via carts for lunch or a hearty Chinese dinner, Mark's Duck House is a popular neighborhood spot. Other good selections: any of the noodle dishes (we especially like the roast pork noodles that have a piercing rice-wine flavor), roast duck and roast pork (like the duck, also sold whole or by the pound for takeout).

> **Chefs** are creative people. Therefore, of course, menus are subject to change. The dishes we describe should give you a good idea of the chef's range and style.

Market Street Bar & Grill Contemporary 13/20

Hyatt Regency Reston, 1800 President St. (Main St.), Reston 20190
703-709-6262, Fax 703-709-6244
Breakfast, Lunch & Dinner daily, Brunch Sun., $$, Casual

This upscale dining room at the Hyatt Regency in Reston is the perfect place for important dinners and special dates, for the setting is country-club casual and the food is downtown elegant. And its convenience to local commerce suits VIPS and others for that breakfast huddle. To make lunches run more smoothly and quickly, the kitchen has instituted specials of simple, ready and hearty fare like macaroni and cheese and seafood and chicken jambalaya. Chef Eric Harmon likes to work with the strong flavors of the Pacific Rim, so expect to find plenty of Asian influences in many of his dishes, like the Chilean sea bass with a red miso crust or sautéed jumbo prawns coated in a green Thai curry paste. But the menu is balanced to satisfy traditional Western palates, too: Try the grilled beef tenderloin infused with a foie gras center. Planning on a breakfast meeting? The wrap with scrambled eggs and chorizo will start the day with a bang.

Matuba Japanese/Sushi 13/20

2915 Columbia Pike (Walter Reed Dr.), Arlington 22204
703-521-2811, Fax 703-521-2811
Lunch Mon.-Fri., Dinner nightly, $, Casual

There aren't many seats or barstools at Matuba, so be prepared for lines. The sushi here is a particular favorite, even though some sound vaguely Western, like the bagel roll or the Boston roll. If you can, grab a seat at the sushi bar—watching the action is a good show. You should also order something off the main menu, like the tempura, which is delicate and crispy. Check out the grilled specials, too. These range from chicken yakitori to hotate yaki (grilled scallops), and for heartier appetites, the grilled seafood combo. The décor is neither glamorous nor funky; but plain, simple, and fresh, just like the sushi. **Also located at** 4918 Cordell Ave., Bethesda, MD, 301-652-7449.

Maxim Palace Chinese 12/20

5900 Leesburg Pike (Rte. 7), Baileys Crossroads, Falls Church 22041
703-998-8888, Fax 703-998-8896
Lunch & Dinner daily, $$, Casual

Under new ownership, this bastion of Chinese treats looks sleekly trim and is a favorite destination for Chinese banquets. Most people come here for the daily dim sum on carts and the decidedly Hong Kong-style food, from seafood dishes (lobster, crab, oyster, conch, squid, abalone, sea cucumber) to the usual delights: Hunan or orange beef, moo goo gai pan and the ubiquitous General Tso's chicken. Don't forget the noodle dishes like the commendable beef chow foon with Chinese broccoli. Keep an eye out for daily specials and maybe even a Vietnamese dish or two.

Mayan Grill & Bar   Tex-Mex/Salvadoran   12/20

2039 Wilson Blvd. (N. Courthouse Rd.), Arlington 22201
703-841-9555, Fax 703-841-9575, *Lunch & Dinner daily, $$, Casual*

A great place for a Latino snack—with an emphasis on Mexican fare—this eatery may be hard to spot unless you keep on the lookout for bright colors. It's small and casual and the food matches the sprightly service and bright décor. You won't find many culinary triumphs here, for the menu offers standard Tex-Mex and Salvadoran food with a short section devoted to Latin American favorites. The pupusas here are good, though not breathtaking, as is the burrito de puerco with its filling of well-seasoned fried pork.

Mexicali Blues   Mexican/Salvadoran   12/20

2933 Wilson Blvd. (Garfield St.), Clarendon, Arlington 22201
703-812-9352, *Lunch & Dinner daily, Brunch Sun., $, Casual*

This restaurant opened to much fanfare and the crowds have barely thinned out since. It's an after-work drop-in place that's easy on the budget. Crowds seem to love the zany bright décor as much as the restaurant's Mexican-Salvadoran cooking. You'll recognize the enchiladas, nachos, and tacos as Mexican, but there are also Salvadoran specialties like fried yuca and pupusas. We'd return often for the bulging burrito, stuffed with grilled pork, chicken, or beef, plus beans and rice and the sopes (thick tortillas) with their choice of toppings are dreamy. Best bet: If you like fried potatoes, you'll love the gutsy textured fried yuca.

Mezza 9   Mediterranean   13/20

Hyatt Arlington
1325 Wilson Blvd. (N. Fort Meyer Dr.), Rosslyn, Arlington 22209
703-276-8999, Fax 703-525-1476
Breakfast, Lunch & Dinner daily, $$, Casual dressy

A Rosslyn hangout for business lunches and a successful drop-in for casual folk at any time, the Hyatt Arlington's Mezza 9 offers a brilliant array of Mediterranean-inspired dishes, many shared in the form of tapas. We recommend the lentil and chickpea salad tossed with bits of roasted tomatoes and eggplant, the honey-glazed lamb and preserved apricot brochette, marinated cheeses served with sausage and Serrano ham with pears and arugula. The dinner menu offers even more of a chance for chef Jeff Foresman to display his talents. Starters include smoked salmon terrine, frutti di mer and roasted tomato and fennel soup. Seamed lobster, grilled veal chop and pistachio-crusted rack of lamb fill out the bill. Desserts are not particularly Mediterranean, but include a warm Alsatian apple tart, mixed berries and a white chocolate crème brûlée.

Mike's American Grill   American   13/20

6210 Backlick Rd. (Cumberland Ave.), Springfield 22150
703-644-7100, Fax 703-866-3769, *Lunch & Dinner daily, $, Casual*

Always crowded no matter when you come, all-brick Mike's is the epitome of the casual American eatery where mighty portions rule. You can choose to pass the time in the lively downstairs bar, but if you want to eat seriously, you'll be escorted to an upstairs table. If you're lucky, you'll secure a table near the kitchen where you can get a close-up of the cooks at work. We recommend the Tex-Mex egg rolls or the eight-layer dip and chips as starters. The bacon-cheddar burger is a must; the steaks are good, too. Other homey foods include meatloaf and mashed potatoes or grilled pork chops and the deep-dish apple and blackberry pie.

Minerva Indian Cuisine Indian 12/20

Village Center at Dulles
2443 Centreville Rd., #G1 (Fox Mill Rd.), Herndon 20171
703-793-3223, Fax 703-793-6519, *Lunch & Dinner daily, $, Casual*
🄰 P 🍴 🥄

Perhaps the most exciting aspect of this restaurant is not the food, but the huge Indian music video that plays out, constantly and loudly, against the back wall. It's a little like being wrapped in "surround sound" while you eat, and a good distraction for the food. This, we found, was inconsistent, with some dishes—namely the butter chicken—far outshining others, such as the bland lamb vindaloo. As any fan of Indian food knows, this should be a dish that screams with flavor and heat, but not here. The menu is lengthy, and actually, some dishes stand out for their rarity. There is hyderabadi kheema, a marinated ground lamb entrée and navaratan khoorma, a vegetarian entrée that's the merging of nine distinct foods, including vegetables, dry fruits and cheese. If you order the full dinner and not à la carte, everything is brought out to you at once on a large metal plate, and you get the chef's choice of dessert, like it or not. **Also located at** 10364 Lee Hwy., Fairfax, VA, 703-383-9200.

Mirage Restaurant Afghan 12/20

6271-A Old Dominion Dr. (Kirby Rd.), McLean 22101
703-734-0909, Fax 703-734-1648, *Lunch & Dinner daily, $, Casual*
🄰 ☎ P 🍴

This Afghan eatery appeals to regulars who want to tackle the cuisine's dumplings, fried potatoes, kebabs and sautéed vegetables. The setting is rather dark and unglamorous—its most outstanding feature is the mural of an Afghan village. The best bets here are the thick, tangy yogurt, the first-rate breads, the sautéed pumpkin and firnee, a cornstarch pudding that's a soothing comfort sweet. We've found other dishes, even the kebabs, inconsistent in flavor.

Morton's of Chicago Steakhouse 14/20 ♔

8075 Leesburg Pike (Aline Ave.), Tysons Corner, Vienna 22182
703-883-0800, Fax 703-883-0673
Lunch Mon.-Sat., Dinner nightly, $$$$, Business casual
🄰 ☎ P 🍸 🍶 ⟳

Morton's has lots of upscale neighbors like Tiffany in Tysons, but the reason to visit for foodies is more compelling than diamonds. It's for one of the aged, top-quality porterhouses, available in one-and-a-half- or three-pound cuts. To avoid ruining your appetite, go easy on the starters—perhaps a house salad or a plate of sliced beefsteak tomatoes with red onion and blue cheese. As a side, one of the football-sized baked potatoes does nicely. The service is excellent, as is the wine list, and, if you are not in the mood for beef, you can secure a good chop or a fresh piece of salmon. **Also located at** 1050 Connecticut Ave. NW, Washington, DC, 202-955-5997; and 3251 Prospect St. NW, Washington, DC, 202-342-6258.

Myanmar Restaurant   Burmese   13/20

Merrifalls Shopping Center
7810-C Lee Hwy. (Hyson Lane), Falls Church 22042
703-289-0013, *Lunch & Dinner daily, $, Casual*

Restaurants that serve Burmese food are rare in the United States. And there are only a few, including this one, in the Washington, DC, area. How local residents will respond to catfish curry and mohingar (the fish soup that is eaten daily in Burma) remains to be seen. However, even if you skip that, we recommend the spicy pork with mango pickles, the squash fritters and the spicy chicken curry, all staples of Burmese home cooking. The kitchen even produces the sweet and intensely rich shweji for dessert and if you ask, the cook will make fa_looda, a sumptuous Indo-Burmese drink that is more dessert than anything else. To keep and please some American clientele, the owner has added such dishes as broiled salmon and kebabs to the menu, but these can't match the Burmese food. Besides the Burmese landscape paintings, there's little décor and nothing at all glamorous about the ambience.

Nam-Viet Pho 79   Vietnamese   12/20

1127 N. Hudson St. (Wilson Blvd.), Arlington 22201
703-522-7110, Fax 703-243-4535, *Lunch & Dinner daily, $$, Casual*

One of Arlington's—and the area's—first Vietnamese restaurants, this old-timer still has plenty of popular appeal. You won't find anything particularly trendy, but you will find a complete assortment of the standards, from caramel pork with black pepper to crispy spring rolls, shrimp barbecued on sugar cane and grilled pork on rice vermicelli. Some dishes, such as the orange beef or chicken and the chicken with cashews, don't sound particularly traditional, and may be the chef's fancy. We've enjoyed the garden rolls and the refreshing shredded green papaya salad with shrimp, but could spend the whole evening mixing and matching items from the menu. The pho, though, the famed noodle soup, did not please us; we've had better in many other restaurants. However, even with all the Vietnamese competition, this place still holds its own.

Nayeb Kabob Restaurant   Persian   12/20

Idlywood Shopping Center, 2190-B Pimmit Dr. (Rte. 7), Falls Church 22043
703-893-6677, Fax 703-893-6674
Lunch & Dinner daily, $, Casual dressy

This very small and hidden Persian eatery serves kebabs and not much else. Maybe the secret to its success is keeping the menu simple with just a full complement of kebabs from chicken and Cornish hen to tenderloin and ground sirloin, the last being a flavorful morsel. Appetizers include the famed kashke bademjan (the sautéed eggplant dish with grilled onions) and shirazi salad. Unlike most Persian places, the kitchen does not bake its bread on the premises but uses instead the flat lavash cut into sheets.

Neisha Thai Cuisine   Thai   **12/20**

Culmore Shopping Center, 6037 Leesburg Pike
(Glen Carlyn Rd.), Baileys Crossroads, Falls Church 22041
703-933-3788, Fax 703-933-3790, *Lunch & Dinner daily, $, Casual*

Named after the owner's daughter, this Thai restaurant is meant to sparkle like a jewel—that's the idea of the cavelike interior in glinting jewel-like colors. The food is also meant to shine, but we were disappointed. The menu does not include many of the better-known Thai dishes and most we sampled were overly sweet; the cook would do well to cut the sugar by half. The best choices here include the fried tofu appetizer and the crispy soft-shell crabs, which come two to an order. The pineapple fried rice served in a hollowed-out pineapple half looks glamorous but seems more Cantonese than Thai. Although not centrally located, it's become a popular place and packs in a hungry lunch crowd of young professionals.

Nizam's   Turkish   **11/20**

The Village Green Center, 523 Maple Ave. W (Nutley St.), Vienna 22180
703-938-8948, Fax 703-938-0453
Lunch Tues.-Fri., Dinner Tues.-Sun., $$$, Casual

No wonder this cheerily decorated spot has gained a name not only for its excellent food, but for its impressive staff: The servers are particularly helpful for those who are new to Turkish cuisine. If that describes you, perhaps the best way to get a handle on it is to start with an appetizer platter: The stuffed grape leaves and fried eggplant with yogurt sauce alone are worthy of a prince's table. A house special is the doner kebab (not available every night). It's praiseworthy, but if unavailable, consider the lamb shank instead, a mildly seasoned dish topped with eggplant, tomatoes and green peppers. For dessert, we recommend a mixed plate for two, which includes an outstanding baklava and kazandibi, another rich pastry.

The NM Café at Neiman Marcus   **13/20**

American
Tysons Galleria, 2255 International Dr.
(Old Dominion Dr.), Tysons Corner, McLean 22102
703-761-1600, Fax 703-821-7794, *Lunch daily, $$, Casual*

Want to know a secret? Neiman Marcus' NM Café, a chic eatery on its first floor, is pure luxury—and affordable. Line up with elegant shoppers to indulge in fresh, yeasty rolls spread with strawberry-sweetened butter, the cheese-thickened and ultra-rich tortilla soup and the upscale California Club layered with avocado. The classic Cobb salad is sensational; a lighter salad is the seasonal fruit platter laced with honey-sweetened yogurt. To finish, how about lingering over the gooey brownie tart with thick hot fudge, whipped cream and vanilla ice cream or just a caffè latté?

Prices are based on a complete dinner for one, including appetizer, entrée, dessert, coffee, tax and tip—but excluding wine or other beverages.

Okra's Louisiana Bistro   Southern   12/20

9110 Center St. (Battle St.), Old Town, Manassas 20110
703-330-2729, Fax 703-330-0899, *Lunch & Dinner Mon.-Sat., $$, Casual*

🅰 🍴 👓 ♿ 🍸

Hip Southern cooking and slick décor that looks just this side of honky-tonk make Okra's an unexpected find in Old Town Manassas. But don't get us wrong: This is all upscale fun and food, with the emphasis on fun. As for the cooking, you'll find mostly such Louisiana classics as dirty rice, gumbo, fried okra, étouffée, Creole jambalaya and that New Orleans' sandwich specialty, muffuletta. The kitchen, however, does throw in a couple of Yankee-influenced dishes, such as the ubiquitous Caesar salad, a charbroiled portobello mushroom, a stylized hamburger and a BLT. Desserts are flamboyantly Southern, and include pistachio praline and caramelized bananas with fried ice cream.

Old Peking Restaurant   Chinese   11/20

2952C Chain Bridge Rd. (Rte. 123), Oakton 22124
703-255-9444, Fax 703-242-2856
Lunch Mon.-Sat., Dinner nightly, Brunch Sun., $$, Casual

🅰 🅿 ♥ 🍴 🍸

This Chinese restaurant is somewhat off the beaten track, but worth searching for if you want solid Chinese food and a menu that offers some healthful choices. The menu notes that no animal fats are used in cooking and that all ingredients are prepared fresh daily. The menu is also a mix of regional cooking, with an emphasis on favorites, such as the ubiquitous General Tso's chicken, orange-flavored beef, sweet 'n' sour pork and Peking duck. Other reliable choices include cold noodles with sesame sauce, a nicely textured hot 'n' sour soup and a mild ma po tofu.

The Oriental Regency   Chinese   13/20   👨‍🍳

8605 Westwood Center Dr. (Rte. 7), Vienna 22182
703-827-9066, Fax 703-556-9597, *Lunch & Dinner daily, $$, Casual*

🅰 ☎ 🅿 🍴 🍸 🍷

For devotées of classic Chinese cooking, this restaurant promises some serious cuisine. Flip to the back pages of its lengthy menu to see why: drunken chicken, mountain seaweed soup and crispy-salty paper-skin chicken garnished with deep-fried mint. The cooking style here is basically Northern and Eastern Chinese. In the menu's first few pages, you'll find the usual orange beef and General Tso's chicken dishes. We recommend the Northern fare, though, and start most meals with the deep-fried dumplings. It's obvious that the restaurant takes itself seriously: Its décor is more formal than at most local Chinese restaurants.

Outback Steakhouse   Steakhouse   11/20

Elden Plaza, 150 Elden St., #100 (Herndon Pkwy.), Herndon 20170
703-318-0999, Fax 703-709-1448, *Dinner nightly, $$, Casual*

🅰 🅿 🍴 🍸

Brazenly Australian on the outside, this popular steakhouse chain is American through and through. But the gimmick works—you will find boomerangs and other Aussie paraphernalia setting the scene for adequate steaks served in fairly generous portions. No meal is really complete here without the

"Bloomin' Onion," an oil-drenched and trademarked appetizer that's had many copycats. Steaks, of course, are the claim to fame, but the choice cuts aren't always tender. If you want beef, pay extra for the prime or select one of the other dishes, including chicken, pork chops, and grilled baby back ribs. You'll probably find a line at mealtimes, so if you want to eat and run, order ahead for the takeout service, available at most locations. **Other locations.**

Pacific
Pacific Rim/Asian   **12/20**

Potomac Run Plaza, 46240 Potomac Run Plaza (Rte. 7), Sterling 20164
703-404-5500, Fax 703-404-8251
Lunch & Dinner daily, Brunch Sun., $$, Casual

In a semitropical setting with a wooden alligator and a splashing waterfall, Pacific gives a taste of Asian experiences with an eclectic menu that's more about fusion cooking than traditional fare. The formula works, for it's drawing crowds of all generations. The menu is studded with such unique dishes as the chicken cocochilenut soup, with its Thai roots, and roast duck spring rolls with a very sweet dipping sauce. The kitchen does a good job with various Vietnamese grilled beef and chicken dishes served with sautéed rice vermicelli cakes and rice paper wrappers. Almost as good is the royal pad Thai, with a non-Thai addition of roast duck. The extensive menu presents something to please all ages. Note that management puts on cooking classes and offers multicultural entertainment.

Palm
Steakhouse   **13/20**

Tysons Galleria
1750 Tysons Blvd. (Chain Bridge Rd.), McLean 22102
703-917-0200, Fax 703-917-6120
Lunch Mon.-Fri., Dinner nightly, $$$, Business casual

Gentler and slightly less political than its downtown high-profile cousin, this suburban steakhouse nonetheless puts steaks, prime ribs, and lobsters on center stage for a power meal. But, the kitchen also plays to the lunchtime ladies and dieters with entrée salads and fancy sandwiches. Try the grilled filet mignon with Gorgonzola and arugula for its mass appeal. The beginning breadbasket offers several assortments, and the dessert tray is a must to at least view if not order samples from. Best bet: the Key lime pie, a successfully creamy tart-sweet slice of pastry. Admire the restaurant's trademark murals, which are caricatures of local, national celebs. **Also located at** 1225 19th St. NW, Washington, DC, 202-293-9091.

Panjshir
Afghan   **11/20**

924 W. Broad St. (West St.), Falls Church 22046
703-536-4566, *Lunch Mon.-Sat., Dinner nightly, $, Casual*

This and its sister restaurant in Vienna are old-timers in the area, and thus, have a loyal following of business folk and suburbanites for lunch and dinner. Worthy dishes include the Afghan noodle soup, aush, and the seib chalow, a dish with apples baked in tomato sauce with Afghan prunes. You may find some interesting kebabs—the shami kebab is very plain—and some hearty vegetarian fare. Desserts include baklava and the delicious pudding, firnee, in both plain and chocolate flavors. **Also located at** 224 Maple Ave. West, Vienna, 703-281-4183.

Paolo's   Italian   12/20

Reston Town Center, 11898 Market St. (Reston Pkwy.), Reston 20190
703-318-8920, Fax 703-318-8928, *Lunch & Dinner daily, $$, Casual*

It's easy to fall in love with a place like Paolo's. Its Reston location looks out over Town Center's central plaza and fountain, and the passing crowds are part of the entertainment. The other part of the attraction, of course, is the good food. It's not classic Italian and includes offerings of duck confit pizza with apple butter coulis and a pulled roasted chicken salad. Another recommendation: the succulent filet mignon with Gorgonzola-walnut asparagus. The restaurant is so popular that you'll probably wait if you don't have a reservation. But in fine weather, enhanced seating means eating outdoors, an ideal option for people watching. At one time Paolo's had a higher profile locally, but now it has only two locations—a pity for those of us who love its lusty and unconventional fare and laid-back ambience. **Also located at** 1303 Wisconsin Ave., NW, Washington, DC, 202-333-7353.

Pars Famous House of Kabob   Persian   12/20

10801 Lee Hwy. (Oak St.), Fairfax 22030
703-273-3508, Fax 703-273-3509, *Lunch & Dinner daily, $$, Casual*

For terrific kebabs, head straight to Pars in Fairfax, a low-key, diner-restaurant featuring a quirky metal statue of a grill-master out front. At lunchtime, there's a nonstop buffet selection of two kebabs plus assorted other Persian fare. We vote that the ground-beef kebabs are some of the area's finest; the juicy, tender chicken kebabs run a close second. The glassed-in tandoori oven is right up front, so you can watch your kebabs and puffy breads cooking to order. If you don't mind Saturday night mobs, come for the weekly special, baghali polo, a tender lamb shank with baby lima beans and basmati rice. To finish, the rose water-scented Persian ice cream is sublime.

Pasha Café   Egyptian/Middle Eastern   13/20

Cherrydale, 2109 N. Pollard St. (Lee Hwy.), Arlington 22207
703-528-2126, *Lunch Mon.-Sat., Dinner nightly, $$, Casual*

This tiny and unglamorous spot is the DC area's only Egyptian restaurant we know. The menu, though, is large. It's a quiet lunch destination, which becomes livelier toward the end of the week when the kitchen gets into full gear. Dinners on weekends attract diners who love culinary adventures. We recommend the howoshi, a richly spicy mixture of ground lamb stuffed inside a large pita. If you want variety, order an assortment of appetizers, mezze style. Or if you have a robust appetite, sample the fetta leb lahma, a rice, bread and lamb dish that Napoleon apparently loved.

Some establishments change **days of operation** without warning. It is always wise to check in advance.

Pat Troy's Restaurant & Pub   Irish/American   12/20

Tavern Square, 111 N. Pitt St. (King St.), Old Town, Alexandria 22314
703-549-4535, Fax 703-549-4614
Lunch & Dinner daily, Brunch Sun., $$, Casual

You'll need no more than maybe three seconds to realize that Pat Troy's Restaurant & Pub is Irish, all Irish, and proud to be wearin' the Green. Almost every square inch is festooned with some Irish trinket. On the slightly elevated stage, a trio fiddles and twangs away at enchanting Irish melodies, emotional enough so you'll raise your glass in a toast. The menu includes Irish and American fare. Those not in the mood for Kilcormac shepherd's pie, Mulligan beef stew or Ferbane Irish breakfast can enjoy burgers, hot and cold sandwiches, soups, salads, appetizers and specials. Bread pudding and a rich cheesecake made with Bailey's Irish Cream are good desserts. Note that owner Pat Troy hosts a weekly Sunday morning Irish radio program with news about what's going on in the local Irish community and, of course, Irish music. Indeed, his place is all about entertainment, too: Check out the monthly calendar of events.

Paya Thai   Thai   11/20

8417 Old Courthouse Rd. (Rte. 123), Tysons Corner, Vienna 22182
703-883-3881, Fax 703-883-3882, *Lunch & Dinner daily, $, Casual*

The cool, pale-jade green walls, mirrored niche containing a golden Buddha and the portrait of Thai royalty make a certain elegant statement. So, too, do the white linen tablecloths and well-dressed staff in this upscale Thai restaurant, a favorite at lunch for the Tysons area business crowd. The management also has gentrified the restaurant's food, paring down flavors, discarding chilies and leaving a selection of dishes lacking the traditional dramatic Thai flavors or heat. Probably the most noteworthy dishes on the menu include the roast duck salad, the drunken noodles and the much-too-mild Penang curry. The black sticky rice pudding made with coconut milk is the best dish on the menu.

Peking Gourmet Inn   Chinese   13/20

Culmore Shopping Center, 6029 Leesburg Pike
(Glen Carlyn Rd.), Baileys Crossroads, Falls Church 22041
703-671-8088, Fax 703-671-5912, *Lunch & Dinner daily, $$$, Casual*

It remains to be seen if it will be like father, like son, but this was a favorite restaurant of George Bush, Sr., while he was president (or at least the one that made the evening news). He had good taste. The restaurant's signature dish is its plump, juicy, and scrumptious Peking duck. It's not inexpensive, but every morsel is succulent, and besides, the chef does it properly: It's carved tableside in the traditional manner. We also recommend the jumbo spring onions tossed with lamb (or beef, shrimp or pork). The onions and some of the other produce is grown at the restaurant owner's farm. Portions of most dishes are enormous, so count on taking home leftovers. It's best to come early or reserve ahead; this restaurant fills up fast and stays that way.

Peking Village   Chinese   **12/20**

Fairfax Plaza, 2962 Gallows Rd. (Rte. 29), Falls Church 22041
703-698-9220/1, *Lunch & Dinner daily, $, Casual*

🅰 🅿 🎋 🍸 🍶

This spot is well off the main road, but well worth seeking out—and usually crowded. Your payoff will be excellent tofu and eggplant dishes and Mongolian lamb sizzling with garlicky flavors. If you arrive at lunchtime, you'll find a popular luncheon buffet plus some lunchtime daily specials, including Hunan lamb, Mongolian lamb and chef's special lamb. General Tso's chicken is a mainstay. In the evenings, note that the menu offers both Peking duck and salted duck.

P.F. Chang's China Bistro   Chinese/American   **12/20**

Tysons Galleria
1716 M International Dr. (Cambridge St.), Tysons Corner, McLean 22102
703-734-8996, Fax 703-734-8997, *Lunch & Dinner daily, $$, Casual*

🅰 🅿 🍽 🎋 🍸 🍶

Disco decibels greet you at P.F. Chang's, where long weekend-night waits are typical and people stack up at the bar in sardinelike conviviality. The fact that the kitchen serves bistro-style Chinese fare is really irrelevant, since most people come here for the casual atmosphere and the merriment. Even the presence of stylized Chinese décor and faux Xian terra-cotta warriors can't change the fact that this is an all-American hangout. Best bets are the salt and pepper shrimp, the red-sauced won tons and the tender beef garnished with strips of fresh orange peel. **Also located at** 11301 Rockville Pike, North Bethesda, MD, 301-230-6933.

Phillips Seafood Grill   Seafood   **12/20**

American Center Office Park
8330 Boone Blvd. (Rte. 7), Tysons Corner, Vienna 22182
703-442-0400, *Lunch Mon.-Fri., Dinner nightly, $, Casual*

🅰 🅿 🍽 🍸 🍶 ↻

At lunchtime, Phillips Seafood Grill has become a must for dealmakers, who want the luxuries of a club atmosphere—dark greens, dark woods, heavy chandeliers and unobtrusive service—without the hassle of downtown traffic. An alfresco patio and a snazzy bar are additional pluses, too. A still-hot sourdough mini loaf arrives at your table as a preamble to an appetizer, like the smooth, herb-spattered lobster bisque. More offbeat fare includes Thai mussels and popcorn shrimp. Crab cakes play big here, even in lunchtime sandwiches, but the crunchy blackened catfish is excellent, too. Other entrées include steak, chicken, and pasta selections, plus plenty of fresh-catch options. Don't run off before checking the dessert tray: The cheesecake or chocolate cake should hit the spot. **Also located at** 900 Water St. SW, Washington, DC, 202-488-8515

P. J. Skidoo's, The American Way   **12/20**

American
9908 Lee Hwy. (Rte. 123), Fairfax 22030
703-591-4516, Fax 703-591-5407
Lunch & Dinner daily, Brunch Sun., $$, Casual

🅰 🅿 🍽 🎋 🦉 🎷 🍸 ↻

Crafted in the tradition of American saloons, this Fairfax restaurant has been promising—and delivering—good times for several decades. It looks as square and solid as a brick barn, and its smoky bar and Tiffany lamps only add a sense of fun. The menu tells the real tale here: big, fat burgers; large entrée salads; and the steak and chicken dishes that have helped make this place popular. We absolutely adore the Mexi burger with its load of beans, jalapeños, and melted cheese but the grilled salmon salad suits less hungry moods. Skidoo's appetizers make ideal bar food: Sip your brew, nibble on the Tex-Mex nachos and watch a game on one of the bar television sets. Don't miss the Sunday brunch.

Planet Wayside   American   13/20

420 W. Colonial Hwy (Hughes St.), Hamilton 22608
540-338-4315, *Lunch & Dinner Wed.-Sat., $, Casual*
No credit cards. P

Planet Wayside is a pleasant surprise. Cooked for and owned by Tim and Suzanne O'Neil, this whimsical little place looks like a ramshackle tool shed, but it's a foodie destination. Looking for all the world like a Berkeley flower child (no chef's garb here), O'Neil cooks a variety of treats. Take the Chili Pluto, a fiery, cheese-drenched, onion-garnished bowl of beans that we loved. From there, move on to the ribs with the best barbecue sauce this side of Tennessee, or maybe the Monte Cristo sandwich with smoked chicken, bacon and Swiss on batter-dipped French bread. Salad greens usually come fresh-picked from the garden in season. For dessert, try the marionberry cobbler, which is luscious, or the Key lime sugar cookie torte. Even the coffee is a surprise: strong, with overtones of cinnamon.

Po Siam Thai Restaurant   Thai   11/20

3807 Mt. Vernon Ave. (Russell Rd.), Alexandria 22305
703-548-3925, Fax 703-548-4683, *Lunch & Dinner daily, $, Casual*

Once upon a time, the crispy duck and the sensational soft-shell crabs made a visit to this restaurant a must. It was also popular with local Thais who loved its many traditional noodle dishes. Now with so many other Thai choices, Po Siam no longer ranks among the best. That said, you'll still find the small dining room crowded with local businesspeople at lunch, and with twenty- and thirtysomething's at dinner. You won't find anything unusual on the menu, except perhaps the country-style noodle soup, packed with thinly sliced beef. This is Thai dining in a pinch, when you don't feel like driving across town for really impressive cuisine. Check the lunch menu for specials, and note that both the standard and the takeout menus are not identical.

Potowmack Landing Restaurant   Seafood   12/20

1 Marina Dr. (George Washington Memorial Pkwy.)
Ronald Reagan National Airport, Alexandria 22314
703-548-0001, Fax 703-548-2296, *Lunch & Dinner daily*
(check on winter hours), Brunch Sun., $$, Business casual

One of the most picturesque restaurants in the Washington area, this place sits on the Potomac River at the side of Reagan National Airport, thus commanding a breathtaking view of the Washington skyline and the river traffic. The view is worth the trip, though the food is staid and predictable. The menu offers a fair smattering of trouble-free seafood dishes from an adequate she-crab soup to crab fritters, a lobster and scallop entrée, and grilled salmon and grouper. You also may want to check out the more robust Potowmack jambalaya. Your best bet may be to drop by for lunch so you can dine al fresco on the wraparound deck and appreciate the view while you enjoy the Potowmack portobello sandwich.

Primi Piatti Ristorante — Italian — 14/20

Fairfax Square
8045 Leesburg Pike (Aline Ave.), Tysons Corner, Vienna 22182
703-893-0300, Fax 703-442-7727
Lunch Mon.-Fri., Dinner Mon.-Sat., $$$, Casual dressy

Why bother to buy a ticket to Italy when you can pamper yourself with authentic Italian food right in the DC area? Dressier and pricier than most local Italian eateries, Primi Piatti has staked out its reputation on quality ingredients that are thoughtfully and well prepared. Always popular here—besides the dense, peasant-style breads and crunchy breadsticks—are the antipasto platters and the robustly sophisticated pastas and lunchtime designer pizzas. This is one restaurant that appeals to yuppie and seniors alike. **Also located at** 2013 I (Eye) St. NW (20th St. NW), Downtown, Washington, DC, 202-223-3600.

Pulcinella Ristorante — Italian — 13/20

6852 Old Dominion Dr. (Rte. 123), McLean 22101
703-893-7777, Fax 703-356-6012, *Lunch & Dinner daily, $$, Casual*

One of McLean's most popular family places, it's not unusual for there to be long lines here. However, once everyone gets seated, service is fast and courteous and everyone seems to enjoy the festive atmosphere, which on Saturday nights, goes on long into the evening. Although people pile in for excellent pizzas such as the pizza bianca with loads of garlic, other dishes are big hits on the menu, too, including pastas with outstanding sauces, and veal, chicken and seafood entrées.

Queen Bee — Vietnamese — 12/20

3181 Wilson Blvd. (Washington Blvd.), Clarendon, Arlington 22201
703-527-3444, Fax 703-525-2750, *Lunch & Dinner daily, $$, Casual*

It probably won't win any design awards, but this utilitarian restaurant near the Clarendon Metro station—one of the earliest Washington area Vietnamese restaurants—is one of the busiest. There's likely to be a wait for a table, but it seems shorter with a bottle of 33 or Amber beer from France. Once you get seated, it's hard to go wrong: crisp spring rolls, chili-flecked green papaya salad, quail roasted to a mahogany brown, chicken in ginger sauce, Hanoi grilled pork and crispy whole fish are some of the stellar choices.

Find the name you are looking for, quickly and easily, in **the index**.

Rhodeside Grill — American — 13/20

1836 Wilson Blvd. (N. Rhodes St.), Arlington 22201
703-243-0145, Fax 703-243-8454
Lunch Mon.-Fri., Dinner nightly, Brunch Sun., $$, Casual

Although both the lunch and the dinner menus feature assorted creative dishes such as grilled tuna club wrap or at dinner, monkfish puttanesca, when you are the Rhodeside Grill, you probably will still get the sense that you are eating in someone's slightly upscale home dining room with Mom doing the cooking. Why? Because you can choose such comfort dishes as a lusty black bean soup striped with sour cream, a basket of warmed and textured sourdough bread and sides of french fries or garlic mashed potatoes. Other elements that add to the casual atmosphere: whimsical oil paintings and a mural. And for dessert? Save up calories for the rich mocha swirl cheesecake.

Rincome Thai Cuisine — Thai — 12/20

Cherry Blossom TraveLodge
3030 Columbia Pike (Highland St.), Arlington 22204
703-979-0144/5, Fax 703-979-0128, *Lunch & Dinner daily, $, Casual*

Although this is an extremely hospitable spot, don't look for dazzle or glamour. The food is plain, though the menu is extensive and you can turn up some treasures. We recommend the crispy duck salad, the fried fish cakes and the roast duck. During mango season, the restaurant serves one of the best sticky rice and mango desserts in town. It's definitely a family place, and it seems always that at least one group is celebrating a birthday or special occasion.

Rio Bravo — Latin American — 12/20

Glen Forest Shopping Center, 5912 Leesburg Pike
(Carlyn Ct.), Baileys Crossroads, Falls Church 22041
703-379-7777, Fax 703-379-7787, *Lunch & Dinner daily, $$, Casual*

This pleasant restaurant puts a pretty face on some macho dishes usually associated with serapes and sombreros. Indeed, although the thrust of the cooking heads south-of-the-boarder, the kitchen staff slips in dishes like baked filet of salmon with sautéed spinach and steamed rainbow trout wrapped with herbs and plantain leaves. There's even a version of surf 'n' turf, with blackened New York steak and grilled shrimp. But the kitchen turns its main energies to such dishes as enchiladas, fajitas and a terrific burrito stuffed with lobster. To start, find ceviche mixto, sopa de tortilla, and pupusas.

Rio Grande Café — Tex-Mex — 13/20

1827 Library St. (Bluemont Way), Reston 20190
703-904-0703, Fax 703-709-5468, *Lunch & Dinner daily, $$, Casual*

A crowd-pleaser, the Rio Grande delights with its lusty fare and lively ambience, yet it's one of the few local places where high decibel levels really do not distract. Weekend nights may be bedlam: At its Reston location, crowds are stacked up in the bar and cluster on the sidewalk, facing probably an hour's wait. But in the end, everyone is served a gratis chips-and-dip combo before the rounds of enchiladas, tacos, sizzling fajitas, chiles rellenos and even broiled quail emerge with baskets of freshly baked tortillas from the kitchen. We recommend the luncheon El Dorado soft tacos and at night select a tortilla soup, carne asada main course and the outstanding chocolate flan for dessert. **Other locations**.

Ristorante Bonaroti   Italian   12/20

Wolf Trap
428 E. Maple Ave. (Beulah Rd.), Vienna 22180
703-281-7550, Fax 703-281-7587
Lunch Mon.-Fri., Dinner Mon.-Sat., $$$, Casual dressy
No credit cards. ☎ P 🍴 Y ▲ ♡

Perhaps when this restaurant opened for business many years ago, it offered suburbanites a glam destination for haute Italian eats. But DC's high-profile Italian destinations overshadow Bonaroti, with its menu that seems more '70s than Y2K. The crowds tell another tale, though, with latecomers being seated even at 9:30 on Saturday nights. It's a full house, and that may account for the rather slow, if well-dressed, waitstaff. Fortunately, the bread with its tapenade spread sustains while you wait. The menu offers few surprises, with its fair share of pastas and chicken dishes, seafood and other red meats. The pasta e fagioli soup lacked the expected garlic and basil punch of versions elsewhere. The abundant bouillabaisse, though, more than made up for the uninspired soup. Lusty with garlic and white wine, this entrée comes with abundant seafood—scallops, mussels, clams, chunks of fish, and shrimp—all cooked to perfection. You may find this more than suffices and a dessert of, say, Italian cheesecake or tiramisu may knock you out—but check out the display before you decline.

Ristorante Geranio   Italian   14/20

722 King St. (Columbus St.), Old Town, Alexandria 22314
703-548-0088, Fax 703-548-0091
Lunch Mon.-Fri., Dinner nightly, $$, Casual dressy
🅰 ☎ P 🍴 Y ▲ ♡

After a period of relative silence from chef Troy Clayton, his fans from his days cooking at the Hyatt Regency in Reston (and previously with famed Jean-Louis Palladin) are undoubtedly happy to find him. He's best when creating at the stove, and his splendid Italian cooking at Geranio shows off his culinary skills. Elements of his lunch menu show up again at dinner, but in general, luncheons are lighter and feature several entrée salads and main-dish pastas. It's easy to be lured right past the appetizers, but you'd miss out on the rather startling broth stocked with five varieties of onions—startling because it looks tame but, unlike French onion soup, packs a peppery punch. Pastas take on a new significance after this light soup, and qualify as perfect light entrées. We recommend the penne with seared fresh tuna, which keeps you just this side of gluttony, thereby saving a tiny bit of room for Clayton's dandy lemon tart. We also recommend the grilled salmon, seared sea scallops, beef ragoût, braised lamb shank, osso buco, venison and Maine lobster with scallops and mussels.

Some establishments change **days of operation** without warning. It is always wise to check in advance.

Ristorante Il Borgo · Italian · 14/20

Marketplace, 1381-A Beverly Rd. (Old Dominion Dr.), McLean 22101
703-893-1400, Fax 703-893-1955
Lunch & Dinner Mon.-Fri., Dinner Sat.-Sun., $$, Casual

This handsome restaurant with its sparkling lights, lush greenery and colorful Italian banners attracts both VIPs and locals alike. All are lured by the elegant Northern and Southern Italian cuisine of chef-owner Vittorio Testa. Our favorites are the classic bean and pasta soup that comes brimming with garlic and fresh Parmesan, the sautéed homemade Italian sausages, peppers and onions on spaghetti and the jumbo shrimp baked with mozzarella cheese. The regal finale is Testa's special "Kiss of Naples," which combines chocolate, zabaglione and ice cream.

Ristorante Il Cigno · Italian · 12/20

1617 Washington Plaza (North Shore Dr.), Lake Ann, Reston 20190
703-471-0121, Fax 703-471-4259
Lunch Mon.-Fri., Dinner Mon.-Sat., $$, Casual dressy

A Reston landmark, Il Cigno has served local clientele for nearly 20 years and flourished under the direction of former owner Silvio Valbussa. Today, new owner Tony Arbid carries on the tradition with many homemade breads, pastas, meat and seafood entrées and desserts. The oven-baked pizzas offer plenty of gastronomic interest. Look for seasonal specials daily. In addition to the good food, the restaurant has one of the prettiest alfresco dining areas around.

Romano's Macaroni Grill · Italian · 12/20

1845 Fountain Dr. (Reston Pkwy.), Reston 20190
703-471-4474, Fax 703-471-8714, *Lunch & Dinner daily, $$, Casual*

Whether you started out in the mood or not, you'll probably have fun at this colorful national chain. Each table has its share of crayons for drawing, and every so often, waiters burst into song. Fun also equals big eats, and giant portions rule. If you want lighter fare, stick to salads or sandwiches for lunch, though pizzas are also popular. Dinners mean heartier beef, veal, and chicken dishes—many are family recipes. If it gets crowded, and it often does on weekend nights, you can sit in the bar area—the atmosphere is not quite as much fun, but then at least you get served. The kitchen offers pretty desserts—check the dessert tray—and the caramel cheesecake is a sure bet. **Also located at** 2641 Prince William Pkwy., Woodbridge, VA, 703-491-3434 and 12169 Fairlakes Promenade, Fairfax, VA, 703-273-6676.

Rosemary's Thyme Bistro · 12/20

Mediterranean/Continental
5762 Union Mill Rd. (Braddock Rd.), Clifton 20124
703-502-1084, Fax 703-502-1017, *Lunch & Dinner daily, $$, Casual*

Rosemary's Thyme Bistro started small some years ago, becoming known for its gutsy pizzas and sandwiches and warm, sunny Mediterranean foods. The restaurant's menu grew and so did the restaurant itself, with two locations now in the metro

149

area. Creole-inspired dishes vie with Mediterranean and some Southwestern ones on a menu that offers something for everyone in the family. You can start with hot or cold appetizers. How about some Mediterranean carpaccio tuna? Then focus on entrée-sized salads, such as the Aegean salad with crawfish tails, or select something meatier, such as one of the grills. We enjoyed the kebab that is served fajita-style on a sizzling platter, with its pairing of ground beef and ground lamb on skewers with a side of grilled vegetables. Made-on-the-premises desserts include crème brûlée, Godiva chocolate cheesecake and profiteroles. **Also located at** 1801 18th St. NW, Washington, DC. 202-332-3200.

Ruth's Chris Steak House — Steakhouse **14/20**

Crystal 3, 2231 Crystal Dr.
(23rd St.), Crystal City, Arlington 22202
703-979-7275, Fax 703-979-3907
Lunch Mon.-Fri., Dinner nightly, $$$, Business casual

The upscale international steakhouse chain that started in New Orleans, Ruth's Chris faces competition in the area, but still makes a splash. The big attraction is the steak, USDA Prime, cut in large portions, cooked to order and dripping in butter, New Orleans-style. But you'll find assorted other dishes, too, such as lobster, veal, chicken and select seafood. There are plenty of vegetable and potato dishes and desserts on the menu, but the appetizers and salads tend to be forgettable. **Other locations.**

Sahara Grill — Lebanese/Middle Eastern **11/20**

8411 Old Courthouse Rd. (Rte. 123), Vienna 22182
703-748-1400, *Breakfast, Lunch & Dinner daily, $, Casual*

It's all flash on the outside. Indoors, find a cafeteria-style restaurant that serves primarily Lebanese foods (chef Hassib Alaoui's worked at Lebanese Taverna). Head to the line and start with appetizers such as hummus and baba ghanouj. The kibbeh hamis is luscious, though the lamb kebab was a little less so. Try the chef's specials, sambosick (meat pie) or fattaer spanigh (spinach pie). The desserts are fresh and tempting, especially the baklava. However, unlike at some other kebab places, the bread is not tandoor-baked.

Saigon House Vietnamese Restaurant — Vietnamese **10/20**

Loehmann's Plaza, 7235 Arlington Blvd. (Rte. 50), Falls Church 22042
703-560-8180, *Lunch & Dinner daily, $$, Casual*

To take the guesswork out of ordering, if you come as part of a couple or larger group, you can order the preset meal. This may be helpful since the menu is long and convoluted, with such unhelpful descriptions as "Shaky Beef" or simply, steamed crabs. The service, too, left much to be desired. It crept along and the order was never fully delivered. If you have the patience, you can wait for such dishes as the soft spring rolls and green papaya salad, the grilled pork with rice noodles and the Vietnamese pancake, the caramel spare ribs and the shrimp sour soup; all are adequate, but nothing more.

Saint Basil Brick Oven Grill   Contemporary 13/20

Tall Oaks Shopping Center
12050-A North Shore Dr. (Wiehle Ave.), Reston 20190
703-742-6466, Fax 703-742-7835
Lunch Mon.-Fri., Dinner Mon.-Sat., $$, Casual

Only a few steps from a supermarket, this mall restaurant surprises with some high-profile, high-end dishes. The menu is Mediterranean- and Italian-inspired. We recommend the classic onion soup with its French bread croutons and melted cheese and the grilled chicken panini with a smear of basil pesto and a layering of pancetta, cheese, chicken and roasted peppers. Wood-fired pizzas (the oven takes up a whole section of the restaurant) are available day and night. Up for something more sophisticated? Dinners also include such pricey dishes as grilled filet mignon and pan-seared sea bass. Listen to the dessert selections if you must, but picking the cheesecake is a wise bet.

Sakoontra Thai Restaurant   Thai   12/20

Price Club Plaza
12300-C Price Club Plaza (West Ox Rd.), Fairfax 22030
703-818-8886, Fax 703-815-2900, *Lunch & Dinner daily, $$, Casual*

Much hyped, this Thai restaurant in a Fairfax shopping center has at least one tourist attraction: a tuk-tuk, the venerable motorized three-wheeler that makes traffic in Bangkok so much fun. Here, it sits serenely by the entrance. We dined here with a friend, and both of us admitted to some puzzlement over a menu that is coded by letters, such as V (a mix of vegetables), M (choice of chicken, beef, or pork), and S (single or combination of seafood—shrimp, scallop, squid, fish)—that does not include some of the items, such as the house duck. We were disappointed with some dishes—a house fried rice with raisins, for example—and were generally pleased with others, such as the duck salad and the steamed dumplings stuffed with pork and shrimp. There's an active bar that serves up loads of somewhat tropical drinks and, because of its pretty décor, Sakoontra has clearly become a popular destination.

Sala Thai   Thai   11/20

2900 N. Tenth St. (Washington Blvd.), Arlington 22201
703-465-2900, Fax 703-465-4406, *Lunch & Dinner daily, $$, Casual*

Preceded by the reputation of its downtown sister restaurant, the new Sala Thai should be the source of some excellent Thai dishes, but alas, that is not the case. The special of soft-shell crabs yielded crabs that were not crispy and lacked assertive flavors; the stir-fried roasted duck was fatty; and the seafood combination was the only dish that saved the day. Filled with a medley of shellfish, it satisfied a Thai craving with right-on flavors. With so many outstanding Thai restaurants in Virginia, we found this one lacking; but the DC location is a pleaser. **Also located at** 2016 P St. NW, Washington, DC, 202-872-1144.

Sam & Harry's   Steakhouse   13/20

8240 Leesburg Pike (Chain Bridge Rd.), Vienna 22182
703-448-0088, Fax 703-448-0104
Lunch Mon.-Fri., Dinner Mon.-Sat., $$$$, Business casual

Most steakhouses look like men's clubs. Sam & Harry's, much awaited in the Northern Virginia 'burbs, looks like a sophisticated California nightclub from the outside. The specialty steak here is a porterhouse, custom-cut for Sam & Harry's by a Chicago packer. If you want something other than steak, alternatives are lamb or veal chops, large lobsters and grilled fish. The wine list is long and impressive. There's also a casual tap room, where you can still get your steaks, but you can also order overstuffed sandwiches and entrée salads. **Also located at** 1200 19th St. NW, Washington, DC, 202-296-4333.

Santa Fe East   Southwestern/New Mexican   13/20

110 S. Pitt St. (King St.), Old Town, Alexandria 22314
703-548-6900, Fax 703-519-0798
Lunch & Dinner daily, Brunch Sun., $$, Casual dressy

Once the "must" destination for anyone in love with New Mexican cooking, the Santa Fe East has become somewhat more obscure since the departure of well-known chef Alison Swope a few years ago. However, just because crowds may have thinned a bit doesn't mean chef Manuel Barahona's cooking doesn't have sparkle. The duck dishes are excellent and we adore such dishes as the green chile stew and the chipotle chicken entrée, a classic of fine almost-hot flavors enveloping a chicken breast. Other good choices are the chile relleno stuffed with goat cheese, the duckling smoked in green tea leaves with a black mole sauce, and the lamb chops smoked in hickory wood. This is food you won't find elsewhere and you will know why once you savor the flavors and textures. Save room for the Mexican chocolate cake. The décor is classic New Mexican, and if you are a Westerner, you'll feel very much at home here.

Sawatdee Thai Restaurant   Thai   12/20

Court House Plaza
2250 Clarendon Blvd. (Courthouse Rd.), Clarendon, Arlington 22201
703-243-8181, Fax 703-527-5858, *Lunch Mon.-Sat., Dinner nightly, $, Casual*

In the middle of downtown Arlington, Sawatdee offers a glitzy take on the Thai theme. Rumor has it that its authentic décor comes straight from Thailand, which immediately puts customers in a Thai mood. The menu presents many of the familiar Thai dishes Westerners have come to love, including lemon grass soup, spring rolls, satay with peanut sauce, and, of course, pad Thai. We recommend the tom yam talay, a seafood soup served over rice noodles—it's hot and filling—and the appetizer garden roll of shrimp and crab meat folded into a soft wrapper. Lunchtimes are particularly crowded.

The Serbian Crown Restaurant   12/20

Russian/French

1141 Walker Rd. (Colvin Run Mill Rd.), Great Falls 22066
703-759-4150, Fax 703-759-6381
Lunch Fri.-Sun., Dinner nightly, $$$, Casual dressy

Gypsy entertainers and an accordionist who resembles an old-time Cossack soldier add a sense of romantic glamour often lacking in suburban eateries. On top of that, The Serbian Crown offers an eclectic array of both Russian and French fare, with a smattering of wild game dishes thrown in for good measure. Given the tenor of the place, it's also not surprising to find listed at least two dozen vodkas, nearly 20 vodka-based drinks, various flavored vodkas and Russian beer. With such a setting, it's no wonder that patrons opt for the heavy, rich dishes better suited to Siberia. Take, for instance, the tender venison cutlets, served with a rich sauce and two poached fruits (good) and green beans (overcooked). The pirozki, tamed sausages wrapped in a flaky pastry and sauced, is a good starter. If you are up to dessert, a server will wheel to you a tiered dessert cart with elegant towering cakes and pastries. Perhaps in the end you may just decide to order shots of vodka and caviar, lean back to soak up the background music and dream of far off lands.

Shamshiry   Persian   12/20

8607 Westwood Center Dr. (Tyco Rd.), Tysons Corner, Vienna 22182
703-448-8883, Fax 703-448-3340, *Lunch & Dinner daily, $$, Casual*

Shamshiry has long been a favorite among local Persians, and its reputation has been built and sustained by its assorted kebabs and rice dishes. In the quiet, mirrored setting you can dine on the shirin polo (sweet rice with sugared orange peel, pistachios, and almonds) and skewers of kubideh (ground beef) or barg (filet mignon) kebabs grilled over a charcoal fire. Usually served over or with rice, many of the meat kebabs also wrap well in the restaurant's bread for a portable sandwich. Enjoy a Persian dessert: rose water-scented noodles and fruit syrup, saffron ice cream, baklava, or a fritter (zulbia-bamieh) with rose water syrup.

Sign of the Whale   American   12/20

Loehmann's Plaza, 7279 Arlington Blvd. (Graham Rd.), Falls Church 22042
703-573-1616, Fax 703-573-5469
Lunch & Dinner daily, Brunch Sun., $$, Casual

This is a neighborhood hangout, and if you drop by in the late afternoon, chances are you'll find a chatty crew at the bar swapping tales with the bartender. Actually, think *Cheers* and you've got the picture. What you should also add to this picture are some of the region's best burgers. If you are not in the mood for one of the innovative Whaleburgers, you can turn your attention to the main menu, where grilled strip steaks, pastas, hefty sandwiches and fried seafood dishes predominate. Our suggestion: Start with the Super Nachos and finish with a Mexican Whaleburger, then add on a wedge of Key lime pie.

Silverado Southwestern 11/20

7052 Columbia Pike (John Marr Dr.), Annandale 22003
703-354-4560, Fax 703-354-8890
Lunch & Dinner daily, $$, Casual

🄰🄿🎪♈🍶♡

Silverado's media hype has put it on the suburban-restaurant map, but the food doesn't always live up to expectations. The crowds do, however, so plan your visit accordingly. The menu draws are the Southwestern and Tex-Mex dishes that have a few interesting twists. We recommend the Tex-Mex egg rolls with avocado dip and the Monterey chicken salad, a good choice for calorie counters. Less inspiring are the house special, the lobster bisque, and the overheated fajitas. Nightly specials—blackened prime rib or soft-shell crab tacos—may prove more satisfying. If you plan on chatting with friends or closing a business deal, the bad acoustics will nix that. Background music and laughter drown out any quiet conversation.

South Austin Grill Tex-Mex 13/20 👨‍🍳

801 King St. (Columbus St.), Old Town, Alexandria 22314
703-684-8969, Fax 703-519-0126
Lunch & Dinner daily, Brunch Sat.-Sun., $$, Casual

🄰🎪♈🍶

Texans know a thing or two about good chili, and chefs at the South Austin Grill have learned the secrets. Their bowls of simmered, shredded beef with ground chiles (anchos and chipotles) are just short of heavenly. It's a rugged dish, with enough fire-breathing potential to stand your hair on end. Fortunately, it comes with four small, warm flour tortillas you can dunk or use for wrapping. The tortillas help tame the flames. Terrific chili is only one of many delights on this funky restaurant's menu: fajitas, enchiladas, burritos, carnitas and quesadillas are all good choices. Check the menu's new seasonal specialties section, too, where you might find lamb chops with pineapple-chipotle glaze. If you need to quench your thirst with all this hot, spicy food, select a cooling tequila drink—there are several interesting margaritas like the signature lime-strawberry one—or a chilled brew. This is the only location called South Austin Grill; others go just by Austin Grill. **Other locations**.

Star Thai Cuisine Thai 12/20

Fair Lakes Shopping Center
13046 Fair Lakes Shopping Ctr. (Fair Lakes Pkwy.), Fairfax 22033
703-222-5452, *Lunch & Dinner daily, $$, Casual*

🄰☎🄿🖥🎪♈🍶

Painted deep blues and orange and lit mostly by tiny sparkly lights at night, this Thai restaurant offers hard-edge décor, a fish mosaic mural, and some trendy and pretty good cooking. This is a well-conceived menu that offers a good sampling of the cuisine. We enjoyed the light and delicate hoi jow appetizers, the larb with hand-minced chicken and the fiery drunken noodles. Tropical drinks are on the menu, too. Clearly popular with locals, this makes a convenient stop-off after a day of exhausting shopping nearby.

Stella's   Contemporary   12/20

1725 Duke St. (Reinekener's Ln.), Alexandria 22314
703-519-1946, Fax 703-519-7610
Lunch & Dinner daily, Brunch Sun., $$, Casual dressy

You'll find flashes of culinary brilliance here, though some-times these are interspersed with less than dazzling food. We have found the portions usually modest. For lunch, you won't go wrong with the crab cake sandwich followed by the blueber-ry crumble in a praline shell for dessert. For dinner, start with a barbecue duck quesadilla or launch directly into entrées: sea bass, yellowfin tuna steak or mango barbecued pork strip. Got a big appetite? Consider the osso buco. Note that the dinner menu changes regularly.

Supee's Kitchen   Thai   11/20

3813 Lee Hwy. (N. Pollard St.), Arlington 22207
703-528-5833, Fax 703-528-7070
Lunch & Dinner daily, $, Casual

Tiny Supee's Kitchen looks like a converted deli/tearoom with its glossy food photos and stands of faux flowers. The Thai tip-off? A Buddhist's altar and a photo of the Thai monarch. Its charm lies with its casual, friendly airs and decent Thai food at affordable prices. Considering the small size of the kitchen, Supee's menu is extensive enough to compete with less modest Thai places, but don't expect surprises. Its basic and familiar dishes are satisfactory and gratify any overwhelming urges for pad Thai or Penang curry in a hurry.

Sushi-Zen Japanese Restaurant   Japanese/Sushi   12/20

Lee Harrison Shopping Center
2457 Harrison St. (Lee Hwy.), Arlington 22207
703-534-6000, *Lunch Mon.-Sat., Dinner nightly, $, Casual*

Sushi is only one part of what the menu offers at this usual-ly crowded spot: We started with a vegetable-shrimp tempura appetizer and gladly accepted the soup and salad. The sushi was roughly cut and not as appealing as we are used to having. Better? A big bowl of pork cutlets over rice.

Tachibana   Japanese/Sushi   14/20

6715 Lowell Ave. (Old Dominion Dr.), McLean 22101
703-847-1771, *Lunch & Dinner daily, $$, Casual*

Moving from Arlington to McLean several years ago has not altered Tachibana's course: The restaurant continues to serve top Japanese fare. It features two sushi bars, which attest to the chefs' skills and the restaurant's food quality. The first choice will always be sushi (sold singly or by assortment). Other choic-es: the big noodle bowls, such as nabeyaki udon or tempura udon, the shabu shabu and the nabemonos. The décor (including a silk kimono mounted on the wall) is cheery.

Tara Thai — Thai — 13/20

United Bank Building, 226 Maple Ave. W (Lawyers Rd.), Vienna 22180
703-255-2467, Fax 703-255-2867, *Lunch & Dinner daily, $, Casual*

A ☎ P 🍴 🍶

Owner Nick Srisawat has ventured where those at many other local Thai restaurants have feared to go. He presents authentic Thai flavors in a flamboyant style. This has made his restaurants magnets for crowds, who return time and again to indulge in honey-roasted duck, green papaya salad, Pattaya noodles and Tara Thai's signature dish, grilled whole rockfish wrapped in banana leaf. A line of refreshing tropical drinks (with or without alcohol) and offbeat tropical sweets, such as the young coconut pie, effectively wrap up a meal at Tara Thai. Also effective: The restaurant's cool aqua colors and deep-sea décor. **Other locations**.

Taste of Saigon — Vietnamese — 11/20

8201 Greensboro Dr. (International Dr.)
Tysons Corner, McLean 22102
703-790-0700, Fax 301-217-5985, *Lunch & Dinner daily, $, Casual*

A ☎ P 🖥 🍴 Y 🍶

This pretty gleaming Vietnamese restaurant in the heart of Tysons is a popular destination for local office workers. They come for the straightforward Vietnamese fare, such as the grilled beef in grape leaves, the Thai-style stuffed chicken wings and the large bowl of noodles with spring rolls and grilled pork. In good weather you can dine outside. Inside, everything sparkles with glass and mirrors. Service is pleasant and quick, which is a feat at crowded lunchtimes. **Also located at** 410 Hungerford Dr., Rockville, MD, 301-424-7222.

Thai Basil — Thai — 14/20 🍳

Chantilly Park
14511-P Lee Jackson Memorial Hwy. (Airline Pkwy.), Chantilly 20151
703-631-8277, Fax 703-631-5283, *Lunch & Dinner daily, $$, Casual*

A P 🍴 🍷

Local Thai cooking teacher and chef around town, Nongkran Daks now has her own place way out in the 'burbs. It's small and pretty, decorated with many of her own artifacts. Here she turns out her smooth curries and peanut-sauced salad khaek, plus a whole range of traditional Thai dishes that don't often appear in local restaurants. Consider the khao tang na tang, an appetizer of ground pork and chopped shrimp with a peanut sauce or the pineapple and shrimp curry with slivers of fresh pineapple. She even offers khao soi, a mild Northern Thai chicken curry served on noodles. Among the more familiar dishes, look for gloriously pudgy tod man and the fried tofu with an exotic apricot dipping sauce. A traditionalist, Daks plays it straight and never falls prey to the labor-saving tricks that destroy good Thai flavors. Incidentally, if there were a pad Thai cookoff among area restaurants, it is our firm belief that Daks would win.

For **Gayot Hot Ten Restaurants in Washington, DC,**
visit: gayot.com

Thai Luang   Thai | 12/20

171 Elden St. (Stuart Rd.), Elden Plaza, Herndon 20170
703-478-2233, Fax 703-478-2234, *Lunch Mon.-Fri., Dinner nightly, $, Casual*

A ☎ P 🍴 Ƴ

One of the pioneers of Thai food in the suburbs long before this cuisine became so trendy, Thai Luang has retained a consistently loyal following, even though its cooks have come and gone. Lunches are popular with local office workers, and dinners beckon the suburban crowd. The décor is understated Thai, with just enough traditional trinkets and portraits of the Thai royal couple to add a certain air of authenticity. The menu has undergone occasional overhauls, but fortunately retains our favorite dish, the soup filled with fresh wide rice noodles and strips of crispy roast duck. We also recommend the duck with sweet basil and the green curry chicken. Ask about the homemade Thai desserts.

Thai Noy Restaurant   Thai | 12/20

Westover Village
5880 N. Washington Blvd. (McKinley St.), Arlington 22205
703-534-7474, Fax 703-534-0196, *Lunch Mon.-Sat., Dinner nightly, $, Casual*

A ☎ P 🖥 🍴 Ƴ ▲

Tucked between a pizza parlor and a Lebanese restaurant, this Thai eatery fits into its ethnic neighborhood just fine. A pretty restaurant with a good selection of dishes, wines, and beers, Thai Noy pleases. It displays some lovely Thai décor, including a Buddhist altar, and these artifacts set the tone for the cuisine. We started with the ubiquitous tod mun (fish cakes). The boneless duck salad with onions, ginger, and cubed pineapple is a spicy sensation. Try the drunken noodles for a luscious and filling main course.

Thai Old Town   Thai | 11/20

300 King St. (S. Washington St.), Old Town, Alexandria 22314
703-684-6503, Fax 703-684-7070, *Lunch & Dinner daily, $, Casual*

A 🍴 Ƴ

Situated on King Street near the waterfront and convenient for tourists and locals alike, this Westernized Thai restaurant hums with activity. At lunchtime especially, you'll likely have to squeeze in for a table in this pretty little place with its splashing fountain and decorative Thai statuary. Its menu is much simpler than the décor and offers few surprises. Nevertheless, the papaya salad is a good appetizer choice as is the mildly spicy grilled beef salad. The red duck curry is not up to par, however, nor is the kway-tiaw nam, a bowl of bland noodle soup that contains many more noodles than broth or seafood. To eliminate menu guesswork at lunchtime, check out the lunch-box specials with spring roll. For dinner, you will find standard Thai offerings.

Thai Pilin   Thai | 11/20

Pike Seven Plaza
8385 Leesburg Pike (Westpark Dr.), Tysons Corner, Vienna 22182
703-556-9191, Fax 703-556-3308, *Lunch & Dinner Mon.-Sat., $, Casual*

A P 🍴

With only minimal ambience and insipid food, Thai Pilin and its sister restaurant Pilin Thai might win the title of the MacDonald's of Thai cooking. The cooking is done so fast in the tiny kitchen that it seems like the cooks sometimes forget essential seasonings and techniques. The cooking is also inconsistent, for at times the red duck curry is delicious; at other times, the duck with basil and the fried tofu is truly forgettable. Nevertheless, the place is popular. There are only a handful of tables and, therefore, Thai Pilin is just as much about carrying out as eating in. **Also located at** 116 Brood St., Falls Church, VA, 703-241-5850.

T.H.A.I. in Shirlington   Thai   12/20

Shirlington Village, 4029 S. 28th St. (Arlington Mill Dr.), Arlington 22206
703-931-3203, Fax 703-931-3205, *Lunch & Dinner daily, $$, Casual dressy*

🅰 ☎ P 🖥 🎎 Y

T.H.A.I. in Shirlington is such an attractive place with its architectural devices and hard-edged colors that you probably will want to come for the setting, if nothing else. And that is apparently part of the owner's concept: To rid patrons of preconceived ideas of Thai décor and Thai cooking. If the design breaks with tradition, so does the menu, filled with dishes with Thai names, but not necessarily with Thai flavors. We've enjoyed the restaurant's roast duck salad and what they called kao soi, which is a Northern Thai specialty, but neither resembles the originals. Presentation, however, is part of the plan, too, and every plate is a staged architectural arrangement that is as pretty as the restaurant.

Thai Square Restaurant   Thai   13/20

Westmont, 3217 Columbia Pike (Glebe Rd.), Arlington 22204
703-685-7040, Fax 703-685-0071, *Lunch & Dinner daily, $, Casual*

🅰 P 🎎 🍶 🥄

This is a small, no-frills restaurant, but the flavors are authentic. We recommend the mussels baked in a clay pot, the tart-sweet green papaya salad, the shredded fish tossed with lime juice, the roasted duck salad with ginger shreds and the crispy pork with Chinese broccoli. If you are stumped about what to order, the cheerful staff is willing to help.

That's Amore   Italian   12/20

150 Branch Rd. (Rte. 123), Vienna 22180
703-281-7777, Fax 703-281-4132
Lunch Mon.-Fri., Dinner nightly, $$, Casual

🅰 ☎ P ♥ 🎎 Y 🥄 ○

Possibly the first Italian restaurant in the DC area to launch the family-size portions plan, this popular eatery embraces the idea that more is more. We applaud such appetizers as the fried mozzarella in carrozza, a luscious and caloric taste of fried and battered Italian bread topped with mozzarella, prosciutto and basil and bathed in marinara and pesto caper cream. That starter plus a salad can make an ample lunch, but then you'd pass up the ultra spicy sausage, peppers, and onions. There's plenty here to appeal to everyone in the family, from pasta dishes to chicken, veal, seafood and steaks. Homemade desserts are good, including tiramisu, cannoli, gelatto, cheesecake, bread pudding and Gelato Paradisio, a dazzling sundae with ice cream and hot fudge. **Other locations**.

Tom Sarris' Orleans House
American   **12/20**

1213 Wilson Blvd. (Lynn St.), Rosslyn 22209
703-524-2929, *Lunch Mon.-Fri., Dinner nightly, $$, Business casual*

🅰🕾🛉🍸▲🗘

For years, this slightly dated restaurant has presented a vastly popular prime rib meal that's helped make it famous. It also sports a somewhat unique look inside and out that vaguely resembles New Orleans. For these reasons alone, you'll find a trip here worthwhile. At lunch, it's a favorite with local business folk who line up for the salad bar and dig into one of the reasonably priced sandwiches and entrées (which even includes the prime rib). Indeed, Tom Sarris' boasts of selling more prime rib than any other restaurant in the country.

Toro Tapas & Grill
Spanish/Tapas   **12/20**

4053 S. 28th St. (S. Quincy St.), Shirlington, Arlington 22206
703-379-0502, Fax 703-379-0915, *Lunch & Dinner daily, $$, Casual*

🅰🅿🖳🛉🍸▲

If you're new to the Spanish tapas concept—little plates of selected dishes, like sampling a mini-meal—then you can satisfy your curiosity and appetite at this eatery. You can order plenty and not worry about overeating, though your bill may add up to more than you'd reckoned. We have enjoyed the gambas al ajillo (roasted shrimp in garlic), the costillitas de cordero (marinated and grilled lamb chops on mashed potatoes), and the puerco a la Mancha (boneless pork steaks with onion in an orange sauce). And if you are hankering for something sweet, the flan is perfectly cooked with its dense yet creamy texture. Thirsty? The sangría is outstanding.

Tortilla Factory
Southwestern   **12/20**

The Pines Center, 648 Elden St. (Monroe St.), Herndon 20170
703-471-1156, Fax 703-318-0390, *Lunch & Dinner daily, $$, Casual*

🅰🅿♥🛉🌜▲

Year after year, locals consistently hold this restaurant in the highest esteem, for it really knows its business: making Southwestern food the old-fashioned way. It should, for once upon a time the Tortilla Factory was really a tortilla factory. Today, as a restaurant it's so popular that management may end up serving gratis chips and dip to the long lines waiting on weekend nights. We return often for the cook's masterful green chili burrito, carne machaca burrito and dark and rich chicken mole. There are plenty of other choices on the menu, too, including the ubiquitous nachos, squash soup with cheese and New Mexico stacked enchiladas. The décor is pleasantly Southwestern, and there may be a piñata or two hanging around. Many of the good sauces and fillings are packaged to sell to-go, too.

Tuscarora Mill
Contemporary   **13/20**   🍸

203 Harrison St. SE (Loudoun St.), Market Station, Leesburg 20175
703-478-1141, Fax 703-771-3987
Lunch & Dinner daily, Brunch Sun., $, Casual dressy

🅰🕾🅿🕴🛉🌜🍸▲🗘

For country chic, it's hard to compete with Leesburg's famed Tuscarora Mill, which occupies a former working mill. Large wooden beams and plank floors, plus a sky-lit dining area, make this a favorite with the local landed gentry—try squeezing into the bar/café area at any mealtime. The restaurant has gone through various chef and kitchen changes in the past, but with executive chef Patrick Dinh in charge, customers can count on outstanding food, from his excellent hamburgers to his upscale veal chop or grilled Argentinian rib-eye steak with jalapeño mashed potatoes. His pork chops are succulent and tender and an appropriate prelude to such gooey desserts as the airy pineapple cheesecake or the ultra-dense triple chocolate torte. An added pleasure: Expect live piano music on Saturday nights.

Union Street Public House   American   12/20

121 S. Union St. (Prince St.), Old Town, Alexandria 22314
703-548-1785, Fax 703-548-0705, *Lunch & Dinner daily, $$, Casual*

With chef Mike Soper overseeing the kitchen, you can be sure that this Old Town favorite will continue its position as a popular "eats and drinks" neighborhood place. Well-known in the metro area, the chef formerly had his own place, Soper's on M, in DC. Here the young and hungry gather from far and wide in a number of dining rooms, though the action focuses around the main barroom with its dark woods. You'll find the ubiquitous TVs tuned to sports and stocks, but the food also draws attention. Many of the dishes have Southern roots, like the Carpetbagger Po' Boy of steak and fried oysters stuffed in a hero roll. The garlic mashed potatoes are a winner. For dessert, who can resist a homemade deep-dish chocolate chip pie. For families, there's a kids' menu with traditional pleasers.

Viet Royale   Vietnamese   12/20

Eden Center, 6795 Wilson Blvd. (Rte. 50), Falls Church 22044
703-533-8388, *Lunch & Dinner daily, $, Casual*

You've arrived a little before the main dinner hour and feel smug that you have a table, while the line out front faces a wait. But business moves briskly here, thanks to very efficient service. That's the only way management can accommodate the crowds who love the casual, ethnic ambience—to say nothing of the authentic flavors—at Eden Center's most popular restaurant. The green papaya salad is refreshing and crispy, really more of an entrée dish. We also recommend the classic hot 'n' sour soup and caramel fish. The restaurant has built a reputation on the traditional "beef seven course" meal, and the noodle dishes are wonderful, too. Looking for inexpensive lunch options? Check out the combination plates.

Village Bistro   American/Italian   12/20

Colonial Village, 1723 Wilson Blvd. (N. Queen St.), Arlington 22209
703-522-0284, *Lunch Mon.-Fri., Dinner nightly, $$, Casual*

The big buzz comes at lunchtime when local media types head here for the superb food and somewhat frenzied ambience. Plan to wait for a table, unless you come way before mealtime or have reservations. The restaurant's American-Italian food is original and interesting. Unusual pasta dishes intrigue the young at heart, but lustier fare comes with the seafood creations: blackened sea bass with potato purée, seared tuna with sesame seeds and lobster ravioli are a few good choices. Plenty of people also love the bistro's lunch sandwiches, some of which come layered on fresh, hot, crusty yet tender French bread. Desserts are very good, especially the berry crème brûlée. Great casual food and a good selection of beers, all at reasonable prices.

The White Tiger   Indian   11/20

146 E. Maple Ave. (Park St.),Vienna 22180
703-242-0500, *Lunch & Dinner daily, $$, Casual dressy*

A ☎ P ♻ ⚡ ⍭ ↻

We have loved the Capitol Hill location so much that when The White Tiger set down roots in the 'burbs, we cheered. But the Virginia restaurant can't compete with its downtown cousin, at least, not yet. What's missing here is what the other location has in spades: skilled service, exquisite tableware, elegant presentation and preparation, and breads you'd drive across town for. We dined here with friends, eager for an Indian experience, starting off with the samosas (here vegetarian) and the papri chaat, enough for one but not enough to share with several. The menu elaborates on the Indian theme with enough offbeat dishes to awaken yearnings, if not taste buds, though the paneer karahi and the dal were sterling renditions. And what about the breads? They are outstanding, especially the Kashmiri naan, a tandoori puffed bread stuffed with nuts. The kulfi is refreshing; the shahi tukra (deep-fried bread with milk), rich and satisfying. **Also located at** 301 Massachusetts Ave. NE, Washington, DC, 202-546-5900.

Yama Japanese Restaurant   Japanese   12/20

328 Maple Ave.W. (Chain Bridge Rd.),Vienna 22180
703-242-7703, *Lunch Mon.-Fri., Dinner nightly, $$, Casual*

A ☎ P ♻

With its aroma of freshly hewn wood, this tiny Japanese eatery specializes in offbeat sushi offerings. Good choices include everything from the classic nigiri sushi wof salmon roe and flounder to such fanciful goods as the crispy salmon skin roll, the holiday roll (with tuna, salmon, avocado, cucumber and scallions) to ther popular spider roll. If you don't get everything you want from the sushi listings, you'll find lots else to enjoy on the main menu, from tonkatsu to soft-shell crab tempura. The only drawbacks are big crowds, long lines and slow service, but that's the price of popularity.

Zeffirelli   Italian   12/20

728 Pine St. (Station St.), Herndon 20170
703-318-7000, *Lunch Mon.-Fri., Dinner nightly, $$$, Business casual*

A ☎ P ♻ ⍭ ▲ ↻

Zeffirelli, Herndon's upscale Italian restaurant, has won fans not so much for its wide-ranging menu but really for the house specialty, a lusty, meaty veal chop cooked to perfection. The lunch menu is basically pastas and a few meatier dishes, which is fine for midday eating. In the evening, the big-gun dishes arrive. There is that veal chop, assorted veal cutlet and veal scaloppine dishes and a grilled beef filet that is an Italian version of pepper steak with Cognac. Often one of the house specials is rack of lamb with garlic and rosemary and it's just about as good as the veal chop. Pastas are prepared in house and are therefore extremely fresh. To start, consider the fried squid, a delicate seafood temptation with cocktail sauce or ask about the soup of the day. Most desserts are pastry-based and ultra rich.

QUICK BITES

AMERICAN

Chicken Out Rotisserie

1443-A Chain Bridge Rd. (Tennyson Dr.), McLean 22101
703-917-8646, Fax 703-917-9116, *Lunch & Dinner daily, $, Casual*

A **P** 🍽 ♥ 🏃

This chicken eatery is a local success story, the kind of "to riches" tale that makes an entrepreneur out of many. From a single location in Maryland, the owners took their simple idea—cook wholesome food from scratch and charge reasonable prices—and spun it into a local empire. Locations are squeaky clean, service is prompt and courteous, and the food, generally as good as (or maybe better than) homemade. Choose this chain for an all-out chicken or turkey feast, or at least a sandwich or salad. We recommend the half-chicken meal with mashed potatoes and fresh vegetables and an apple crisp for dessert. Everything is available for takeout. **Other locations.**

Flatbreads Food Shop

315 Madison St. (N. Royal St.), Old Town, Alexandria 22314
703-836-9165, Fax 703-836-3751, *Lunch Mon.-Sat., $, Casual*

A **P**

This off-the-beaten-path sandwich shop reflects the bohemian nature of the art school that is its neighbor. In this very dressed-down atmosphere, high-end sandwiches come dressed with special homemade marinades, house cilantro spreads, mole sauces and other exotica. The menu of idiosyncratic offerings includes chili, German potato salad and big Cubana and muffuletta sandwiches. Follow up with delicious baked goods for dessert and chase with some delicious tea.

Fuddruckers

1030 Elden St. (Herndon Pkwy.), Herndon 20170
703-318-9438, Fax 703-318-6637, *Lunch & Dinner daily, $, Casual*

A **P** 🏃

Fuddruckers' corporate motto says simply that they make the world's best hamburgers. And if you've ever had a Fuddruckers' burger, then you've just tasted burger nirvana. Tender, juicy, and flavorful, the burgers come in several sizes (the latest: one pounders) and are the main reason to eat here. Adding fries, onion rings and a milk shake only make the experience more heavenly. The menu has evolved over the years and chicken and salads are also included on the simple menu, plus hot dogs and special brews. You can stack your meal—burger or otherwise—with heaps of condiments and greens from the fixings bar and squirt everything with melted cheese. End your meal with a brownie or giant cookie. **Other locations.**

We're always interested to hear about **your discoveries and to receive your comments on ours.** Please let us know what you liked or disliked; e-mail us at gayots@aol.com.

Hard Times Café

Super K-Mart Centre, 428 Elden St. (Van Buren St.), Herndon 20170
703-318-8941, Fax 703-318-8942, *Lunch & Dinner daily, $, Casual*

A P 🍴 ♨ ♦

One of the first major chili houses in the area, Hard Times still excels at what it does best: making power-packed chili in three styles—Texas, Cincinnati and vegetarian. In each category there are more choices to for you to make: with spaghetti, with beans, with cheese and/or with onions. Our favorite is the tried-and-true Texas chili with coarse-ground meat, served with beans and topped with cheese and onions. Non-chili dishes include sandwiches and salads, but why bother? Responding to America's love for the chili bowl, each café sells pints, quarts and gallons of chili to-go, plus its sweet cornbread. You can also find Hard Times T-shirts, hot sauces and spice mixes. At this location, you can play pool. **Other locations.**

Johnny Rockets

Pentagon City Mall
1100 S. Hayes St. (Army Navy Dr.), Arlington 22202
703-415-3510, *Lunch & Dinner daily, $, Casual*

A P 🍴

If you could turn the clock back a few decades, you'd be eating at a place like Johnny Rockets. You'd listen to the jukebox, eat underdone fries and overdone burgers and sip Cokes or milk shakes. And that's just what today's twenty- and thirtysomethings are doing. This is really a glorified soda fountain, offering a big dose of nostalgia plus casual eats for every generation. You'll find more than just burgers: club sandwiches, BLTs, hot dogs, chili dogs and grilled cheese sandwiches are also on the menu. Service may be disjointed and slow; on the other hand, the place is not about haute cuisine. A good destination for a slow trip down memory lane. **Also located at Union Station Food Court, 50 Massachusetts Ave. NW, Washington, DC, 202-289-6969; and 3131 M St. NW, Washington, DC, 202-333-7994.**

Lake Anne Coffee House

Washington Plaza
1612-1614 Washington Plaza (Baron Cameron Ave.), Reston 20190
703-481-9766, *Breakfast, Lunch & Dinner daily, $, Casual*

A P 🔲 📷 ♥ 🍴 ⚲

Under new management, this lakeside coffeehouse has al fresco seating and a glorious lake and plaza view. It's an ideal spot for breakfast or lunch due to the view and good pastries and sandwiches. Want to rent a boat for the lake? Ask inside.

Luna Park Grille

5866 Washington Blvd. (McKinley St.), Westover, Arlington 22205
703-237-5862, *Lunch & Dinner daily, Brunch Sun., $, Casual*

A P 🍴 ⚲ Y

Like any neighborhood hangout, the Grille has a bunch of regulars who seem to know each other well. You'll probably find a group clustered at the bar, sipping brews and feasting on big burgers while they chat or watch the big-screen TV. We recommend a bowl of chili with kaiser roll and maybe a slice of chocolate cake. Other good choices include jalapeño poppers as starters and then barbecue beef ribs or a steak platter. The place is smoky, friendly and cooled by ceiling fans.

Philadelphia Mike's

Plaza America Shopping Center
11652 Plaza America Way (Sunset Hills Rd.), Reston 20190
703-481-8847, Fax 703-481-5033, *Lunch & Dinner daily, $, Casual*

[A][P][symbols]

Talk about crowds! Lunchtime is a madhouse, with lines snaking out the door. Local office workers have tapped into a good thing: cheap eats, American-style, and have made the Philly steak and cheesesteak sandwiches the top sellers here. A Philadelphia Mike's Philly steak sandwich in case you've never been lucky enough to taste one is meat cooked on a hot grill with chopped mushrooms, onions and green peppers (cheese, too, if you want it) and scooped into a hoagie loaf (three sizes available). Burgers, house special sandwiches (clubs, Reubens, and beef barbecue), hot dogs and overstuffed deli sandwiches fill out the menu. Gooey brownies make an indulgent dessert. **Other locations.**

Ramparts

1700 Fern St. (Quaker Ln.), Alexandria 22302
703-998-6616, Fax 703-998-2942, *Lunch & Dinner daily, $, Casual*

[A][P][symbols]

Ramparts is a sports bar for the whole family. What started as a basic neighborhood watering hole has expanded to include a smoking pub and a connecting California-style smoke-free restaurant. If you want to join a group of cheering sports fans at the bar or in the pub, your less enthusiastic friends can dine in comfort just through a doorway. Burgers and lots of other choices highlight the menu.

The Vienna Inn

120 E. Maple Ave. (Mill St.), Vienna 22180
703-938-9548, *Breakfast & Lunch daily, Dinner Mon.-Sat., $, Casual*

[A][P][symbols]

Popular for its cozy, all-American atmosphere—smoky and shirt-sleeves casual—this pub makes it a family affair. For breakfast, the menu hits the basics with egg dishes, like steak and eggs and country ham and eggs. Lunches and dinners are pub-style fare, although the kitchen has adapted to modern tastes with chicken fajitas and blackened tuna sandwiches. But this is a place known for its outstanding chili dog and that's more representative of the overall menu. When you're ready to leave, you can buy a keg of beer to go.

Wrap Works

1820 Discovery St. (Reston Pkwy.), Town Center, Reston 20190
703-318-5200, Fax 703-318-5062, *Lunch & Dinner daily, $, Casual*

[A][P][symbols]

These little sandwich shops show how creative cooks can turn bread and filling into magic. Wraps have become something of a cliché, but not when you bite into something like the Coat & Thai chicken (spicy peanut chicken with fresh spinach plus extras) in a red chile-flavored tortilla or Kung Pao-Wow chicken in a sesame wheat tortilla. You can also create your own wrap from a selection of ingredients. Another good bet: the silken, chilly smoothies. **Other locations.**

BAKERIES/CAFÉS

Alexandria Pastry Shop & Café

Bradlee Shopping Center
3690-H & I King St. (Quaker Ln.), Alexandria 22302
703-578-4144, *Breakfast, Lunch & Dinner daily, $, Casual*
A P

Location, location, location—definitely a plus for this pastry shop/café. This neighborhood was in desperate need of a place to go for a good sandwich. Unfortunately, this café often disappoints. The sandwiches are small and dry, the service is painfully slow and the bread is ordinary. The bakery side of the shop is a different story and does a brisk business. Fresh ingredients and the best Belgian and French chocolates are used.

Best Buns Bread Co.

4010 S. 28th St. (Quincy St.), Village of Shirlington, Arlington 22206
703-578-1500, *Breakfast, Lunch & Dinner daily, $, Casual*
A P

Best Buns is a delicious meeting place, whether you like boules, focaccia, brioche, ciabatta, sweet baguettes, sourdough, bread with dill and potato, raisin bread, scones or cakes. The open bakery is welcoming, and fresh coffee is available to accompany a slice of your choice with a schmear of goat cheese, Brie or sun-dried tomato spread. The only disappointment is the limited selection of prepared luncheon foods. It's easy to imagine a variety of delicious sandwiches on such great breads and buns, but there are only a few.

Bread & Chocolate

611 King St. (Washington St.), Old Town, Alexandria 22314
703-548-0992, *Breakfast, Lunch & Dinner daily, $, Casual*
A P ⛄

The idea of combining a wedge of freshly baked, buttered and cinnamon-sprinkled bread with a mug of hot chocolate probably is enough to tempt even the most stubborn dieter. Those are the kind of combinations available at Bread & Chocolate. Consider the special morning eye-opener, the french toast, which has chocolate added to the batter mix. You'll find plenty more chocolate options—try the chocolate cake—but you can also sample such savory dishes as a chicken, mozzarella and pasta salad, French onion soup and Hungarian goulash in cup or bowl. This is a comfort-food mecca. **Other locations.**

Cenan's Bakery

122 Branch Rd. SE (Maple Ave.), Vienna 22180
703-242-0070, *Breakfast, Lunch & Dinner daily, $, Casual*
A P ⛁ ⛄

Cenan offers a full line of breads, muffins, cakes, scones, brioche, bagels and luscious, crunchy cinnamon swirls, plus some interesting breads like garlic-Parmesan, jalapeño-cheddar, walnut sourdough and potato dill. This place is popular, too, for designer sandwiches. Salads and potent coffees round out the menu. Freshness and top ingredients are hallmarks here. Also see review in *Gourmet Shops & Markets/Bakeries.*

Corner Bakery

1790 International Dr. (Chain Bridge Rd.), McLean 22102
703-821-4224, *Breakfast, Lunch & Dinner daily*, $, *Casual*

A P 🏃

It seems no matter how early we get to Corner Bakery, the big, fat, squishy cinnamon rolls are gone. Fortunately, there is a lot more on the menu. Start with breakfast: coffee, fruits, and a bowl of granola, bagels, muffins, and yogurt. Later, the kitchen is turning out heartier goods: ample bowls of soups, sandwiches, pizzas and salads, to eat in or takeout. The sweets still beckon, but now they're transformed into brownies, cookies and cakes. Fresh baked loaves of bread are also a staple here. **Other locations.**

Firehook Bakery & Coffee House

105 S. Union St. (King St.), Old Town, Alexandria 22314
703-519-8021, *Breakfast, Lunch & Dinner daily*, $, *Casual*

A 🏃

Stunningly successful, these bakeries have grown from one to many locations, each with its share of pastries, pies, tarts, breads and casual sandwiches to eat in or takeout. Many folks drop in for morning coffee and a sweet roll, but sandwiches are just as much of a lure. An overstuffed tuna salad sandwich on one of the designer breads, hot coffee and a pastry make for a great midday meal. **Other locations.**

Heidelberg Bakery

2150 N. Culpeper St. (Lee Hwy.), Arlington 22207
703-527-8394, *Breakfast & Lunch daily, Dinner Mon.-Sat.*, $, *Casual*

A P 🏃

Renowned for its hearty whole-grain and designer breads that are baked on the premises each day, plus its range of fine European pastries, cookies and desserts, this bakery is a favorite for discerning party hosts who want to serve an exquisite dessert. It's also a favorite drop-in spot for breakfast goodies, especially the strudels, and for coffee breaks during the day. Lunchtime sandwiches include such classics as tuna melt and Reubens. Also see review in *Gourmet Shops & Markets/Bakeries*.

Krispy Kreme Doughnuts

6328 Richmond Hwy.
(Fairview Dr.), South of Alexandria on Rte. 1, Alexandria 22306
703-768-0300, *Open 24 hours*, $, *Casual*

A P

A legend long before it was immortalized on film in *Primary Colors*, Krispy Kreme has a presence in the metro area. A visit here is worth a detour. The doughnuts, available in many different flavors and varieties, are sweetly squishy and delicious, a caloric delight from the chocolate-iced custard ones to the glazed blueberry, our favorite.

We're always interested to hear about **your discoveries and to receive your comments on ours.** Please let us know what you liked or disliked; e-mail us at gayots@aol.com.

Panera Bakery & Café

Hechinger Commons
3201 Duke St. (Quaker Ln.), Alexandria 22314
703-751-1800, *Breakfast, Lunch & Dinner daily, $, Casual*

A P ♥

This large national chain straddles the fence by thinking locally and mobilizing nationally. The store motto dwells on the notion that the European neighborhood bakery is alive and well, but the Web site identifies Panera locations across the country. The ersatz Tuscana-Americana interior is pleasant—it's a good place to have lunch with your grandmother. There's plenty of flexibility and variety in the combinations of half sandwiches, half salads and a bowl of soup. Unfortunately, our meals haven't lived up to homemade: The soups were salty and the bread a bit doughy. **Other locations.**

Upper Crust Bakery

4 N. Pendleton St. (Main St.), Middleburg 20118
540-687-5666, *Breakfast & Lunch Wed.-Sun., $, Casual*

A P 🍴 🛒 🎂

Stroll up to the wooden front porch and find it crowded with folks enjoying a casual country lunch of sandwiches and iced tea. It's a nice environment and the food is good, too. The baked goods are fresh and delicious. For breakfast you'll find croissant sandwiches and eggs; for lunch, chicken, ham, egg and tuna salad sandwiches, as well as roast beef, turkey and country ham on croissant or homemade breads and rolls.

BARBECUE

Barbeque Country Jamboree

Super K-Mart Centre, 470 Elden St. (Jonquil Ln.), Herndon 20170
703-437-7621, Fax 703-437-1461, *Lunch & Dinner daily, $, Casual*

A P 🎂

When a craving for ribs strikes, we often turn to this long-time chain. We can stand outside and smell its hickory smoke trailing on the breeze, and that's enough to whet anyone's appetite. You'll find sandwiches of pulled pork or beef and platters of sausages and cut-up chickens, but why fool with perfection? Ribs come in generous, meaty portions and the juicy half slab is more than enough for two people or two meals—if they last that long. Add on sides like vinegary greens and sweet-spicy barbecue beans. The décor is low-key and not at all glamorous, but then you probably will be too busy enjoying the ribs to notice. **Other locations.**

Ben's Whole Hog Barbecue

7422 Old Centreville Rd. (Yorkshire Ln.), Manassas 20111
703-331-5980, Fax 703-331-2142, *Lunch & Dinner daily, $, Casual*

A P 🎂

In this red-roofed log cabin, Ben Mooris smokes meats slowly in a brick oven, using hickory and sometimes applewood or wild cherry to impart a delicate flavor. Gnaw on tender ribs or pulled pork as is, or slather on Ben's own blend of barbecue sauce, sweet with apple cider. Sides are yummy: sweet potato soufflé (goes well with the smoked turkey), baked beans with bits of bacon and onion and a delicious moist cornbread.

Bo Dean's Pit B.B.Q.

14303-B Sullyfield Cir. (Rte. 50), Chantilly 20151
703-968-7775, Fax 703-968-7263
Lunch Mon.-Sat., Dinner Thurs.-Sat., $, Casual

Often crowded at lunch with local office workers, Bo Dean's deserves its fan club: The ribs are terrific, with a crisp-charred exterior that seals the meat juices to the bones. There's plenty else to whet the appetite, from the feisty black bean and sausage soup to the steamed shrimp and fried fillet of fish. But we always return for the ribs, to enjoy the full, smoky flavor. Sauces come in varying degrees of heat, so pick your poison. The décor might be called "good ol' boy-style." It stars a mounted deer's head.

Bubba's Bar-B-Q

Merri Falls Plaza, 7810-F Lee Hwy. (Hyson Ln.), Falls Church 22042
703-560-8570, Fax 703-560-8572, *Lunch & Dinner Mon.-Sat., $, Casual*

Pigs are glorified in pictures and collectibles. Whether this puts one in the mood to eat pork or simply say, "Oh, isn't that cute" we're not sure. But the pulled pork sandwich is mighty tasty, a jumbo meal loaded with smoky flavor. Ribs come with a good sauce, but could be more meaty. Sides include coleslaw, barbecued beans and green beans, which tend to be overcooked. Also on the menu are smoked chicken, brisket of beef, burgers and chili. Lots of people drop by at lunch to pig out, so finding a seat may be difficult. Planning a party? You can buy the hickory-smoked meats by the pound.

Crisp & Juicy

Lee Heights Shopping Center
4540 Lee Hwy. (Woodrow St.), Arlington 22207
703-243-4222, *Lunch & Dinner daily, $, Casual*

The food here is pollo a la brasa, or charbroiled chicken. It's a Latino cooking method that's caught on in a big way here, but these eateries offer more than delicious and crispy chickens: The menu includes Argentinean steaks and sausages in sandwiches, and even trendy Gruyère chicken breast sandwiches. But those in the know will stick to the basics: cut-up chickens sold solo or a chicken platter with two sides. We love the fried yuca and plantains, the most traditional combos with Latino chicken. You can buy and eat plenty here, all for about $10. Don't come for the ambience or décor—there isn't any. **Also located at** 913 W. Broad St., Falls Church, VA, 703-241-9091; and 1331-G Rockville Pike, Rockville, 301-251-8833.

Dixie Bones

Woodbridge Center Plaza
13440 Occoquan Rd. (Rte. 1), Woodbridge 22191
703-492-2205, Fax 703-492-6535, *Lunch & Dinner daily, $, Casual*

One of the contenders for best barbecue in the DC area, Dixie Bones draws customers from far and wide. The menu includes pork, beef and catfish sandwiches and platters of pork, chicken, beef, catfish and rib racks with assorted sides. We recommend the ribs with a side of greens and Muddy

Spuds (a baked potato that's been chopped into small pieces and seasoned with barbecue sauce). Owner Nelson Head proudly asserts that his meat is hickory-smoked over logs for 12 to 14 hours. The cooks are busy, because they also make all the pies and concoct their own barbecue sauce that runs to mild rather than hot.. Save room for pie. Décor? Patriotic and all things pig.

Dixie Pig

1225 Powhatan St. (Bashford Ln.), Old Town, Alexandria 22314
703-836-0605, *Breakfast, Lunch & Dinner Tues.-Sat., $, Casual*
A P 🍴

Also known as Miss Dixie Pig, this quirky little eatery in historic Old Town features barbecue and some rather unusual non-barbecue dishes, including Belgian waffles, Texas french toast and eggs Benedict. If you're hankering for some North Carolina-style ribs (wet only), you'll find them in full and half racks later in the day. The kitchen also dishes out pulled or chopped pork, a Reuben steak sandwich, grilled shrimp and a smoked ham quesadilla. Prices are low and the food is good, two reasons why this Miss Piggy has been around for so many years.

El Pollo Rey

3610 Columbia Pike (Glebe Rd.), Arlington 22204
703-486-1200, Fax 703-486-3007, *Lunch & Dinner daily, $, Casual*
No credit cards. P 🍴

Does El Pollo Rey (translated as "The Chicken King") rule? It claims to be the best chicken place around and definitely is a contender. Besides chicken, you can pick up grilled steak with fries, several vegetarian dishes, Salvadoran favorites including pupusas and fried yuca, and hearty breakfast fare. If you want to be efficient while you eat, do your washing at the laundromat next door.

El Pollo Rico

2917 N. Washington Blvd. (Tenth St.), Arlington 22201
703-522-3220, Fax 703-522-3282, *Lunch & Dinner daily, $, Casual*
No credit cards. P 🍴

Don't be surprised if you're the 40th person in line—and don't give up and leave. The chicken here is worth the wait, and the line moves fast. You'll have just enough time to marvel at the enormous rotisserie grills filled with chickens, sacks of charcoal for cooking and mounds of potatoes ready for the fryer. The service is like a chicken conveyor belt, with kitchen staff roasting, chopping, and filling plates as fast as they can. The menu offers chicken halved, quartered, or whole, so your choices are simple: What size and which drinks? You can eat in or take away, but the sizzle and aromas are so overpowering you'll probably decide to grab a table and feast. It's no-frills eating with a decided Latino beat. The Wheaton location is much more subdued. **Also located at** 2541 Ennalls Ave., Wheaton, MD, 301-942-4419.

Hog's Breath

Glyndon Shopping Center, 153 Glyndon St. SE (Rte. 123), Vienna 22180
703-281-7487, Fax 703-281-7599, *Lunch & Dinner Mon.-Sat., $, Casual*
A P 🍴

Owner-cook Johnny Crone does barbecue right: He smears a secret-formula dry rub on everything and slow-smokes meats for hours over a mix of hickory and oak. Meats, such as the North Carolina ribs and Texas beef brisket, are imbued with a heavenly aroma and the flavor is outstanding. When trying the house sauces, remember that hot here is really hot. There are no desserts, but who has room?

Memphis Bar-B-Q

Ballston Commons
4238 Wilson Blvd. (Glebe Rd.), Ballston, Arlington 22203
703-875-9883, Fax 703-875-2283, *Lunch & Dinner daily, $, Casual*

A **P** 🍴 **Y**

You can choose wet or dry ribs, and the dry ribs are nicely seasoned. On our visits, though, the ribs were not consistently meaty. Good sides are the seasoned fries and barbecued beans. You'll also find barbecued pizzas, burritos, chicken and beef. If you like your calories from chocolate, hold out for the Tennessee Mudd, made of Oreo cookies and chocolate pudding. The décor is meant to conjure up images of Elvis in his heyday as well as a Southern country store. **Also located at** 13067 Lee Jackson Hwy., Fairfax, VA, 703-449-0500; and 11804 Baron Cameron Dr., Reston, VA, 703-435-5116.

Old Hickory Grille

Loehmann's Plaza
7263 Arlington Blvd. (Graham Rd.), Falls Church 22042
703-207-8650, Fax 703-207-9140, *Lunch & Dinner daily, $, Casual*

A **P** 🍴 **Y**

The Falls Church location of Old Hickory is quieter than its sister restaurant in Burtonsville, MD, but it offers the same menu and a full bar with lots of interesting brews. The slightly funky Southern and Tex-Mex formula really works. You may find the smothered chicken poblano with fries or grits mighty good, but we swear by the ribs—try the monster rack. For a change of pace, combine the ribs with some grilled chicken. Don't skip desserts, especially the custard-style banana-chocolate bread pudding. **Also located at** 15420 Old Columbia Pike, Burtonsville, MD, 301-421-0204.

Red Hot & Blue

4150 Chain Bridge Rd. (Judicial Dr.), Fairfax 22030
703-218-6989, Fax 703-218-6994, *Lunch & Dinner daily, $, Casual*

A **P** 🍷 🍴 ▲

When this barbecue group opened years ago, good barbecue— smoky, juicy, and prepared by pros—was hard to come by. Thus this group of restaurants became an instant hit and a ribs meal from here was almost worth its weight in gold. Times change, and as others brought the barbecue theme to the area, RH&B has suffered and several of its outlets have closed, a loss to its many fans. Those fans appreciate the ribs offered wet or dry. We love the intense heat of the dry-rubbed ribs with a side of beans, and then call it a day with a serving of banana pudding. **Other locations.**

Rockland's Barbeque & Grilling Company

4000 Fairfax Dr. (N. Quincy St.), Ballston, Arlington 22203
703-528-9663, Fax 703-528-9732, *Lunch & Dinner daily, $, Casual*

A **P** 🍷 🍴 🍖

This second location of Rockland's has become as popular for its pool tables as for its crunchy ribs. The menu is uncomplicated, and basically offers the smoky ribs in whole, half or quarter slabs and several interesting sides. The quarter slab of ribs with Texas corn pudding is an excellent meal, but for a change of pace, you may prefer chicken, fish or vegetables grilled to order. There aren't many desserts—but there are plenty of bottled hot sauces you can purchase. **Also located at** 2418 Wisconsin Ave. NW, Washington, DC, 202-333-2558.

Three Pigs Barbecue

Langley Shopping Center
1394 Chain Bridge Rd. (Old Dominion Dr.), McLean 22101
703-356-1700, Fax 703-356-5777, *Lunch & Dinner daily, $, Casual*
No credit cards. P ⊟ ⛽

With its dancing pig motif, this eatery has offered up a special East Carolina-style barbecue for years, with an emphasis on baby-back ribs and barbecued chicken. Since it is budget-priced, Three Pigs has a devoted following, who drop in for minced pork or beef sandwiches, a slab of baby-back ribs, or—in cold weather—a hearty cup or bowl of stew.

BREWPUBS

Capitol City Brewing Co.

2700 S. Quincy St. (28th St.), Shirlington, Arlington 22306
703-578-3888, Fax 703-820-7320, *Lunch & Dinner daily, $, Casual*
A P ⊟ ⛽ Y

Billing itself as "The first brew pub in the nation's capital since Prohibition," Capitol City Brewing Co. is a welcoming place. It's large and spacious, with room for diners who don't want to watch the sports channels that are always on at the central bar. As soon as you sit down at one of the roomy booths, freshly made, warm, salted pretzels are brought to the table. The menu is varied: Bratwurst, crab cakes, fish 'n' chips and homemade meatloaf are listed right next to each other. The portions are large, well presented, and give good value. The only surprise is that you'd expect such a place would have a burger to rave about, but sorry to say, that's not the case. The price range allows you to save cash, yet eat well on large sandwiches; otherwise, splurge on heftier meals and call it dinner. **Also located at** 2 Massachusetts Ave. NW, Washington, DC, 202-842-2337; and 1100 New York Ave., Washington, DC, 202-628-2222.

The Old Brogue, an Irish Pub

Village Centre
760-C Walker Rd. (Georgetown Pike), Great Falls 22066
703-759-3309, Fax 703-759-7874
Lunch & Dinner daily, Brunch Sun., $, Casual
A P ⊟ ⛽ ⊠ ⚗ Y ▲ ⬡

You don't need to travel to Ireland to wear a little o' the green. Just come to The Old Brogue, a suburban watering hole that has been treating its customers to jolly drinking fests and hearty pub-style food for years. Even though its shining hour comes on St. Paddy's Day, the Old Brogue seems like a perpetual party. Best culinary bets include big, juicy burgers with fries, crab-cake sandwiches (or entrées, depending on the time of day), and some of the house Irish specialties at night. Why not enjoy a Guinness beef pie with some stout and dance some Irish jigs? It's a casual place, with the requisite smoky atmosphere.

171

Sweetwater Tavern

3066 Gatehouse Plaza (Rte. 50), Merrifield, Falls Church 22042
703-645-8100, Fax 703-645-8108, *Lunch & Dinner daily, $$, Casual*

Despite the faux Western décor mimicking a frontier barroom, this restaurant serves anything but rustic, frontier foods: We love the "big salads," but most people probably favor the very big entrées, starring pork chops, filet mignon, rib-eye steaks and assorted seafood dishes, served with the kitchen's luscious basil redskin mashed potatoes or other sides of your choice. The cook also whips up a treacherously delicious white chocolate cheesecake that puts other desserts to shame. One of the notable draws of this restaurant is its microbrews prepared on site in the vast copper tanks. These provide some of the freshest, liveliest beers around—and consequently, one of the liveliest bar scenes. **Also located at** 14250 Sweetwater Lane, Centreville, VA, 703-449-1100.

COFFEE SHOPS & DINERS

Bob & Edith's Diner

2310 Columbia Pike (S. Wayne St.), Arlington 22204
703-920-6103, *Open 24 hours, $, Casual*
No credit cards. P

For the past three decades, this unadorned diner has served basic, plain food, calories and all, in the American way: big portions. Unlike many of its modern counterparts, this is the real McCoy with no contemporary frills. It's also one of the best bargain-eats places in town: You can enjoy a full dinner of, say, four pieces of fried chicken with mashed potatoes, gravy and veggies plus a beverage for less than you might pay for a fancy-restaurant appetizer elsewhere. The staff knows many customers by name. Breakfasts of eggs with steak, corned beef hash or pork chops, or possibly a pecan waffle, can start or finish your day. Otherwise, find hefty meat and seafood entrées, sandwiches, subs and fresh baked goods. The chocolate meringue pie is mighty tempting.

Four Seasons

557 S. Van Dorn St. (S. Pickett St.), Van Dorn Station, Alexandria 22304
703-823-9767, *Breakfast, Lunch & Dinner daily, $, Casual*

This Greek-American diner has "authentic" written all over it. The signature dish is an outstanding Greek salad. Also good are the Mediterranean fish dinner, moussaka and stew. American dishes include turkey, chicken and roast platters, sandwiches, soups and salads.

Metro 29 Diner

4711 Lee Hwy. (Glebe Rd.), Arlington 22207
703-528-2464, *Breakfast, Lunch & Dinner daily, $, Casual*

Serving a cross-section of suburbia, this gleaming-metal diner sticks to diner tradition with hearty budget meals. Patrons can settle into a comfy booth or perch at the counter for an eating marathon. Start with french toast and Belgian waffles (the latter with sausages, Canadian bacon or two scoops of ice cream), muffins and omelets, or pancakes with all the trimmings. For mid- to late-day savories, count on finding over-stuffed sandwiches (our favorite: the Reuben deluxe with gobs of melted cheese and sauerkraut). Also try the baked Virginia ham, sirloin steak, Italian specialties and entrée-sized salads. Stick around for dessert, if you want a towering slice of home-made pie, cake, diet-busting pastry, gooey banana royale or a comforting, calorie-dense sundae. This is a bit of delicious, homey Americana.

Mike's Diner & Lounge

8401 Digges Rd. (Rte. 234), Manassas 20110
703-361-5248, *Open 24 hours, $, Casual*
🅰 P ♥ 🍴 🐮 ♈

Keeping it simple, Mike's offers a wood-and-brick ranch house setting rather than the more traditional gleaming metal shed of most diners. But underneath its rustic exterior lurks a true, old-fashioned diner with homemade eats and big, comfy booths, plus waitstaff who treat you like family. In keeping with its basic American menu, cooks whip up creamed chipped beef and pancakes for breakfast; pizzas, soups, salads and sandwiches for midday; and hearty dinner entrées like meatloaf, turkey and dressing and baked fish. Desserts, of course, are rich and worth saving room for.

Payne's

13846 Lee Hwy. (Rte. 28), Centreville 20120
703-830-8935, *Breakfast daily, Lunch Mon.-Fri., Dinner Fri., $, Casual*
No credit cards. P 🍴

A real Virginia tradition, Payne's isn't exactly a diner, but it fits into the category. Serving for decades as a pit-stop for truck drivers hauling into DC from rural Virginia, Payne's basic American home-cooking will make you feel as though you've dropped by Mom's. The place even has squeaky front doors. Cook-owner Abdo serves breakfast—grits, home-fries, hot cakes, chipped beef or sausage gravy—and adds plain but hearty fare for lunch and dinner. Sit at the lunch counter or slip into a booth for a filling meal.

Silver Diner

Fair Oaks Mall, 12250 Fair Lakes Pkwy. (West Ox Rd.), Fairfax 22033
703-359-5941, *Breakfast, Lunch & Dinner daily, $, Casual*
🅰 P ♥ 🍴 🐮

Reminiscent of an earlier America, the Silver Diner offers individual jukeboxes, '50s music and down-home cooking at affordable prices. It's no surprise that everyone from students to grandparents loves this place. No matter what hour you stop in, booths and counter stools are filled, but the turnover is quick, and you can always order takeout. We go back for the classic meatloaf and the chocolate cream pie, but the menu is extensive, and there's plenty to please. You'll find light fare as well, including lots of salads. Breakfast service starts at the crack of dawn and lasts all day. **Other locations.**

29 Diner

10536 Lee Hwy. (Rte. 123), Fairfax 22030
703-591-6720, Fax 703-934-4731, *Open 24 hours, $, Casual*
No credit cards. P 🍴 🐮

Fred (or make that Fredy) and Ginger have been together again since the '40s at this legendary locale. That's Fredy and

Ginger Guevara, who helm what is one of Northern Virginia's oldest eateries. Seating no more than 40 people, 29 Diner is a relic from pre-fast-food-joint America, when people would flock here (or to places like it) to listen to the jukebox and down such basic eats as burgers and fries, grilled ham steak and home-style desserts. You can hunker down at the counter or grab one of the few booths for your trip down memory lane.

DELIS & BAGEL SHOPS

The Bagel Café

F & M Bank Centre, 300 Elden St. (Herndon Pkwy.), Herndon 20170
703-318-7555, Fax 703-318-7582, *Breakfast & Lunch daily, $, Casual*
A **P** 🍽 🛗

This is one of our favorite places for bagels and bagel sandwiches, with a full-scale sandwich, salad and soup menu, plus desserts and pastry snacks. The bagels are made from scratch on the premises daily and include such flavors as pumpkin, jalapeño, chocolate chip, raspberry, egg and sourdough. To our way of thinking, there's nothing more wonderful than the "everything" bagel with cream cheese and smoked salmon. There are lots of options for breakfast, including eggs, bagel french toast, French and Greek omelets, and eggs Benedict.

Celebrity Delly

Loehmann's Plaza
7623-A Arlington Blvd. (Allen St.), Falls Church 22042
703-573-9002, Fax 703-573-0721
Breakfast, Lunch & Dinner Mon.-Sat., $, Casual
A **P** ❤ 🛗

A typical New York-style deli, the Celebrity covers the full spectrum of basic American eats, from breakfasts of bagels with whitefish or kippered salmon through dinners of hot brisket, hot corned beef, bulging heroes and kosher dogs. Seat yourself and get ready to eat well. Great pickles! **Also located at** 12215 Nebel St., Rockville, MD, 301-881-4422.

Chesapeake Bagel Bakery

6815 Old Dominion Dr. (Chain Bridge Rd.), McLean 22101
703-506-0536, Fax 703-506-8798, *Breakfast, Lunch & Dinner daily, $, Casual*
No credit cards. P 🛗

Imagine the crowds at a fire sale, and you'll have an idea of what this place is like on a Saturday morning. Everyone is smiling and happy, and once they get their bagels and coffee (or tea, juice or hot chocolate), they grab a booth or table and spread out the newspaper for reading. When they are ready to eat, they will be happy to know that the menu has been expanded to include a croissant with eggs, sides of sausage and bacon and cereal with milk. Lunches and late-in-the-day meals include specialty sandwiches, bagel sandwiches, hot sandwiches, and focaccia sandwiches, plus soups and salads. Purists, however, can stick to bagels served plain or with a variety of cream cheese spreads. **Other locations.**

For **Gayot Hot Ten Restaurants in Washington, DC,**
visit: gayot.com

Einstein Bros Bagels

1829 Fountain Dr. (Bowman Towne Dr.), Reston 20190
703-787-0600, *Breakfast, Lunch & Dinner daily, $, Casual*

🅰🅿 ♥ 🍴

If you're a New Yorker and mad for bagels, you'll appreciate this group of bagel restaurants that sells classic bagels and good toppings. We love the onion bagel with salmon "shmear" (salmon cream cheese). Even if you're not a New Yorker, how can you go wrong with a wild blueberry bagel and some fruit shmear? Einstein Bros isn't just about bagels: In the tradition of sensible eateries, it offers a little something for everyone, including wraps, muffins, yogurts, iced and hot coffee, salads and, naturally, bagel sandwiches—try the hot BBQ chicken. Remember, if you want to eat bagels for dinner, most stores close in the early evening. **Other locations.**

ETHNIC FLAIR

Afghan

Charcoal Kebab

Super K-Mart Centre, 394 Elden St. (Herndon Pkwy.), Herndon 20170
703-435-2400, Fax 703-435-2350, *Lunch & Dinner daily, $, Casual*

🅰🅿 🍴

This popular Herndon hangout lures locals with good, cheap Afghan food and excellent breads. Seasonings tend to be fiery, so ask about spiciness before you order. There are a number of kinds of kebabs. But if you like things hot, the best bet is the highly seasoned chapli kebab; it might bring tears to your eyes. Note: They make a great mango lassi, the famous yogurt-mango drink.

Armenian

Ann MeMe's Bakery & Café

2419 Mt. Vernon Ave. (Uhler Ave.), Del Rey, Alexandria 22301
703-683-6638, *Breakfast, Lunch & Dinner daily, $, Casual*

🅰🅿

Ann MeMe's is a wonderful little island of flavors in the flatlands of Alexandria. The chefs take pride in serving homemade treasures. A wide variety of flatbreads includes Armenian peda, fougasse, lavash, lahmajoon and a fabulous focaccia. Salads and sandwiches are enhanced with Mediterranean elements including hummus, mint, couscous, yogurt and tabbouleh. Desserts include small fruit tartlets for individual servings, as well as larger tarts and cakes for families and groups.

Chinese

China King

141 Spring St. (Herndon Pkwy.), Herndon 22070
703-478-3757, Fax 703-742-9561, *Lunch & Dinner daily, $, Casual*
No credit cards. 🅿 🍴

The first of a small but expanding group of Virginia-based Chinese eateries, this casual place has made its reputation on serving good, fast food using quality ingredients. For that reason, it has become a regular for many locals who depend upon such dishes as the popular General Tso's chicken and somewhat fiery orange beef for lunch and dinner carryout. Don't get stuck as we have: no credit cards are accepted, so bring plenty of cash. It's easy to over-order. **Other locations**.

Wok & Roll Chinese Café

1371 Beverly Rd. (Elm St.), McLean 22101
703-556-8811, Fax 703-556-8812, *Lunch Mon.-Fri., Dinner nightly, $, Casual*
A P 🖴 🍴
Lines are almost inevitable at mealtimes, so you might want to call ahead for takeout. The kitchen here short-order cooks excellent Hunan and Szechuan food. The lemon and sesame chicken and orange beef dishes are reliably good. The lunch specials are platters that are worthy choices, too, and include Hunan chicken and sweet 'n' sour shrimp.

Cuban

Caribbean Grill

5183 Lee Hwy. (N. George Mason Dr.), Arlington 22207
703-241-8947, *Lunch & Dinner daily, $, Casual*
No credit cards. P 🍴
This is Arlington's answer to Little Havana, and despite the name, you'll find mostly Cuban food here—its sister restaurant/nightclub in Washington is Havana Breeze. We like to stop by whenever we crave the Cuban favorite, ropa vieja (shredded flank steak simmered in a seasoned broth) or a Cuban sandwich. For a hearty and delicious soup, consider the black bean chorizo, which will warm you up on the coldest day. The short menu also includes several non-Cuban selections, including Bolivian empanadas, Caribbean burritos and salteñas.

French

la Madeleine French Bakery & Café

1833 Fountain Dr. (Reston Parkway), Reston 20190
703-707-0704, *Breakfast, Lunch & Dinner daily, $, Casual*
A P 🍴 ⟐
When this French-inspired café-bakery hit town, residents cheered. It offers decent basic French cooking, warming bowls of soup, fresh-baked breads and pastries, all at bargain prices. Countless people find this combination irresistible for a nourishing breakfast, speedy lunch or cozy dinner. Food is served cafeteria-style: be sure to check both the blackboard and the menu before making a final decision. Among the most popular dishes are the tomato basil soup, which has become a signature dish, and the rosemary roasted chicken. Innovations include a bevy of Provençal dishes with hearty country-French flavors. **Other locations.**

Très Joli

Hunter Mill Plaza
2952 A Chain Bridge Rd. (Hunter Mill Rd.), Oakton 22124
703-242-8752, Fax 703-242-0475
Breakfast Mon.-Sat., Lunch daily, Brunch Sun., $, Casual
A P 🖴 ♥ 🍴
Pastry chef William Eash has carved out his own niche, bringing city fare to the 'burbs. He's best known for his

authentic French and Viennese pastries, but his breads, muffins and bistro lunches and special-order dinners have made this cozy, sunny restaurant a favorite among locals. Some linger over the newspaper and coffee; others are in and out in 30 seconds flat for their fix to-go. When you do have time to spend, take note that Eash is known for his weekend brunches, starring crêpes and tortas rusticas. Also see review in *Gourmet Shops & Markets/Gourmet Shops & Gourmet To-Go.*

Indian/Pakistani

Shiney's

Seoul Plaza, 4231-D Markham St. (Rte. 123), Annandale 22003
703-642-0460, Fax 703-920-8321, Lunch & Dinner daily, $, Casual
A P

About as bare-bones as it gets, this eatery has been a well-kept secret. There are many reasons to add this to your restaurant list: The tandoori breads are sensational, the curries and kabobs are outstanding, and the prices are low. Just don't come here expecting glitz. The décor is limited to a poster or two. For sheer gluttony, tackle Shiney's eat-all-you-want buffet. Or, from the menu, sample the cholle bhature salad and the lamb and chapli kebabs. While you eat, think about how you can tackle the towering stack of rainbow-colored Pakistani candies for dessert.

Tandoori Kabob House

607 Randolph St. North (Wilson Blvd.), Ballston, Arlington 22203
703-525-0999, *Breakfast, Lunch & Dinner daily*, $, *Casual*
A P

The Indian answer to a fast-food, Tandoori Kabob House is following the local trend towards exotic takeout featuring wholesome ethnic food. Don't just start and stop with the steam table; check out the extensive printed menu for inspiration. Kebabs are a good starting point, though the lamb shish kebab has a startlingly pungent taste; however, the dal as a separate dish comes as a mildly spiced several-bean mixture. Thanks to the handiness of the tandoor, you can also get any number of oven-baked breads, including a good onion kulcha. The range of curries is notable, and the butter chicken is especially good. There are no desserts, but after all, the kitchen does offer mango lassi, the famed yogurt beverage that is always a good sweet substitute.

Italian

Bruscato's

814 N. Fairfax St. (Madison St.), Old Town, Alexandria 22314
703-684-3613, Fax 703-684-0203, *Breakfast & Lunch daily*, $, *Casual*
No credit cards.

Some places are known for subs, others for pizza and yet others for paninis. Bruscato's, however, does them all well. Subs topped with the sensational house-made olive oil/oregano dressing is memorable. And if you're interested in a midweek picnic, you're just a block away from Oronoco Park on the banks of the Potomac. Tucked in among the office buildings, Bruscato's does a brisk lunch business with regular customers, so be prepared for a wait if you visit at prime time.

The Italian Store

Lyon Village Center
3123 Lee Hwy. (Spount Run Pkwy.), Arlington 22201
703-528-6266, Fax 703-524-8361, *Lunch & Dinner daily, $, Casual*

🅐🅟💺🍴

Most people come here because The Italian Store stocks hard-to-find Italian ingredients and also bakes outstanding pizzas. But those in the know are drawn by the store's substantial subs (Philadelphia-style, specialty and Italian) and gourmet sandwiches, including pâté and Brie on the bread of your choice. If you want something whopping, consider the napoli with spicy pepperoni and capacola ham paired with mozzarella cheese. Also see review in *Gourmet Shops & Markets/Ethnic Markets/Italian*.

Pica Deli Gourmet

4536 Lee Hwy. (Lorton Ln.), Lee Heights, Arlington 22207
703-524-5656, Fax 703-522-3507, *Lunch & Dinner Mon.-Sat., $, Casual*

🅐🅟💺📷🍴

As busy as a Saturday yard sale, this Arlington restaurant balances delicately between being a deli and a sandwich shop. Cooks in search of Italian fixings can fill up their shopping bags, while the hungry masses head to the back counter and wait their turn for a super hero. The cook's big specialty sandwiches include the Caesar Augustus, with capacola ham, aged salami, pepperoni and provolone, a yummy feast made slightly piquant with crushed red chilies. The sandwich list is extensive, but if you want something special, the staff will make it for you on one of the freshly baked breads.

Primo Italiano

Plaza America Shopping Center
11688 Plaza America Dr. (Reston Pkwy.), Reston 20190
703-471-0016, Fax 703-471-0302, *Lunch & Dinner Mon.-Sat., $, Casual*

🅐🅟💺🍴

If you work nearby, you'll probably lunch here often. If you live nearby, you'll probably pick up a pizza or two and a hunk of cheesecake after work. And if you want to stock up on deli meats, cheeses and salads, plus assorted Italian grocery items, you'll make this a frequent destination. Those in the know come primarily for the wood oven-baked gourmet pizzas. The crusts are thin and chewy, the toppings top quality, and the topping choices interesting. We love the white pizza with ricotta, olives, prosciutto and Gorgonzola. For the fastest service, call ahead, or plan to eat at the restaurant at off-peak hours. It's a suburban taste of Little Italy.

Japanese

Atami

3155 Wilson Blvd. (Highland St.), Clarendon Metro, Arlington 22201
703-522-4787, Fax 703-522-1289, *Lunch & Dinner Tues.-Sun., $, Casual*

🅐🅟

In spite of the very visible sushi bar and the rice paper lampshades, it's easy to get the feeling that long before seaweed and rice were rolled and wrapped in this venue, the kitchen was spooning out lots of chow mein. Maybe it's the tall maroon booths that give the dark interior a '50s Chinese-restaurant look. But today, Atami is a favorite for sushi, and the fish is fresh, the knives sharp, and the sushi chefs busy. Prices are quite reasonable. Vegetarians and those who like Vietnamese food also get some menu choices.

Bonsai

4040 S. 28th St. (S. Quincy St.), Shirlington, Arlington 22206
703-824-8828, *Lunch & Dinner daily, $, Casual*

A ☎ P ⌨

One thing is certain: The key ingredient for good sushi is freshness. Bonsai meets that standard. This small, (it seats only 50, including tables and sushi barstools) charming restaurant offers basic sushi fare—no fusion or other faddish approaches. The printed menu doesn't change, but a chalkboard highlights the fresh fish of the day.

Mr. Hibachi

2313 Wilson Blvd. (Adams St.), Arlington 22201
703-524-6548, Fax 703-524-6549, *Lunch & Dinner Mon.-Sat., $, Casual*

A P 👖

This little rice and noodle place makes a big deal out of several basic Asian ingredients, from fried tofu to bean sprouts, fish cakes, clear soup stock and pan-fried dumplings, plus, of course, rice and noodles. Although the fare is primarily Korean and Japanese, the kitchen has slipped in two good peanut-mustard dishes that seem vaguely Western and Thai. Servings tend to be on the small side and the stock overly salty, but this is portable, casual, enjoyable food. **Also located at** 150 Elden St., Herndon, VA, 703-472-6768.

Miyagi

6719 Curran St. (Chain Bridge Rd.), McLean 22101
703-893-0116, *Lunch Mon.-Fri., Dinner Mon.-Sat., $, Casual*

A ☎ P 👖

Top-quality sushi and a tiny dining room mean large crowds. A minimalist décor of blond woods and Japanese prints is the backdrop for the almost all-sushi menu created by two knife-wielding chefs. Start with some non-sushi appetizers: The hot tofu and the beef negimaki are both good preambles to a blowout sushi meal. All the presentations are delicious, but the chirashi sushi is a particular favorite, as much for its ultra-fresh fish as for its artistic appeal. Finish with the green tea ice cream, smooth as a spring breeze and just as refreshing.

Mediterranean

Amphora Restaurant

377 Maple Ave. W. (Nutley St.), Vienna 22180
703-938-7877, Fax 703-938-1720, *Open 24 hours, $, Casual*

A P ♥ 👖 🐱 ▼ ▲

Family-owned and -operated, Amphora appeals to a family clientele, who love the casual atmosphere, super-friendly staff and substantial meals. The Vienna location looks like an old-fashioned country restaurant, but it's really a diner at heart, staying open 24 hours a day and serving everything from soup to nuts—spaghetti, broiled or fried seafood, gyro platters drizzled with yogurt and hamburgers. Given the diverse American, Greek and Italian menu, don't be surprised to find college students dropping by in the wee hours for a coffee break. Check out the nonstop breakfast menu, with everything from Belgian waffles to sugar-cured ham steaks. There's a small, but complete, affiliated bakery next door. **Also located at** 1151 Elden St., Herndon, VA, 703-925-0900.

Knossos

341 E. Market St. (Catoctin Cir. SE), Leesburg 20176
703-771-9231, *Breakfast, Lunch & Dinner daily, $, Casual*
A P 🍴

Many patrons swear by the big and bulging gyro platter, a meal in itself for two dainty eaters. The grilled meat is wrapped in pita bread and the plate is piled high with fries and fried zucchini. As the name suggests, Knossos features primarily Greek-style food, although the staff whips up American staples such as hamburgers, cheeseburgers, crab-cake sandwiches and, for breakfast, hotcakes. You'd have to search pretty far to find a better gyro or souvlaki, so stick with what the Greeks do well: make a meal of these flavorful, herb-zapped, meat sandwiches.

Mediterranean Bakery

Trade Center Shopping Mall
352 S. Pickett St. (Duke St.), Alexandria 22301
703-751-0030, *Breakfast, Lunch & Dinner daily, $, Casual*
A P ♥

A bakery and market well-stocked with Middle Eastern foods, this place also is a good spot to enjoy such traditional Middle Eastern fare as falafel, gyros, shwarma, spanakopita, vegetable pies, cheese and tomato pies and salads. For breakfast, you will find bagels and croissants. Also see reviews in *Gourmet Shops & Markets/Bakeries and Ethnic Markets.*

Mexican

Anita's Mexican Food

521 Maple Ave. E (East St.), Vienna 22180
703-255-1001, Fax 703-255-1005, *Lunch & Dinner daily, $, Casual*
A P 🍴

It's late and you don't feel like cooking. Worse yet, the kids are starving. If you are lucky, you'll live near one of Virginia's seven Anita's restaurants, and your dinner problems are solved—and at rock-bottom prices. Established about 25 years ago, these eateries are local institutions, frequented by generations of Virginians who have grown up eating the generous enchiladas and tacos. Today's menu is so complete that there are very few popular combinations that you won't find. Our favorites include the classic carne adovada and the excellent chile relleno. Check the blackboard for daily specials, though you can never go wrong with any of the burritos. **Other locations.**

Find the name you are looking for, quickly and easily, in **the index.**

Baja Fresh Mexican Grill

12150 Fairfax Towne Center (W. Ox Rd.), Fairfax 22030
703-352-1792, Fax 703-352-1793, *Lunch & Dinner daily, $, Casual*

A P ♟

This scrubbed-clean West Coast-based eatery is a favorite of moviegoers, mall shoppers and students, who hang out over newspapers and a spicy meal. Burritos are king and come with so many different fillings that return visits are a must. You can eat your way through the house dishes: the Baja burrito (melted Jack cheese, guacamole, fresh salsa, grilled chicken or steak) or the burrito Mexicano (rice, beans, onion, cilantro and grilled chicken or steak). Our favorite is the Burrito Ultimo, which is pretty much the ultimate, with melted Monterey Jack and cheddar cheeses, chicken or steak, beans, chiles, rice and fresh salsa in a flour tortilla wrapper. The kitchen also cooks up tacos, nachos, tostadas, quesadillas and other snacks. No desserts, but no microwaves, no can openers, no MSG and no freezers either. Excellent fast food at bargain prices. **Other locations.**

Chevys Fresh Mex

Pentagon Center
1201 S. Hayes St. (Army Navy Dr.), The Pentagon, Arlington 22202
703-413-8700, Fax 703-413-0061, *Lunch & Dinner daily, $, Casual*

A P ♟ Y

This restaurant chain offers kitschy just-North-of-the-Border décor, bright and vivid colors, and some good Mexican fare. We always judge by the chiles rellenos, and these are cheese filled, batter dipped, and best of all, reasonably priced—that means ordering more than one. Not every dish, like the chicken Caesar salad, is totally Mexican, but so much on the menu is that you can pick your way through to a real fiesta. Freshness is the motto: No canned food is used. This means all sauces are made fresh and all fillings that call for vegetables are made with fresh vegetables. It's a happy place that serves happy food at very reasonable prices. **Other locations.**

El Sabor Latino

Super K-Mart Centre, 408 Elden St. (Jonquil Ln.), Herndon 20170
703-437-8796, *Lunch & Dinner daily, $, Casual*

A P ♟

Pared free of refinements, this shirts-sleeves place suits big happy groups and sprawling families looking for a dining bargain. And every so often, just when there's a lull in the conversation, the jukebox bursts into loud Latino music. Appetizers are basically the Salvadoran selections of pupusas, tamales, fried plantains and fried cassava with pork skin. (The food is mainly Mexican with a nod toward some Salvadoran dishes) Entrées zero in on such bests as chicken hard and soft tacos, enchiladas, fajitas, chimichangas and wonderfully plump cheese burritos. It's all a family affair, and everyone works hard to make this a place worthy of return visits. **Also located at** 6051 Centerville Crest lane, Centreville, VA, 703-815-2709; and 119 Fort Evans Rd. NE, Leesburg, VA, 703-777-7755.

Picante! The Real Taco

14511-B Lee Jackson Memorial Hwy. (Airline Pkwy.), Chantilly 20151
703-222-2323, Fax 703-222-5996, *Lunch & Dinner daily, $, Casual*

A P ♥ ⚑

Whenever local families or office workers need their spirits lifted, they head to this gaily decorated eatery that offers terrific, inexpensive food. The menu features an assortment of zesty tacos, burritos, enchiladas and fajitas with authentic flavor. And the kitchen surprises everyone with some offbeat dishes as well, such as chilies en nogada (meat-stuffed jalapeños) and caldo tlalpeño (chicken consommé with chipotle chilies, chicken and chick peas). We're hooked on the chile verde tacos and the carne guisada tacos made with lean beef simmered in a dusky, chili-flavored sauce. Also a must: the chicken mole. Dieters can find light fare, including a cactus salad. Kids have their own menu, and they eat free with a paying adult on Mondays. Sometimes it looks too crowded to venture in, but the takeout service is fast and efficient.

Taqueria Poblano

2400 B Mount Vernon Ave. (Oxford Ave.), The Flats, Alexandria 22301
703-548-8226, Fax 703-548-2824, *Lunch & Dinner Wed.-Mon., $, Casual*

A P 👪

Taqueria Poblano is a cheerful, friendly establishment, usually crowded with families. The owners are proud of their fresh salsas and they should be. Each one—green, red and the hot habañero—has a rich flavor that goes well with the chips and fresh jícama that appear on your table. The simple menu offers tacos, of course, plus taquitos, quesadillas, cowboy-style frijoles, burritos and several char-grilled meat dishes. For dessert, try the muy bueno chocolate fritters.

Middle Eastern

Atilla's

2045 Wilson Blvd. (Courthouse Rd.), Courthouse, Arlington 22201
703-525-7979, *Lunch & Dinner daily, $, Casual*

A P

Travelers know that snacks are some of the best culinary experiences, like noodles off a cart in Thailand, ice cream in the old city of Copenhagen or falafel across from the main bus station in Tel Aviv. It's a struggle to match those tasty memories in restaurants back home, but Atilla's comes close, serving up gyros, falafel and other Middle Eastern quick bites. The atmosphere can't compare to the blasting sun and chaos at the Tel Aviv bus station, and you won't find those terrific pickles, but the pocket bread is wonderful and the hot sauce will remind you of faraway places.

Bread & Kabob

3407 Payne St. (Leesburg Pike), Baileys Crossroads, Falls Church 22041
703-845-2900, *Lunch & Dinner daily, $, Casual*

A P ⚑

This sturdy and worthy old-timer seems like the prototype for the casual kebab eateries that have sprung up in recent years. Although lacking charm, it more than compensates with its tender lamb and succulent kubideh kebab and delicious homemade hummus, a dish that in some hands can emerge overpowered with garlic. The kebabs, cooked-to-order over gas flames while your bread bakes in the corner clay oven, have made the restaurant's reputation. But the menu includes other specialties as well: If you time your visit right, you can satisfy a bigger appetite with hearty dizi, a traditional Persian lamb stew that includes everything but the kitchen sink. You'll also find Persian pickles, tea from a samovar and Persian sweets. What you won't find is table service and other amenities. **Other locations.**

Kabob Place Café & Bakery

9904 Georgetown Pike (Walker Rd.), Great Falls 22066
703-757-7788, Fax 703-757-7789, *Lunch & Dinner daily, $, Casual*

A P 🖥 🍽

Persian cook and caterer Partoo Hagian Golesorkhi and master kebab chef Alborz have relocated to Great Falls from Vienna, and the locals must be celebrating. Noted for her great Persian foods and pastries, Golesorkhi has slightly updated her restaurant menu so that it offers numerous kebab dishes—we adore her subtly seasoned and juicy kubideh kebabs—and she's included several Persian sandwiches and some western and Persian salads. Ask about specials of the day, and if her rich, filling aush (a Persian vegetable soup) is available, order one to eat and one to go. Add some Persian pastries and an order of creamy Persian rice pudding, minus the rosewater.

Lebanese Taverna Market

4400 Old Dominion Dr. (Lorcom Ln.), Arlington 22207
703-276-8681, Fax 703-276-6877, *Lunch & Dinner daily, $, Casual*

A P 🍽

Why pick dandelions in the wild? We'd prefer to have them here in our favorite dish. It's hendbi made with chicory, caramelized onions and dandelion leaves. We also enjoy the lamb kebabs and any one of the many Lebanese salads that are fresh, complicated, and very exotic. While you wait, stroll around the grocery section for imported delicacies, teas and luscious Lebanese pastries and sweets. Curb your appetite or your tab may run up by the time you check out. Interested in learning about Lebanese food? Inquire about the Market's ongoing cooking classes. Also see review in *Gourmet Shops & Markets/Ethnic Markets/Middle Eastern.*

Moby Dick House of Kabob

6854 Old Dominion Dr. (Beverly Rd.), McLean 22101
703-448-8448, Fax 703-448-6061, *Lunch & Dinner daily, $, Casual*

P 🍽

Moby Dick has made its name serving kebabs and fresh breads. It used to be a secret, but its reputation has spread so much that now all of Washington is in on it. Depending on the hour, getting a table may be a challenge. Plan to order ahead, otherwise you may join a line waiting for the terrific kebabs wrapped in fresh-baked breads. We're addicted to the kubideh kebab in hot bread with its side of tangy yogurt. Add a shirazi salad and you've got a meal. Always check out the specials Monday through Friday; these are full-blown Persian entrées that are more substantial than a sandwich. **Other locations.**

Samadi Sweets Café

5916 Leesburg Pike
(Glen Forest Dr.), Baileys Crossroads, Falls Church 22041
703-578-0606, Fax 703-578-1757
Lunch Mon.-Sat., Dinner nightly, Brunch Sun., $, Casual

A P 🛒

Many people drop by to enjoy the Lebanese savories, from shish kebab served with almond-garnished rice to a shwarma plate with chicken. But those with a sweet tooth come for the array of Lebanese pastries—glorious, golden and usually gleaming with honey. Best bet: Point and ask about the ones that look the most delicious to you. We've loved the ones with crushed nuts or with creamy custard fillings—maybe the ideal is to ask for a sampler plate.

Simply Grill

1835 Fountain Dr. (Reston Pkwy.), Reston 20190
703-471-1410, Fax 703-471-1571, *Lunch & Dinner daily, $, Casual*

A P 🍽 ❤ 🛒

Don't expect American ribs or steaks at this excellent spot because the food that will be simply grilled here is Persian. You'll savor family recipes of owner Ali Nafidi for ground beef or chicken kebabs served on fresh tandoori bread. You may also find at least one of his mother-in-law's famed Persian specials each day, and in winter, the hearty aush soup is essential for beating the chill. Nafidi makes the rose-flavored Persian ice cream. For customers who want American-style food, Nafidi offers several familiar sandwiches and salads, but his Persian treats, especially the lamb kebabs, have proved immensely popular.

Peruvian

Pollos Inka

The Pines Center, 1151 Elden St. (Monroe St.), Herndon 20170
703-481-9090, Fax 703-318-7454, *Lunch & Dinner daily, $, Casual*

A P 🛒 🍴

This tiny Herndon eatery was one of the first in the DC metro area to introduce diners to Peruvian-style roasted or grilled chicken. There are other distinguished Peruvian and Latino dishes, too, at this excellent quick-dine spot.

Vietnamese

Bay Lo

Eden Center, 6757 Wilson Blvd., Ste. 21 (Rte. 7), Falls Church 22044
703-241-4094, *Lunch & Dinner daily, $, Casual*

A P 🛒

Intrepid gourmands know about the Vietnamese Eden Center in Falls Church and about the cluster of restaurants along its interior corridors. The informal Bay Lo is one of the best. Begin with starters such as soft spring rolls with shrimp (goi cuon) or pork (bi cuon) or the soft-wrap bo bia. Entrées include assorted noodle and rice dishes, and the highlighted special, bun bo Hué, turns out to be a steaming broth filled with beef and thick egg noodles. For a change of pace, try the bun cha Ha Noi, a grilled pork soup. Another must: the refreshing fresh lemonade.

Kim Son Restaurant

3103-D Graham Rd. (Rte. 50), Falls Church 22042
703-641-0008, *Breakfast, Lunch & Dinner daily, $, Casual*

A P 🍴

Starting off as a bakery, Kim Son quickly evolved into a dandy fast-food spot with a Vietnamese-only menu. There's a mini-buffet spread at the steam table, plenty to order from the menu, and an assortment of ready-to-go snacks, such as the ever-popular summer rolls (goi cuon). These are some of the best in town, and most of the other snack items offer good quality and great flavors, too.

Pho Gourmet

Sudley Manor Square
7829 Sudley Rd. (Sudley Manor Dr.), Manassas 20109
703-530-9693, Fax 703-530-9704, *Lunch & Dinner daily, $, Casual*

A P 🍴

It seems that everywhere you look in the DC metro area you'll find another Vietnamese soup place, even as far west as Manassas. This place, like most other soup restaurants, stars the popular pho with many variations on the beef theme. There are also a limited number of rice and noodle entrée dishes, plus spring rolls and several desserts that should keep the interest of those who don't want pho. This helps if you want soup and your companion craves something heartier. Both the fresh and the fried spring rolls are good, and for an extra treat, order the crispy butter wings, chicken wings that really are crunchy.

Pho 75

3103 Graham Rd., # B (Arlington Blvd,), Falls Church 22041
703-204-1490, *Breakfast, Lunch & Dinner daily, $, Casual*

A P 🍴

A few years ago, this local restaurant group helped introduce Washingtonians to the glories of the Vietnamese soup bowl, the pho. Now pho places are all the rage in the metro area, and Pho 75 has five locations. Who would have guessed that so many would fall in love with this hearty meal-in-a-bowl? Some soup places offer other dishes, too, but this group sticks to the basics: Order your soup with a choice of meat combinations in small or large bowls. Your order comes with chopsticks, soup spoon and loads of vegetables; it's up to you to add chopped chilies, cilantro and chili sauce to your taste. **Other locations.**

Pho Tay Ho

Culmore Shopping Center, 6015 Leesburg Pike (Glen Carlyn Dr.)
Baileys Crossroads, Falls Church 22041
703-578-3037, *Lunch & Dinner daily, $, Casual*

A P 🍴

The soup here is full-bodied and flavorful, and we've enjoyed the rich, steaming broth. It comes with several different beef-topping options, and the menu gives you the choice of various chicken soups as well. The owners, however, also make an effort to accommodate the American palate with soup combinations that both do and do not include tendon and tripe. Like most Vietnamese restaurants, this one offers traditional Vietnamese drinks, from the intensely potent sweet coffee to fresh coconut juice.

Vietnam 75 Noodle Restaurant

5731 N. Lee Hwy. (Lexington St.), Arlington 22207
703-536-1000, *Lunch & Dinner daily, $, Casual*

A P 🍴

Sweeping the Northern Virginia area, this local group of Vietnamese restaurants features an adequate soup (pho) menu plus a few other light-fare items, such as the fried and soft spring rolls, beef salad and chicken wings. There are also several large noodle entrées with meat or spring roll toppings. The kitchen also puts out several typical desserts, including the wonderful three-flavors pudding. Vietnamese coffee, tea and fresh lemonade are on the menu, too. There's nothing fancy about the food or the place, but it's clean, bright, cheerful and the food is good and reasonably priced. **Other locations**.

HEALTHY/VEGETARIAN

Sunflower Vegetarian Restaurant

2531 Chain Bridge Rd. (Nutley St.), Vienna 22181
703-319-3888, Fax 703-242-7331, *Lunch & Dinner daily, $, Casual*

A P ♥ 🍴

You get the idea: The cheerful yellow flower is everywhere, brightening the interior of this very popular vegetarian restaurant. A throwback to the '60s, the Sunflower is dedicated to providing you with commune-type food with flair and obvious Asian overtones. Most dishes have a strong Japanese influence, although they also offer General Tso's Surprise (soy protein, not chicken), Curry Paradise (all ingredients are vegetables, not meat), and Chinese ma po tofu, which here obviously is not cooked with ground pork. It would be hard to come away hungry—there are flavors that should please all palates, vegetarian or not.

ICE CREAM & MORE

Lazy Sundae

2925 Wilson Blvd. (N. Garfield St.), Clarendon, Arlington 22201
703-525-4960, *Lunch & Dinner daily, $, Casual*
No credit cards. 📺 🍴

As the name implies, they're all about ice cream here. But not just any ice cream: This stuff is unlike any other kind of frozen treat you'll find in town. Maybe it's the offbeat décor, the cool staff, the wacky flavors or the fact that all ice creams are made on the premises. Flavors rotate often, but our favorite—when we can find it—is the caramel swirl. Also available: sundaes, shakes and plenty of topping choices, plus glass jars filled with candies and gums. Seating is very limited, so you may want to pack up a quart and eat at home. The kitchen here also makes assorted cakes and other dessert items.

Lee's Ice Cream & Deli

Reston Town Center, 11917 Freedom Dr. (Library St.), Reston 20190
703-471-8902, Fax 703-471-0430
Breakfast, Lunch & Dinner daily, $, Casual
No credit cards. P 🖥 🍴

A hangout for strollers who like to eat ice cream and people-watch at the same time, this popular place has lots of flavors on tap, plus nonfat and soft-serve ice creams, and "flavor bursts" (toppings such as Blue Hawaiian coconut or cotton candy are drizzled over vanilla soft-serve ice cream). Arbuckle (vanilla with crystallized gourmet chocolate syrup) is a top seller, but all flavors are outstanding. There's also an assortment of deli foods and some baked goods, making this a popular lunch spot for business folk in the area. **Also located at** Tysons Corner, Leesburg Pike, Vienna, VA, 703-761-3131.

Maggie Moo's Ice Cream & Treatery

Bradlee Shopping Center
3610 King St. (Braddock Rd.), Alexandria 22302
703-671-4799, *Lunch & Dinner daily, $, Casual*
A **P** 🍴

It's hard to say the name of this establishment with a straight face, but who cares? The ice cream at Maggie Moo's is terrific! Freshly made at the shop, it's deliciously creamy. There's always a line, but it's worth the wait, and while you're waiting you can make some decisions about what you want mixed into your favorite flavor. A variety of candy bars, sprinkles, fruits and nuts are offered. If you don't want a mixture and don't have time to wait for a scoop, there are packages in the freezer. **Also located at** 6575-N Frontier Dr., Springfield, VA, 703-921-0380; and 533 N. Frederick Ave., Gaithersburg, MD, 301-926-4239.

Milwaukee Frozen Custard

Sully Plaza
13934 Lee-Jackson Memorial Hwy. (Centreville Rd.), Chantilly 20151
703-263-1920, Fax 703-263-0335, *Lunch & Dinner daily, $, Casual*
No credit cards. P 🖥 🍴

Frozen custard—a concentration of egg yolk, creams and butterfat—is king in Milwaukee. And it looks as though this ultra-smooth ice cream is going to start ruling here, too. Chocolate and vanilla are always available and, according to a calendar schedule (ask at the counter of this bright, white store), a third flavor such as marionberry or chocolate malt ball may be on tap for the day. The malt ball tastes just like those movie favorites. **Also located at** 8411 Sudley Rd., Manassas, VA, 703-393-9990.

Yum Yum Ice Cream Café

12164 Fairfax Towne Center (W. Ox Rd.), Fairfax 22033
703-218-0300, Fax 703-218-0309, *Breakfast, Lunch & Dinner daily, $, Casual*

Yum Yum deserves a loud cheer for its bright colors and rows of handsome baked goods, from apple strudel to dainty baklava from the Tivoli at the Watergate. Its upscale soda-fountain look triggers ice cream fantasies, and may transport adults back to childhood dreams of great gallons of ice cream for everlasting cones. There are about 24 flavors of Lee's brand frozen delights, including ice cream, yogurts and soft-serves. Should you decide to balance your diet, they also carry Mediterranean sandwiches, soups, salads and gourmet coffees.

PIZZA

California Pizza Kitchen

7939 Tysons Corner Center/Lower Level (Rte. 7), McLean 22102
703-761-1473, *Lunch & Dinner daily, $, Casual*

You have to have a sense of humor to enjoy CPK's outrageous pizza toppings. They are innovative, offbeat and likely to raise eyebrows among traditionalists. That's probably a quick and then forgotten reaction, though, since this is one of the country's most popular chains. We enjoy the rosemary-chicken-potato pizza, the tandoori chicken and the Thai chicken pies. Not everything is so ingenous: Sticklers for the conventional will find pepperoni; vegetarian; and five-cheese-and-fresh-tomato pies. Hungry for more? Check out the menu for soups, salads, sandwiches and pasta dishes. This tiled, shiny-clean restaurant is casual, fun and often crowded. **Other locations.**

Emilio's Brick Oven Pizza

Dulles Square Shopping Center
22207 Shaw Rd., Unit A-10 (Church St.), Sterling 20166
703-444-2555, Fax 703-444-0366
Lunch & Dinner Mon.-Sat., $, Casual

If you'd go to the ends of the earth for a good pizza, save time and stop by Emilio's. It's a small and attractive place, with a prominent brick oven for baking pizzas as well as some excellent calzones. The dough and the sauces are made fresh daily from top ingredients. You can create your own pie from a list of tempting toppings or order one off the menu—like the Julian with fresh mozzarella and Italian sausage or the Al Forno with fresh mozzarella, roasted eggplant and yellow squash. Supplement your order with one of those tasty calzones or a sub. Add a biscotti or cannoli for dessert and you'll be in heaven.

Ledo Pizza

Battlefield Shopping Center
1037 Edwards Ferry Rd. NE (Rte. 15 Bypass N.), Leesburg 22075
703-777-9500, *Lunch & Dinner daily, $, Casual*

A restaurant group that started with its first store in College Park, MD, these popular pizza restaurants have a devoted following among students, families and anyone who likes hearty

Italian-style meals. The menu offers salads, pasta entrées, over-stuffed subs, sandwiches, and burgers. Its pizzas, however, have made its name and fame: The dough and sauce are prepared fresh daily; toppings are high-quality ingredients. Expect to find clean, busy restaurants for sit-down meals. **Other locations.**

Lost Dog Café

Westover Shopping Center
5876 N. Washington Blvd. (McKinley Rd.), Westover, Arlington 22205
703-237-1552, Fax 703-237-0477, *Lunch & Dinner daily, $, Casual*

This funky "gourmet pizza deli" has an obvious dog theme with paw prints on walls. It offers 22 pies and 30 toppings for create-your-own. Choose Pedigree Pie (garlic butter, artichokes, tomatoes, spinach, cheeses); Perro Pie (salsa, grilled chicken breast, spinach, fresh tomato, cheeses); Polynesian pie (shrimp, ham, pineapple, bacon, cheese); and other unusual combos. Or you can play it safer with a straightforward plain pie or any of the restaurant's non-pizza offerings.

Papa Petrone's

West Springfield Center
6222 Rolling Rd. (Old Keene Mill Rd.), W. Springfield 22152
703-866-4343, Fax 703-866-4368, *Lunch & Dinner Mon.-Sat., $, Casual*
No credit cards. P ♥ 🍴

A community favorite, Papa Petrone's has devised a unique way of serving up pizzas: Pies are assembled with toppings strewn over a secret-formula crust, then everything is wrapped up for easy carryout, and you, the cook, bake it at home for the very freshest pizza. This guarantees a perfect pie, right out of the oven. One of the most popular and biggest-selling items is the Scramble Bread, which combines pizza dough with a choice of pizza toppings. Check out Papa's desserts; they're rich and tempting.

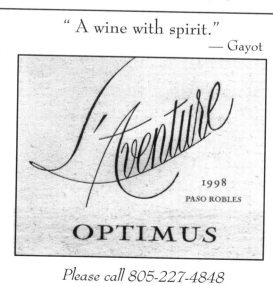

GOURMET SHOPS & MARKETS

BAKERIES

Cenan's Bakery

122 Branch Rd. SE (Maple Ave.), Vienna 22180
703-242-0070, Fax 703-242-0091, *Open daily*

A **P**

This popular bakery in the bedroom community of Vienna is best known for its baguettes, which are not as crusty as those from some other bakeries. The farmer's bread draws raves, and the Pugliese has many of the porous characteristics of the rustic breads. On a Saturday morning the business is brisk with families (toddlers attached) running their weekend errands. Cenan's breads are served in several of the area's finer restaurants. Also see review in *Quick Bites*.

Grace's Pastries

Big K-Mart Centre, 434 Elden St. (Herndon Pkwy.), Herndon 20170
703-318-0286, *Open Mon.-Sat.*

A **P**

Grace's breads and coffeecakes were such big sellers at local farmers markets that she started her own retail operation. Here freshly baked goods include a variety of white and multigrain breads and sweet items such as a raspberry-blackberry coffeecake.

Great Harvest Bread Co.

785 Station St. (Alder St.), Herndon 20170
703-471-4031, Fax 703-471-5580, *Open Tues.-Sat.*

A **P**

Part of a nationwide chain of nutritionally correct bread and muffin bakeries, this store is usually thronged with people who love the free bread samples they can spread with jam, butter, and/or honey. Loaf flavors are interesting and the breads wholesome and delicious. Our favorite: the honey whole-wheat and the raisin cinnamon. Muffins, scones, quickbreads, and thick, chunky cookies taste homemade. **Other locations.**

Heidelberg Bakery

2150 N. Culpeper St. (Lee Hwy.), Arlington 22207
703-527-8394, Fax 703-528-5061, *Open daily*

A **P**

Looking for German baked goods? Stop in at this bakery for a wide selection of delicious strudels, creamy almond pastries made with marzipan and loads of European-style baked goods. From wedding cakes, candies, cookies and coffeecakes to daily fresh bread, Heidelberg rarely disappoints. Keep an eye out for the seasonal items that include fabulous hot cross buns, Christmas stollen and Easter breads. Once you find this Arlington secret, it will be a regular stop. Also see review in *Quick Bites*.

Mama Lavash

Idylwood Shopping Center
2190-A Pimmit Dr. (Leesburg Pike), Falls Church 22043
703-827-7788, Fax 703-827-8291, *Open Mon.-Sat.*
A P

The breads of Mama Lavash appear in many of the fine Middle Eastern restaurants around town. For home cooks, the retail store is a good source for the entire line of Iranian breads, from the well-known lavash to the thicker, sesame-seed-topped barbari. The storefront isn't fancy, but if you're lucky enough to be there when the bread is coming out of the oven, who cares?

Mediterranean Bakery

Trade Center Shopping Village
352 S. Pickett St. (Duke St.), Landmark, Alexandria 22304
703-751-1702, Fax 703-823-5007, *Open daily*
A P

This is a veritable supermarket for Middle Eastern goods—both cooked and raw, sweet and savory. Among baked goods, you'll find a variety of phyllo-based sweets laden with syrups, honey and rose water and filled with pistachios and filberts. Also see review in *Gourmet Shops & Markets/Ethnic Markets* and in *Quick Bites*.

Mom's Apple Pie

296 Sunset Park Dr. (Herndon Pkwy.), Herndon 20170
703-471-6266, *Open Mon.-Sat.*
A P

After 20 years of baking terrific pies, just like Mom might, this bakery garners plenty of praise for its moderately priced pies and other baked goods, including sturdy whole-grain breads. Everything is made from scratch with all natural ingredients.

Pie Gourmet

Green Village Center, 507 Maple Ave. W. (Nutley St.), Vienna 22180
703-281-7437, Fax 703-281-7488, *Open daily*
A P

Whenever we visit here, we can't avoid taking away at least one slice of the chocolate cream pie, probably the best homey dessert in the area. This little baking gem can confuse the issue with its multitudinous choices: Its menu displays more than 50 pie flavors, some of which are seasonal only. You'll also find cheesecakes, muffins, specialty items, savory dinner pies (chicken pot pie and zucchini-mushroom pie, for example), tea loaves and cookies. But why fool around? The pies are simply scrumptious: the best in town. Ask about the pie delivery service for out-of-town friends.

For **updated Gayot Washington, DC restaurant reviews,** visit: digitalcity.com/washington/dining

CANDY & CHOCOLATES

De Fluri's Fine Chocolates

425 Maple Ave.W (Nutley St.), Vienna 22180
703-938-2133, Fax 703-938-2137, *Open Mon.-Sat.*

A P

Owner, pastry cook and candy crafter Brenda Casabona's candy shop/bakery has been one of Vienna's best-kept secrets. One whiff of the store and the experience of chocolate hits you in the palate. Sample her truffles, all handmade and ultra-rich and chocolatey. Like most candy stores, De Fluri's is big on holidays, but unlike others, De Fluri's is stocked with unusual chocolates and other seasonal sweets. Easter plays big here—this is the home of the giant gourmet Easter Bunny.

Giant Gourmet Someplace Special

1445 Chain Bridge Rd. (Laughlin St.), McLean 22101
703-448-0800, Fax 703-506-0531, *Open daily*

A P

Your first stop at this gourmet market should be the glass candy counter where seasonal specialties beckon. Throughout the year, you'll find the classy Belgian chocolates by Neuhaus and Belusa and such delicacies as sugared edible flowers. It's a fully stocked counter, so take your time and browse. Also see review in *Gourmet Markets & Gourmet To-Go.*

COFFEE & TEA

Greenberry's Coffee & Tea Company

McLean Corner, 6839 Redmond Dr. (Old Dominion Rd.), McLean 22101
703-821-9500, *Open daily*

A P

This popular coffee emporium combines a friendly neighborhood feel with world-class coffee beans roasted by the local store's master coffee roaster. The buyers are always looking for new beans on the market, including a recently noted New Guinea Tagari, an unusual coffee typified by a winey sweetness. The store sells and serves only Arabica. Last count also showed 10 different decaffeinated beans for sale, including a Sumatra. Teas are a second thought now, but the collection appears to be growing with each visit though primarily this is a coffee haven.

ETHNIC MARKETS

Asian

Apsara Oriental Gourmet Market

Sunset Business Park, 291 Sunset Park Dr. (Spring St.), Herndon 20170
703-471-9194, *Open daily*
No credit cards. P

Owned and operated by a Cambodian family, this pan-Asian market has expanded into a warehouse-sized location and stocks almost anything an Asian cook could want. Most customers are Asian, but friendly staff help any mystified Westerners trying to figure out which chili paste or frozen fish to buy. The only thing the store lacks is a complete produce department, but you can usually find Thai herbs, fresh chilies and shredded green papaya.

Dong y China Herbs

Eden Center, 6763 Wilson Blvd. (Rte. 50), Falls Church 22044
703-536-3339, Fax 703-536-2326, *Open daily*
A P

The combination of culinary and medicinal herbs makes Dong y China a mysterious adventure for the person unacquainted with the complexities of Asian culture. Move beyond the herbal prescriptions and you can find ingredients like black sesame seeds, cardamom, coriander seeds and dried mushrooms to finish off your favorite recipe. Asian teas are featured with the herbs.

Duangrat's Oriental Food Mart

5888 Leesburg Pike
(Glen Forest Dr.), Baileys Crossroads, Falls Church 22041
703-578-0622, Fax 703-820-6206, *Open daily*
A P

Around the corner from Duangrat's (see review in *Restaurants*) sits a small market that has many of the ingredients used in the restaurant's daily preparations. The compact store offers a full line of the noodles, spices and jasmine rice needed for a good Thai meal. Also check out the freezer cases, which have items for Lao and other Asian cuisines. The lemon grass, fish sauce and items such as basil seed make this an important stop for Thai cooks on this side of the Beltway. The market's reputation as a number-one destination for Thai cooks is well-deserved.

Eden Supermarket

Eden Center, 6763 Wilson Blvd. (Rte. 50), Falls Church 22044
703-532-4950, Fax 703-532-1842, *Open daily*
A P

The Eden has one of the area's most extensive selections of Asian (mostly Vietnamese and Chinese) canned goods, seasonings and rices. You also can expect to find all the fruits and vegetables you'll ever need for any Asian dish. Where else can you find a durian in season? From the hoisin sauces to the rice-paper wrappers, the roast meats (duck and pork) and iced fresh fish—it's all here. Eden even sells the utensils, cookwares and serving dishes you need.

Han Ah Reum

8103 Lee Hwy. (Gallows Rd.), Falls Church 22041
703-573-6300, *Open daily*
A P

Han Ah Reum is truly a bargain hunter's paradise, attracting many restaurant owners for its great, inexpensive produce in mass quantities. Most packaged goods are either Korean or Japanese, but the fresh produce and refrigerated meats and noodles will fit into any Asian meal. Check out the kimchi: Koreans are known for their kimchi, the traditional standard condiment made from cabbage, cucumbers and assorted other vegetables with a secret blend of spices, often unique to the family of origin. The store can be a bit bewildering to those unfamiliar with the Asian cuisines, and the staff may not speak much English; but price and variety are big drawing cards. A caveat: Expect crowds on the weekends. **Also located at** 12015 Georgia Ave., Silver Spring, MD, 301-942-5071.

Lotte

Lotte Plaza, 3250 Old Lee Hwy. (Fairfax Cir.), Fairfax 22030
703-352-8989, Fax 703-352-7850, *Open daily*

A P

One of the largest Asian supermarkets in the area, Lotte is primarily a Korean market, but they stock a full range of Asian ingredients. Customers love the meat and produce departments, and the fresh fish is some of the best in town and at prices that may convert you to seafood. Sushi-quality fish is particularly special here. Like kimchi? You'll go wild for the large selection of this Korean staple.

Mabuhay Oriental Store & Bakery

7016 Commerce St. (Backlick Rd.), Springfield 22150
703-451-8986, Fax 703-451-8986, *Open daily*

A P

One of the friendliest of the ethnic markets, this Virginia home for Filipino food has a reputation for teaching about the culture as you shop in the store. The shelves are filled with preserves, sauce and soup mixes and canned specialties. The freezer always has some stuffed ensaymadas, the savory filled pastry. The bakery has a selection of sweets that include a sponge cake shaped in a loaf, iced with sugar and butter. Meats and bacon are available frozen.

Saigon Supermarket

Saigon West Mall, 6795 Wilson Blvd. (Rte. 50), Falls Church 22044
703-533-9430, Fax 703-450-8967, *Open daily*

A P

True to its name, the Saigon Supermarket has become an important source for all those hard-to-find items needed for Vietnamese cookery. You can even find all the fixings for the famous national soup, the pho, although you may find that just stopping at one of the area's numerous pho shops is easier. Check out all the seasoning ingredients, too, especially the line of fish sauces.

Sukhothai Oriental Market

1904 Mt. Vernon Ave. (Howell St.), Del Ray, Alexandria 22301
703-683-4016, *Open daily*
No credit cards.

This small, well-stocked market in the Del Ray section of Alexandria sells Thai staples. Jasmine rice is a bargain in 5- to 25-pound bags. Coolers have Thai herbs—always a fresh bundle of lemon grass. For beginners, mixes and spice blends are on every shelf. One corner of the store is overflowing with Asian movies for rent. From basil seeds to frozen squid, Sukhothai is a one-stop Thai market.

German

German Gourmet

7185 Lee Hwy. (S. Washington St.), Falls Church 22046
703-534-1908, Fax 703-237-6302, *Open Mon.-Sat.*
A **P**

The Gourmet has all you'd expect of an authentic German market, from the cured meats to the German beers and wines. Start with the Black Forest and Westphalian hams, then check the famous bratwurst, which has lured many patrons away from the ordinary supermarket variety. Grab a loaf of pumpernickel and inquire about the variety of meats—this will turn into a lesson in German culinary culture. The staff is helpful, and don't worry if German is the spoken word; English is welcome at the German Gourmet.

Indian

Indian Spices & Appliances

3000 N. Tenth St. (Pollard St.), Arlington 22203
703-522-1555, Fax 703-522-5232, *Open Thurs.-Tues.*
A **P**

A long life of more than 25 years in the area makes this friendly place one of the leading home resources for the herbs and spices to make the masalas of Indian cuisine. The chutneys are a glorious extension beyond the narrow band found in most stores. Rice, a host of Indian pickles and all the fixings for any curry make this a must-stop for Indian food lovers. For the less ambitious, there is a freezer full of prepared foods. The Indian flat breads come in a myriad of varieties.

Italian

The Italian Store

Lyon Village Center
3123 Lee Hwy. (Spount Run Pkwy.), Arlington 22201
703-528-6266, Fax 703-524-8361, *Open daily*
A **P**

This place is the ravioli king of the Italian markets—you can find more than a dozen at any time here. Favorites include shrimp and lobster, but plenty of shoppers prefer the good old-fashioned cheese-filled pastas. While you're here, buy a sauce to go, a bottle of wine and some Italian bread. The tiramisu is store-made and worth it. Also see review in *Quick Bites*.

Latin American

Americana Market

6128 Columbia Pike (Blair Rd.), Falls Church 22041
703-671-9625, Fax 703-6711-0059, *Open daily*
A **P**

The aromas from a Latino market are cause for a case of sensory overload, and Americana Market is no exception. All the spices, peppers, fruits and meats mingle into a symphony of Latin food harmonies. The chorizos of Americana are rich and thick—and spicy, and come in as many styles and flavors as you'll find in the Washington area. From jicama to chayote to plantains, the busy produce section is always a source for good values compared with chain market prices. **Also located at** 8541 Piney Branch Rd., Silver Spring, MD, 301-495-0864.

Middle Eastern

Lebanese Taverna Market

4400 Old Dominion Dr. (Lorcom Ln.), Arlington 22207
703-276-8681, Fax 703-276-6877, *Open daily*

A P

Owned and managed by a family who has been in the restaurant business for more than 20 years in Washington, the Marketplace opened in 1991 in a bright space with high ceilings and modern fixtures. You can always find at least 25 salads, 12 kinds of olives, cheeses and even a selection of Lebanese wines, both red and white, in stock—plus Almaza, the favorite Lebanese beer. The olive oils, dry goods and spices are excellent values, as are the cooking classes on Wednesday and Thursday evenings; the class price includes wine and the meal you prepare. Ingredients used in the class are available in a package to go, so you can practice your new-found skills at home. Also see review in *Quick Bites*.

Mediterranean Bakery

Trade Center Shopping Village
352 S. Pickett St. (Duke St.), Landmark, Alexandria 22304
703-751-1702, Fax 703-823-5007, *Open daily*

A P

A supermarket for Middle Eastern goods—cooked and raw, sweet and savory—this store has more than 70 kinds each of olive oil, vinegar and hot sauce, as well as lots of cheeses and tea. You'll need many visits to sample all the large selection of pickles and olives. Many shoppers think the hummus here can't be topped for its bold, rich flavors. Among other items available are gyros, falafel, shwarma, spanakopita, vegetable pies, cheese and tomato pies and salads. Also see reviews in *Gourmet Shops & Markets/Bakeries* and in *Quick Bites*.

Russian

Russian Gourmet

Langley Shopping Center
1396 Chain Bridge Rd. (Old Dominion Rd.), McLean 22101
703-760-0680, Fax 703-760-0411, *Open daily*

A P

You can't see this store from the street, but when you see the Three Pigs barbecue restaurant, you'll know you're at the right shopping strip. Located directly behind the restaurant, this deli-market offers a complete selection of Russian and Eastern European goods that are representative of the culture and the cuisine. You can find Russian brands of meats and sausages as well as staples like butter and dried and smoked fish. The store is packed with everything from videos to innumerable candies. Of course, there's caviar, too.

FARMERS MARKETS

Neighborhood Farmers Street Markets

TUESDAY
Fairfax—10480 Main St., 8 a.m.-12:30 p.m. (May-Nov.), 703-642-5173.
Alexandria—Government Center Parking Lot, 2511 Parkers Ln., 8:30 a.m.-12:30 p.m. (May-Nov.), 703-642-5173.

WEDNESDAY
Vienna—9601 Courthouse Rd., 8:30 a.m.-12:30 p.m. (May-Oct.), 703-642-5173.
Arlington—Clarendon Metro Park (Highland St. & Clarendon Blvd.), 3 p.m.-7 p.m. (May-Oct.), 703-276-0228.

THURSDAY
Annandale—Mason District Park, 6621 Columbia Pike, 8 a.m.-12:30 p.m. (May-Oct.), 703-642-5173.
Herndon—Old Town, Spring St. (next to Red Caboose), 8:30 a.m.-12:30 p.m. (May-Nov.), 703-642-5173.

FRIDAY
McLean—Lewinsville Park, 1659 Chain Bridge Rd., 8:30 a.m.-12:30 p.m. (May-Nov.), 703-642-5173.

SATURDAY
Arlington—N. 14th St. & N. Courthouse Rd., 8 a.m.-12 p.m. (Apr.-Dec.), 703-228-6400.
Burke—VRE Parking Lot, 5671 Roberts Pkwy., 8 a.m.-12 p.m. (May-Oct.), 703-642-5173.
Falls Church—300 Park Ave., 8 a.m.-12 p.m. (May-Nov.), 703-248-5027.
Reston—Lake Anne Plaza, North Shore Dr., 8 a.m.-12 p.m. (May-Nov.), 703-642-5173.
Alexandria—Oxford Ave. & Mt. Vernon Ave., 8 a.m.-12 p.m. (May-Nov.), 703-683-2570.
Alexandria—Market Square, 301 King St., 5 a.m.-10 a.m., (Mar.-Dec.), 703-370-8723.

SUNDAY
Arlington—Columbia Pike & S. Walter Reed Dr., 10 a.m.-2 p.m. (May-Nov.), 703-892-2776.

FISH, MEAT & POULTRY

Cannon's Seafood

Village Center, 762-A Walker Rd. (Georgetown Pike), Great Falls 22066
703-759-4950, Fax 703-759-2180, *Open Tues.-Sat.*
A P

Going strong for 60 years in Washington, Cannon's is the source for any cook looking for ultrafresh seafood. The market has a large selection of lobsters, crabs and jumbo lump crab meat, spiced shrimp and smoked fish. You can buy your fish—from Chilean sea bass to the local favorite, rockfish—whole or fileted. There's always a good selection of favorites such as tuna, halibut and salmon. If you want something you don't see, ask the fishmonger; he'll do his best to find it on the market—even that six-pound lobster you crave. **Also located at** 1065 31st St. NW, Washington, DC, 202-337-8366.

Springfield Butcher

6816 Bland St. (Backlick Rd.), Springfield 22150
703-451-3033, Open Mon.-Sat.

A P

Eager to show the new customer the benefits of a good relationship with a butcher, the Springfield Butcher is a small, consumer-friendly meat-cutting shop. In this strip mall, the staff breaks down sides of beef with care and skill. Looking for a strip steak for a barbecue? They can cut it for to your specifications. Roasts and crown cuts are a specialty.

GOURMET MARKETS & GOURMET TO-GO

Fresh Fields

143 Maple Ave. E. (Park St.), Vienna 22180
703-319-2000, Fax 703-319-2001, Open daily

A P

Fresh Fields is part of Whole Foods Market, which claims to be the world's biggest retailer of natural and organic foods. Here you will find a large, creatively merchandised produce department, an in-house bakery, extensive prepared-foods counters and large wine and cheese departments. Most stores have a wide-open feel and a welcoming ambience. Home of the best grocery salad bar—with couscous, bean and tofu salads for the health-conscious—Fresh Fields also has one of the area's finest butcher shops, featuring naturally raised beef, lamb and pork. Shoppers can find the favorite chicken brands of local chefs: Eberly and Bell and Evans. Some locations have coffee and juice bars, the latter run by Jamba Juice, featuring its California-created power smoothies. **Other locations.**

Giant Gourmet Someplace Special

1445 Chain Bridge Rd. (Laughlin St.), McLean 22101
703-448-0800, Fax 703-506-0531, Open daily

A P

The gourmet extension of Giant Food has become an institution for Northern Virginia foodies. This was one of the first groceries to venture into the gourmet market, and a staunchly loyal local following has supported Someplace Special while the market competition has expanded fiercely. Known for its extensive cheese department and the wine and specialty food section, the store also has an excellent meat department, where customers are on a first-name basis with their favorite butcher. Also see review *Gourmets Shops & Markets/Candy & Chocolates.*

Harris Teeter

Hyde Park Plaza, 600 N. Glebe Rd. (Randolph St.), Arlington 22203
703-526-9100, Fax 703-292-5966, Open daily

A P

This place represents a new breed of upscale grocery that stops just short of claiming the title "gourmet" yet provides shoppers with an extensive selection of fresh, frozen and freshly cooked items and a broad range of natural and organic products. The chain is expanding in the Washington area with stores that promote improved customer service and large specialty food lines. The Arlington store has an extensive wine department, flower department and coffee shop on a mezzanine level, an elevator ride away. Now that's upscale! **Other locations**.

Sutton Place Gourmet

6655 Old Dominion Dr. (Old Chain Bridge Rd.), McLean 22101
703-448-3828, Fax 703-448-3829, *Open daily*

A P

Sutton Place Gourmet was one of the first specialty gourmet markets in the Washington metro area. An expansion has added components of Hay Day Markets and Balducci's, the ultimate snazzy gourmet market from New York City. Special Balducci's selections include lentils from Castelluccio in Umbria and Arborio rice, grown in the Po Valley of northeastern Italy. Hay Day has brought open-produce sections to the center of the stores. Only Dean & DeLuca competes at this price level—this is no place to shop if you're looking for a bargain. **Other locations**.

Trader Joe's

5847 Leesburg Pike
(Columbia Pike), Baileys Crossroads, Falls Church 22041
703-379-5883, *Open daily*

A P

Trader Joe's has recently moved east of the Mississippi from its West Coast origins. Customers speak of the private-label marketing of specialty coffees, nuts, candies and beverages with a cultlike fanaticism. These fanciful stores feature Hawaiian-shirted staff and beachcomber décor. Trader Joe's only buys when the price is right, so you will find bargains; but variety can be limited and brands not always available. Quality is high and the frozen food department is exceptional, with finds like the salmon stir-fry with all the veggies and seasonings in the bag. Many products are considered "natural," such as the yogurt-covered blueberries packed with no preservatives or artificial coloring or flavors. While the Virginia stores have a selection of wine and beer at good prices, the Maryland stores cannot sell beer or wine. **Other locations.**

Très Joli

Hunter Mill Plaza
2952-A Chain Bridge Rd. (Hunter Mill Rd.), Oakton 22124
703-242-8752, Fax 703-242-0475, *Open daily*

A P

Très Joli's staff would like the whole world to slow down a moment to enjoy food in the leisurely French way. One way is to lunch on the croque monsieur, with its Gruyère, ham and béchamel sauce on country white bread. Quiches with tender, flaky crusts and savory fillings are also popular. The menu is extensive, and the pastries—such as the simply luscious bittersweet chocolate croissant—may tempt you to go overboard for the day. It's possible to sit and sip coffee all day, but this is also a bakery and café to go. Also see review in *Quick Bites*.

KITCHEN EQUIPMENT

Kitchen Etc.

46301 Potomac Run Plaza, Ste. 150 (Leesburg Pike), Sterling 20164
703-433-2390, *Open daily*

A P

Truly a cooking and dining headquarters, this warehouse-sized store holds every kitchen and household gadget and appliance you might ever want—and newly discovered treasures to take home. Also among the inventory are table linens, glassware and a small but interesting collection of cookbooks. It's a dream place for the new bride.

La Cuisine

323 Cameron St. (Royal St.), Alexandria, VA 22314
703-836-4435, Fax 703-836-8925, *Open Mon.-Sat.*

A

This Old Town kitchen store is the delight of epicures on the hunt for the unusual, the exotic and the practical kitchenware. Owner Nancy Purves Pollard scours the globe for the very best.

Marketplace Kitchen & Coffee

1375 Beverly Rd. (Old Dominion Rd.), McLean 22101
703-761-2224, Fax 703-761-1606, *Open daily*

A P

In suburban McLean, foodies can find a kitchen-gadget heaven in Marketplace Kitchen & Coffee. Imagine any gadget that might ease your cooking tasks, and this store either will have it or will find it for you. It also stocks one of the area's largest selections of cookie cutters (while other stores have reduced their inventories of these low-ticket items), which will delight those seeking the small kitchen treat. The store has appliances like rice cookers and toasters for the serious shopper, but it's the fun items (and the active owner) that give the store its character. If you can't find it in the store, the search begins with catalogs and then it's on to the Internet. The mission is a satisfied customer who walks out with a kitchen tool.

Williams-Sonoma

Tyson's Galleria, 1833-G International Dr. (Rte.7), McLean 22102
703-917-0005, Fax 703-917-0021, *Open daily*

A P

With about ten stores in the metro area, this classy kitchenwares purveyor has its own distinctive look and collection of cookware. It usually stocks seasonings, kitchen gadgets, cookbooks and small culinary whatnots that will please devoted cooks. **Other locations**.

WINE & SPIRITS

Arrowine

Lee Heights Shopping Center
4508 Lee Hwy. (Glebe Rd.), Arlington 22207
703-525-0990, Fax 703-525-2218, *Open Mon.-Sat.*

A P

This store's expansive shelves hold wines from South Africa to Australia along with fine Virginia and California selections,

Champagne and Spanish sherry. You also can buy wine accessories, good beers, fine cheeses, charcuterie items (salami, pâté) and other gourmet goods. Wine tastings are held Friday and Saturday evenings.

Bostetter's Wine & Gourmet

Bradlee Shopping Center
3690-J King St. (S. Taylor St.), Alexandria 22302
703-820-8600, Fax 703-820-8601, *Open Mon.-Sat.*
A **P**

David Bostetter and his friendly staff will help customers find fine wines for any occasion from their vast selection. Besides wine, there are 200 types of beer. Gourmets will be tempted by such additional items as cheeses, gourmet pasta and chocolate, smoked fish, cigars and Riedel stemware. Free wine tastings are held every Wednesday night, and there are occasional formal, private tastings. Visit www.wineandgourmet.com for the events calendar.

Ceciles Finewine.com

Salona Village, 1351 Chain Bridge Rd. (Rte. 123), McLean 22101
703-356-6500, Fax 703-356-6502, *Open Mon.-Sat.*
A **P**

Formerly known as Cecile's Wine Cellar, this shop always has provided personal wine service but also specializes in hard-to-find American and international cheeses and gift baskets for its Fortune 500 client list. The staff conducts regular classes, wine dinners and tastings in the store and at area restaurants and hotels. There's also an extensive selection of wines and gift baskets at its expanding Web site, www.finewine.com. **Also located at** 20 A Grand Corner Ave., Gaithersburg, MD, 301-987-5933.

Classic Wines of Great Falls

9912-C Georgetown Pike (Walker Rd.), Great Falls 22066
703-759-0430, Fax 703-759-0448, *Open daily*
A **P**

Owner Tom Casmay is the catalyst for the strong wine business that passes through this small Virginia store. He knows and loves wine, and he understands giving people what they want. He's an expert taster, wine judge and member of wine boards, and he spends time in the shop sharing his expertise with customers. This is one of the state's leading retailers of Virginia wines and also has a good selection from small California wineries. It's also one of the best shops for giving personal service, including special-order wines.

Daily Planet

2004 Mt. Vernon Ave. (Howell Ave.), Del Ray, Alexandria 22301
703-549-3444, Fax 703-549-8520, *Open Mon.-Sat.*
A

Friendly and knowledgeable staff make this neighborhood wine store a pleasure for buyers. Owned by the popular Evening Star restaurant next door, the store has regular tastings, wine dinners and events. Fresh breads and baguettes, fine cheeses, carryout from the restaurant and a fine specialty food inventory make this a quick-stop gourmet heaven. Sampler packs are always a good buy for those trying one of each of the six wine specials for the month. The monthly newsletter is one of the best in the area for store news and informative wine descriptions.

Fern Street Gourmet

Fairlington Center
1708 Fern St. (Quaker Lane), Fairlington, Alexandria 22302
703-931-1234, *Open Mon.-Sat.*

A

In business for 14 years, this small but select store offers more than 12,000 different wines from all over the world, including a great selection of dessert wines and ports. Locals also get their cheese fix here (over 75 choices). Owner Geoff Romine holds free, informal themed wine tastings on Saturdays from noon to 5 p.m.

Rick's Wine & Gourmet

Hechinger Commons, 3117 Duke St. (Quaker Ln.), Alexandria 22314
703-823-4600, Fax 703-823-4605, *Open Mon.-Sat.*

A P

Yes, there is a Rick, and he's on the floor of this busy Alexandria wine shop most days of the week—unless he's on a California scavenger hunt for new wines or an excursion to France or Italy looking for unknown premium producers. The store conducts regular wine dinners for Washington and Virginia restaurants as well as weekly in-store tastings. To accompany the wines is an extensive line of beers, fine cheeses and locally baked breads. The gourmet specialty department is growing.

Total Beverage

1451 Chain Bridge Rd. (Old Dominion Dr.), McLean 22101
703-749-0011, Fax 703-331-3813, *Open daily*

A P

A supersized warehouse for beer and wine, this store is a great source for the depth of its beer selection and wines of all price ranges. On the weekend you can find most staff on hand to help with your selections and small tasting clusters with wines being poured by local distributors. With its cut-rate prices, it's a good place for stocking up on your favorite wines and for finding some obscure labels.

The Wine Seller

F & M Bank Centre, 304 Elden St. (Herndon Pkwy.), Herndon 20170
703-471-9649 Fax 703-733-0202, *Open daily*

A P

The Wine Seller has a strong history as a local store with a select inventory of great wines and great buys. Strongest in California wines, it has a good representation of local wineries (more than 50 in Virginia) and a more than adequate import collection. For many, this is their home-brew supply store, one of the best in the area. It has a superb collection of microbrew beers and imports, ranging from Brooklyn Brewery to England's Samuel Smith. The store is small, but the staff is always accessible, friendly and knowledgeable.

Find the name you are looking for, quickly and easily, in **the index**.

Maryland Suburbs

INTRODUCTION   204

RESTAURANTS   204

QUICK BITES   235

    AMERICAN   235

    BAKERIES/CAFÉS   238

    BARBECUE   238

    BREWPUBS   240

    CAFÉS & COFFEEHOUSES   241

    DELIS & BAGEL SHOPS   241

    ETHNIC FLAIR   242
       (Caribbean, Chinese, Indian, Italian,
       Japanese/Sushi, Mexican, Middle Eastern,
       Pan-Asian, Peruvian, Thai, Vietnamese)

    ICE CREAM & MORE   254

    PIZZA   254

GOURMET SHOPS & MARKETS   256

    BAKERIES   256

    COFFEE & TEA   257

    ETHNIC MARKETS   257
       (African, Asian, Indian, Kosher, Latin American/
       Caribbean, Middle Eastern, Portuguese)

    FARMERS MARKETS   260

    FISH, MEAT & POULTRY   261

    GOURMET MARKETS & GOURMET TO-GO   261

    WINE & SPIRITS   263

INTRODUCTION

From **Rockville** to **Frederick** to **Hyattsville** to **Wheaton**, suburban Maryland offers a wealth of restaurants. But perhaps some of its greatest treasures are its outstanding ethnic restaurants, everything from Thai and Chinese to Persian, Cuban and Jamaican, and just about everything in between. Another treat: browsing along **Bethesda's** restaurant-dense streets, with one after another of some of the DC area's best eateries beckoning.

RESTAURANTS

Acajutla   Mexican/Salvadoran   **12/20**

124 Plaza Shopping Center
18554 Woodfield Rd. (Snoufer School Rd.), Gaithersburg 20879
301-670-1674, *Lunch & Dinner daily, $, Casual*

Despite its pleasant service and family-style ambience, this Mexican-Salvadoran restaurant holds no real allure, although the kitchen has come up with an ambitious menu and some fairly tasty refried beans. As expected when restaurants blend these two cuisines, you'll find such standards as the Salvadoran pupusa and the mariscada (seafood soup with shrimp, clams and crabs) that here is an anemic version of others around town. On the other hand, the taquitos and minichimi appetizers, plus assorted other Mexican dishes (the cheddar cheese enchiladas were particularly good), are fine but not arresting. For dessert, the Salvadoran flan or Mexican apple chimichanga are your best bets, but forget the fried ice cream. Kids have their own menu.

Addie's   Contemporary   **14/20**

11120 Rockville Pike (Edson Rd.), Rockville 20852
301-881-0081, Fax 301-881-0082
Lunch Mon.-Sat., Dinner nightly, $$, Casual

Hats off to an adventurous cook and kitchen staff who dare to experiment. As a result, the menu is uniquely eclectic. Many dishes are wood-grilled (you can smell the smoke in the parking lot), and we love the lunchtime grilled quesadilla with grilled vegetables and the mighty grilled hamburger with bacon and blue cheese—both of these are simply all-American. Dinners are another thing altogether: Look for Dijon mustard-glazed pork chops or grilled ostrich with sweet potato purée or the Angus rib-eye with a Cabernet sauce, either a must if available. Desserts—could be crème brûlée or a torte of some sort— sound utterly caloric, so save some room. And while you wait with your fellow diners, enjoy the funky décor. The main room boasts ten different zany clocks, and only one seems to work. Black's Bar & Kitchen in Bethesda is its hip sister restaurant.

Andalucia — Spanish — 13/20

4931 Elm St. (Arlington Rd.), Bethesda 20814
301-907-0052, Fax 301-907-9750
Lunch Mon.-Fri., Dinner nightly, $$, Casual

This restaurant brings to life the romance and adventure of Spain's Andalucia region, rich in history. The focus is on the garlicky foods of southern Spain with their Mediterranean influences. Lamb, chicken and seafood dishes, some splashed with golden olive oil, are particularly good, especially the chicken al ajillo, flavored with loads of garlic and sherry, and the red snapper baked in rock salt. Another good choice: Seville-style duck with green olives, ham and dry sherry. Enjoy the crusty breads and be sure to indulge in some of the well-chosen wines. Flan is a good choice for dessert.

The Andaman Restaurant & Bar — Thai — 12/20

4828 Cordell Ave. (Woodmont Ave.), Bethesda 20814
301-654-4676, Fax 301-654-0611, *Lunch & Dinner daily, $, Casual*

Self-described as serving both contemporary and traditional Thai foods, Andaman goes even one step further: It serves tapas, a rather Mediterranean concept for an Asian eatery. Can Thai food translate to tapas? Naturals for this treatment are the rolls—the duck roll needs more duck and fewer greens—and the small salads. The kitchen also works out menu items that are more typical, with full entrée servings of seafood, noodles, chicken, lamb chops and whole fish. For an entrée, we recommend the stir-fried boneless duck with basil and chilies, infused with just enough heat to make for interesting mouthfuls. Some other dishes we found too salty perhaps due to an overload of fish sauce. Desserts include cakes, coconut custard and fresh fruit such as mango.

Austin Grill — Tex-Mex — 13/20

7278 Woodmont Ave. (Elm St.), Bethesda 20814
301-656-1366, Fax 301-656-1398
Lunch & Dinner daily, Brunch Sat.-Sun., $$, Casual

Texans know a thing or two about good chili, and chefs at the Austin Grill have learned the secrets. Their bowls of simmered, shredded beef with ground chiles (anchos and chipotles) are just short of heavenly. It's a rugged dish, with enough fire-breathing potential to stand your hair on end. Fortunately, it comes with four small, warm flour tortillas you can dunk or use for wrapping. The tortillas help tame the flames. Terrific chili is only one of many delights on this funky restaurant's menu: fajitas, enchiladas, burritos, carnitas and quesadillas are all good choices. Check the menu's new seasonal specialties section, too, where you might find lamb chops with pineapple-chipotle glaze. If you need to quench your thirst with all this hot, spicy food, select a cooling tequila drink—there are several interesting margaritas like the signature lime-strawberry one—or a chilled brew. The Alexandria location is the only location called South Austin Grill; others go just by Austin Grill. **Other locations.**

Bacchus   Lebanese   **13/20**

7945 Norfolk Ave. (Del Ray Ave.), Bethesda 20814
301-657-1722, Fax 301-657-4406
Lunch Mon.-Fri., Dinner nightly, $$, Casual

Whether you dine in the original little dining room near Dupont Circle in DC or under the tented ceiling of the two-tiered pavilion at this Bethesda branch, you're in for the best Lebanese cuisine in town. The menu is long, and it's best to come with a group and share. Start with baba ghanouj or hummus, or make an entire meal of mezze, a selection of Middle Eastern appetizers that might include stuffed grape leaves, pickled turnips, stuffed baby eggplant with pomegranate sauce, and miniature fried meat turnovers. Main course recommendations include kebabs, stuffed cabbage with pomegranate sauce or pilafs topped with slices of lamb or chicken. **Also located at** 1827 Jefferson Pl. NW, Washington, DC, 202-785-0734.

Bangkok Garden   Thai   **14/20**

4906 St. Elmo Ave. (Norfolk Ave.), Bethesda 20814
301-951-0670, Fax 301-951-0671
Lunch & Dinner daily, $$, Casual

An old-timer in Bethesda and one of the first Thai restaurants in the area, Bangkok Garden serves traditional Thai meals that wow even those used to the most authentic fare. Always good: the soft-shell crab, the crispy fried whole fish and the chicken in basil; some people swear the crispy duck is the best in town. Chicken tendons or a northeastern soup containing vegetables and tripe may be an acquired taste, but the crispy pork with Chinese broccoli and the shredded catfish salad appeal to most people. Bring along a Thai friend to translate. The food is delicious and the décor, with plenty of Thai and Buddhist art, captures the atmosphere and sounds of Bangkok.

Black's Bar & Kitchen   Contemporary   **14/20**

7750 Woodmont Ave. (Old Georgetown Rd.), Bethesda 20814
301-652-6278, Fax 301-215-6781
Lunch Mon.-Fri., Dinner nightly, $$, Casual

If you're looking for a Bethesda restaurant with a certain edginess and style, don't look any farther. Its aquatic décor suggests a wharf-side eatery and its bar is a happening place. A sister restaurant to the funky Addie's in Rockville, its menu goes in a slightly different direction, with some outstanding Gulf Coast dishes. Try the stellar Texan duck enchilada appetizer. For a lighter beginning, consider the New Orleans chopped salad, which is just what it sounds like: a salad of chopped lettuce tossed with fried crawfish tails, roasted corn kernels and grilled sweet potatoes. Entrée choices include unusual pasta inventions, a few meat-based dishes and some high-class seafood main courses. You might fall for the tortilla-crusted Gulf snapper, but if you're a softie for crabs, you won't find better soft-shells. Dessert choices change often, but if the chocolate-caramel-toffee cheesecake is on the menu, grab it and run—it's sensational.

Bombay Bistro — Indian — 14/20

98 W. Montgomery Ave. (S. Adams St.), Rockville 20850
301-762-8798, Fax 301-762-8799, *Lunch & Dinner daily, $$, Casual*

One of the very early Indian restaurants in the area, the Rockville Bombay Bistro (really like a bistro) has always been a big hit. It's all about casual fun and good times, and often there's a young crowd enjoying curries, naans and dosas. We recommend the consistently good lamb vindaloo, which here is appropriately hot and sour—and in generous portions—and the outstanding, smoky-flavored dal makhani. We've also discovered the very good South Indian masala dosa (potato-stuffed pancake) and swear by the delicious tandoori-baked breads. The famous buffets make a good excuse for overeating. Whatever you do, save room for the mango ice cream. **Also located at** 3570 Chain Bridge Rd., Fairfax, VA, 703-359-5810.

Bombay Gaylord — Indian — 11/20

8401 Georgia Ave. (Bonifant St.), Silver Spring 20910
301-565-2528, *Lunch & Dinner daily, $$, Casual*

Inconsistency has been the main ingredient when we've visited Bombay Gaylord. One time the dishes are superbly seasoned, with the chef hitting the right balance between creamy and textured and mild and searing hot. Another time the food is drab, as we discovered at one dinner when some of the meat samosas were still cold, the lamb biryani was unmemorable and the Goan fish curry—which could be a signature dish when made with salmon—was leaden. Even the breads, which can excel, may not live up to expectations. So eating here can be chancy and may really depend on who's in the kitchen: If it's good, though, the food is outstanding. But you have to give the owners credit for tackling a restaurant business in the ever-changing environment of Silver Spring.

Café Deluxe — American — 13/20

4910 Elm St. (Woodmont Ave.), Bethesda 20814
301-656-3131, Fax 301-656-0466
Lunch & Dinner daily, Brunch Sun., $$, Casual

Like its older sister restaurant downtown, this Bethesda site features an American-casual menu, which judging from the noise level, appeals to a large audience, from toddlers in strollers to businessmen at the bar: The place resounds with chattering voices and tinkling cutlery as loads of people either bar hop or simply overeat. As for appetizers, we found that the creamed spinach dip and chips featured more chips than dip, so you might look at the goat cheese salad or possibly the crispy chicken spring rolls as better starters for the entrées. The kitchen offers several sandwich selections—we found the roasted lamb and goat cheese mediocre—and such appealing full meals as an herb-roasted chicken with mashed potatoes (real comfort food) and chicken potpie, steamed mussels and grilled meatloaf also with mashed potatoes. Desserts don't deserve gold stars, the apple pie with caramel sauce was rather mushy, and the lackluster chocolate chip cookie pie has been replaced with a brownie dessert. Yet even if every dish doesn't ring true, the whole place is fun and convivial, a true neighborhood happening. **Also located at** 3228 Wisconsin Ave. NW, Cleveland Park, Washington DC, 202-686-2233.

Café Europa   Italian   **12/20**

7820 Norfolk Ave. (St. Elmo Ave.), Bethesda 20814
301-657-1607, Fax 703-734-0661, *Lunch & Dinner daily, $$, Casual*

It's sleek and chic, this little Bethesda eatery, and lures in the young, trendy and all others who are looking for some decidedly European ambience served up alongside their Italian casual food. Because of its centrally located wood-burning brick oven, it would seem that pizzas are the main game here. The portobello pie is pleasing, but you'll find several other traditional pies as well. Heartier fare includes the grilled salmon or jumbo crab cakes, neither of which seem particularly Italian. But the pasta dishes do, featuring ravioli stuffed with mushrooms and cheese tortellini with rock shrimp and spinach. Dinners include such hearty entrées as roast duck with raspberry sauce and a roast rack of lamb. At either meal, hold out for the ricotta cheesecake. The décor looks like a mini-gallery for avant-garde artworks.

Café Mileto   Italian/Contemporary   **12/20**

18056 Mateny Rd. (Great Seneca Hwy.), Germantown 20874
301-515-9370, Fax 301-515-9378
Lunch & Dinner daily, Brunch Sun., $$, Casual

The cooks at this Italian restaurant have mastered the art of assembling terrific antipasto platters and baking excellent crusty and flavorful pizzas. If you end up here for lunch, check the specials menu: spinach and penne, shrimp salad, chicken cacciatore and a grilled eggplant sandwich. Too bad the Sunday brunch buffet has ended, but regulars can still enjoy some unusual breakfast fare from the shortened brunch menu: Tuscan french toast, Belgian waffles, a fresh-fruit platter and omelets with a choice of toppings. The décor is fetching: mustard yellows and corals, hanging plants and ceiling fans set the stage for this small yet upscale eatery.

Café Roval   American/Mediterranean/French   **13/20**

Potomac Village, 9812 Falls Rd. (River Rd.), Potomac 20854
301-299-3000, *Lunch Mon.-Sat., Dinner nightly, $$, Casual*

Chef-owner Fritz Siegfried makes it all look so simple: Classically trained in Switzerland, he assembles lovely meals and has made a permanent impression on the Potomac community that has patronized this restaurant for years. The menu has undergone some changes over the decades—it gets infused more and more often with the sunny flavors of the Mediterranean—but we'd always put our money on Siegfried's French onion soup, free-range chicken with pomme frites and (surprisingly), his hefty hamburger. His chicken club sandwich is also good, with layers of applewood-smoked bacon and tomatoes. Desserts are mandatory here—if the Chocolate Decadent Cake appears on the menu, snap it up: It's a masterful layering of chocolate on chocolate.

For Gayot Hot Ten Restaurants in Washington, DC,
visit: gayot.com

Caspian Café   Persian   13/20

20100 N. Frederick Rd. (Middlebrook Rd.), Germantown 20876
301-353-0000, *Lunch & Dinner daily, $, Casual*

A P

As unpretentious as any hamburger joint, this startlingly good Persian restaurant is a roadside wonder. Who would expect to find such gently seasoned meats, delicately saffron-spattered rice and crunchy shirazi salads from such a tiny kitchen? The formula works, for the place never seems empty, especially when local businesspeople want a generous midday meal. Start with garlic-spiked hummus, then work your way through the vegetable-and-pasta aush soup to the lamb and chicken kebabs. Check the specials menu: If you are lucky, you'll feast on tah-diq (the crusty rice from the bottom of the cooking pot) topped with a ladle of yellow split peas and cubed beef. If it's available, ask for a serving of bademjan, or stewed eggplant, swirled with Persian yogurt. All in all, it's fine bargain dining in the suburbs.

Centro Italian Grill   Italian   13/20

4838 Bethesda Ave. (Arlington Rd.), Bethesda 20814
301-951-1988, Fax 301-951-7022
Lunch Mon.-Fri., Dinner nightly, $$$, Casual

A

Brought to you by the same group who dreamed up Bethesda's Red Tomato Café and DC's glamorous Red Tomato restaurant, this charming desert-colored bistro is a perfect backdrop for ultra-glamorous (read chic and wealthy) patrons as well as the casual drop-ins who are beguiled by the skylights and open front windows. Passersby might wonder about the unusual foods served in such a cheery setting. The authentic Italian dishes are true to their origins. Look for lusty pasta dishes such as penne with salmon and zucchini in a light vegetable cream sauce and weightier grilled foods, like grilled beef tenderloin with mashed potatoes. Lunch guests might prefer a sandwich, and we can recommend the luscious grilled artichoke, eggplant, pepper and ricotta on focaccia. Desserts are sumptuous including a chocolate terrine with layers of chocolate on chocolate or the filo dough shell stuffed with semolina, ricotta and candied fruit.

Cesco Trattoria   Italian   14/20

4871 Cordell Ave. (Norfolk Ave.), Bethesda 20814
301-654-8333, Fax 301-654-8874
Lunch Mon.-Fri., Dinner nightly, $$$, Casual dressy

A P

It's enough for gastronomes to hear the name Francesco Ricchi to understand that they are about to experience an explosion of flavors and textures. A noted area chef, he opened DC's Etrusco and I Ricchi and has put some dishes on the local culinary map. Cesco Trattoria features his sublime northern Italian cooking in a pretty corner setting. Particularly nice: an alfresco lunch on the covered patio. Splurge on the signature prosciutto with fried bread or the tomatoes with fresh mozzarella drizzled with extra virgin olive oil. The grilled salmon special may tempt, but skip straight to the pastas, for example, the homemade cavatelli with broccoli rabe, minced sausage and tomato. The breads are impressive, too, and one— a focaccia with roasted tomatoes as a topping—is luscious. And how about the osso buco in white wine sauce, topped with crunchy angel hair pasta? So many choices, so many calories.

The Cheesecake Factory American **13/20**

White Flint Mall
11301 Rockville Pike (Nicholson Ln.), North Bethesda 20895
301-770-0999, Fax 301-230-9280, *Lunch & Dinner daily, $$, Casual*

If you don't want to wait forever for a table, plan to visit during the off-hours. Everyone loves the hip atmosphere, mammoth portions of funky foods and outstanding cheesecakes at this upscale national chain. You'll face two dilemmas: what to choose from the multipage menu and how to avoid overeating. Choices include everything from zany pizzas to overstuffed sandwiches to overflowing salad bowls. We've enjoyed the Santa Fe and Thai noodle salads, all of the burgers and the mix of Tex-Mex eats. Whatever you do, pace yourself so you can enjoy one of more than 30 varieties of cheesecake. Or pack up a whole cappuccino-white chocolate cheesecake or other gem to-go. **Also located at** Chevy Chase Pavilion, 5345 Wisconsin Ave. NW, Washington, DC, 202-364-0500,

China Canteen Chinese **12/20**

808 Hungerford Dr. (Mannakee St.), Rockville 20850
301-424-1606, *Lunch & Dinner daily, $, Casual*

China Canteen is not glamorous, nor a real hot spot for trendy Chinese fare. You come here for basic family cooking with an emphasis on the little-known Yangchow style of cooking, which means pot stickers, steamed and pickled fish, fish head stews and crispy jellyfish to start. Some of the best dishes here come from the Chinese side of the menu, and this is one place where even the skittish should skip past the familiar and ask for the Chinese menu. We have loved the bean curd noodles with cabbage slaw and the soft tofu with shrimp, the Peking duck, orange beef and sesame chicken. Check out the weekend Northern dim sum.

China Chef Chinese **12/20**

11323 Georgia Ave. (University Blvd.), Wheaton 20902
301-949-8170, *Lunch & Dinner daily, $$, Casual*

Popular for its weekend dim sum, China Chef also serves a consistently good Chinese menu with a wide range of popular traditional dishes. We recommend the orange beef , General Tso's chicken, boneless duck stuffed with taro and the eggplant in garlic sauce. The menu has an extensive seafood and a vegetarian section—try the ma po tofu. For cold weather dining, you can warm up with one of the assorted hot pot dishes.

Clyde's of Chevy Chase Contemporary **13/20**

Chevy Chase Center
70 Wisconsin Circle (Wisconsin Ave.), Chevy Chase 20815
301-951-9600, Fax 301-656-4586
Lunch & Dinner daily, Brunch Sun., $, Casual

This is a great place for kids, who are mesmerized by the toy train that chugs around overhead and the numerous miniature airplanes suspended from the ceiling. As with all Clyde's restaurants, the menu offers certain core items (chili and hamburgers, for sure), but menus change daily, and also feature seasonal favorites, from Maine lobsters in the fall, to Copper River salmon and fresh asparagus in the spring, to local farm-fresh produce come summer. Favorites include their crispy Thai spring rolls, stuffed with shredded cabbage and pork and the sausage and chard rigatoni, an ample pasta dish suited to a farmer's country meal. Few dishes though surpass the soft-shell crab sandwich or the blackberry pie, both available only in season. **Other locations.**

Comus Inn American 12/20

23900 Old Hundred Rd. (Comus Rd.), Comus, Dickerson 20842
301-349-5100, Fax 301-349-5319
Lunch & Dinner Wed.-Sun., Brunch Sun., $$, Casual

The upstairs dining room offers a view of Sugarloaf Mountain, and for sheer country splendor you'd be hard-pressed to find an equally fetching vista. On weekends, particularly at Sunday brunch, Comus Inn is an all-in-the-family place, where generations join together for fun. The brunch buffet includes sweet rolls, Danish, bagels, a cheese display and both fruit and green salads. Heartier fare includes country biscuits and cornbread; bacon, sausage, country potatoes and scrambled eggs; bran and regular waffles with fruit and maple syrups; and hot meats and a rice pilaf. A dessert table with three different kinds of cake concludes the feast. Lunches consist of a black Angus burger with bacon and/or cheese and the classic club. Dinners are fancier meals, at which you might find dishes such as chili-roasted chicken and almond-crusted trout. The inn does a brisk reception and special-events business, and as long as the owners can keep the developers at bay, it makes a bucolic destination not too far from downtown DC.

Copeland's of New Orleans Southern 12/20

1584 Rockville Pike (Halpine Rd.), Rockville 20852
301-230-0968, Fax 301-230-0949
Lunch Mon.-Sat., Dinner nightly, Brunch Sun., $$, Casual

Let the good times roll at Copeland's of New Orleans, a Southern-style restaurant with a mighty big menu. Starring such New Orleans flavors as the Creole andouille sausage, red beans and rice, shrimp etoufée and blackened chicken and red fish. Most of the main courses have a Louisiana lilt, but you can find mainstream dishes like burgers, prime rib and Caesar salad. The menu rotates dishes several times a year, but one mainstay seems to be the Cajun Gumbo Ya Ya, a stew with shrimp, scallops and seasonings. It's a lusty combo of zingy flavors, and if you want an inkling of what New Orleans cooking is all about, you might want to start here. Like to begin your Sundays with a bang? Drop in for brunch and load up on some beignets, eggs Sardou and French toast stuffed with a bananas Foster-style mixture. **Also located at** Old Centreville Crossing, 13810 E. Braddock Rd., Centreville, VA, 703-222-0089; and 4300 King St., Alexandria, VA, 703-671-7997.

For **updated Gayot Washington, DC restaurant reviews,**
visit: digitalcity.com/washington/dining

Cottonwood Café   Southwestern   12/20

4844 Cordell Ave. (Woodmont Ave.), Bethesda 20814
301-656-4844, Fax 301-656-0517
Lunch Mon.-Sat., Dinner nightly, Brunch Sun., $$, Casual

   Southwestern-style Cottonwood Café, with its psychedelic-bright colors, is quite a pretty eatery.. True to its Southwestern roots, it offers such oddities as rattlesnake meat, along with more familiar Latino fare: chili, enchiladas and chimichangas stuffed with achiote-rubbed duck strips and sprinkled with cheese. For an entrée, you won't go wrong with their Sonoran seafood paella, bursting with ultra-fresh seafood. Go hog wild with the desserts: Try the Mexican chocolate silk pie or the fruit cobbler.

Crisfield Seafood Restaurant   Seafood   13/20

8012 Georgia Ave. (East-West Hwy. & Rte. 410), Silver Spring 20910
301-589-1306, Fax 301-589-8378, *Lunch & Dinner Tues.-Sun., $$$, Casual*

   As longtime residents will tell you, Crisfield Seafood Restaurant is an institution. Unlike its fancier competitors, this place sticks to its shirtsleeves informality, and just about anything goes. Its décor suggests a fisherman's hangout, with prints of sailing sloops gracing the walls. Its seafood comes the way ships' hands would eat it, without any downtown fussiness. Evenings can be crowded, and you may find yourself squeezed onto a barstool at the main counter—tables are at a premium. Wait patiently for the kitchen's bonanza: its very basic seafood dishes, from fried oysters (in season) and flounder stuffed with crab meat to fried sea scallops and fish dishes cooked in the Norfolk style. The seafood bisque is a creamy-chunky mixture loaded with fish; soft-shells are treated with great respect and fried quite crisply. Desserts are limited; try the moist house pound cake.

Cuban Corner   Cuban   13/20

825 Hungerford Dr. (Washington St.), Rockville 20850
301-279-0310, *Lunch & Dinner Mon.-Sat., $$, Casual*

   Crowds reflect a growing American interest in Cuban cooking, which sounds similar to Tex-Mex fare, but is pure Caribbean in essence. Try the empanadas de carne and the tostones if you doubt it. Go for other Cuban specialties, too: the ropa vieja of shredded stewed flank steak that resembles old rags, and the holiday dish, puerco asado, of roasted pork doused with a vinegary sauce. There are plenty of other island choices—from fried fish to shrimp cooked with fresh tomatoes, capers and wine—so dig in and eat. Traditional desserts include flan, rum cake and medallions of egg in syrup. The whole experience is a tropical treat.

Delhi Dhaba   Indian   12/20

7236 Woodmont Ave. (Elm St.), Bethesda 20814
301-718-0008, Fax 301-718-0113, *Lunch & Dinner daily, $, Casual*

   This Indian restaurant group has made its mark locally with its budget prices and daringly seasoned food. Don't expect bland curries or insipid vegetable dishes. Indeed, its vindaloo can be astonishingly hot. Make no mistake: This is honest food with lusty curries, hot-from-the-tandoor plain breads and fiery chutneys. Hits include the well-seasoned chicken tikka and the very pungent goat meat curry. The dal is slightly runny but its flavors are robust. Crowds return over and over again for the honest and basic food. Also a draw at this location: the stylish interior décor and the friendly curbside, alfresco dining. **Other locations.**

Don Pablo's, The Real Enchilada   Tex-Mex   12/20

14600 Laurel Pl. (Mulberry St.), Laurel 20707
301-725-1993, Fax 301-725-2208, *Lunch & Dinner daily, $$, Casual*

Suggestive of ranchos and rancheros, bandidos and tacos, this small group of Tex-Mex eateries is as much about cheery ambience as about food. You'll find that plenty of the dishes are more north than south of the border, but as the menu states, this was grub cooked for Texas cowhands. It's plain and simple fare—with some notations about fat grams—that won't win gold medals, but it obviously appeals to a mass crowd of the young and hungry and those in between. We can recommend the chiles rellenos, the refried beans and the freshly made tortillas. There's plenty more here to whet your whistle and curb your appetite, from freshly made lemonade to iron-skillet pie. Prices are reasonable, flavors fine, atmosphere fun: That equals a good night out.

El Aguila   Salvadoran   12/20

Spring Center, 8649 16th St. (Spring St.), Silver Spring 20703
301-588-9063, *Lunch & Dinner daily, $, Casual*

This little mini-mall restaurant offers basically Tex-Mex eats, but you can see its heart lies with El Salvador: Salvador prints and beers predominate. The owner must be a soccer fan, for part of the restaurant logo is soccer balls. We like the courteous service as much as the Santa Fe burrito filled with beef rolled in a flour tortilla and topped with enchilada sauce. The chile relleno also is good. For a taste change, try the pupusas in their thick cornmeal wrap or fried plantains with cream and beans. You can have a seated meal or do take-out for a burrito or taco on the run.

Fairmont Bar & Dining   American   13/20

4936 Fairmont Ave. (Old Georgetown Rd.), Bethesda 20814
301-654-7989, Fax 301-654-6180
Lunch & Dinner Mon.-Sat., Brunch Sun., $$, Casual

Despite the decibel level, Fairmont offers a terrific dining experience: The waiters are cheery and helpful, and the food is nothing short of spectacular. That's high praise for a place that's becoming an affordable neighborhood destination. You'll find the requisite bar with big-screen TVs, the Bruce Willis wannabes and the unglamorous décor befitting a neighborhood hangout. But you won't find predictable bar fare: For one thing, breads come from Marvelous Market, so they're outstanding. For another, executive chef Rob Campbell has concocted a seasonal menu that pulls together Italian, Mediterranean and Asian influences under one big American umbrella. Bring a group, and you can share crispy risotto poppers, beer-battered shrimp and chicken satay with a spicy peanut-lime dipping sauce. Solo? Consider the two-soups-in-one, which is a must: It's a combo of puréed roasted red and yellow tomatoes. At dinner, you have the choice of big meals such as steak frites or herb-roasted chicken with mashed potatoes or lobster mashed potatoes. Lighter fare includes grilled pizzas, big and small salads and sandwiches. We adored the grilled lamb wrapped in homemade pizza dough. Desserts—especially the cookies—are also terrific.

Full Key Restaurant   Chinese   12/20

Wheaton Manor
2227 University Blvd. W. (Amherst Ave.), Wheaton 20902
301-933-8388, *Lunch & Dinner daily, $, Casual*

A P 🚻

Want a Chinese meal at midnight? You can head here for a Cantonese splurge of congee with pork, squid and peanuts or more likely the predictable sweet 'n' sour pork or shredded beef, Szechuan-style. If you can read Chinese characters, check out the specials board, which may offer codfish with bean curd in a casserole or salty fish, chicken and eggplant. The place is not much to look at, but the prices are so low that families can eat well on a low budget, which explains why the restaurant is so popular.

Good Fortune   Chinese   12/20

2646 University Blvd. (Viers Mill Rd.), Wheaton 20902
301-929-8818, *Lunch & Dinner daily, $$, Casual*

A P 🚻 � ♡

An enduring institution among Chinese restaurants, Good Fortune continues serving luscious weekend dim sum plus abundantly good Cantonese fare from the regular menu. On weekends, it may be hard to get a table, as the Chinese community often turns out in full force. From the regular menu, look for an assortment of atypical dishes, including shredded abalone and duck soup, marinated cuttlefish, boneless duck stuffed with taro and duck feet with black mushrooms hot pot. On the more familiar side, you'll find the usual Po Po platter (aka Pu Pu platter), kung pao chicken, Peking duck, ma po bean curd and the ubiquitous orange beef. But your best bet here is to experiment, as the menu embodies some of the better dishes from the Cantonese kitchen. They often host large Chinese banquets, so you know the food is good.

Grapeseed   American   13/20   👨‍🍳

4865-C Cordell Ave. (Norfolk Ave.), Bethesda 20814
301-986-9592, Fax 301-652-6463
Lunch Mon.-Fri., Dinner Mon.-Sat., $$, Casual

A ☎ P 🍷 🍸

Chef Jeff Heineman, owner of Bethesda's only wine bistro, has chalked up a sure winner with this tidy, bright, cheerful tapas/full-meal restaurant. About the size of a handkerchief, Grapeseed offers a unique twist: Many of Heineman's dishes have been inspired by a specific wine. If you order a tapas chimichuri roasted mussels, he'll suggest sipping the complementary Bonny Doon Le Cigare Volant; on the other hand, if you select a dinner entrée of breast of turkey stuffed with Fontina, almonds and olives, he'd want you to pair that with a Mission Saint Vincent Bordeaux from France. Many of the dishes are inventive and offbeat, such as the white grape gazpacho once offered; others are too tricky to work right, such as the bland mango chiffon pie. But you'll never be bored eating and drinking here.

Green Field Churrascaria   Brazilian   **11/20**

1801 Rockville Pike (Twinbrook Pkwy.), Rockville 20852
301-881-3397, Fax 301-881-3398, *Lunch & Dinner daily, $$, Casual*

Brazilian barbecue plays big in the Washington area, where value for money makes a difference. Here customers can eat all they want from the salad and entrée bar and from the skewers of grilled meats carried from table to table by waitstaff. Salads include the usual greens, grains, pastas and beans, tossed with seasonings and dressings, but the entrées are more authentic and include fried yuca, oxtail stew, chicken with garlic, farofa, mashed potatoes, fried bananas and rice. As for the grilled meats, your choices may include chicken, sausage, pork loin, bacon-wrapped turkey, lamb, duck, rabbit or beef ribs. Desserts are a truly lackluster selection of cakes and pastries and worth skipping. Somber, with its dark woods and formal furniture, Green Field lacks the spirited gaucho flair you might expect for such informal eating.

Green Papaya   Vietnamese   **13/20**

4922 Elm St. (Woodmont Ave.), Bethesda 20814
301-654-8986, Fax 301-654-2220
Lunch Mon.-Sat., Dinner nightly, $$, Casual
No credit cards.

With a cheerful and often charming blend of East and West, the Green Papaya restaurant stakes itself out as a player in the roiling Bethesda restaurant scene. Maybe this place won't make its mark as an outstanding purveyor of Vietnamese eats, but it will garner praise for glamorized food and décor that are pretty, if not exactly authentic. And as for the food, make no mistake: You probably will be delighted. Consider this kitchen's version of garden rolls, plump and well wrapped, and served with a flavorful peanut sauce alongside, though the roll lacks some of the more traditional greens wrapped up with the noodles. Less intriguing, and skimpy to boot, is the bowl of rice vermicelli topped with fried spring roll; it is not flavorful enough and comes with more greens than noodles. Although not lengthy, the menu takes you through some of the classics of the Vietnamese kitchen with flavors tidied up for the Western palate. You may find crowds aplenty, so you can opt to sit and eat at the classy bar with its splashy waterfall cascading over sea-green tiles.

Gringada Mexican Restaurant   Mexican/Tex-Mex   **11/20**

12300 Baltimore Blvd. (Ritz Way), Beltsville 20705
301-210-3010, *Lunch & Dinner daily, $, Casual*

Shirtsleeves casual and definitely low-key, this Mexican-style eatery has been a real draw for family crowds and even in midafternoon, pulls in the few stragglers who order up margaritas and Mexican beer to accompany their Tex-Mex dishes. This is not gourmet fare. Instead, it's the usual mix of burritos and fajitas, nachos and chimichangas, all cooked and served with little of the upscale seasonings you'll find at downtown restaurants. Nevertheless, the grub must be a crowd-pleaser, because this place has withstood the test of time and hung on in its Beltsville location for years. Perhaps the best bet here is the green chile burrito or maybe the crab burrito with chili con queso. If someone tags along and doesn't seem to warm to most things on the menu, they may want some breaded and butterflied fried shrimp or a chicken tender cheddar melt. Good desserts: fresh pies and cakes and fried ice cream.

Haandi — Indian — 12/20

4904 Fairmont Ave. (Norfolk Ave.), Bethesda 20814
301-718-0121, Fax 301-718-0123, *Lunch & Dinner daily, $$, Casual*
🅰 ☎ 🅿 👭 🍸

Much acclaimed and well-established, the Haandi Indian restaurants offered one of the first Indian dining experiences in the metro area and continue to hold their own against a flood of upstarts. Its menu reads like a familiar guidebook to Indian eats, and you won't find much that's unfamiliar or jolting. All foods are mildly spiced; if you want to turn up the heat, you'll have to ask for it. So this may appeal to diners who love temperate and familiar dishes. We enjoyed the unusual daal masala, a simmer of various lentils cooked in mild spices and credit the tandoor cook with making decent bread. We usually like fiery vindaloos lavished with chilies, but this one was too mild. **Also located at** 1222 W. Broad St., Falls Church, VA, 703-533-3501.

Hamburger Hamlet — American — 12/20

Georgetown Square
10400 Old Georgetown Rd. (Democracy Blvd.), Bethesda 20814
301-897-5350, Fax 301-897-8238
Lunch & Dinner daily, Brunch Sun., $$, Casual
🅰 🅿 ➰ ♥ 👭 🍸 ♨

You have to hand it to a place that's built its reputation on hamburgers. From a plain burger to a sautéed mushroom burger to a Cajun-spiced burger, there are 15 burgers in all. The rest of each menu consists of an all-American assortment of dishes that caters to every taste. Salads include Chinese chicken, Santa Fe chicken and turkey pasta. Other good choices: chicken and seafood entrées, pasta and New York strip steak. Fresh fruit shakes are chilled and flavorful and a substitute for dessert. Otherwise, select among cheesecake, hot fudge sundae and a baked apple crisp. Don't overlook the Sunday brunch, with its interesting egg dishes. **Other locations.**

Hollywood East Café — Chinese — 13/20 👨‍🍳

2312 Price Ave. (Fern St.), Wheaton 20902
301-942-8282, Fax 301-946-8821, *Lunch & Dinner daily, $, Casual*
🅰 ☎ 👭 🐱 🍷 ♻

Certainly one of the area's hottest Chinese restaurants, this humble Wheaton eatery has won its devoted following by sticking to Hong Kong-style dishes and keeping the setting as low-profile as possible. The kitchen staff leans to such exotica as fried tofu cooked with the braised hearts of bamboo stalks. As in many traditional Chinese restaurants, the chef posts the specials on red paper strips—if you can't translate, ask about the jumbo prawns cooked in a red wine sauce, sautéed spinach with triple eggs (egg, salted egg and thousand-year-old egg) and a spicy clam casserole with scallions. Clearly successful, this restaurant has nearly doubled its space, a lucky break for the many fans who would otherwise have to wait for tables.

House of Chinese Delights   Chinese   **12/20**

16240 Frederick Rd. (Shady Grove Rd.), Gaithersburg 20877
301-948-9898, Fax 301-948-3572, *Lunch & Dinner daily, $, Casual*

🅰🅿🍴

Separate menus for Chinese-speaking and English-speaking patrons, plus weekend dim sum, equals diversified eating at this eclectic Chinese restaurant. Since you have a choice of such familiar dishes as chicken chow mein, lemon chicken, and a rather lackluster orange beef, you can stick to what you know. But if you feel like experimenting, switch gears and dive into some truly authentic fare. We've enjoyed a delicate dish called bamboo shoots with loofah (a spongy material) and eggplant with bean curd, but the Chinese menu compels with other unusual dishes such as braised eel with yellow leek, sea cucumber in brown sauce, water spinach with garlic, and if you can handle it, live shrimp.

Houston's   American   **12/20**

7715 Woodmont Ave. (Cheltenham Dr.), Bethesda 20814
301-656-9755, Fax 301-656-9754, *Lunch & Dinner daily, $$, Casual*

🅰🅿🍴

Want good casual food that's reliable, if not trendy? That's the hallmark of Houston's, an old favorite locally for its predictably good salads, burgers (including a vegetable burger made with oat bran) and fries, steaks and barbecued ribs. Check under the "This and That" section, where you'll find such add-ons as cheddar Parmesan toast and couscous, plus a grilled artichoke medley that's sensational. **Also located at** 12256 Rockville Pike, Rockville, MD, 301-468-3535, and 1065 Wisconsin Ave. NW, Washington, DC, 202-338-7760.

Hunan Palace   Chinese   **12/20**

9011 Gaither Rd. (Shady Grove Rd.), Gaithersburg 20877
301-977-8600, *Lunch Mon.-Fri., Dinner nightly, $$, Casual*

🅰🅿🍴🍸

Housed in an ample space with few frills, this popular Chinese eatery has a Taiwanese foundation and many Taiwanese dishes. But it also considers the diners who come for the more familiar General Tso's chicken, sweet 'n' sour spareribs or orange beef. For something a little more adventurous, consider the Yellow Birds, an ingenuous wrap of dried bean curd skin enclosing shredded vegetables or the ma po tofu. For a culinary challenge, you can order from the Chinese menu, which offers choices such as cuttlefish with garlic, pig's kidney with soy sauce, pork with fermented cabbage, leek with duck red soup and sea cucumber with pig tendon.

Il Pinito Trattoria   Italian   **12/20**

5071 Nicholson Ln. (Nebel St.), Rockville 20852
301-881-0085, *Lunch Mon.-Fri., Dinner nightly, $, Casual*

🅰🅿🍴

Although this tiny Rockville eatery has garnered much hype, we feel it falls far short of the high standards of classic rustic Italian cooking. Using a favorite of sausages and peppers as a benchmark, we found this sauté completely bland and undistinguished and in need of a few shakes of crushed red pepper to perk it up. That goes, too, for the cold antipasto platter to start, so perhaps you should turn your attention to the fried calamari or zuppa di mussels to kick off your meal. It would be better to try a pasta or pizza dish. Dessert options include homemade tiramisu.

India Bistro   Indian   12/20

9031 Gaither Rd. (Shady Grove Rd.), Gaithersburg 20877
301-212-9174, Fax 301-212-9370, *Lunch & Dinner daily, $$, Casual*

A P ⚲

Indian restaurants have become almost commonplace in the area, but Nepalese cooking is a rare jewel, and something to savor. Inconsistency, however, marks the food here, which can be glorious or mediocre. But, to its credit, the kitchen does offer a short selection of truly divine Nepalese dishes. The masu curry (lamb with yogurt) is stunning. Other offerings include Nepali kukhura (chicken marinated in yogurt), tandooried fish in a rich curry, lentils with vegetables, and grilled prawns. The Indian menu holds no surprises, with its usual pakoras, tandoori dishes, vindaloos (lamb, beef and chicken, all of which are too tame to win medals), biryanis and curries. The most economical way to enjoy this restaurant's food is to attack the lunch buffet. The second best bet, after the Nepalese food, is the bread. Want something sweet? Drink a mango lassi (a yogurt beverage) and call it quits. **Also located at** 239 Muddy Branch Rd., Gaithersburg, MD, 301-330-0484.

The Inn at Brookeville Farms Contemporary 14/20 ♟

19501 Georgia Ave. (Rte. 108), Brookeville 20833
301-924-6500, Fax 301-260-2594
Lunch Mon.-Fri., Dinner nightly, $$$, Casual dressy

A ☎ P ⚲ ♟ Y ♦ ⬦

Located at almost the farthest uppermost corner of Montgomery County, this farm-turned-inn may become one of that area's most sought-after destinations. Expanded and gentrified, the old house forms the basis for the new inn, and offers plenty of spacious and quaint dining areas. In the building's midsection stands a small bar with several tables. All this provides a dressy setting for chef Richard Ade's able cooking and interesting seasonal American menu. We tackled his lusty Maryland-style corn and crab chowder decorated with a crab hush puppy that's more crab than corn. Thick with cream, corn and crab meat, this successful soup pairs well with something lighter for the lunch entrée, but we found the Asian-style grilled salmon salad somewhat short on any flavor other than Tamari soy sauce. Better but much richer is his main-dish quiche, elevated beyond the ordinary by its soft custard filling textured with crab meat and Virginia ham. Desserts are a bit trickier to contemplate, and to settle on a favorite may require several more meals. The apple-cheddar crisp tastes comforting and old-fashioned but the cheddar cheese ice cream is a bit hard to figure out. Yet at meal's end, we still felt pampered and satisfyingly full.

Inn at Glen Echo   American   13/20 ♟

6119 Tulane Ave. (MacArthur Blvd.), Glen Echo 20812
301-229-2280, Fax 301-229-2518
Lunch & Dinner daily, Brunch Sun., $$, Casual

A ☎ P ♣ ⚲ ◻ ♟ ⚖ Y ♦ ⬦

Sometimes the eight dining rooms at this funky old inn really swing. Head here on a Sunday afternoon with a group of friends for live jazz and noisy camaraderie. If you're seeking tranquility, request a table in one of the quieter rooms upstairs and settle down to a substantial, all-American meal, kicked off with a hot pumpernickel-raisin loaf. Dinners offer some fairly interesting yet plain food, with such starters as grilled quail or a sensual roasted butternut squash soup. Depending on the season, main courses may include grilled sea bass, pork loin stuffed with pears or the delicious lamb shank, slow-roasted with herbs and served with a Gorgonzola polenta. A good dessert selection would be the warm chocolate soufflé cake. Although the inn feels like a neighborhood pub, it's a destination for city dwellers who want country ambience without a long drive.

Jean-Michel Restaurant   French   12/20

Wildwood Shopping Center
10223 Old Georgetown Rd. (Democracy Blvd.), Bethesda 20814
301-564-4910, Fax 301-564-4912
Lunch Mon.-Fri., Dinner nightly, $$, Business casual

🅰 ☎ P 🍷

If you're looking for French-inspired cooking but haven't the time or energy to cope with downtown traffic, this Bethesda eatery may be your salvation. However, be warned that the staff can be somewhat brusque. The menu is not replete with many classic French dishes, offering instead corn soup with lobster to start and continuing on with clams casino, calamari tempura with aïoli sauce, and grilled and aged New York strip steak. Medallions of lamb with herbs is a good French choice, but steer clear of the forgettable pistou soup and choose the pâté maison instead as a starter. Desserts include soufflés, an apple tart with caramel ice cream, and, of course, crème caramel. Ask about the pastries—some of them are wonderful enough to make the meal.

Joe's Noodle House   Chinese/Korean   12/20

Chesapeake Plaza
1488-C Rockville Pike (Templeton Pl.), Rockville 20852
301-881-5518, *Lunch & Dinner daily, $, Casual*

🅰 ☎ P 🖥 🍴

After a change in ownership, this little place retains its charm, but the menu has undergone a radical change, from all-Chinese to a mix of Chinese and a few Korean dishes. Probably the best time to eat here is weekend mornings, when the kitchen pulls off an array of northern Chinese dim sum dishes, from sweet soy milk and sesame balls to turnip cakes and fried dumplings. We also recommend the scallion crêpe, the least oily and puffiest one we've enjoyed. Also good are the beef chow fun and the cold sesame noodles with shredded chicken. You can skip the predictable lemon chicken and maybe sample the duck tongue with basil. At lunch, don't be surprised to find a handful of Thai dishes.

Levante's   Middle Eastern/Turkish   12/20

7262 Woodmont Ave. (Elm St.), Bethesda 20814
301-657-2441, Fax 301-657-2458
Lunch & Dinner daily, Brunch Sun., $, Casual

🅰 🍴 🍸

With its bold blues and yellows, this Middle Eastern restaurant has taken the DC area by storm. Drop in at lunch or

219

dinner and scan around for a vacant table. It seems everyone has stopped by for a glass of wine, a loaf or two of the restaurant's superb hot bread dunked in golden olive oil and one of the oversized Turkish pides—a "pizza boat" loaded with your choice of toppings. We are addicted to the red lentil soup to start and always end up with an order of garlicky hummus and the lamb pide. Bigger appetites will enjoy the moussaka, kebab or veal and lamb chop entrées. The staff is very friendly and helpful, and that attitude is contagious: Everyone seems to have a good time. **Also located at** 1320 19th St. NW, Washington, DC, 202-293-6301.

Los Chorros Restaurant   Mexican/Salvadoran   12/20

2420 Blueridge Ave. (Georgia Ave.), Wheaton 20902
301-933-1066, Fax 301-949-2353, *Lunch & Dinner daily, $$, Casual*

If you drop by on Sunday for a hearty repast, you'll find that you and plenty of others have sat down to one of the restaurant's remarkably popular and inexpensive dishes. Most dishes are Salvadoran, although the menu does have a Mexican component, where you'll find hefty burritos of beef, chicken or beans or combos thereof, plus enchiladas, fajitas and assorted seafood dishes. Of the latter, it seems everyone orders the mariscada, a seafood soup chock-full of lobster meat, shrimp, clams and scallops. It's a whopping order, enough to share, and that allows you to sample the nachos, taquitos and the chili relleno, Salvadoran style. Don't forget the dessert selection: The flan is outstanding and, for the uninitiated, the Salvadoran chilate con nuegado is a special treat. It's a lively group and often noisy—everyone is having a fiesta.

Louisiana Express   Southern   12/20

4921 Bethesda Ave. (Arlington Rd.), Bethesda 20814
301-652-6945, Fax 301-654-4852
Breakfast Mon.-Sat., Lunch & Dinner daily, Brunch Sun., $, Casual

Hardly fashionable, tiny Louisiana Express has been a consistent winner in everyone's book for its exciting, spicy fare and rock-bottom prices. As the name suggests, its menu is all fast Louisiana food, which makes its takeout service a reasonable option if you've double-parked. Otherwise, sit back in this casual place and enjoy the dark and potent gumbos; the over-stuffed Po' Boys with oysters, catfish or assorted other fillings; and other Louisiana staples such as étouffée and jambalaya. Although it's not Southern, the house hamburger with rémoulade, Creole mustard and peppers is a real winner. So, too, the hot dog with andouille sausage. Breakfast fare is less Southern, but you'll find eggs Sardou and beignets.

Mamma Lucia   Italian   12/20

Federal Plaza
12274 Rockville Pike, Ste. M (Twinbrook Pkwy.), Rockville 20852
301-770-4894, Fax 301-770-2541, *Lunch & Dinner daily, $, Casual*

The premise here is a simple yet glorified take on the cafeteria where patrons help themselves. Though here, patrons line up at the kitchen counter, make a selection or selections from the posted menus, and when the order is ready a waiter delivers the food. Or, if you prefer, they will prepare it for takeout.

As the name indicates, this place serves home-style Italian food that can be good, or just slightly off. We've rhapsodized over the tiramisu, a triumph here of sponge cake and a rich, creamy filling. But we also found the calzone with its ricotta cheese filling lacking flavor. Perhaps the key is to stick to the New York-style pizza or the meat-based entrées such as the chicken with prosciutto and mozzarella. You may love the food, but you'll really love the prices; management keeps them low, so whole families can dine out (or in) without breaking the bank. **Also located at** 18224 Village Mark Dr., Olney, MD, 301-570-9500.

Mandalay Restaurant & Café Burmese **13/20**

9091A Baltimore Ave. (Cherokee St.), College Park 20740
301-345-8540, *Lunch & Dinner daily, $, Casual*

A P

Fans of exotic Asian cooking will celebrate the arrival of a third Burmese restaurant in the metro area, and this is about as good as it gets outside of the capital city, Rangoon. To make this restaurant even more unique, it doubles as a doughnut shop, which must perplex both sets of customers. Every dish we tried rang true, and we loved the pickled green tea leaf salad—a favorite refreshing snack for Burmese—and the pork with mango pickles, a hot yet sour dish that is apparently ranked as the restaurant's top-selling dish. Not so interesting, and more Chinese than anything else, was the shrimp with hot and spicy sauce, which was neither hot nor spicy. Save room for the golden shweji, a cake made with cream of wheat baked with sugar and coconut milk—it's rich, filling and authentic.

Mark's Kitchen American/Asian **12/20**

7006 Carroll Ave. (Laurel Ave.), Takoma Park 20912
301-270-1884, *Breakfast, Lunch & Dinner daily, $, Casual*

A P ♥

A throwback to the '60s, this hippie restaurant in hip downtown Takoma Park offers both vegetarian and nonveg dishes. You can start your day with an unlikely, though delicious, Mark's Tofu Breakfast; we more enjoyed the more traditional eggs over easy with sausage, home fries and toast. Other choices: pancakes, omelets and waffles. Later in the day, fresh fruit juices and vegetable blends can accompany vegetable curry with rice, Korean short ribs, crabcakes, sesame noodles or a tofu club sandwich. This is an ideal destination after the Sunday morning farmers market.

Matuba Japanese/Sushi **13/20**

4918 Cordell Ave. (Old Georgetown Rd.), Bethesda 20814
301-652-7449, Fax 301-365-5991, *Lunch & Dinner daily, $, Casual*

A ☎

The second location of Arlington's immensely popular sushi restaurant, this Bethesda branch is larger and just as crowded. The sushi here is a particular favorite, even though some sound vaguely Western, like the bagel roll or the Boston roll. If you can, grab a seat at the sushi bar—watching the action is a good show. Unlike the Arlington restaurant, this one has no grill, so you'll be sticking to sushi, tempura and the like. The décor here is slightly more upscale and overtly Japanese than at the sister restaurant, but people don't come for atmosphere; they come to eat. **Also located at** 2915 Columbia Pike, Arlington, VA, 703-521-2811.

Meadow Lark Inn American 12/20

19611 Fisher Ave. (Beall St.), Poolesville 20837
301-428-8900, Fax 301-349-2676
Lunch & Dinner Tues.-Sun, $$, Casual dressy

Ⓐ 🎁 P 🍴 ♻

Your great-grandparents would probably feel right at home in this restaurant that harkens back to an earlier, more tranquil America. Once in the middle of Maryland farmland, the inn sits on the roadside today, and it does have a local history— read the story on the menu. The menu reflects a staid approach to cooking, minus any downtown flourishes. It's farm home cooking, with fresh fruit cup or bacon-wrapped scallops to start, then veal Parmigiano with ziti, broiled lamb chops or roast turkey as entrées. The flashiest dish may be the twin crab cakes with tartar sauce. Desserts include a brownie with ice cream and chocolate sauce, cheesecake and apple cobbler with ice cream.

Mi Peru Restaurante Peruvian 12/20

Flower Hill
18216 Flower Hill Way (Woodfield Rd.), Gaithersburg 20879
301-926-8736, *Lunch & Dinner daily, $, Casual*

Ⓐ P 🍴

Grilled, sautéed, battered and boiled, sturdy authentic Peruvian food emerges from this tiny kitchen. The national soup, chupe, is offered here, chock-full of shrimp, potato chunks, cooked eggs and a section of corn on the cob. A filling dish, this lusty soup vies with such dishes as the various potato (papas) appetizers: The traditional papas rellenas come as a scoop of mashed potatoes shaped around a spicy ground meat filling; the whole packet is deep-fried until crispy and golden. Another best: the papas a la huancaina, a platter of sliced cooked potatoes topped with a peppery red sauce, that may be too much for timid palates to handle. Main courses are simple fish, steak or chicken dishes (charcoaled chicken Peruvian-style is a featured item here) dressed up with typical sauces and accompaniments. The bistec a la limena is a familiar beef filet with fries, fried eggs and rice; however, other dishes seem more exotic and mysterious. Dessert choices are limited to flan, the alfajores (traditional cookies with a caramelized filling), and cake.

Mykonos Grill Greek 12/20

121 Congressional Ln. (Rockville Pike), Rockville 20852
301-770-5999, Fax 301-770-5949, *Lunch & Dinner Tues.-Sun., $, Casual*

Ⓐ 🎁 P 🍷 Ⓨ ♻

Splashy Aegean blues, moderately good Greek food, and sometimes-grumpy service are the typical experience here. Yet the place is popular, and you'll find plenty of fellow diners wrestling with the appetizers—the winners are feta-stuffed mushrooms and the spanakopita—and aggressively dipping chunks of bread into the green-gold olive oil. The menu lists an uninspiring selection of dishes and you may find that the rare lamb in the kebab is almost too raw to eat and the cooked vegetables quite limp. The Greek desserts, especially the creamy rice pudding, help end the meal on a sweeter note. For a finale, try the Greek coffee or a coffee drink called Zorba that will wake you right up.

Nam's of Bethesda   Vietnamese   13/20

4928 Cordell Ave. (Norfolk Ave.), Bethesda 20814
301-652-2635, Fax 391-652-7937, *Lunch & Dinner daily, $$, Casual*

A P 🍴 🍸 🍶 ⟺

An almost-elegant Vietnamese eatery—fresh flowers at each table and pale peach walls—with outstanding food, this Bethesda restaurant obviously has a kitchen staff who knows the right stuff. The nongreasy and plump fried spring rolls make a good beginning, as does the grilled beef wrapped in grape leaves. If you happen by at lunchtime, you can order a luncheon special, but your best bet is to explore the menu, which includes grilled pork on vermicelli, caramel fish, frogs' legs and the always-popular fisherman's soup with fish, pineapple and bean sprouts. It's worth many return trips, especially if you can't make it to the Eden Center in Virginia.

New Fortune Chinese Seafood Restaurant   12/20

Chinese/Seafood
Walnut Hill Shopping Center
16515 S. Frederick Ave. (Shady Grove Rd.), Gaithersburg 20877
301-548-8886, Fax 301-926-6603, *Lunch & Dinner daily, $$, Casual*

A P 🍴 🍷 🍸 ⟺

This is a huge Hong Kong-style restaurant, a popular banquet destination for the Chinese community with full-tilt dim sum service (more than 100 choices on the carts) for everyone during the day. As much as we love the dim sum, we're just as captivated by the solid Cantonese cooking: The menu has about 250 dishes, most of which go far beyond the usual General Tso's chicken category. We've enjoyed the lobster with ginger and onions, the beef chow foon and several of the hot pots, but you may prefer the more familiar kung pao chicken or Hunan beef. Because the menu is so vast and the cooking so good, this is one place to explore some of the outer limits of this cuisine. Weekends are mobbed, so if dim sum is your choice, try going during the week.

The Nibbler   Peruvian   12/20

124 Plaza Shopping Center
18556 Woodfield Rd. (Snoufer School Rd.), Gaithersburg 20879
301-417-0233, Fax 301-548-9515, *Lunch & Dinner daily, $$, Casual*

A 📞 **P** 🍴

We love this tiny place, as much for its imaginatively painted interior (looks like a Peruvian countryside scene) as for its original menu. There is a good selection of dishes. Whatever else you select, be sure to sample the llapingachos, an appetizer of fried mashed potato cakes filled with melted cheese, and the unusual papa a la huncaina (steamed potatoes submerged in a cheese sauce). For a main course, try the chupe, the national dish of Peru, a savory stew of seafood and potatoes. We also recommend the lomo saltado, a stew of shredded flank steak cooked with tomatoes and seasonings. End your meal with something sweet, such as the irresistible banana tres leches, a dish of custard cream and bananas with a sponge cake.

For **guidebooks to other cities worldwide,**
visit: gayot.com

Old Angler's Inn — Contemporary — 14/20

10801 MacArthur Blvd. (Brickyard Rd.), Potomac 20854
301-365-2425, Fax 301-983-0630, *Lunch & Dinner Tues.-Sun., $$$$, Casual*

A favorite of generations of Washingtonians, more for its location than its cooking, the Old Angler's Inn sits just across the road from the C&O Canal. In summer, the deck is about as picturesque as any outdoor dining spot in the Washington metro area. In winter, the ambience is made even cozier by the roaring fire in the downstairs sitting room, where you can have a pre- or post-dinner drink. Ingredients are good, preparations are simple and cooking times are near-perfect. Roast fish and meats are well executed. You might also consider ordering a tasting menu for the entire table. It might start with a Maine lobster tail with Thai curry sauce, continue with a silken pumpkin soup, followed by peppercorn-crusted tuna and rack of lamb and a hazelnut-chocolate cake for dessert.

Old Siam Restaurant — Thai — 11/20

108 E. Diamond Ave. (Summit Ave.), Old Town, Gaithersburg 20877
301-926-9199, Fax 301-926-9132
Lunch Mon.-Sat., Dinner nightly, $$, Casual

We loved the Thai predecessor of this Gaithersburg restaurant and looked forward to eating here once again. But we found the new one rather disappointing, a shadow of what went before. The décor remains, but the kitchen has taken a turn toward some westernized Thai dishes. We found, for example, the fish salad, which at most other places is cooked and chopped-up catfish, here is a tuna that tastes canned and is stirred with fixings that turn it into a sandwich filling. Equally unmemorable were the khanom jeeb (steamed dumplings, with a shrimp, crab meat and ground pork filling), they were easily left uneaten. The best part of the meal was the fried soft-shell crabs; the requested curry was not available.

Oriental East — Chinese/Dim Sum — 12/20

1290 East-West Hwy. (Colesville Rd.), Silver Spring 20910
301-608-0030/1/2, *Lunch & Dinner daily, $, Casual*

We wish that places like Oriental East existed in every neighborhood. Not only is the daily dim sum delicious, but we've also enjoyed many dishes on the menu, most of which are Cantonese inspired. We adore the Mongolian lamb (which isn't Cantonese), Chinese broccoli with oyster sauce and the orange beef, and have returned often for the dim sum offerings, which come rattling past the tables on carts at regular intervals. It's best to arrive early on weekends—the crowds line up fast and if you straggle in later, you'll surely wait for your dim sum. Weekends are the most fun for families, and everyone seems to have a great time.

Outback Steakhouse — Steakhouse — 11/20

7720 Woodmont Ave. (Cheltenham Dr.), Bethesda 20814
301-913-0176, Fax 301-913-0248, *Dinner nightly, $$, Casual*

Brazenly Australian on the outside, this popular steakhouse chain is American through and through. But the gimmick works, even though you won't even find grilled kangaroo. You will find boomerangs, Aussie paraphernalia adequate steaks served in fairly generous portions. No meal is really complete here without the "Bloomin' Onion," an oil-drenched and trademarked appetizer that's had many copycats. Steaks, of course, are the claim to fame, but the choice cuts aren't always tender. If you want beef, pay extra for the prime. Or select one of the other dishes, including chicken, pork chops, and grilled baby back ribs. You'll probably find a line at mealtimes, so if you want to eat and run, order ahead for the takeout service, available at most locations. **Other locations.**

Persimmon, An American Bistro Contemporary 14/20 ♀

7003 Wisconsin Ave. (Leland St.), Bethesda 20815
301-654-9860, Fax 301-654-9272
Lunch Mon.-Fri., Dinner Mon.-Sat., $$$, Business casual

🅰 ☎ 🅿 ♨

As bistros go in this town, Persimmon is making waves and attracting a sophisticated crowd, making hometown owner-chef Damian Salvatore the toast of the town. A graduate of Maryland's L'Académie de Cuisine, Salvatore has constructed a menu that emphasizes seafood but also offers several offbeat treatments of pasta and hearty meat dishes. Start with the very fine mushroom and blue cheese ravioli or the mussels. Then, at lunch, dig into his hangar steak frites, a luscious beef indulgence with a heady wine sauce. At dinner, consider the Caribbean-style pork rack or perhaps the Atlantic bouillabaisse. And if Salvatore whipped it up for the day, insist on a slice of his cheesecake, one of the best on the East Coast. Or you can end simply with the delicate crème brûlée. Reservations are essential at night.

Pho New Saigon Vietnamese
Restaurant Seafood & Grill   Vietnamese   12/20

Langley Hampshire Shopping Center
1167-C University Blvd. (New Hampshire Ave.), Takoma Park 20783
301-408-4545, Fax 301-408-4545, *Lunch & Dinner daily, $, Casual*

🅰 🅿 ♨

Maryland residents won't have to make the long trek to Virginia's Eden Center for good Vietnamese food. Now they can just drive to Takoma Park to this capacious restaurant, which serves several outstanding dishes. Its menu is pages long and loaded with such Vietnamese classics as caramel fish, shrimp on sugar cane and fish with ginger sauce. One of the house specials is the famous pho—clear and free from oily slicks—and it's available in numerous variations. The menu offers help if you're entertaining a group of friends: Two back pages list dinners ideal for various-sized groups.

Pinto & Mazzilli   Italian   12/20

Ritchie Center
785-K Rockville Pike (Wootten Pkwy.), Rockville 20852
Lunch Mon.-Sat., Dinner nightly, $$, Casual
301-838-0077, Fax 301-838-0197

🅰 🅿 ♨ ♨

Bare of decorative flourishes, this Rockville eatery makes a pretty picture with its bar and stools around the open kitchen and its flame-breathing oven. Otherwise, you can pick a table next to the windows to watch the passing scene. Why not order the house special—a crisp-skinned half or whole chicken that arrives at the table glistening with juices? You can also have the roasted chicken sliced up and served in a panini of pizze bread. Start with the chopped salad, a wonderfully healthful bowl of greens, salami and Fontina cheese tossed with pepperoncini, garbanzo beans and sun-dried tomatoes. Freshly baked pastries sit on a counter display, winking at you in their golden glory. Add to the meal with the ricotta tart, a tiny circle of rich pastry dough filled with a creamy ricotta.

Rio Grande Café   Tex-Mex   13/20

4919 Fairmont Ave. (Norfolk Ave.), Bethesda 20814
301-656-2981, *Lunch & Dinner daily, $$, Casual*

A sure crowd-pleaser, the Rio Grande seems to delight patrons of all ages with its lusty fare and lively atmosphere: It's one of the few local places where high decibel levels really don't distract. As expected, weekend nights are jam-packed. But gratis chips-and-dip combos are usually served before the rounds of enchiladas, tacos, sizzling fajitas, chiles rellenos and even broiled quail emerge with baskets of freshly baked tortillas from the kitchen. We recommend the luncheon El Dorado soft tacos and at night select a tortilla soup, carne asada main course and the outstanding chocolate flan for dessert. **Other locations.**

Ruan Thai   Thai   14/20

11407 Amherst Ave. (University Blvd.), Wheaton 20902
301-942-0075, Fax 301-942-0075
Lunch Mon.-Fri., Dinner nightly, $$, Casual

The terrific, authentic cuisine prepared by the owner-cook and family members at the simple, no-frills Ruan Thai draws crowds. The flavors concocted by chef Krisana Suchotinunt come straight from the streets of Bangkok. The adventurous will enjoy the smoky eggplant salad with cut-up shrimp and the exquisitely savory larb pla (cooked and crumbled fish salad with chilies, ground rice and sliced shallots). Other favorites? The hoy tod (pan-fried mussels), the house special duck with its crispy skin and succulent sauce, and the whole crispy fish with three-flavor sauce, best when it's red snapper. They may ask if you want it hot—this is the time to experiment with some fire. It's easy to overeat here, so take along some friends and order wisely and well.

Ruth's Chris Steak House   Steakhouse   14/20

Air Rights Bldg., 7315 Wisconsin Ave. (Elm St.), Bethesda 20814
301-652-7877, Fax 301-718-8463, *Dinner nightly, $$$, Business casual*

The upscale international steakhouse chain that started in New Orleans, Ruth's Chris faces competition in the area, but still makes a splash. The big attraction is the steak, USDA Prime, cut in large portions, cooked to order and dripping in butter, New Orleans-style. But you'll find assorted other dishes, too, such as lobster, veal, chicken and select seafood. There are plenty of vegetable and potato dishes and desserts on the menu, but the appetizers and salads tend to be forgettable. **Other locations.**

Sabang · Indonesian · 13/20

Triangle Shopping Center
2504 Ennalls Ave. (Viers Mill Rd.), Wheaton 20902
301-942-7859, Fax 301-942-9681, *Lunch & Dinner daily, $$, Casual*

One of the very few Indonesian restaurants in the metro area, Sabang is a destination for those who appreciate this rather spectacularly hot Southeast Asian cuisine. We head here for the rendang, a very rich and spicy beef dish with a coconut milk base and for the lighter and rather sweet gado-gado, the famous Indonesian salad composed of cooked vegetables and dressed with peanut sauce. We also adore the es chendol, a chilled and sweet coconut milk-based drink speckled with pressings of rice flour. Some careful decoration has gone on to dress up the interior with plenty of woodcarvings, parasols and tropical wood furniture.

Saigon Gourmet · Vietnamese · 12/20

1326 Gude Dr. (Southlawn Lane), Rockville 20850
301-309-0444, *Lunch & Dinner daily, $, Casual*

When you know a restaurant has the potential to excel, and the staff (family members) work hard to please, you may be disappointed when the quality isn't always up to par. Saigon Gourmet won't win any design awards with the homespun décor of a few Vietnamese trinkets and the big-screen TV dominating one corner, and the food is also homespun. Best bets are the above-average summer rolls and the delicious shrimp sour soup, good enough for seconds. Sometimes a dessert like fried bananas just appears on the table for free, but only sometimes.

Sam Woo · Korean/Japanese · 13/20

Edmonston Shopping Center
1054 Rockville Pike (W. Edmonston Dr.), Rockville 20852
301-424-0495, Fax 301-294-9266, *Lunch & Dinner daily, $$, Casual*

This Rockville eatery is one of those places that melds two cuisines under one roof—with good results. Although the décor is Japanese, the menu consists of many hearty Korean dishes, including the popular meun kalbi tang (short ribs dish in which the meat—bones and all—comes in a boiling hot broth). "Hot," warns the waitress, and if you can't deal with chilies, you'd better head to cooler eats. You'll have plenty other Korean choices, and maybe one of the noodle soups, beef, or fish dishes might make more sense. There's also a sushi bar and the Japanese portion of the menu, which includes yakitori, teriyaki, tempura and Japanese noodle soups. You can rely on this restaurant for its good and reasonably priced fare, as the crowds will attest.

Seibel's Restaurant · American · 12/20

15540 Old Columbia Pike (Rte. 29), Burtonsville 20866
301-384-5661, Fax 301-421-1428
Breakfast, Lunch & Dinner daily, $$, Casual

Something of a local landmark, Seibel's epitomizes family food at its most wholesome. There's a low-fat, heart-healthy section on its menu, with calorie and fat gram counts included.

But if you prefer more traditional fare, you can order up a roast turkey dinner with all the trimmings, then move on to the homemade pies and cakes. Better yet, ask for some scoops of the made-on-the-premises ice creams, which are justifiably famous. Dozens of flavors are available, but if yours is not among them, when the staff makes it, they'll let you know.

Seven Seas · Chinese/Japanese · 12/20

1776 East Jefferson St. (Montrose Rd.), Rockville 20852
301-770-5020, Fax 301-770-5083, *Lunch & Dinner daily, $$, Casual*

Popular in the Chinese community, this restaurant also has a dedicated following among many others who've come to enjoy its various seafood dishes, Taiwanese-, Northern- and Cantonese-style dim sum (we liked the fried bean curd and turnip cakes) and its smattering of Japanese sushi. They even take into account those who might usually avoid Chinese food because of dietary concerns: There's a health-conscious section on the menu, featuring dishes low in oil and salt and cooked without MSG.

Shanghai Café · Chinese · 12/20

7026 Wisconsin Ave. (Woodmont Ave.), Bethesda 20815
301-986-5140, *Lunch & Dinner daily, $$, Casual*

You may come for the weekend dim sum, only to find that you can't turn down a whole slew of menu items, including a limited assortment of Japanese sushi and sashimi. You undoubtedly will ponder long and hard between the Lion's Head stew and sesame beef; in fact, the length of the menu may bog you down. Many of the dishes are not standard fare, so plan to experiment with Shanghai-style cold sesame noodles, crispy walnuts and crispy chicken to start. Move on to big-dish items like shredded chicken with spicy pickled vegetables and shrimp in chili sauce. For a real taste adventure, consider ordering most dishes prepared Shanghai-style, a way of cooking not often found in these parts. To make lunchtimes easier for office workers, the restaurant has a special combination menu for easy ordering and quick service.

South Beach Café · American/Cuban · 13/20

7921 Norfolk Ave. (Cordell Ave.), Bethesda 20814
301-718-9737, Fax 301-718-2664
Lunch Mon.-Fri., Dinner nightly, $$, Casual

Chef-owner John Richardson has attitude and so does his food—a Cuban-Floridian attitude reflected in the peppery Cuban black bean soup smoothed with a cilantro cream stirred over top and the soft-shell crab sandwich or the pork loin with Swiss cheese and cucumber relish on Cuban bread. We've loved the pepper-glazed pork chop served with baked plantains and are happy to save some room for the chocolate tort with chocolate sauce, or a piece of some of the best Key lime pie anywhere.

For **Gayot restaurant reviews in other U.S. cities,**
visit: digitalcity.com/dining

Summit Station Restaurant & Brewery   12/20

American/Southern

227 E. Diamond Ave. (Summit Ave.), Old Town, Gaithersburg 20877
301-519-9400, Fax 301-519-7307
Lunch & Dinner daily, Brunch Sun., $$, Casual

If y'all like your Cajun flavors hot and snappy and your Creole gumbo loaded with peppery flavors, you'll count this place as a real find. Of course, Southern cooking (specifically, Crescent City-style) is not the only theme that runs through the menu: You can start with a three-cheese focaccia, fresh vegetable rolls with pickled ginger, or a hearty crab and poblano cheese dip. But maybe the best way to set up for the coming courses is with a bowl of the black bean chile. "You want only half a portion," the waitress asked of our skimpy order of the bourbon-barbecued crispy shrimp salad. Sure, we smiled, but never again, because this puts other salads to shame with its jumbo crispy prawns tossed with loads of flavor extras. But since the call of the South is strong, you might want to tackle the real Louisiana boudin with Cajun pork air-freighted in from New Orleans. And, yes, many beers are brewed on the premises, which have retained their historic character and charm.

Suporn's Thai Restaurant   Thai   13/20

2301 Price Ave. (Fern St.), Wheaton 20902
301-946-7613, *Lunch & Dinner Tues.- Sun., $$, Casual*

This is a charming restaurant with a lengthy menu. Steer a straight course, however, to the shredded roast duck salad, a balance of sweet and hot flavors, then consider the sakooh sai gai, a traditional snack of pearl tapioca wrapped around minced chicken. If it's available, order some Chinese water spinach (pak boong), any of the curry dishes and a big bowl of duck noodle soup. You'll have to make this a frequent destination if you ever hope to eat through the menu.

Sweet Basil   Thai   13/20

4910 Fairmont Ave. (Norfolk Ave,), Bethesda 20814
301-657-7997, Fax 301-657-7998
Lunch Tues.-Fri., Dinner Tues.-Sun., $$, Casual

As far as Thai restaurants go, Sweet Basil takes the concept one step further, and openly avows that what they serve should be considered "new Thai cuisine." While the kitchen staff keeps traces of authentic flavors running through each dish, you'll note that they add a hefty portion of creativity: Appetizers include grilled portobello mushrooms and fried zucchini served with satay sauce, and for entrées, you'll find marinated grilled lamb or baked salmon filet with a light soy sauce to dress it up. Purists might not be charmed with such culinary liberties (for instance, honey is used instead of sugar), but it works. Plates are picture pretty (which is a traditional Thai culinary trait) and the décor suggests a light and airy tearoom.

Taipei Tokyo Café #2   Chinese/Japanese   12/20

Metro Center, 1596-A Rockville Pike (Halpine Rd.), Rockville 20852
301-881-8533, Fax 301-881-8538, *Lunch & Dinner daily, $, Casual*
No credit cards. P 🍴

The newer of the two Taipei Tokyo Cafés, this looks more like a tearoom than a dual-purpose Asian restaurant. The drill, the prices and the menu are the same as with its older sister restaurant, but it's less crowded (you'll probably always find a seat) and weekends mean a limited dim sum selection. You also won't find the noodle maker on display; all the kitchen work goes on behind closed doors. The sushi bar is quite attractive, and in addition to a bowl of handmade noodles in a soup or stew, you may want to order the handsome dragon roll or other sushi creation. Any of the hot pot dishes are good for a chilly day. **Also located at** 11510-A Rockville Pike, Rockville, MD, 301-881-8388, see review in *Quick Bites*.

Tako Grill   Japanese   13/20   🍴

7756 Wisconsin Ave. (Cheltenham Dr.), Bethesda 20814
301-652-7030, Fax 301-907-0338, *Lunch Mon.-Fri., Dinner nightly, $$, Casual*
🅰 P 🍴

As you might guess by the name, grill cooking comes naturally here—there's even a separate menu for checking off the grilled items you want—rather like selecting sushi. Choices are unusual and range from grilled ginko nuts to grilled whole flounder. The more familiar grilled dishes include chicken and beef teriyaki and negimaki (scallions wrapped in thinly sliced beef). If you prefer sushi, your options include the usual shrimp and mackerel, maguro (tuna) and California roll. Before you make a final choice, read the whole menu so you understand all your options. One option not to miss: the green tea ice cream for dessert.

Tara Thai   Thai   13/20   🍴

4828 Bethesda Ave. (Arlington Rd.), Bethesda 20814
301-657-0488, Fax 301-657-1896, *Lunch & Dinner daily, $$, Casual*
🅰 🕾 P 🍴 Y 🍸

Owner Nick Srisawat has ventured where those at many other local Thai restaurants have feared to go. He presents authentic Thai flavors in a flamboyant style. This has made his restaurants magnets for crowds, who return time and again to indulge in honey-roasted duck, green papaya salad, Pattaya noodles and Tara Thai's signature dish, grilled whole rockfish wrapped in banana leaf. A line of refreshing tropical drinks (with or without alcohol) and offbeat tropical sweets, such as the young coconut pie, effectively wrap up a meal at Tara Thai. Also effective: The restaurant's cool aqua colors and deep-sea décor. **Other locations.**

Tel-Aviv Café   Mediterranean   13/20   🍴

4867 Cordell Ave. (Norfolk Ave.), Bethesda 20814
301-718-9068, Fax 301-718-9069
Lunch Mon.-Sat., Dinner nightly, $$, Casual
🅰 🚳 🍴 🐮 ⚡ Y 🔄

This sand-and-sun-colored restaurant with splashes of turquoise is a pleasant surprise. The food is so genuinely delicious that you wonder why the dining rooms aren't always overflowing. The falafel, hummus, kibbeh and foule m'damas, loaves of puffy Bethlehem pita, succulent lamb kebabs and the dazzling entrée salad made with chicken shawarma are all outstanding. Even the gratis dark-green olive oil and pita served with drinks rates high marks. Portions are generous enough to feed two. For dessert, check out the pistachio-based pastries, cheesecake and double chocolate mousse cake. Chances are you'll leave with a doggie bag and will want to return as soon as the next day.

Temari Japanese Café   Japanese   12/20

Talbott Center, 1043 Rockville Pike (Edmonston Dr.), Rockville 20852
301-340-7720, Lunch & Dinner Wed.-Mon., $, Casual

Surprisingly small, this café caters to a mostly Japanese crowd, who congregate for some unique little dishes: soy beans boiled within the pod, deep-fried oysters with rice, chicken and eggs served over rice, rice balls with seasoned seaweed and a wafu (a Japanese-style hamburger). We also recommend the assorted rolls, including an innovative oshinko roll, donburi bowls (we relished the avocado-tuna donburi, with its picture-perfect presentation), and tonkatsu (deep-fried breaded pork). There are also distinctive desserts. As charming as a picture postcard, this quirky little eatery offers interesting eats in a super-casual setting.

Thai Leela   Thai   11/20

4733 Bethesda Ave. (Woodmont Ave.), Bethesda 20814
301-654-0262, Fax 301-654-0267, Lunch Mon.-Sat., Dinner nightly, $$, Casual

Located down a flight of stairs near a main Bethesda intersection, this little eatery serves a genteel version of the Southeast Asian cuisine, with all the fire tamped out. Lunchtime means a preset menu of soup, appetizer and entrée with a very diluted iced tea as a beverage. Should you choose to order off the regular menu, the horizons expand to include satays and fried tofu, pineapple fried rice, noodle dishes and assorted curries. It's an ideal "starter" restaurant for those not familiar with Thai cuisine: the chili heat is low and extremely exotic ingredients are kept to a minimum.

Thanh Thanh   Vietnamese   13/20

Wheaton Center
11423 Georgia Ave. (University Blvd.), Silver Spring 20902
301-962-3530, Lunch & Dinner daily, $, Casual

An unusually bright and perky Vietnamese restaurant, this pretty little place offers a complete menu, including the full-meal soup pho, in many variations. The kitchen does itself proud with above-average cooking, turning out dishes that are delicate yet flavorful. We recommend the fried and the soft spring rolls, but would steer clear of the mediocre ginger chicken, which lacked much of the desired punch from fresh ginger. We would head back here at any time, for the menu is lengthy and that means finding ample dishes for all-out feasting.

Find the name you are looking for, quickly and easily, in **the index**.

That's Amore — Italian — 12/20

15201 Shady Grove Rd. (Corporate Blvd.), Rockville 20850
301-670-9666, Fax 301-670-0810
Lunch Mon.-Fri., Dinner nightly, $$$, Casual

A ☎ **P** ♥ 🍴 **Y** ▮

Possibly the first Italian restaurant in the DC area to launch the family-size portions plan, this popular eatery embraces the idea that more is more. We applaud such appetizers as the fried mozzarella in carrozza, a luscious and caloric taste of fried and battered Italian bread topped with mozzarella, prosciutto and basil and bathed in marinara and pesto caper cream. That starter plus a salad make an ample lunch, but then you'd pass up the ultra spicy sausage, peppers, and onions. There's plenty here to appeal to everyone in the family, from pasta dishes to chicken, veal, seafood and steaks. Homemade desserts are good, including tiramisu, cannoli, gelatto, cheesecake, bread pudding and Gelato Paradisio, a dazzling sundae with ice cream and hot fudge. **Other locations.**

Thyme Square — American — 11/20

4735 Bethesda Ave. (Woodmont Ave.), Bethesda 20814
301-657-9077, Fax 301-657-4505, *Lunch & Dinner daily, $, Casual*

A 🍽 ♥ 🍴 **Y** ▮

This is not one of our favorite destinations, mainly because we find many of the flavors insipid and the pairing of some ingredients odd. But you can't fault the restaurant's underlying philosophy, to serve healthful dishes constructed from locally grown and organic ingredients. The kitchen would do well to liven up its cooking, though. The juice bar menu is outstanding, however, and you can refuel on such fresh concoctions as the Lava Lamp, made with berries and cranberry juice; many drink selections come with alcohol, too, if desired. The crowded tables suggest that the restaurant has plenty of fans.

Tiffin, The Indian Kitchen — Indian — 13/20 🍽

Unilang Shopping Center, 1341 University Blvd. E.
(New Hampshire Ave.), Langley Park, Hyattsville 20783
301-434-9200, Fax 301-434-3772, *Lunch & Dinner daily, $$, Casual*

A **P** 🍴 **Y** ⟳

If you're a fan of Indian cooking and don't want to spend big bucks for good curries, you should head here. Such words as "bargain," "terrific," and "variety" don't begin to capture the essence of this special experience. The all-you-can-eat buffet dazzles the imagination: three curries; five side dishes, including rice, dal and vegetables; two desserts; and assorted chutneys. But the Indian food connoisseur will turn to the menu, which promises a variety not often found in local eateries. We recommend the Bengali fish curry, redolent with mustard seeds, and the goan lamb vindaloo, with its hot-dusky flavor, breathes its own kind of fire. Breads are oven-fresh and plump—the onion kulcha is a knockout. Your only regret may be that Tiffin is not right next door to your house.

Chefs are creative people. Therefore, of course, menus are subject to change. The dishes we describe should give you a good idea of the chef's range and style.

Timpano Italian Chophouse Italian/Steakhouse 13/20

Montrose Crossing
12021 Rockville Pike (Randolph Rd.), Rockville 20852
301-881-6939, Fax 301-881-6731
Lunch & Dinner daily, Brunch Sun., $$, Casual

Crowded, noisy and immensely popular with every age group, Timpano's offers a menu packed with lusty, impossibly generous dishes. You'll know the cooking is good because the aromas of garlic and Parmesan cheese permeate the air. We love the antipasti platter—enough for two—and the grilled portobellos with fried polenta. As for the main course, lunches don't offer many steak and chop options, so if that's what you want, wait for dinner. Timpano's New York strip, Delmonico, filet mignon and New York bone-in strip steaks are succulent and perfectly cooked. The 9-ounce filet comes to the table bathed in garlic. Order a side of mashed potatoes, with your choice of garlic or Gorgonzola as an added ingredient. The Italian gelato, a truly rich and creamy ice cream, is an outstanding dessert, as is the tartuffo, an ice cream ball encased in chocolate.

Turning Point Inn   American   13/20

3406 Urbana Pike (Hwy. 355), Urbana 21704
301-874-2421, Fax 301-831-8092
Dinner Tues.-Sun., Brunch Sun., $$$, Business casual

Surrounded by farmland, this country inn offers a sleek menu that's in sharp contrast to the rustic, country views out its windows. For cozy seating, ask for the casual dining area with its whitewashed walls, greenery and eclectic décor—a perfect setting for a sunny Sunday brunch. The menu changes seasonally under the direction of chef Nigel Coleman, but the lobster bisque is a house-specialty fixture. The brunch menu showcases some unusual breakfast choices: You may find a frittata with wild mushrooms, caramelized onions and Parmesan cheese, which rates thumbs up. Sturdier brunch entrées include game birds, seafood and beef dishes with all the trimmings. At dinners, look for the leg of lamb stuffed with sausage, an oven-roasted sea bass, prime rib, slow-roasted pork shank and a pan-seared salmon fillet. Desserts are inventive, including the ultrarich chocolate terrine with its coating of toasted and crushed rice, crème brûlée and mocha mousse.

Udupi Palace   Indian/Vegetarian   13/20

1329 University Blvd. E. (New Hampshire Ave.), Hyattsville 20783
301-434-1531, Fax 301-434-4139, *Lunch & Dinner daily, $$, Casual*

Because South Indian vegetarian cooking is not common in these parts, many of the dishes may sound unfamiliar, but even if you have no idea what you're ordering, you won't be disappointed. We recommend the sambar and the alu bonda appetizers, and crave the masala dhosas (thin rice crêpes filled with piquant potatoes and onion slices). The mango lassi is a delicious drink, and if you want to overindulge on sweets, stop by the sweetmeats counter on the way out; it features numerous Indian candies and pastries. This place is a real treat; chances

233

are you'll have better luck getting a seat during the week or at off-hours. Weekends are especially busy.

West End Grill   American/Italian   **12/20**

7904 Woodmont Ave. (St. Elmo Ave.), Bethesda 20814
301-951-9696, Fax 301-951-6161
Lunch Mon.-Fri., Dinner nightly, $$, Casual

With all the fine dining in the neighborhood, West End Grill will have to toe the mark to keep its fans coming in. We've found the menu inconsistent. However, many of the pasta dishes are fine, and if you stop by at lunchtime, you might want to investigate the burdened buffet table rather than order off the menu. One good bet: the salmon sandwich.

Wok Inn   Pan-Asian   **12/20**

4924 St. Elmo Ave. (Old Georgetown Rd.), Bethesda 20814
301-986-8590, Fax 301-986-8490
Lunch Mon.-Sat., Dinner nightly, $, Casual

If you know little about Asian food, the Wok Inn may be a good place to start. Its menu is accessible, and the dishes are described well enough to banish confusion. The décor is vaguely Asian, with a Singapore T-shirt tacked to one wall and a television over the mini-bar tuned to Asian dramas. Waitstaff are very pleasant and accommodating. The offerings span Asia, with representative samples from China, Malaysia, Thailand, Singapore, Indonesia and Japan. Tackling such diverse cuisines is a daunting task, and old Asian food hands may find that the flavors fall short of the mark: Fried tofu appetizers ring true, but the Vietnamese summer roll unwraps as you eat it, and the ipoh chow fun noodles from Malaysia need a chili boost. Better choices are the Singaporean kway teow mee with shrimp. For heartier appetites, order something from the grill or one of the Thai curries.

Wurzburg Haus Restaurant   **13/20**

German/Continental
Red Mill Shopping Center
7236 Muncaster Mill Rd. (Redland Rd.), Rockville 20855
301-330-0402, Fax 301-963-6822, *Lunch & Dinner daily, $$, Casual*

Beloved by many Washingtonians, this bustling and colorful German restaurant provides a lively break from the workaday world—especially with its drinking songs and bouncy music when musicians are on hand. Otherwise, people are charmed by the Germanic décor and hearty, stout dishes that almost demand an accompanying stein of beer. We enjoyed the freshly baked rolls and bread the various sausage platters served with sauerkraut. Even though you may leave feeling overfed, don't skip past the appetizers: We can heartily recommend the robust and peppery goulash. If some dishes, like the tomatoes with mozzarella, seem a bit out of place, just stick to the real reason for coming here, a plate or two of the chefs' (duties are shared by Henning Lorenzen and Peter Gruenfelder) cooking. Octoberfest, of course, is a festive (and delicious) time of year at Wurzburg Haus.

QUICK BITES

AMERICAN

The Broadway Diner Restaurant

Wintergreen Plaza
895 Rockville Pike (W. Edmonston Dr.), Rockville 20852
301-424-5008, Fax 301-424-5485
Open 24 hours, $, Casual

🅰️ 🄿 ♥ 👗 🦉 🍸

This diner's menu is so large that you might need the 24 hours to read through it. The lengthy listing takes you all the way from breakfast, served round the clock, to snacks, soups, sandwiches, and main dishes such as porterhouse steak and the Greek pastitsio. We've had the Greek gyro sandwich, which you may want to complement with a Greek salad. Visit the dessert counter before sitting down: That way, you can figure out which home-baked goodies—such as baklava, Boston cream pie, or New York-style cheesecake—you desire. Like soda fountain treats? You'll find milk shakes and even malts here.

Chicken Out Rotisserie

Cabin John Shopping Center
11325 Seven Locks Rd. (Tuckerman Ln.), Potomac 20854
301-299-8646, Fax 301-299-9840
Lunch & Dinner daily, $, Casual

🅰️ 🄿 ♥ 👗

This chicken eatery is a local success story, the kind of "to riches" tale that makes an entrepreneur out of many. From a single location in Maryland, the owners took their simple idea—cook wholesome food from scratch and charge reasonable prices—and spun it into a local empire. Locations are squeaky clean, service is prompt and courteous, and the food, generally as good as (or maybe better than) homemade. Choose this chain for an all-out chicken or turkey feast, or at least a sandwich or salad. We recommend the half-chicken meal with mashed potatoes and fresh vegetables and an apple crisp for dessert. Everything is available for takeout. **Other locations.**

eatZi's Market & Bakery

11503-B Rockville Pike (Nicholson Ln.), Rockville 20852
301-816-2020, Fax 301-816-0332
Lunch & Dinner daily, $, Casual

🅰️ 🄿 🍽️ 👗

This is one place that has it all, and we mean everything— from flowers to cigars to designer brews to chef-made meals. Although it's a food-wine-cigar market, management has thoughtfully provided an ample eating area so you can sip your gourmet coffee, eat your overstuffed sandwich or voluminous salad, gingerly sample the fresh sushi or nibble on a delicate, flaky pastry before, during and/or after you've shopped. Everything is available for take home as well. The good food here is no secret; the place is often bulging with people. Also see review in *Gourmet Shops & Markets/Gourmet Markets & Gourmet To-Go.*

Fuddruckers

1300 Rockville Pike (Edmonston), Rockville 20852
301-468-3501, Fax 301-483-7478, *Lunch & Dinner daily, $, Casual*

A P 👥

Fuddruckers' corporate motto says simply that they make the world's best hamburgers. And if you've ever had a Fuddruckers' burger, then you've just tasted burger nirvana. Tender, juicy, and flavorful, the burgers come in several sizes (the latest: one pounders) and are the main reason to eat here. Adding fries, onion rings and a milk shake only make the experience more heavenly. The menu has evolved over the years and chicken and salads are also included on the simple menu, plus hot dogs and special brews. You can stack your meal—burger or otherwise—with heaps of condiments and greens from the fixings bar and squirt everything with melted cheese. End your meal with a brownie or giant cookie. **Other locations.**

Hard Times Café

Woodley Gardens Plaza, 1117 Nelson St. (Rte. 28), Rockville 20850
301-294-9720, Fax 301-424-7116, *Lunch & Dinner daily, $, Casual*

A P 👥 ♡

One of the first major chili houses in the area, Hard Times still excels at what it does best: making power-packed chili in three styles—Texas, Cincinnati and vegetarian. In each category there are more choices to for you to make: with spaghetti, with beans, with cheese and/or with onions. Our favorite is the tried-and-true Texas chili with coarse-ground meat, served with beans and topped with cheese and onions. Non-chili dishes include sandwiches and salads, but why bother? Responding to America's love for the chili bowl, each café sells pints, quarts and gallons of chili to-go, plus its sweet cornbread. You can also find Hard Times T-shirts, hot sauces and spice mixes. At the Herndon location, you can play pool. **Other locations.**

The Original Pancake House

7700 Wisconsin Ave. (Old Georgetown Rd.), Bethesda 20814
301-986-0285, Fax 301-986-1517, *Breakfast & Lunch daily, $, Casual*

A P 🍽 👥

Sunday breakfasts can be crowded, but there's no better way to relax than over a stack of hot pancakes with loads of butter and syrup. Why all the fuss? It must be over the 16 pancake selections as well as the multiple varieties of waffles and crêpes. Chocoholics rave about the chocolate chip stack with tiny chips melting slowly under sweetened whipped cream, but our favorites are the Hawaiian pancakes, filled with crushed pineapple and bathed in an intense orange syrup. Delicious breakfast sausages are made from a secret recipe. **Also located at** 12224 Rockville Pike, Rockville, MD, 301-468-0886; and 370 W. Broad St., Falls Church, VA, 703-891-0148.

Roy's Place

2 E. Diamond Ave. (Chestnut Ave.), Gaithersburg 20877
301-948-5548, Fax 301-948-4840, *Lunch & Dinner daily, $, Casual*

A P 👥 ❦

Sandwich places should be casual, and Roy's hits the mark. The dark walls, ceiling fans, Tiffany-style lamps and kitschy bric-a-brac make this a shirtsleeves kind of place. No one else prepares sandwiches quite like Roy's, where overstuffed breads and more than 200 wacky combinations are available. Detailed menu descriptions will get you through the ordering process. Fillings range from fried oysters and grilled knockwurst to thick bacon, melted cheese and lobster meat. Solid American desserts, like the thickly crusted apple pie, put an exclamation point on your meal.

Silver Diner

Mid-Pike Plaza, 11806 Rockville Pike (Randolph Rd.), Rockville 20852
301-770-2828, *Breakfast, Lunch & Dinner daily, $, Casual*

A P ♥ 🏠 ▥

Reminiscent of an earlier America, the Silver Diner offers individual jukeboxes, '50s music and down-home cooking at affordable prices. It's no surprise that everyone from students to grandparents loves this place. No matter what hour you stop in, booths and counter stools are filled, but the turnover is quick, and you can always order takeout. We go back for the classic meatloaf and the chocolate cream pie, but the menu is extensive, and there's plenty to please. You'll find light fare as well, including lots of salads. Breakfast service starts at the crack of dawn and lasts all day. **Other locations.**

Star Diner

Kentlands Market Sq., 705 Center Point Way (Kentlands Rd.), Gaithersburg 20878
301-921-8222, Fax 301-963-6141, *Breakfast, Lunch & Dinner daily, $, Casual*

A P ♥ 🏠 Y

Like most classic American diners, this place offers a seemingly endless menu of comfort foods. Breakfasts are the typically sturdy egg/pancake/bacon/sausage varieties, with, of course, cereals, bagels and Belgian waffles as well. Sandwiches seem to be the kitchen's favorite with everything from a classic Reuben to the always popular burgers in a choice of styles. As for entrées, you can stick to Mom's home cooking with a choice of liver and onions or a plate of meatloaf with mashed potatoes or opt for something fancier like a tuna steak. Desserts, as you might expect, are caloric and decadent. Want something that tastes rich but aims to promote health? Try the fitness shake with yogurt, wheat germ and fresh fruit.

Tastee Diner

7732 Woodlawn Ave. (Norfolk Ave.), Bethesda 20814
301-652-3970, Fax 301-652-0767, *Open 24 hours, $, Casual*

A P 🏠 ▥

This spot, open since 1935, epitomizes what old-fashioned home-style cooking that is devoid of frills and gastronomic ploys is all about. Starting with eggs and pancakes for breakfast, the menu expands on that homey theme with sandwiches, subs, burgers and heartier meals, including daily specials like ham and cabbage and fried chicken. Some desserts, like the bread and rice puddings, are made on the premises; they're a better bet than the very starchy cherry pie. **Also located at** 8601 Cameron St., Silver Spring, MD, 301-589-6477; and 118 Washington Blvd., Laurel, MD, 301-953-7567.

Find the name you are looking for, quickly and easily, in **the index.**

BAKERIES/CAFÉS

Bread & Chocolate

7704 Woodmont Ave., Bethesda 20814
301-986-9008, *Breakfast, Lunch & Dinner daily, $, Casual*

A

The idea of combining a wedge of freshly baked, buttered and cinnamon-sprinkled bread with a mug of hot chocolate probably is enough to tempt even the most stubborn dieter. Those are the kind of combinations available at Bread & Chocolate. Consider the special morning eye-opener, the French toast, which has chocolate added to the batter mix. You'll find plenty more chocolate options—try the chocolate cake—but you can also sample such savory dishes as a chicken, mozzarella and pasta salad, French onion soup and Hungarian goulash in cup or bowl. This is a comfort-food mecca. **Other locations.**

Corner Bakery

Westlake Crossing
10327 Westlake Dr. (Democracy Blvd.), Bethesda 20817
301-469-8774, *Breakfast, Lunch & Dinner daily, $, Casual*

A P

It seems no matter how early we get to Corner Bakery, the big, fat, squishy cinnamon rolls are gone. Fortunately, there is a lot more on the menu. Start with breakfast: coffee, fruits, and a bowl of granola, bagels, muffins, and yogurt. Later, the kitchen is turning out heartier goods: ample bowls of soups, sandwiches, pizzas and salads, to eat in or takeout. The sweets still beckon, but now they're transformed into brownies, cookies and cakes. Fresh baked loaves of bread are also a staple here. **Other locations.**

Pastry Designs

4927 Elm St. (Arlington Rd.), Bethesda 20814
301-656-0536, *Breakfast & Lunch daily, Dinner Mon.-Sat., $, Casual*

A P

The glamorous pastries here are the work of pastry chef Karin Corazzini, who not only creates fantasy cakes and sweets—such as the frog-shaped pastries—but also piña colada cakes, apple bread pudding, mousse and much more. But before you indulge in dessert at this low-key shop that plays classical music in the background, sample the potato-artichoke heart salad, a small pizza or one of the outstanding sandwiches such as ham and Brie, grilled eggplant or tuna with capers and peppers. Also see review in *Gourmet Shops & Markets*.

BARBECUE

Charlie's Open Pit Barbecue

Gude Plaza, 1314 E. Gude Dr. (Norbeck Rd.), Rockville 20850
301-340-0584, *Lunch & Dinner Mon.-Sat., $, Casual*

A P

Located in an obscure strip mall, Charlie's may not attract huge crowds, but those who don't show up miss out on true wood-smoked meats. The large, open-hearth, wood-fueled pit stands at the front of the place. The menu's not much to talk about, unless you like ribs and plenty of them, although Charlie's does smoke chunks of beef and whole chickens for use in its barbecue sandwiches and platters. You'll also find assorted sandwiches, soups and salads, but most people come for the large slabs of meaty ribs with barbecue beans, baked potato and greens.

Crisp & Juicy

1331-G Rockville Pike (Edmonston Dr.), Rockville 20852
301-251-8833, Fax 301-251-9693, *Lunch & Dinner daily, $, Casual*

Ⓐ🅿️🍴

The food here is pollo a la brasa, or charbroiled chicken. It's a Latino cooking method that's caught on in a big way here, but these eateries offer more than delicious and crispy chickens: The menu includes Argentinean steaks and sausages in sandwiches, and even trendy Gruyère chicken breast sandwiches. But those in the know will stick to the basics: cut-up chickens sold solo or a chicken platter with two sides. We love the fried yuca and plantains, the most traditional combos with Latino chicken. You can buy and eat plenty here, all for about $10. Don't come for the ambience or décor—there isn't any. **Also located at** 4540 Lee Hwy., Old Dominion Dr., Arlington, VA, 703-243-4222, and 913 W. Broad St., Falls Church, VA, 703-241-9091.

Levi's Restaurant & Carry-out

Oxon Hill Plaza, 6201 Livingston Rd. (Oxon Hill Rd.), Oxon Hill 20745
301-567-0050, Fax 301-839-1113, *Lunch & Dinner Tues.-Sun., $, Casual*

Ⓐ🅿️🍴⬭

If you remember nothing else about Levi's, you'll remember the ribs. They are huge and meaty, barbecued North Carolina-style with a sultry-sweet sauce that's got just a hint of pepper around the edges. Overall, this is old-fashioned Southern home cooking at its best: fried fish, fried chicken, mounds of mashed potatoes, lots of greens, sugary sweet potatoes, hush-puppies, pigs' feet, chicken wings and those fantastic barbecued beef ribs. It's all served cafeteria-style—if you hit a busy time of day, you'll line up with a crowd just for a chance to overeat (it's hard to say no to anything on the line). No meal here is complete without at least one order of the banana pudding, a triumph of Southern comfort. Levi's takes its Southern food seriously.

O'Brien's Pit Barbecue

387 East Gude Dr. (Calhoun Dr.), Rockville 20850
301-340-8596, Fax 301-424-5391, *Lunch & Dinner daily, $, Casual*

Ⓐ📷🅿️🍴

This barbecue old-timer is as popular at lunch for local business folks as it is on Sundays, when families drop in for a mid-day meal. Service is cafeteria-style—with delicious foods on display in all their glory. O'Brien's is best known for its ribs, but we have found them inconsistent. The fork-tender smoky beef brisket, though, has always been excellent. All the barbecuing is authentic hickory-smoking, Texas-style. There are plenty of sides to choose from, but the barbecue beans and coleslaw pair best with any barbecue meal. Desserts are not homemade and are worth skipping. O'Brien's has an active catering business for those parties when barbecue will do. **Also located at** 46005 Regal Plaza, Sterling, VA, 703-450-8490.

Old Hickory Grille

15420 Old Columbia Pike (Rte. 29), Burtonsville 20866
301-421-0204, Fax 301-421-9761, *Lunch & Dinner daily, $, Casual*

🅰️🅿️🍴

Prepare to wait for a table at this popular spot. There's an active take-out section, though—an option to make your visit much more brief. The smothered chicken poblano with fries or grits is mighty good, but we swear by the ribs. Try the monster rack—which you should eat sitting in the privacy of your bathtub; they're coated with some drippy sauce and come with extra for dunking. For a change of pace, you can combine the ribs with some grilled chicken, but we prefer the ribs solo. Don't skip desserts, especially the custard-style banana-chocolate bread pudding. **Also located at** 7263 Arlington Blvd., Falls Church, VA, 703-207-8650.

Red Hot & Blue

677 Main St (Seventh St.), Laurel 20707
301-953-1943, Fax 301-953-1987, *Lunch & Dinner daily, $$, Casual*

🅰️🅿️🍴🍷

When this barbecue group opened years ago, good barbecue—smoky, juicy, and prepared by pros—was hard to come by. Thus this group of restaurants became an instant hit and a ribs meal from here was almost worth its weight in gold. Times change, and as others brought the barbecue theme to the area, RH&B has suffered and several of its outlets have closed, a loss to its many fans. Those fans appreciate the ribs offered wet or dry. We love the intense heat of the dry-rubbed ribs with a side of beans, and then call it a day with a serving of banana pudding. **Other locations.**

Texas Ribs & BBQ

7701 Old Branch Ave. (Kirby Rd.), Clinton 20735
301-877-0323, Fax 301-877-0365, *Lunch & Dinner daily, $, Casual*

🅰️🅿️❤️🍴🔑🍷

For a barbecue joint, Texas Ribs serves a diverse menu of other foods, too. The menu includes quesadillas and chili, steamed shrimp, steak and more. We've even watched light eaters nibbling on salads. But why not enjoy what this restaurant does best? Ribs. Dry-rubbed and smoky, they come in the usual full or half racks. If you're hungry, order the whole rack, plus the "pit potato"—a baked potato that cooks with the meat and soaks up the drippings. Even if you overeat, be sure to take home one of their made-on-the-premises pies. Everyone loves this food, so the place is apt to be crowded—you may even hear some Texas drawls. If the food doesn't convince you of its Western roots, the cowboy posters will. **Also located at** 108 Smallwood Village Center, Waldorf, MD, 301-843-8400.

BREWPUBS

Rock Bottom Brewery

7900 Norfolk Ave. (St. Elmo Ave.), Bethesda 20814
301-652-1311, Fax 301-652-5888, *Lunch & Dinner daily, $, Casual*

🅰️🍺🍴🐱🦉🍷🍦🚌

If you're looking for solid stouts, polished porters and fizzy handmade beers, join the happy crowd at Rock Bottom, who come for the pub grub and the beer. The food's not bad, either. We like the two-fisted burgers, especially the hickory burger with cheese and bacon. Other choices include brick-oven pizzas, ribs, chicken and alder-smoked fish and chips. If the photos on the wall tell any story, it would be that the rugged décor and wood-cabin look appeal to sports fans and the outdoorsy set. **Also located at** 4238 Wilson Blvd., #1256, Arlington, VA, 703-516-7688.

Willie & Reed's

4901-A Fairmont Ave. (Norfolk Ave.), Bethesda 20814
301-951-1100, Fax 301-986-0505, *Lunch & Dinner daily, $, Casual*

A ☎ P 🍴 ♟ Y ♨

Twentysomethings, maybe older, drop by for a brew and a burger and to bask in plenty of sports memorabilia and game broadcasting. About a dozen screens are tuned to sports events, so even the biggest enthusiast can overdose. With exposed pipes and plenty of bar seats, this Bethesda destination opens its doors to good times, good food and good brews.

CAFÉS & COFFEEHOUSES

Kefa Café

963 Bonifant St. (Georgia Ave.), Silver Spring 20910
301-589-9337, *Breakfast & Lunch daily, $, Casual*

A P ♨

Ethiopian siblings Lene and Abeba Tsegaye saw a niche that needed filling—the neighborhood coffeehouse—and opened this charming, flower-bright place several years ago. It's the ideal spot for friends, family and neighbors to stop in for a friendly chat or to talk, listen to music, read and sip coffee. You'll find several brews, a full espresso bar, a number of flavored coffees, pastries, bagels, scones, sandwiches and salads and take-home tea leaves and coffee beans.

DELIS & BAGEL SHOPS

Einstein Bros Bagels

19114 Montgomery Village Ave (Stedwick Rd.), Gaithersburg 20879
301-926-8509, Fax 301-926-5619
Breakfast, Lunch & Dinner daily, $, Casual

A P ♥ ♨

If you're a New Yorker and mad for bagels, you'll appreciate this group of bagel restaurants that sells classic bagels and good toppings. We love the onion bagel with salmon "shmear" (salmon cream cheese). Even if you're not a New Yorker, how can you go wrong with a wild blueberry bagel and some fruit shmear? Einstein Bros isn't just about bagels: In the tradition of sensible eateries, it offers a little something for everyone, including wraps, muffins, yogurts, iced and hot coffee, salads and, naturally, bagel sandwiches—try the hot BBQ chicken. Remember, if you want to eat bagels for dinner, most stores close in the early evening. **Other locations.**

Hofberg's Deli

4917 Elm St. (Arlington Rd.), Bethesda 20814
301-654-5200, Fax 301-654-9798, *Breakfast & Lunch daily, $, Casual*

A P ♥ 🍴

With just a nod to mainstream fare such as chicken quesadillas and buffalo wings, since 1938, the Hofberg menu has focused on New York-style delicatessen food. We love coming here for that ultimate New York meal: crunchy kosher dill pickles and a huge Rueben sandwich slathered with mustard. And there's plenty more that smacks of Manhattan, from smoked whitefish and triple-deckers with hot corned beef and pastrami to braised brisket of beef, stuffed cabbage and the New York-style breakfasts of lox, eggs and onions, plus much more. New York-style cheesecake is available in all its glory—creamy, smooth wedges of various flavors, like Oreo, strawberry and cherry. And don't miss the rich and crumbly rugalach.

Katz's Kosher Supermarket

4860 Boiling Brook Pkwy. (Nicholson Ln.), Rockville 20852
301-468-0400, *Breakfast & Lunch Sun.-Fri., Dinner Sat.-Thurs., $, Casual*

A P 🍴

Unlike the average supermarket, Katz's offers an in-store deli counter that serves both regular shoppers and those who want to take a break from shopping to eat. Hungry shoppers can order sandwiches, soups and sweets and grab a table in an adjoining eating area. You have plenty of choices such as corned beef sandwiches, matzoh ball soup or a cold fish platter. Check out the deli case or scan the blackboard menu for suggestions. The big, soft black-and-white cookies make a good snack. After you eat, you can do your day's shopping without leaving the premises.

Parkway Deli & Restaurant

8317 Grubb Rd. (East-West Hwy.), Silver Spring 20910
301-587-1427, *Breakfast, Lunch & Dinner daily, $, Casual*

A P 🍴 🍷

This is a great place to break the fast on Yom Kippur or to eat any day of the year. You can make a takeout selection—from baked chicken and mashed potatoes to a cheesecake of your choice—from the front deli counter. But savvy patrons head to the restaurant in back for a full-fledged and very casual sit-down meal. Breakfasts, with their staggering portions, are immensely popular. Later in the day, meals get big and tempting such as matzoh ball soup or chopped chicken liver and stuffed cabbage or roast fresh brisket of beef. Lighter fare includes triple-decker clubs and kosher dogs. The milk shakes are thick and creamy—a perfect partner to any meal.

ETHNIC FLAIR

Caribbean

Caribbean Café

Flower Shopping Center
8482 Piney Branch Rd. (Flower Ave.), Silver Spring 20901
301-585-9388, *Lunch & Dinner Mon.-Sat., $, Casual*

A P 🍴

They claim to serve "the best Jamaican food in town," and if great aromas have anything to do with it, you'll agree. Roasted jerk chicken leads off the menu, and there are plenty of curry dishes, including curried goat. The menu branches out with sandwiches of jerk chicken or fish, plus a non-Caribbean steak and cheese and three kinds of roti: chicken, goat and vegetables. Other good choices: beef, chicken or vegetable patties, calaloo and coco bread. Many of the juices are made on the premises—you might want a refreshing mauby or sorrel to quench the heat. Sweets? Carrot or Jamaican cakes, coconut drops and sweet potato or bread puddings. Check the board for daily specials.

Caribbean Delight

7811 Riggs Rd. (University Blvd.), Adelphi 20738
301-439-1270/1, *Lunch & Dinner daily, $, Casual*
🅐🅟👥

Weekends are jam-packed with patrons looking for black pudding, cassava pone, coco bread, Guyanese-style Creole rice and goat. Stumped about choices? Ask the staff, or just mix and match. Try the cow heel soup, ackee and salt fish and calaloo on the side. Also good: curry beef roti and the pine tart appetizer. Daily and weekend specials may turn up such temptations as curried kingfish or kingfish with green bananas and dumplings. Hanging plants, Caribbean photos and plenty of island patois add color and character. **Also located at** 11000 Baltimore Ave., Beltsville, MD, 301-595-4687/8.

Caribbean Feast Restaurant & Catering

Saah Plaza, 823 Hungerford Dr. (Frederick Ave.), Rockville 20850
301-315-2668, Fax 301-314-2669, *Lunch & Dinner Mon.-Sat., $, Casual*
🅐🅟👥

You won't soon forget the slow burn after a jerk chicken dinner here. "It's hot," warns the counterman as he chops and serves up your chicken. "That's fine," we say, not understanding the meaning of hot. The chicken is the trademark dish. Other good choices: ox tail, curried goat, brown stew chicken and loads of sides. The décor consists of a showy assortment of Jamaican prints and posters, but you probably will be too busy eating to notice. Dessert is a treat if it's mango or passion fruit ice cream that's made at York Castle Tropical Ice Cream in Silver Spring and sold here.

Caribbean Palace

Takoma Park Shopping Center
7680 New Hampshire Ave. (University Blvd.), Hyattsville 20783
301-431-1563, *Lunch & Dinner daily, $, Casual*
No credit cards. 🅟👥

One of the tiniest eateries in town, this no-frills place offers a bare-bones menu of curries and rotis, and not much more. Without chairs and tables, this is strictly a carry-out venture, but you may find that satisfactory. For appetizers, choose fried plantains or an order of beef or chicken patties. We rave about the roti meals. Curries, like jerk chicken, beef, goat, kingfish, shrimp, oxtail and salt fish, are good, too. Vegetarians eat well, too.

Some establishments change **days of operation** without warning. It is always wise to check in advance.

Negril

965 Thayer Ave. (Georgia Ave.), Silver Spring 20910
301-585-3000, Fax 301-585-6303, *Lunch & Dinner daily, $, Casual*

A P

One of the granddaddies of local Caribbean fare, Negril helped point the way for today's flock of casual Caribbean restaurants, where good food at bargain prices attracts loyal fans. We've often stopped in to pick up a goat roti, but you may want to tackle one of Jamaica's big-flavor specialties: jerk chicken. You can eat in at one of the few tables, but chances are you'll carry out, as many customers do. Either way, pick up a coconut custard tart or one of the other cakes on display. Since its first days in Washington, DC, Negril has expanded to several other locations, making it easy to satisfy a roti craving at many points around the Beltway. **Also located at** 2301 Georgia Ave., NW, Washington, DC, 202-332-3737; and 18509 N. Frederick Ave., Gaithersburg, MD, 301-926-7220.

Chinese

A & J Restaurant

Woodmont Station
1319 C Rockville Pike (Edmonston Dr.), Rockville 20852
301-251-7878, *Lunch & Dinner daily, $, Casual*
No credit cards. P

One of the very few northern-style dim sum restaurants in the area, A & J offers an extensive menu. If you know only Cantonese dim sum, some of the dishes may give you pause: beef tendon with garlic sauce, beef tripe soup and bean curd with thousand-year-old egg are some of the less familiar offerings. But the majority of patrons are Chinese, and there's rarely an empty table here, at least not on weekends. To keep busy until a table empties, customers head next door to the Chinese bookshop. But once seated, you probably will want to linger over such dishes as scallion pancakes and spicy won tons with hot sauce. It's nonstop dim sum, so don't expect General Tso's chicken.

Asia Café

Burgundy Park Shopping Center
703 1st St. (Baltimore Rd.), Rockville 20851
301-610-7899, Fax 301-610-7829, *Lunch & Dinner daily, $, Casual*

A P ♥

A bright, cheery little restaurant offering a very long menu, this café is all about Chinese eats on the run. Although you can dine in at one of the very few tables, most people get their food to-go. Like similar restaurants, the emphasis here is on speed, not necessarily on haute flavors. We found the beef with broccoli with its dash of star anise better than average, but bemoaned the lemon meringue-pie quality of the lemon chicken, too sweet and gooey by far. We started with the ubiquitous pu pu platter. This starred two of everything: spring rolls, fried wontons, chicken wings, skewered chicken and shrimp toast. **Also located at** 12819 Wisteria Dr., Germantown, MD, 301-528-6610.

For **Gayot Hot Ten Restaurants in Washington, DC,**
visit: gayot.com

Bamboo Buffet

Twinbrook Shopping Center
2010 Veirs Mill Rd. (Twinbrook Pkwy.), Rockville 20851
301-279-9600, Fax 301-279-9698, *Lunch & Dinner daily, $, Casual*

A P 🍴

Like at a bargain basement sale, customers attack the various counters as if everything will soon disappear. Instead, this buffet restaurant manages its constant supply of buffet items with regimental precision: Cooks bustle from the kitchen carrying filled trays as soon as those on the counters empty. And what a lavish amount of food: Chinese, Japanese, Mexican and American dishes (including drinks, salads, desserts and non-stop dim sum on weekends) overflow their containers before the onslaught of the crowds. It's enough to feed several armies. In fact, it's a feeding frenzy, with perhaps the best deals being the barbecued beef ribs and the dim sum offerings. Don't expect gourmet fare, but do expect plenty to eat—and at bargain prices. **Also located at** 3501-C S. Jefferson St., Falls Church, VA, 703-671-8788.

Eastern Empire Buffet-Restaurant

11575 Old Georgetown Rd. (Rockville Pike), Rockville 20852
301-881-7822, Fax 301-881-7868, *Lunch & Dinner daily, $, Casual*

A P ♥ 🍴 **Y** 🍵

Want to eat 'til you drop? Check out this Chinese/Continental spread, with about 150 items to whet your appetite. Choices range from lobster and dim sum to a salad bar, hot pot items in winter and Mongolian barbecue. Desserts are also popular, although not particularly exotic, and may include cakes, cookies and ice cream. All this unfettered eating is part of the restaurant's effort to hold its own in the burgeoning Chinese-buffet restaurant competition in the metro area. The big winners are the patrons, who can spend one low price and eat plentifully. Eastern Empire also sells buffet items by the pound, if you want to pick up dinner (or lunch) on the way home.

Peking Eastern House Restaurant

Midway Shopping Center
16041 Frederick Rd. (Redland Rd.), Rockville 20855
301-527-8558, Fax 301-527-8559, *Lunch & Dinner daily, $, Casual*

A 🕾 **P** 🍴

The handmade noodles are the stars of the menu, which also features numerous stews characteristic of the cooking of Eastern and Northern China. Although the menu makes a point of including Chinese-American favorites, the exotic lamb dishes are more noteworthy, and, of course, the soup noodle dishes with the thick yet tender handmade noodles. These include lamb stew soup (a clear, hearty broth touched with chile fire and brimming with pungent lamb slices), beef stew, Mandarin beef stew soup and noodles with Peking sauce. The Eastern Pots (or hot pots) make good group dishes and run the gamut from assorted seafood to lamb with sour cabbage, each bubbling in a rich and wholesome broth. Standout appetizers include Eastern-style pancakes with spring onions and assorted boiled, steamed or fried dumplings. Want northern-style dim sum? It's served here daily from a special dim sum menu. The Chinese doughnut with pancake is a knockout.

The Vegetable Garden

White Flint Station Center
11618 Rockville Pike (Marinelli Rd.), Rockville 20852
301-468-9301, Fax 301-468-1518, *Lunch & Dinner daily, $, Casual*

A P ♥ ⅰ

This small and unpretentious place offers several dishes stamped with a heart-healthy seal of a local hospital, plus assorted vegetarian and macrobiotic dishes, mostly of Chinese and Japanese origin. The menu also explores several hot pot items, but you won't find a lick of beef or a shred of chicken going into the bubbling broth. Carnivores may not thrill to the food, but such dishes as the kung pao tofu will surely delight vegetarians. There's mock duck and beef, too (in a dish mimicking orange beef, for instance). Non-vegetarians may find the fare a bit bland, as we did.

Yuan Fu Vegetarian

798 Rockville Pike (Mt. Vernon Pl.), Rockville 20852
301-762-5937, *Lunch & Dinner daily, $, Casual*

A P ♥ ⅰ

If you like gluten as a substitute for beef and tofu skin replacing fish, you'll love this place. Carnivores and those accustomed to more familiar tastes and textures may not warm up to this kind of cooking, but there's plenty to enjoy in the Crispy Eggplant, with its orange-flavor overtones, or sesame noodles and steamed dumplings.

Indian

Madras Palace

Giant Shopping Complex
74 Bureau Dr. (Quince Orchard Rd.), Gaithersburg 20878
301-977-1600, Fax 301-840-8558, *Lunch & Dinner daily, $, Casual*

A P ♥ ⅰ

Very much in vogue, Indian vegetarian food has many proponents in the area, and such restaurants as Madras Palace only underscore how popular this kind of food has become. If you are comfortable with the smooth, silken curries of North Indian cooking and the subtly complex seasonings, vegetarian dishes may startle you, for flavors are generally hotter and more intense (typical of South Indian cooking). It looks like Sunday is the big day here, for most seats were taken by large Indian families taking advantage of the eat-all-you-want buffet with its set number of offerings. But the menu holds so many more promises, from the uthapam (pancakes made with rice and lentils) and vegetable curries (North and South Indian-style) and the assorted rice specialties, to say nothing of the various variations of dosas. Desserts are the standard rasmalai and ice creams, but include a South Indian specialty as well, the Madras special payasam made from milk and sugar boiled with very thin vermicelli.

Prices are based on a complete dinner for one, including appetizer, entrée, dessert, coffee, tax and tip—but excluding wine or other beverages.

Woodlands

8046 New Hampshire Ave.
(University Blvd.), Langley Park, Hyattsville 20783
301-434-4202, Fax 301-434-4107, *Lunch & Dinner daily, $, Casual*

A P ♥ ☷

Despite its stark décor and cafeteria-style setting, Woodlands has a special charm, emphasized by vivid Indian paintings. And you most likely will be charmed, as we were, by the restaurant's abundant menu, beginning with that South Indian favorite, idli (steamed rice and lentil patties). We love a good masala dhosa (a rice-flour crêpe stuffed with potatoes and herbs—the South Indian answer to french fries), and this ones is as flavorful as any in town. Try the Mysore Royal Thali (dinner special), which includes samples of appetizers and main dishes. Whatever else you do, start with rasam, the traditional South Indian sour-spicy soup, a flavorful broth that will jar your taste buds awake. Desserts are predictable: rasmalai, halvah, ice cream and payasam. **Also located at** 4078 Jermantown Rd., Fairfax, VA, 703-385-1996.

Italian

Red Tomato Café

4910 St. Elmo Ave. (Norfolk Ave.), Bethesda 20814
301-652-4499, Fax 301-652-9643, *Lunch Mon.-Sat., Dinner nightly, $, Casual*

A P ☷

Colorful and sleek, this tiny Italian eatery attracts upscale patrons seeking terrific, fast Italian meals, along with some American-inspired dishes. Among luncheon sandwiches, the Red Tomato Special with fresh mozzarella, sun-dried tomatoes and artichoke hearts tops the bill. Dinners include entrée salads and plenty of pasta choices. For any meal, the pizzas from wood-burning oven are among the hottest going in town. We've loved the Brie pizza and the spicy Italian sausage pizza, but you won't go wrong with any selection. Cheerful and colorful, this is a good place to relax over a glass of wine. **Other locations.**

Japanese/Sushi

Momo Taro Sushi

16051 Frederick Rd. (Redland Rd.), Rockville 20855
301-963-6868, *Lunch Mon.-Sat., Dinner nightly, $, Casual*

A P ☷

Like many sushi places, this sushi spot is all decked out in blond woods and cutsey Japanese décor with the seating arranged by stools at the sushi bar and at tables. Unlike some other sushi places, the sushi chefs love to talk with customers and with each other. However, what it does not offer is anything that is offbeat or different. Nevertheless, with its selection of good sushi combinations, and its interesting sushi specials such as toro (fatty tuna), white tuna and ankimo (monkfish), patrons are assured of a good sushi meal. They can also count on hearty bowls of soup and assorted other Japanese favorites, from tempura to teriyaki. The food is not consistently good, nor does every dish sparkle with creativity, but the staff is pleasant, and the service is competent.

Sushi Sushi

4915 Fairmont Ave. (Norfolk Ave.), Bethesda 20814
301-654-9616, *Lunch Mon.-Fri., Dinner Mon.-Sat., $, Casual*

As its name implies, this little place deals strictly in sushi—and lots of it. Small and unpretentious, it has few chairs and just a couple stools around the sushi bar, where two chefs are hard at work. You can buy sushi in several different ways: by the piece, as chirashi sushi, as cone rolls or as maki sushi. The lunch special of soup, salad and two rolls is a big bargain, but you can afford to splurge here: Order the sushi of your dreams with Japanese beer and green tea ice cream, and leave refreshed.

Taipei Tokyo Café

11510-A Rockville Pike (Nicholson Ln.), Rockville 20852
301-881-8388, *Lunch & Dinner daily, $, Casual*
No credit cards.

The older of the two Taipei Tokyo Cafés resembles a bargain sale at mealtimes, and you'll be lucky to find a seat, or even standing room. The draw is the split character of this very casual place: One section features sushi; the other, assorted Chinese dishes with an emphasis on handmade and hand-cut noodles. Grab a menu, place your order, and wait for your food. To pass the time, watch the noodle maker at work in the front window. Noodle dishes are the best bet here. Another standout: the terrific beef noodle soup. The table turnover is fast, but you may end up sharing space with a stranger. **Also located at** 1596-A Rockville Pike, Rockville, MD, 301-881-8533, see review in *Restaurants.*

Mexican

Baja Fresh Mexican Grill

Congressional Plaza
1607 Rockville Pike (Halpine Rd.), Rockville 20852
301-770-4339, Fax 301-770-4537
Lunch & Dinner daily, $, Casual
No credit cards.

This scrubbed-clean West Coast-based eatery is a favorite of moviegoers, mall shoppers and students, who hang out over newspapers and a spicy meal. Burritos are king and come with so many different fillings that return visits are a must. You can eat your way through the house dishes: the Baja burrito (melted Jack cheese, guacamole, fresh salsa, grilled chicken or steak) or the burrito Mexicano (rice, beans, onion, cilantro and grilled chicken or steak). Our favorite is the Burrito Ultimo, which is pretty much the ultimate, with melted Monterey Jack and cheddar cheeses, chicken or steak, beans, chiles, rice and fresh salsa in a flour tortilla wrapper. The kitchen also cooks up tacos, nachos, tostadas, quesadillas and other snacks. No desserts, but no microwaves, no can openers, no MSG and no freezers either. Excellent fast food at bargain prices. **Other locations.**

Find the name you are looking for, quickly and easily,
in **the index.**

California Tortilla

4862 Cordell Ave. (Norfolk Ave.), Bethesda 20814
301-654-8226, Fax 301-654-8237
Lunch & Dinner daily, $, Casual

A P ♿

Few places take such an edgy approach to creating tacos and burritos as this eatery with the California free spirit. That must account for its immense popularity, making it one of the busiest places on Bethesda's restaurant row. Once you've fought your way to the counter, consider your many choices: Thai chicken, blackened chicken Caesar, Buffalo chicken wing burritos, fajita platters or BBQ chicken. Burritos come in small or regular sizes, but they all look overstuffed. Everything is made fresh daily, and the cooks don't use lard or animal fats— a concession to weight watchers. Love to experiment? Try the Hot Mango Burrito. **Also located at** 199 E. Montgomery Ave., Rockville, MD, 301-610-6500.

Chevys Fresh Mex

668 Clopper Rd. (Quince Orchard Rd.), Gaithersburg 20878
301-926-6646, Fax 301-926-1934
Lunch & Dinner daily, $$, Casual

A P ♿ ♿ Y

This restaurant chain offers kitschy just-North-of-the-Border décor, bright and vivid colors, and some good Mexican fare. We always judge by the chiles rellenos, and these are cheese filled, batter dipped, and best of all, reasonably priced—that means ordering more than one. Not every dish, like the chicken Caesar salad, is totally Mexican, but so much on the menu is that you can pick your way through to a real fiesta. Freshness is the motto: No canned food is used. This means all sauces are made fresh and all fillings that call for vegetables are made with fresh vegetables. It's a happy place that serves happy food at very reasonable prices. **Other locations.**

Chipotle Mexican Grill

7600 Old Georgetown Rd. (Woodmont Ave.), Bethesda 20814
301-907-9077, Fax 301-907-7905
Lunch & Dinner daily, $, Casual

A ♿

With its slightly industrial, clean-lines look, this Bethesda burrito/taco takeout spot makes life a little easier for all the hungry folks who like a quick Mexican pick-me-up. It's also casual enough so that rollerbladers can skate right in, order their burrito (or taco or fajita) and skate away. It would be difficult to find any place more casual, except a backyard barbecue. In fact, there's not even wait service: You place your order at the counter, and if the fixings seem puzzling, the line cook will explain what's what. The menu is short and streamlined and revolves around a few basic items: flour tortillas; steak, chicken, carnitas and vegetarian fillings; salsas, guacamole and chips; and beverages. It's up to you to combine the basics into your favorite; our favorite is the Barbacoa—shredded beef braised with chipotle chiles and seasonings and served with coriander rice and beans in a hot flour tortilla with a scoop of guacamole. We also like the carnitas burrito with two salsas. **Other locations.**

El Mexicano

10412 Baltimore Ave. (Sunnyside Ave.), Beltsville 20703
301-572-4000, *Lunch & Dinner daily, $, Casual*

🅰️🅿️💚🍴

This Maryland eatery has put Mexican fast food on a different footing, raising the flavors and options a few notches. It offers an entire vegetarian menu and there's a menu in Spanish and English. Those menus feature some tempting fare like the cheese- and calorie-dense Sunken Burrito, which is a meat-filled (chicken or beef) burrito submerged in a bath of salsa and melted cheese. From there, you can eat your way through chimichangas, chiles rellenos, fajitas, tamales and that all-American favorite, the chili dog. As an added bonus, you can request hotter seasonings, whole-wheat tortillas or black beans. The counter service is so speedy you won't even have time to find a seat. **Also located at** 12150 Darnestown Rd., Gaithersburg, MD, 301-330-5620; and 12922 Middlebrook Rd., Germantown, MD, 301-972-0500.

Pollo Casero

1835 University Blvd. E. (Riggs Rd.), Langley Park, Hyattsville 20783
301-431-6666, *Lunch & Dinner daily, $, Casual*
No credit cards. 🅿️💚🍴🍸

Putting its own spin on the local chicken wars, this casual eatery offers Mexican-style marinated and grilled chickens cooked over coals, calling them a heart-healthy food guaranteed to keep the doctor away. Although that's the main offering at this restaurant, you also can fill up on beans, corn on the cob and assorted burritos filled with meat, chicken, beans and cheese.

Taco Fiesta

Campus Village Shopping Center
8145-C Baltimore Ave. (Navajo St.), College Park 20740
301-441-1661, Fax 301-441-8061, *Lunch & Dinner Mon.-Sat., $, Casual*

🅰️🅿️🍴

A hangout for local college kids, this taco spot boasts a television, a couple of tables and a salsa bar—and the kitchen, of course, wide open to view. Doesn't sound like much, but, because the freshest ingredients are used, the food sings. Beans, guacamole and salsas are made from scratch daily. The short menu includes such sure-fire favorites as a bean and cheese burrito, chimichangas, taquitos, taco salads and enchiladas.

Middle Eastern

The Kabob House

Chesapeake Plaza
1488-A Rockville Pike (Montrose Rd.), Rockville 20852
301-984-0005, Fax 301-984-8757, *Lunch & Dinner daily, $, Casual*

🅰️🅿️🍴

Next door to the busy Yekta Deli Imported Grocery, this family-casual eatery features various kebab platters. The menu has pictures that will help you decide what looks most tempting. We like the lean and juicy kubideh kebab. (Note that you can substitute thin lavash for a mound of rice.) Try one of the Persian-style starters, such as stuffed grape leaves, and check out the array of Persian sandwiches. The trick here is not to wait for table service but to place your order at the counter and await its arrival. You can amuse yourself by reading newspapers or taking a quick tour of the market next door.

Lebanese Taverna Café

Congressional Plaza
1605 Rockville Pike (Congressional Ln.), Rockville 20852
301-468-9086, Fax 301-468-9296, *Lunch & Dinner daily, $, Casual*
A P

Mall shoppers have a new dining destination in Rockville. The newest of the Lebanese Taverna's family of eateries, this small place has a much-diminished menu and offers counter service only. Not everything is listed on the blackboard, so be sure to check the paper menus before ordering. The staff is eager to please and even more eager to be sure customers understand and like Lebanese cooking. Make a meal of appetizers—we loved the falafel and kibbeh—and then continue with your shopping. **Other locations**.

Mediterranean House of Kabob

White Flint Station Center
11616 Rockville Pike (Nicholson Ln.), Rockville 20852
301-881-5956, *Lunch & Dinner daily, $, Casual*
A P

It calls itself Mediterranean, and this casual eatery offers a polyglot cuisine. You'll find the traditional Persian kubideh and chenjeh kebabs, as well as a Greek gyro and a nicely seasoned Greek salad. So take a tip from the menu: mix and match cuisines, and you'll come away with a budget-priced meal with plenty of interesting tastes and textures.

Moby Dick House of Kabob

7027 Wisconsin Ave. (Leland Ave.), Bethesda 20815
301-654-1838, Fax 301-907-6994, *Lunch & Dinner daily, $, Casual*
No credit cards. P

Moby Dick has made its name serving kebabs and fresh breads. This first location in Bethesda has been a popular hangout for years for young people who dig high-quality cheap eats. Now all Washington is in on the secret, because they've expanded to several other locations. Depending on the hour, getting a table may be a challenge. Plan to order ahead, otherwise you may join a line waiting for the terrific kebabs wrapped in fresh-baked breads. We're addicted to the kubideh kebab in hot bread with its side of tangy yogurt. Add a shirazi salad and you've got a meal. Always check out the daily specials Monday through Friday; these are full-blown Persian entrées that are more substantial than a sandwich. **Other locations.**

Pan-Asian

Fortune Garden

Potomac Village, 9812 Falls Rd. (River Rd.), Potomac 20854
301-299-2022, Fax 301-299-2299, *Lunch & Dinner daily, $, Casual*
A P

The fact that the main piece of art here is a picture of Wyoming mountains underscores the split personality of the menu, which is predominately Thai but salted with such interesting nuggets as salmon teriyaki, Vietnamese lime chicken, assorted sushi and an Indonesian beef satay lontong. But mostly you'll find such popular Thai dishes as tod mun, panang curry and roast duck salad.

Oodles Noodles

4907 Cordell Ave. (Old Georgetown Rd.), Bethesda 20814
301-986-8833, Fax 301-986-8818, *Lunch Mon.-Sat., Dinner nightly, $, Casual*

🅰 ▯ ▮

It's rare for a pan-Asian restaurant to excel in several cooking styles, but Oodles Noodles manages to do so. The menu offers Thai, Vietnamese, Japanese and Chinese noodle dishes, all in serving pieces authentic to the country of origin. Any of these dishes make for a satisfying lunch or a light dinner: Thai drunken noodles, spicy Japanese seafood ramen, or rice-noodle soups in a Chinese clay pot. If you're nuts about noodles but on a budget, you can have just about any of the dishes here plus an appetizer or salad for far less than what pasta would cost you at one of the nearby upscale Italian restaurants. There's a reason for the distinguished feats here: The owner is Jessie Yan, who also owns DC's hot spots Spices and Yanÿu. **Also located at** 1120 19th St. NW, Washington, DC, 202-293-3138.

Peruvian

The Chicken Place

2418 University Blvd. (Georgia Ave.), Wheaton 20902
301-946-1212, Fax 301-946-1986, *Lunch & Dinner Wed.-Mon., $, Casual*

🅰 ▯ ▮ 𝚼

Its logo of a plump chicken dressed in Peruvian garb tells the tale: a Peruvian roast-chicken place with a slightly Latino look (it took over from a Southwestern restaurant). But despite the name, you don't have to stick to chicken. In fact, that's the least part of the menu, which has all sorts of Peruvian dishes, including the famed chupe soup, assorted steak and tripe dishes, and a whole range of sautéed and fried seafood. If you want to keep things simple, however, a charbroiled chicken with a side of fries, salad or rice plus the Peruvian sweet—alfajores (shortbread cookies usually filled with a thick caramel spread)—make a perfect eat-in or to-go meal. **Also located at** 117 N. Frederick Ave., Gaithersburg, MD, 301-519-9100.

Thai

Asian Foods

Wheaton Manor
2301 University Blvd. W. (Amherst Ave.), Wheaton 20902
301-933-6071, *Lunch & Dinner daily, $, Casual*

🅰 🅿 ▮

Attached to a longtime favorite Thai market, this small eatery/carry-out serves home-style Thai food and does a thriving business. You can contribute to that by ordering pad Thai, pad-se-ieu, rad-na, pad kee mao, noodle soup with stewed duck and much more. Don't ignore the prepared foods counter—you may find such typical offerings as red curry with Thai eggplant, pork with bittermelon soup, fried rib bellies and fried fish cakes. Needless to say, the authenticity factor is quite high here. Also see review in *Gourmet Shops & Markets/Ethnic Markets/Asian.*

Thai Spice Café

8223 Georgia Ave. (Thayer Ave.), Silver Spring 20910
301-589-8233, *Lunch Mon.-Sat., Dinner Tues.-Sat., $, Casual*
A P 🍴

Thai Spice Café may look like Anywhere, USA, but don't be deceived: You can pick up bargain-basement Thai food here that's packed with traditional flavors. It's a popular stop-and-shop spot for Thais who come weekdays to pick up dinner items. Check for unusual offerings at the steam table or ask about dishes on the takeout menu. We love the steamed red fish curry and the sizzling rice noodles with pork or beef. This hidden gem also offers daily lunch specials. It's a great place to linger over a newspaper and a Thai curry.

Vietnamese

Pho 95

Ritchie Center
785-H Rockville Pike (Wootten Pkwy.), Rockville 20852
301-294-9391, *Lunch & Dinner daily, $, Casual*
A P ♥ 🍴

As Vietnamese restaurants go, this eatery offers few surprises, except that the kitchen prepares quail and frog (goat has been deleted from the menu). The popular soup, pho, comes in several hearty, beefy versions, accompanied by a mound of bean sprouts and basil leaf. Standards such as the soft spring rolls (goi cuon) are better than most, as are the grilled beef in grape leaves and the entrée-size rice noodles made with coriander, shredded carrots and a sweet broth that binds it all together. The special rice crêpe with grilled pork, shrimp and spring roll is a knockout. Beverages include fresh and salty lemonade; desserts include grass jelly with coconut milk and longan.

Pho 99 Restaurant

2065 University Blvd. E. (Riggs Rd.), Hyattsville 20783
301-445-1431, *Lunch & Dinner daily, $, Casual*
A P 🍴

Pho 99 has undergone several changes in ownership, and, currently, the menu and food are much less upscale than they were. This has not stopped the stampede, however. There are lots of customers. The menu seems shorter than before, but if you stick to such tried-and-true dishes as the spring rolls or the bowls of pho, you'll do just fine. We liked the grilled shrimp on vermicelli but would pass next time on the shrimp and pork salad.

Pho 75

University Place
1510 University Blvd. (New Hampshire Ave.), Hyattsville 20783
301-434-7844, *Breakfast, Lunch & Dinner daily, $, Casual*
No credit cards. P 🍴

A few years ago, this local restaurant group helped introduce Washingtonians to the glories of the Vietnamese soup bowl, the pho. Now pho places are all the rage in the metro area, and Pho 75 has five locations. Who would have guessed that so many would fall in love with this hearty meal-in-a-bowl? Some soup places offer other dishes, too, but this group sticks to the basics: Order your beef soup with a choice of meat combinations in small or large bowls. Your order comes with chopsticks, soup spoon and loads of vegetables; it's up to you to add chopped chilies, cilantro and chili sauce to your taste. **Other locations.**

ICE CREAM & MORE

Gifford's Ice Cream Company

7720 Wisconsin Ave. (Woodmont Ave.), Bethesda 20814
301-907-3436, *Lunch & Dinner daily, $, Casual*

🅰 P 🖥 ♥ 🍴

    This longtime favorite has pleased crowds young and old since 1938, making it one of the oldest ice cream stores in the metro area. The high-quality, high-fat ice cream is cranked on the premises—no wonder crowds line up out the door. In the summer you can count on sherbets as well. Eat at tables or grab a wooden bench out back.

Kohr Brothers

Saah Plaza, 827 Hungerford Dr. (Campus Dr.), Rockville 20850
301-762-4343, Fax 301-762-4344, *Open daily, $, Casual*
No credit cards. P 🖥 🍴

    Frozen custard seems to taste best after a hot meal or when the temperature soars, but even in the dead of winter, at Kohr Brothers it tastes pretty darn good. Soft-serve smooth custard comes in limited flavors at this vendor, including vanilla-chocolate, mint-chocolate and peanut butter-chocolate. Our favorite is the vanilla-orange, which pairs a slightly tart orange with a creamy-sweet vanilla. We thought the peanut butter-chocolate tasted more like a candy bar than frozen custard. **Other locations.**

York Castle Tropical Ice Cream

9324 Georgia Ave. (Seminary Rd.), Silver Spring 20910
301-589-1616, *Open daily, $, Casual*
No credit cards. P 🖥 🍴

    After relocating here from Jamaica, the Headley family opened this quirky little ice cream parlor with its unusual tropical flavors, from banana and mango to passion fruit (nicely tart). Other flavors here are much more traditional, and maybe even as delicious, but why not take a fling with something exotic? Jamaican savories, such as jerk chicken wings and beef or chicken patties, are also sold here. The ice cream is sold at Rockville's Caribbean Feast restaurant, too.

PIZZA

California Pizza Kitchen

Montgomery Mall
7101 Democracy Blvd (Westlake Dr.)., Bethesda 20817
301-469-5090, Fax 301-469-0869, *Lunch & Dinner daily, $$, Casual*

🅰 P 🖥

    You have to have a sense of humor to enjoy CPK's outrageous pizza toppings. They are innovative, offbeat and likely to raise eyebrows among traditionalists. That's probably a quick and then forgotten reaction, though, since this is one of the country's most popular chains. We enjoy the rosemary-chicken-potato pizza, the tandoori chicken and the Thai chicken pies. Not everything is so ingenous: Sticklers for the conventional will find pepperoni; vegetarian; and five-cheese-and-fresh-tomato pies. Hungry for more? Check out the menu for soups, salads, sandwiches and pasta dishes. This tiled, shiny-clean restaurant is casual, fun and often crowded. **Other locations**.

Il Forno Pizzeria

Walnut Hill Shopping Center
8941 N. Westland Dr. (Rte. 355), Gaithersburg 20877
301-977-5900, Fax 301-977-5902, *Lunch & Dinner daily, $, Casual*

Ⓐ🅿 🚎 👬

Time and time again, when we think of pizza, we think of the pies that emerge from this wood-burning oven. The restaurant is tiny, but the pizzas have giant flavor and texture. You won't find unusual toppings, just straightforward ones. Ask about daily specials. **Also located at** 4926 Cordell Ave., Bethesda, MD, 301-652-7757.

Ledo Pizza

2638 W. University Blvd. (Georgia Ave.), Wheaton 20902
301-929-6111, Fax 301-929-0065, *Lunch & Dinner daily, $, Casual*

Ⓐ🅿 👬

A restaurant group that started with its first store in College Park, MD, these popular pizza restaurants have a devoted following among students, families and anyone who likes hearty Italian-style meals. The menu offers salads, pasta entrées, over-stuffed subs, sandwiches, and burgers. Its pizzas, however, have made its name and fame: The dough and sauce are prepared fresh daily; toppings are high-quality ingredients. Expect to find clean, busy restaurants for sit-down meals. **Other locations.**

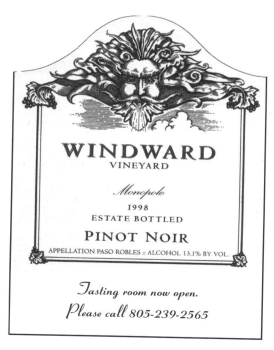

GOURMET SHOPS & MARKETS

BAKERIES

Creative Cakes

8814 Brookville Rd. (Lyttonsville Rd.), Silver Spring 20910
301-587-1599, Fax 301-1598, *Open Mon.-Sat.*

A **P**

Cakes! Cakes! Cakes! The self-proclamation says it all—Creative Cakes is about custom cakes for all occasions. It's known for its "edible images" of well-known characters and designs. A recent visit found a happy mom picking up her daughter's birthday cake with a Barbie motif. Want to taste a cake before ordering? Come to an open house, held varying Sundays each month except December, and sample the cake flavors. The shop does children's create-a-cake birthday parties at the store on Sundays, if you're lucky enough to get a booking.

Great Harvest Bread Co.

219 N. Washington St. (Beall Ave.), Rockville, 20850
301-762-6533, *Open Mon.-Sat.*

A **P**

Part of a nationwide chain of nutritionally correct bread and muffin bakeries, this store is usually thronged with people who love the free bread samples they can spread with jam, butter, and/or honey. Loaf flavors are interesting and the breads wholesome and delicious. Our favorite: the honey whole-wheat and the raisin cinnamon. Muffins, scones, quickbreads and thick, chunky cookies taste homemade. **Other locations.**

Le Bon Pain

7637 New Hampshire Ave. (Holton Ln.), Hyattsville 20783
301-434-3911, *Open daily*
No credit cards.

This classic bakery has all the favorites—croissants, danish, cakes, fruit tarts and cookies. Latin and Caribbean favorites like coconut bread, Caribbean fruitcake and butter bread adorn the shelves on the weekend. Known particularly for specialty breads and wedding cakes, its variety goes beyond any other bakery in the area. Each visit brings a new smorgasbord of rich, fresh-baked aromas.

Pastry Designs

4927 Elm St. (Arlington Rd.), Bethesda 20814
301-656-0536, Fax 301-652-7244, *Open daily*

A **P**

Like delicious food art, beautiful cakes grace the shelves of this Bethesda bakery. Pastry Design has become a regular stop for those celebrating special occasions with sweet tributes. Its popular chocolate truffle rests at the top of the menu with its dark chocolate mousse, layers of chocolate génoise and a touch of raspberry preserve. A larger version serving 10-12 is covered with poured chocolate. For only $1 you can personalize a greeting on a marzipan plaque. Many shoppers swear the French apple tart is the best anywhere in the Washington area—here the bakers use their own apple compote under the sliced apples. Not always the friendliest staff, but who cares when the work is so deliciously sweet. Also see review in *Quick Bites*.

COFFEE & TEA

Quartermaine Coffee Roasters

4817 Bethesda Ave. (Woodmont Ave.), Bethesda 20814
301-718-2853, Fax 301-718-9458, *Open daily*

A

Quartermaine roasts top-quality green beans and sells them from their Maryland stores and to leading area restaurants and groceries. Quartermaine's founder, owner and coffee buyer Roger Scheumann regularly visits the world's coffee-growing regions, buying from mostly small estates. Roasting in small batches, the stores never use vacuum packaging to extend life. They roast it, you buy it and you brew a good cup of fresh coffee. One of their most popular choices is the Clyde's Blend made for the popular Clyde's restaurants (see review in *Restaurants*). **Also located at** 36 Wisconsin Circle, Chevy Chase, MD, 301-951-0132.

ETHNIC MARKETS

African

Eko Food Market

Capital Plaza, 6507 Annapolis Rd. (Baltimore-Washington Pkwy.)
Landover Hills 20784
301-341-5050, Fax 301-341-5052, *Open daily*

A **P**

Among the area's wealth of uncommon international markets, Eko Food Market is a rich resource for West African foods and spices, as well as staples like goat and by-products like cow's feet and beef neck bones. Yams and plantains always can be found in the store. Seafood (fresh, smoked and dried) is plentiful, as one would expect in a native West African market. Service is friendly and helpful for those new to this cuisine.

Asian

Asian Foods

Wheaton Manor
2301 University Blvd. W. (Amherst Ave.), Wheaton 20902
301-933-6071, Fax 301-933-1100, *Open daily*

A **P**

Asian Foods has been in business for 25 years, offering products from many corners and outposts of Asia, especially Thailand as the owners are Thai. You'll find the expected lemon grass, chilies, kaffir lime leaves and specialty blends of spices, as well as noodles and mixes for sauces too numerous to count. An experienced regular pointed out a generous supply of Indonesian grocery items. Carryout Thai food is available. Also see review in *Quick Bites*.

Find the name you are looking for, quickly and easily,
in **the index**.

Daruma

6931 Arlington Rd. (Bradley Blvd.), Bethesda 20814
301-654-8832, Fax 301-654-7745, *Open Tues.-Sun.*

A P

There's not a finer Japanese market in the Washington area.
The store is immaculately stocked with groceries of Japan as
well as local and imported produce and fresh and frozen fish.
If it's noodles you're seeking, you can find them at Daruma in
innumerable varieties, both frozen and dried. In accordance
with the Japanese entrepreneurial spirit, you'll even find eggs
raised by a Japanese farmer. Don't overlook the traditional
sweets made with a red bean paste.

Han Ah Reum

12015 Georgia Ave. (Randolph Rd.), Silver Spring 20902
301-942-5071, *Open daily*

Han Ah Reum is truly a bargain hunter's paradise, attracting
many restaurant owners for its great, inexpensive produce in
mass quantities. Most packaged goods are either Korean or
Japanese, but the fresh produce and refrigerated meats and
noodles will fit into any Asian meal. Check out the kimchi:
Koreans are known for their kimchi, the traditional standard
condiment made from cabbage, cucumbers and assorted other
vegetables with a secret blend of spices, often unique to the
family of origin. The store can be a bit bewildering to those
unfamiliar with the Asian cuisines, and the staff may not speak
much English; but price and variety are big drawing cards. A
caveat: Expect crowds on the weekends. **Also located at** 8103
Lee Hwy., Falls Church, VA, 703-573-6300.

Maxim

640 University Blvd. (Piney Branch Rd.), Silver Spring 20901
301-439-0110, Fax 301-439-0111, *Open daily*

A P

Maxim is one of the original Chinese markets in town; here
it's really a supermarket. All the ingredients and equipment
needed for preparing Chinese and almost any Asian dish can
be found in this Silver Spring sister to the Rockville store.
Complete with a produce department, it has everything from
the soy sauce to the sesame oil to the bean curds needed for
authentic recipes. Not ready to tackle the kitchen rituals?
Check out the prepared foods in the freezer. From cabbage to
pork, this is the one-stop Asian food store. **Also located at** 460
Hungerford Dr., Rockville, MD, 301-279-0110.

Thai Market Oriental Grocery & Carryout

902 Thayer Ave. (Georgia Ave.), Silver Spring 20910
301-495-2779, Fax 301-565-8038, *Open daily*

A P

This friendly market has all the produce you need to make
Thai or Asian dishes. The lemon grass stalks are always fresh
and fragrant. Looking for fast food to go? Try the carryout
counter for some fine spicy beef and spring rolls. Rolling your
own? Pick up spring roll skins and oyster sauce for your
favorite recipe. If pad Thai is your weakness, you can buy the
dry rice noodles, fresh bean sprouts and fish sauce to make it
all come together. The staff is cooperative, although the language barrier may be a challenge.

Indian

Dana Bazaar

Congressional Plaza
1701-K Rockville Pike (Halpine Rd.), Rockville 20852
301-231-7546, *Open daily*

A P

Dana offers the herbs and spices Indian food enthusiasts need for a cooking adventure. Rice, chutneys, pickles and a host of Indian products make this a good resource. An excellent produce department adds to the overall appeal of the market for the many who shop in this Rockville store.

Kosher

Shalom Kosher

Wheaton Manor, 2307 University Blvd. (Amherst Ave.), Wheaton 20902
301-946-6500, *Open Sun.-Fri.*

A P

Everything under one roof for an all-kosher kitchen is stocked in this market. Stop by the bustling bakery corner for cookies, pastries and cakes.

Latin American/Caribbean

Americana Market

8541 Piney Branch Rd. (Arliss St.), Silver Spring 20901
301-495-0864, *Open daily*

A P

The aromas from a Latino market are cause for a case of sensory overload, and Americana Market is no exception. All the spices, peppers, fruits and meats mingle into a symphony of Latin food harmonies. The chorizos of Americana are rich and thick—and spicy—and come in as many styles and flavors as you'll find anywhere in the Washington area. From jicama to chayote to plantains, the busy produce section is always a source of good values compared with chain market prices. **Also located at** 6128 Columbia Pike, Falls Church, VA, 703-671-9625.

Brazilian Market

11425 Grandview Ave. (University Blvd.), Wheaton 20902
301-942-8412, Fax 301-942-8432, *Open daily*

A P

Fresh fish, cured hams, sausages and smoked bacon are prominently displayed. You also will find oils, cheeses and rice of the region and soft drinks and canned items from Brazil. Among the baked goods, there's a nice inventory of Portuguese breads and pastries.

Some establishments change **days of operation** without warning. It is always wise to check in advance.

Caribbean Market

7505 New Hampshire Ave.
(University Blvd.), Langley Park, Hyattsville 20783
301-439-5288, Fax 301-439-5283, *Open daily*

A

This market covers the basics of West Indian cookery, from the staple goat and other meat products to root vegetables and okra and spices that are critical to the cuisine. If you're looking for hot peppers, this is the place for an extensive selection of hot (!) Scotch bonnet peppers—with a flavor that gives the food depth as well as heat. Native breads, including spice buns, are available, as well as carryout foods and tropical drinks.

Middle Eastern

Yekta Deli Imported Grocery

Chesapeake Plaza
1488-A Rockville Pike (Congressional Ln.), Rockville 20852
301-984-1190, Fax 301-984-8757, *Open daily*

A P

This wonderful Persian grocery is attached to The Kabob House (see review in *Quick Bites*) and contains much fresh, hard-to-find produce and loads of nuts, dried herbs and other seasonings. There are selections of Persian teas, dried fruits, pastries, breads, grains, halvah and other Persian sweets. The refrigerator cases are stocked with olives, cheese and yogurt drinks.

Portuguese

European Market

Redland Shopping Center
17605 Redland Rd. (Muncaster Mill Rd.), Rockville 20855
301-417-0788, Fax 301-417-0788, *Open daily*

A

The European Market is devoted to the foods of Portugal and Brazil. Fresh fish, cured hams, sausages and smoked bacon are abundant, and there's a good inventory of Portuguese breads and pastries, as well as oils, cheeses and rice. Guava drinks and pastes are among items stocked from Brazil.

FARMERS MARKETS

Neighborhood Farmers Street Markets

TUESDAY
Bethesda—Parking Lot 41-Bethesda National Institutes of Health Complex (near Medical Library), 9000 Rockville Pike, 2 p.m.-6 p.m. (May-Nov.), 301-590-2823.

WEDNESDAY
Bethesda—7155 Wisconsin Ave., 7 a.m.-3 p.m. 301-652-2291.
Takoma Park—Carroll Ave. (Takoma Junction), 4 p.m.-7 p.m. (June-Oct.), 301-270-1700.

THURSDAY
Beltsville—USDA Farmers Market, 5601 Sunnyside Ave., 10 a.m.-2 p.m. (June-Nov.), 301-504-1776.

SATURDAY
Bethesda—7155 Wisconsin Ave., 7 a.m.-3 p.m.. 301-652-2291.
Silver Spring—Wayne Ave. & Fenton St., 7 a.m.-1 p.m. (June-Oct.), 301-590-2823.
St. Michael's—Waterfront at Willow & Green Sts. (one block off Talbot St.), 8:30 a.m.-12:30 p.m. (May-Oct.). 202-331-7300.
Kensington—Howard Ave. Train Station Lot, 8 a.m.-12 p.m. (June-Oct.), 301-949-2424.

SUNDAY
Takoma Park—Old Town, Laurel Ave. (between Eastern & Carroll Aves.), 10 a.m.-2 p.m. (Apr.-Dec.), 301-422-0097.
Wheaton—Grandview Ave. & Reedie Dr., 8 a.m.-1 p.m. (June-Oct.), 240-777-8122.

FISH, MEAT & POULTRY

Cameron's Seafood Market

8603 16th St. (Spring St.), Silver Spring 20910
301-585-5555, Fax 301-585-0000, *Open daily*

A P

These Montgomery County seafood houses conjure up images of the Eastern Shore, and anyone who's looking for clean jumbo crab meat will head to Cameron's. It won't be cheap, but good crab meat never is. You can pick up some salads to take home, from a traditional shrimp salad with celery and mayonnaise to tasty cool squid and mussel offerings. The cream of crab soup is popular among the locals. If it's fin fish you're after, there's always a clean selection of the latest catch—from salmon and tuna to mahi mahi. **Other locations.**

HoneyBaked Ham Company

The Shops of Wisconsin Ave.
6831 Wisconsin Ave. (Bradley Blvd.), Chevy Chase 20815
301-657-1900, Fax 301-657-1906, *Open Mon.-Sat.*

A P

The company's signature spiral-cut honey-baked ham is still the far-and-away favorite for seasonal holiday carryout. There is a following for the ham, which is both tastier and sweeter than anything you can prepare at home—and people still marvel at the way the slices fall away from the bone. If you have any doubt about the store's popularity, check out the lines before any holiday. Today, HoneyBaked is more than ham—the shops offer turkey, pork and even steaks. Diversification means sandwiches, side dishes and frozen desserts, too. But in the end, it's the ham. **Other locations.**

GOURMET MARKETS & GOURMET TO-GO

eatZi's Market & Bakery

11503-B Rockville Pike (Nicholson Ln.), Rockville 20852
301-816-2020, Fax 301-816-0331, *Open daily*

A P

This is carryout with a twist: chef-prepared meals. The Dallas-based eatZi's has 30-40 cooks preparing foods for working professionals—or anyone—to take home. On any given day, shoppers can find 100 different entrées. Match an entrée with a choice from the impressive collection of breads (you pass the bakery on the way in the front door)and some cheese, wine and fresh produce, and the meal is complete. Forget flowers? They're here, too, along with cigars. Find a meat or seafood item you like—they'll grill it for you while you wait—or go to the carving station for sliced meats or a whole roasted chicken. eatZi's brings some pizzazz to the otherwise sterile world of home-cooked-meal replacement. Also see review in *Quick Bites*.

Fresh Fields

Kenwood Center
5269 River Rd. (Little Falls Pkwy.), Bethesda 20816
301-984-4860, Fax 301-984-4870, *Open daily*

A P

Fresh Fields is part of Whole Foods Market, which claims to be the world's biggest retailer of natural and organic foods. Here you will find a large, creatively merchandised produce department, an in-house bakery, extensive prepared-foods counters and large wine and cheese departments. Most stores have a wide-open feel and a welcoming ambience. Home of the best grocery salad bar—with couscous, bean and tofu salads for the health conscious—Fresh Fields also has one of the area's finest butcher shops, featuring naturally raised beef, lamb and pork. Shoppers also can find the favorite chicken brands of local chefs: Eberly and Bell and Evans. Some locations have coffee and juice bars, the latter run by Jamba Juice, featuring its California-created power smoothies. **Other locations.**

Magruder's Grocery

Quince Orchard Shopping Center
602-A Quince Orchard Rd. (Clopper Rd.), Gaithersburg 20878
301-948-2165, Fax 301-948-2167, *Open daily*

A P

In business since 1875, Magruder's stores have maintained a neighborhood feel yet moved into the 21st century with ease. The stores have built their reputation on a strong produce department, known for its product freshness and variety to suit the many cuisines of the multicultural communities in the metro area. You also will find an extensive selection of cheeses that will satisfy the gourmand seeking variety and quality. **Other locations.**

Sutton Place Gourmet

Wildwood Shopping Center
10323 Old Georgetown Rd. (Democracy Blvd.), Bethesda 20814
301-564-3100, Fax 301-493-5947, *Open daily*

A P

Sutton Place Gourmet was one of the first specialty gourmet markets in the Washington metro area. An expansion has added components of Hay Day Markets and Balducci's, the ultimate snazzy gourmet market from New York City. Special Balducci's selections include lentils from Castelluccio in Umbria and Arborio rice, grown in the Po Valley of northeastern Italy. Hay Day has brought open-produce sections to the center of the stores. Only Dean & DeLuca competes at this price level—this is no place to shop if you're looking for a bargain. Also see review in *Wines & Spirits*. **Other locations.**

Trader Joe's

Shops of Wisconsin Avenue
6831 Wisconsin Ave. (Bradley Blvd.), Bethesda 20815
301-907-0982, *Open daily*

A **P**

Trader Joe's has recently moved east of the Mississippi from its West Coast origins. Customers speak of the private-label marketing of specialty coffees, nuts, candies and beverages with a cultlike fanaticism. These fanciful stores feature Hawaiian-shirted staff and beachcomber décor. Trader Joe's only buys when the price is right, so you will find bargains; but variety can be limited and brands not always available. Quality is high and the frozen food department is exceptional, with finds like salmon stir-fry with all the veggies and seasonings in the bag. Many products are considered "natural," such as the yogurt-covered blueberries packed with no preservatives or artificial coloring or flavors. Note that the Maryland stores cannot sell beer or wine; however, the Trader Joe's stores in Virginia do have a selection of wine and beer at good prices. **Other locations**.

Vace Delicatessen

4705 Miller Ave. (Bethesda Ave.), Bethesda 20814
301-654-6367, *Open Mon.-Sat.*

A

A Bethesda extension of the Cleveland Park deli in DC, Vace exudes old world charm. Focaccias are layered with tomato and onion, and hearty slices of pizza will remind you of New York City. The sandwiches are made with generous slices of deli meats like mortadella, salami and ham. Try one of the pasta salads or buy the pasta and choose a sauce from variety in the freezer. Pick up a cannoli on the way out for the trip home. **Also located at** 3315 Connecticut Ave. NW, Washington, DC, 202-363-1999.

WINE & SPIRITS

Why do you have to look so hard for a store dedicated to wine in Montgomery County, Md.? Decades ago Montgomery County took control of alcoholic beverage sales through its Department of Liquor Control. In recent years, that control has been a topic for many public political discussions as controversy surrounds the pros and cons of having a public agency governing the exclusive sale and distribution of all alcohol in the county. The consumer is affected in two ways: limited selection compared to Virginia and Washington, DC, and higher prices. The stores noted here stand out as those that serve wine customers well in a difficult market.

Bradley Food & Beverage

6904 Arlington Rd. (Bradley Rd.), Bethesda 20814
301-654-6966, Fax 301-654-1685, *Open daily*

A **P**

Known for its gift selections, specialty foods and deli, this popular Bethesda neighborhood store has developed over the years a diverse selection of wines, in large part due to its gift-basket business. In an area where wine shops are scarce and Bethesda residents drive into Washington for wine, Bradley is a welcome find. You're on your own for wine advice, but there is something to be found for all occasions and gifts.

Georgetown Square Wine Shop

10400 Old Georgetown Rd. (Democracy Blvd.), Bethesda 20814
301-530-4555, Open daily

A P

Georgetown Square has established itself as a source for a wide selection of wines with a specialty in California estates. The staff shares wine knowledge in a friendly manner and understandable terms. A wide price range is served here—from a $6 quaffing wine to $100-plus Champagnes. Look for an extensive selection of beers, especially for some of the harder-to-find microbrews and imports. Nearby stores charge $3-$4 more for the same wines found on the shelves here.

Rodman's Gourmet Foods

White Flint Plaza
5148 Nicholson Ln. (Rockville Pike), Kensington 20895
301-881-6253, Open daily

A P

Don't be dismayed when you pull into White Flint Plaza and see the large Rodman's sign dark and the store empty—it has moved a few doors down from its first location. Slightly smaller now, Rodman's still has a good inventory of wines ranging from low-cost jugs to harder-to-find selections such as $55 bottles of Kistler Carneros Chardonnay. You will find good sections of South African, Australian, Italian and California wines. The gourmet food shelves have a changing inventory, from imported cookies to some cooking supplies and specialty foods, such as Gordon's Red Crab Soup. Other locations.

Silesia Wine Cellar

10909 Livingston Rd. (Fort Washington Rd.), Fort Washington 20744
301-292-1542, Fax 301-292-6973, Open Mon.-Sat.

A P

The Fort Washington Silesia Wine Cellar sits across the river from Alexandria and has become a hidden treasure for serious wine lovers in the Washington area. Silesia received the "favorite wine store" distinction in one recent poll of wine buyers that covered Maryland, Washington and Northern Virginia. Brothers Ray and Mike Tilch co-own the wine store and the liquor store that has served the area since 1933. Among the friendliest and most knowledgeable members of the wine trade in the area, they hold frequent in-store tastings and are a great source for difficult wine questions. Wines are their passion, so check in to hear the latest in wine news and buys from their frequent visits to the wine regions of the world.

Sutton Place Gourmet

Wildwood Shopping Center
10323 Old Georgetown Rd. (Democracy Blvd.), Bethesda 20814
301-564-3100, Fax 301-493-5947, Open daily

A P

One of the few groceries in Montgomery County permitted to sell beer and wine, Sutton Place applies the same top-quality profile to its wine section as it does to other departments. Selections represent a broad cross section of California boutique wineries and key offerings from the bottle portfolio of such respected wine importers as Terry Thiese and Robert Kacher. The service can be a bit abrupt, and the bargains are scarce. **Other locations.**

GLOSSARIES

WINE SAVVY   266

    INTRODUCTION   266
    WINE TOURING   266
    VINTAGE WINE CHART   270
    GLOSSARY OF TASTING TERMS   271
    GLOSSARY OF GRAPES   272
    FOOD & WINE PAIRINGS   277
    FOOD & WINE EVENTS   281

WATER SAVVY   285

    INTRODUCTION   285
    THE MAJOR BRANDS   286

WINE SAVVY

Thomas Jefferson Would Be Proud

Thomas Jefferson is known as one of the most successful men in history. However, when it came to planting grapes for wine at his Monticello estate, success was elusive.

Jefferson was one of the most vocal proponents of wine in the New World; indeed, in his associations with France, he had tasted many of the great vintages of the time. It was his feeling that the New World could produce as great a variety of wine as Europe, not necessarily the same varietals, but just as good.

Unfortunately, his experimentation with European grapes resulted in frustration. The vinifera (as the European varietals are called) vines fell prey to mildew, Pierce's Disease and found the winter climate hostile as well. Native American vines, called labrusca, were hardy but produced inferior wine.

Later, in the 19th century, hybrids, a crossing of French and American vines, became popular because they supposedly provided Eastern grape growers/winemakers with the best of both worlds. Vidal Blanc, Seyval Blanc and Chambourcin vineyards dotted the landscape.

Extensive fighting in the countryside during the Civil War destroyed vineyards, and, later, Prohibition kept the industry from growing significantly in the first half of the 20th century.

The growth of the Virginia wine industry (Maryland has some vineyards, too, but Virginia is the real success story of the entire South) in the 1960s coincided with Americans' growing interest in wine. In the 1970s, vinifera varieties (Cabernet Sauvignon, Chardonnay, Merlot and Riesling are examples) began to be planted alongside (and in place of) the French hybrids of earlier Eastern U.S. vineyards.

Today, there are more than 60 wineries in Virginia (up from six in 1979). Due to improved knowledge in vineyard planting, technological advances and less restrictive regulations, Virginia wineries have proved their mettle. Even niche varietals, like Viognier, Cabernet Franc, Barbera and Pinot Grigio, have found a home here.

Wine Touring

The hustle and bustle of urban Washington is uniquely juxtaposed with the rolling countryside of Northern Virginia. Once outside the Beltway, you'll find green hills, horse farms, bucolic gentrified estates and, of course, vineyards and wineries. Tourism is a burgeoning industry and most wineries welcome visitors to their tasting rooms (plenty of Civil War historical sites also beckon, as well as Jefferson's Monticello and James Madison's Montpelier). Among the better-known, quality wineries are Barboursville, Gray Ghost, Horton, Oasis, Piedmont and Prince Michel.

Touring the wine country is simple. In Virginia, many of the wineries are in the central and northern part of the state, and grape cluster highway signs point the way to them. In Maryland, the wineries are an easy day trip from DC.

Call ahead when planning a wine-touring trip. Many of the wineries are small, family-run enterprises and consequently may only be open limited hours during weekends; some are open by appointment only.

Virginia

Eastern Virginia

Ingleside Plantation Vineyards
5872 LEEDSTOWN RD.
OAK GROVE 22443
804-224-8687, www.ipwine.com

Williamsburg Winery
5800 WESSEX HUNDRED
WILLIAMSBURG 23185
757-229-0999
www.williamsburgwineryltd.com

Central Virginia

Afton Mountain Vineyards
234 VINEYARD LN., AFTON 22920
540-456-8667

**Autumn Hill Vineyards/
Blue Ridge Winery**
301 RIVER DR.
STANDARDSVILLE 22973
804-985-6100

Barboursville Vineyards
17655 WINERY RD.
BARBOURSVILLE 22923
540-832-3824
www.barboursvillewine.com

Burnley Vineyards
4500 WINERY RD.
BARBOURSVILLE 22923
540-832-2828
www.burnleywines.com

Chermont Winery
ROUTE 1, ESMONT 22937
804-286-2211

Cooper Vineyards
13372 SHANNON HILL RD.
LOUISA 23093
540-894-5253

Dominion Wine Cellars
NUMBER ONE WINERY AVE.
CULPEPER 22701
540-825-8772

Grayhaven Winery
4675 E. GRAY FOX CIR.
GUM SPRING 23065
804-556-3917

Horton Cellars Winery
6399 SPOTSWOOD TRAIL
GORDONSVILLE 22942
540-832-7440, www.hvwine.com

Jefferson Vineyards
1353 THOMAS JEFFERSON PKWY.
CHARLOTTESVILLE 22902
804-977-3042
www.jeffersonvineyards.com

Lake Anna Winery
5621 COURTHOUSE RD.
SPOTSYLVANIA 22553
540-895-5085, www.lawinery.com

Misty Mountain Vineyards
STATE ROUTE 2, MADISON 22727
540-928-4738

Montdomaine Cellars
ROUTE 6
CHARLOTTESVILLE 22902
804-971-8947, www.hvwine.com

Mountain Cove Vineyards
1362 FORTUNE COVE LN.
LOVINGSTON 22949
804-263-5392

Oakencroft Vineyard & Winery
1486 OAKENCROFT LANE
CHARLOTTESVILLE 22901
804-296-4188
www.oakencroft.com

**Prince Michel Vineyards/
Rapidan River Vineyards**
HC ROUTE 4, LEON 22725
540-547-3707
www.princemichel.com

Rebec Vineyards
2229 NORTH AMHERST HWY.
AMHERST 24521
804-946-5168

Rockbridge Vineyard
30 HILLVIEW LN., RAPHINE 24472
540-377-6204
www.rockbridgewine.com

Rose Bower Vineyard & Winery
ROUTE 686
HAMPDEN-SYDNEY 23943
804-223-8209

**Rose River Vineyards
& Trout Farm**
ROUTE 648, SYRIA 22743
540-923-4050

Stonewall Vineyards & Winery
ROUTE 2, CONCORD 24538
804-993-2185

Totier Creek Vineyard & Winery
1652 HARRIS CREEK RD.
CHARLOTTESVILLE 22902
804-979-7105

White Hall Vineyards
5190 SUGAR RIDGE RD.
WHITE HALL 22987
804-823-8615

Windy River Winery
20268 TEMAN RD.
BEAVERDAM 23015
804-449-6996
www.windyriverwinery.com

**Wintergreen Vineyards
& Winery**
462 WINERY LN., NELLYSFORD 22958
804-361-2519
www.wintergreenwinery.com

Northern Virginia

Breaux Vineyards
36888 BREAUX VINEYARDS LN.
HILLSBORO 20132
540-668-6299, Fax 540-668-6283
www.breauxvineyards.com

Chrysalis Vineyards
23876 CHAMPE FORD RD.
MIDDLEBURG 20117
540-687-8222, Fax 540-687-8666
www.chrysaliswine.com

Farfelu Vineyard
13058 CREST HILL RD.
FLINT HILL 22627
540-364-2930
www.farfeluwine.com

Gray Ghost Vineyards
14706 LEE HIGHWAY
AMISSVILLE 20106
540-937-4869

Hartwood Winery
345 HARTWOOD RD.
FREDERICKSBURG 22406
540-752-4893

Linden Vineyards
3708 HARRELS CORNER RD.
LINDEN 22642
540-364-1997
www.lindenvineyards.com

Loudoun Valley Vineyards
38516 CHARLESTOWN PIKE
WATERFORD 20197
540-882-3375
www.loudounvalleyvineyards.com

Meredyth Vineyards
ROUTE 628, MIDDLEBURG 20118
540-687-6277

Naked Mountain Vineyard
2747 LEEDS MANOR RD.
MARKHAM 22643
540-364-1609
www.nakedmtn.com

Oasis Winery
14141 HUME RD., HUME 22639
540-635-7627
www.oasiswine.com

**Piedmont Vineyard
& Winery**
ROUTE 626, MIDDLEBURG 20118
540-687-5528
www.piedmontwines.com

Shadwell-Windham Winery
14727 MOUNTAIN RD.
HILLSBORO 20132
540-688-6464

Sharp Rock Vineyards
5 SHARP ROCK RD.
SPERRYVILLE 22740
540-987-9700

**Spotted Tavern Winery
& Dodd Bros. Cider Mill**
P.O. BOX 175, HARTWOOD 22471
540-752-4453, Fax 540-752-4611

Swedenburg Estate Vineyard
23595 WINERY LN.
MIDDLEBURG 20117
540-687-5219

Tarara Vineyards & Winery
13648 TARARA LANE
LEESBURG 20176
703-771-7100, www.tarara.com

Willowcroft Farm Vineyards
38906 MT. GILEAD RD.
LEESBURG 20175
703-777-8161
www.willowcroftwine.com

Shenandoah Valley

Deer Meadow Vineyard
199 VINTAGE LANE
WINCHESTER 22602
540-877-1919

Guilford Ridge Vineyard
328 RUNNING PINE RD.
LURAY 22835
540-778-3853

Landwirt Vineyards
8223 SIMMERS VALLEY RD.
HARRISONBURG 22802
540-833-6000,
www.valleyva.com/landwirt.html

**North Mountain Vineyard
& Winery**
4374 SWARTZ RD.
MAURERTOWN 22644
540-436-9463

Shenandoah Vineyards
3659 OX RD., EDINBURG 22824
540-984-8699

Southwest Virginia

Château Morrisette Winery
287 WINERY RD., MEADOES OF
DAN 24120
540-593-2865
www.chateaumorrisette.com

Dye's Vineyards
ROUTE 2, HONAKER 24260
540-873-4659

Tomahawk Mill Winery
9221 ANDERSON MILL RD.
CHATHAM 24531
804-432-1063

Maryland

Basignani Winery
15722 Falls Rd., Sparks 21152
410-472-0703
www.basignaniwinery.com

Boordy Vineyards
12820 Long Green Pike,
Hydes 21082
410-592-5015, www.boordy.com

Catoctin Vineyards
805 Greenbridge Rd.
Brookesville 20833
301-774-2310

Elk Run Vineyards
15113 Liberty Rd.
Mt. Airy 21771
410-775-2513, www.elkrun.com

Fiore Winery
3026 Whiteford Rd.
Pylesville 21132
410-879-4007
www.fiorewinery.com

Linganore Winecellars
13601 Glissan Mill Rd.
Mt. Airy 21771
410-795-6432
www.linganore-wine.com

Loew Vineyards
14001 Liberty Rd.
Mt. Airy 21771
301-831-5464

Woodhall Vineyards
17912 York Rd.
Parkton 21120
410-357-8644

Vintage Wine Chart

VINTAGE CHART: The World's Wines																		
FRANCE												GER.	ITALY		CALIFORNIA			
Red Bordeaux	White Bordeaux	Sauternes	Red Burgundy	White Burgundy	Beaujolais	Côtes-du-Rhône	Provence	Alsace	Loire: Anjou, Muscadet	Pouilly, Sancere	Champagne	Rhine, Moselle, Nahe	Piedmonte	Chianti	Cabernet Sauvignon	Chardonnay	Pinot Noir	Zinfandel
1998 3	3	3	3	3	3	5	4	5	3	3	—	4	4	3	2	4	3	3
1997 3	3	4	3	3	3	4	4	4	3	3	—	4	5	4	5	5	4	5
1996 4	3	3	4	4	3	3	4	4	5	4	5	5	5	3	4	4	4	4
1995 5	4	3	3	4	4	4	5	4	4	3		4	4	3	5	5	4	Ex
1994 4	3	2	2	4	3	3	4	5	3	3	—	4	2	3	Ex	5	5	Ex
1993 4	3	3	3	3	4	3	4	4	4	4	4	5	4	2	5	5	4	5
1992 3	3	3	3	5	2	3	3	3	3	3	—	5	3	2	5	5	4	5
1991 3	3	2	4	4	Ex	4	3	3	1	3	1	4	2	2	4	5	4	5
1990 5	4	5	Ex	4	4	5	5	5	5	5	Ex	5	5	5	5	5	4	5
1989 5	4	Ex	5	5	Ex	5	5	Ex	5	5	5	5	5	2	4	3	4	4
1988 4	4	Ex	5	5	4	4	4	5	4	4	5	5	5	3	4	4	4	4
1987 3	4	1	4	3	2	1	2	3	3	2	3	4	4	2	4	3	4	5
1986 5	5	5	3	3	3	3	4	3	5	4	3	4	3	4	5	4	4	4
1985 5	5	2	Ex	5	5	5	3	5	5	5	5	4	5	5	Ex	4	4	5
1983 5	5	Ex	3	5	—	5	4	Ex	4	4	5	5	2	3	3	4	4	3
1982 Ex	4	3	2	4	—	4	—	2	5	5	5	3	5	4	4	3	4	3
1981 4	5	4	—	—	—	3	—	3	5	5	5	4	3	3	4	4	4	4

EX: EXCEPTIONAL   2: MEDIUM
5: VERY GREAT   1: PASSABLE
4: GREAT   —: SMALL YEAR
3: GOOD

*   This is only meant to be a general guide. Start by learning which regions and years are better than others; once you develop a good knowledge, buy according to your preferences.

The European wines are categorized by the region in which the grapes were grown. This is their "appellation," displayed on the label along with the phrase *Appellation controlée* or *Denominazione di origine contrallata* to guarantee the wine's authenticity. The California wines are categorized by grape name, as they are throughout the United States.

Glossary of Tasting Terms

Acidity: a principal component of wine that shows up as a sharpness or tartness, giving it snap

Aroma: the smell the wine acquires from the grapes themselves and fermentation process

Astringency: the mouth-puckering quality found in many young red wines

Austere: a wine unusually high in acidity; lacking roundness or wholeness

Balanced: no individual component of the wine stands out; all the elements contribute to a harmonious whole

Berry: taste characteristic found in many red wines, it resembles the taste of fruit like blackberry, blueberry and cherry

Body: the weight of the wine in the mouth; usually manifested by a richness, fullness or viscosity

Bouquet: the smell that develops from the process of aging wine in the bottle

Buttery: a component that gives white wines a rich roundness that resembles the taste of butter

Chewy: a rich red wine with big body and dense flavor

Clarity: the appearance of a young wine should be clear, not cloudy

Complex: a wine that displays many levels of flavor

Dry: a wine with no apparent residual sugar. Novice wine drinkers may describe this as "sour"

Earthy: positive characteristics of loamy topsoil, mushrooms or truffles sometimes found in red wines. In French, "goût de terroir"

Fat: a wine with good fullness and length, although it may lack finesse

Floral: flowery aromas and tastes, usually associated with white wines

Fruity: the taste of the fruit of the grapes themselves; it often manifests itself as other fruit flavors, such as apples, strawberries or black currants

Grassy: an herbaceous flavor, like new-mown grass, common to Sauvignon Blanc; negative if extreme

Hard: a wine that does not have generous flavors; applied to red wines that have excessive tannins

Herbaceous: a general term descriptive of various herbal flavors in wine, recognized by aroma and taste

Hot: a wine in which the high level of alcohol is out of balance with the other elements

Intense: powerful, dense, and rich in flavor

Jammy: in red wines, intense fruitiness combined with berry-like flavors

Nose: all the elements detected by the sense of smell, including both the aroma and bouquet

Oaky: flavors of the oak in which the wine is fermented and/or aged

Smoky: a roasted aroma or taste characteristic attributable to aging in oak barrels

Spicy: descriptive of the spicelike flavor elements found in wine such as pepper, cardamon, clove and cinnamon

Supple: a wine that tastes soft and smooth; easy to drink

Tannic: a mouth-puckering astringency found in young red wines

Glossary of Grapes
Red Wine Varietals

Barbera

Originated in Italy, Barbera grapes can be found in many generic red wine blends. The grape is hearty and grapey without a lot of nuances, but helps punch up the flavors of these blends. Well-cultivated and low-cropped Barbera vineyards, however, can produce flavorful grapes that result in a charming wine when bottled separately. This grape is part of the "Cal-Ital" varietal trend in California, but East Coast producers are experimenting with it as well including Barboursville in Virginia.

Cabernet Franc

Cabernet Franc is one the five varietals that account for the stellar reputation of red Bordeaux. A cousin to the more well known Cabernet Sauvignon, this grape is normally used in minute quantities, blended with both Merlot and Cabernet Sauvignon to create a sum that is greater than its parts. While American vintners also use the grape as a blending component, many have found a modicum of success with bottlings of 100 percent Cabernet Franc. The latter tend to show dark berry/cherry flavors with a certain chalkiness. Good examples from this part of the country are Barboursville, Gray Ghost and Prince Michel in Virginia.

Cabernet Sauvignon

The king of red wines, Cabernet's reputation was established decades ago by the great estates of Bordeaux, although it has proved distinctive in other regions as well. While sometimes a bit harsh in its youth, it has the ability to mature into a most complex and full-bodied red wine. Its flavors are comfortable with simple grilled meats as well as more complex dishes like venison in mushroom sauce. Great and consistent producers of Cabernet can be found in Napa, Sonoma and Long Island, as well as Australia, Chile, and, of course, the châteaux of Bordeaux, which produce the true benchmark of this varietal. From this part of the country, good producers include Oasis and Boordy in Maryland.

Catawba

This was perhaps the earliest discovered native American grape, growing wild in Ohio and New York valleys, but it has since been surpassed by the Concord as the most widely planted native East Coast grape varietal. It primarily is used to make off-dry or sweet red wines, with a pronounced foxy labrusca flavor sometimes described as wild and musky. A number of producers also utilize this grape to make sparkling wine.

Chambourcin

A French hybrid that is native to the East Coast, Chambourcin is usually fashioned in a claret or Bordeaux style as a dry red wine. It is also used to make rosé.

Concord

This native American grape varietal (of the genus vitis labrusca) is used in making old-fashioned, "rustic" country-style red wines, often displaying what most people think of as a "grape jelly aroma." In fact, the Concord widely used in the production of jellies and jams. This East Coast varietal produces wines often described as foxy, or wild and musky. Mogen David in New York is perhaps the quintessential Concord wine.

Merlot

This variety was once relegated to blending status, but in the last 20 years it has taken on an identity of its own. When varietally bottled, Merlot has herbal and fruity flavors similar to Cabernet, but also has a smooth and supple character in the mouth without the bite of tannins. It complements the same type of foods that Cabernet does, albeit less distinctively. Top producers hail from Bordeaux (where the wine is still predominantly blended with Cabernet), Napa, Sonoma and Washington State. Merlot has become the easy-drinking red wine of choice in the last five years. Among top producers in this area are Williamsburg, Prince Michel and White Hall in Virginia.

Muscadine

A species of native American vines, these were first discovered by European explorers, who found them growing along the low-lying Southern coastal regions. Most Muscadine wines (reds and whites) are blends, usually given proprietary names by the winery (e.g., "Vintners' Blend"), and vinified in the sweet or semi-sweet style. Muscadines and blends are usually sweet and foxy, an aroma/flavor profile also described as wild and musky. For Muscadine and offshoots, look for producers such as Château Elan and Habersham in Georgia, Bryant and Perdido in Alabama and Beachaven and Tennessee Valley Winery in Tennessee. Scuppernong is the Southern name for the grape and the first wine made in the United States. Producers include Duplin in North Carolina and Smoky Mountain in Tennessee.

Norton

In 1835, Dr. Daniel Norton of Virginia developed this grape varietal that was originally known as the Virginia Seedling. Widely planted in the Midwest (where it is sometimes called Cynthiana), it has become a source of interest to East Coast vintners in recent years. It produces a dark, inky wine with flavors of plums and cherries. Horton Vineyards in Virginia is particularly interested in reviving the grape's reputation. In the South, look for Norton (or Cynthiana) from Moonrise Bay in North Carolina, Three Sisters and Tiger Mountain in Georgia and Tennessee Valley and Mountain Valley in Tennesse.

Pinot Noir

Pinot Noir has the potential to be the most seductive, beguiling red wine in existence. In the past decade or so, however, Pinot Noir has shown the greatest increase in quality of any varietal in America. The perseverance of younger winemakers and traditional winemaking methodology is resulting in Pinots that can stand side by side with the benchmark wines of Burgundy. Lighter than Cabernet, Pinots have a richness and intensity of fruit that is unparalleled. The best of them drink like velvet and accompany a wide variety of foods. Top French Burgundies are bottled under different names and labels, depending on region, vineyard and producer. In America, considerable success with this Burgundian varietal has been from the cooler regions of Napa, Sonoma (Carneros), Santa Barbara and Oregon. A fickle grape that needs the proper growing conditions and climate to reach its potential, it is cultivated by only a smattering of vintners in Virginia (try Tarara, Afton or Shenandoah).

Syrah

The great grape of the Rhône Valley has become more widely planted in California, Washington, Arizona and Virginia, in the last ten years. Highly aromatic wines with meaty, smoky, spicy and peppery flavors are the trademark of the Syrah grape. When made in a lighter style, it's a good quaffing wine to pair with simple bistro food. When made in a richer style, it's a good accompaniment to lamb and wild game. Syrah is the grape found in French Côte Rôtie, St. Joseph and Cornas, and plays a major role in the spicy Châteauneuf-du-Papes of the southern Rhône, too. In California, the Syrah grape is being cultivated in such diverse regions as Santa Barbara, Sonoma, Monterey, and the Amador Foothills. In this part of the country, Horton in Virginia is a specialist in Syrah and other Rhône varietals.

Zinfandel

Real Zinfandel is red, a fact many wine drinkers are rediscovering now that the trend for "white" Zinfandel has stabilized. "Peppery," "briary," "brawny" and "chewy" are only a few of the adjectives used to describe this mouth-filling wine. It has a real zest for matching up with tomato-based pasta dishes. It is one varietal that the first Italian winemakers propagated and cultivated when they came to California. Its origins are obviously European, but today it's a grape variety that is unique to California. Vintners in Napa, Sonoma and Amador seem to do the best job with it.

White Wine Varietals

Chardonnay

In the '80s it became de rigeur to ask for "a glass of Chardonnay" in a restaurant and passé to simply request "a glass of white wine." Chardonnay is the most popular wine in America for a reason: It's cold, fruity and easy to drink. It's pleasant with just about any dish involving cheese, eggs, fish or fowl. Winemakers have divided into two camps over the style of Chardonnay; one school of thought emphasizes the high-toned, steely, fruitlike qualities of the wine with little or no use of oak, while the other emphasizes barrel and malolactic fermentation in addition to the fruit characteristic, which lends the wine a rounder, buttery taste. Benchmarks for Chardonnay are (rich and extracted) white Burgundies and (steely and crisp) Chablis. There are fine Chardonnays from many parts of California including Napa, Sonoma, Mendocino, Monterey, Santa Cruz and Santa Barbara. Top producers in this area include Williamsburg, Gray Ghost, Oasis, Piedmont, Château Morrisette, Wintergreen and Rockbridge, all in Virginia.

Gewürztraminer

This so-called "aromatic" varietal is making a minor comeback with wine consumers who are looking for something different. "Gewürz" translates as "spice" and it's immediately detectable when poured into a glass. The flavors echo the fragrant and flowery nose echoes, while providing an additional punch from a piquant, spicy component. Made with some residual sweetness, the wine seems to be a good counterpoint for spicy Chinese and Thai dishes. The Alsatian region of France has about four centuries of experience in producing these wines in the traditional style. In the U.S., cooler growing regions, such as Sonoma, Mendocino and Santa Barbara, do well with this grape. Rapidan River and Afton are top Virginia producers.

Muscadine

The South has a heavy concentration of this grape that is used for both white and red wines. See description under Red Wine Varietals.

Niagara

A native American grape varietal, the Niagara is often referred to as the "white Concord." Widely grown in New York, it is a popular table wine, vinified in a slightly sweet style, though the best producers tend to minimize its inherent foxy, or musky, qualities. Château Morrisette in Virginia is the benchmark for this varietal, though many smaller producers do a good job with it.

Pinot Grigio

Pinot Grigio has become a favorite in America because the Italian Santa Margherita label is seen on the wine list of almost every Italian restaurant. But Pinot Grigio is just another name for Pinot Gris, a grape widely planted in eastern Europe, particularly in northern Italy. Many of the Italian versions are bland and innocuous, but New World producers are more interested in extracting the maximum amount of flavor from the varietal. California and Oregon vintners are enjoying success with Pinot Grigio, while several Virginia wineries, such as Barboursville and Piedmont, are experimenting with it.

Riesling

Another "aromatic" that is also gaining in popularity, Riesling can be a particularly refreshing alternative to the Chardonnay/Sauvignon Blanc white wine tandem. Unlike its cousin, Gewürztraminer, this varietal has little spice and instead relies on its delicate aromas and subtle flavors for its special niche. Usually lighter in style and sometimes with residual sweetness, it's better paired with lighter fare. The Riesling is a mainstay of German winemaking and also ripens to full maturity in Alsace. The top American producers have generally been those who have also had success with Gewürztraminer. Top producers in this area include Virginia's include Rapidan River, Oasis, Swedenburg, Willowcroft and Rockbridge wineries.

Sauvignon Blanc

This variety is often considered the poor man's Chardonnay; it can be vinified similarly but costs only half as much. But Sauvignon Blanc has a number of identities ranging from a clean, slight grassy white wine to an herbaceous, full-bodied wine backed up with oak aging. It does its best service at the table when paired with strong, forceful, herbal flavors like goat cheese and raddichio salad. Unheralded but excellent examples come from Sancerre and Pouilly-Fumé in the Loire Valley. In California, just about every region produces a Sauvignon Blanc, although the North Coast counties seem to have a real knack for it. It's not as widely regarded in Virginia, but look for Naked Mountain and Linden.

Seyval Blanc

A French hybrid, Seyval Blanc often is thought of as "East Coast Chardonnay," or at least an alternative to same. Produced in a crisp, dry style, this white wine is often fermented or aged in oak to enhance the rather neutral flavors of the grape itself. It lends itself to service at the dining table and is food-friendly. Seyval Blanc is often used in proprietary blends; good examples can be found in this part of the country from Linden, Oakencroft, and Willowcroft in Virginia, and Fiore and Woodhall in Maryland.

Sparkling Wines

Domaine Chandon (owned by Moët & Chandon) set up shop in Napa Valley about 25 years ago, and after its initial success, almost every Champagne house has come to California to establish its foothold. The main reason for their interest in the New World is that Champagne is a geographically limited area, which is almost fully planted, and California was virgin territory for sparkling wine. While the legacy of Champagne seems to be tiny pinpoint bubbles that reveal delicate and subtle flavors, their California counterparts are more often bold, upfront and fruity with their flavors. The prevailing wisdom is that the delicate nuances of the wine (in particular, Champagne) get lost when paired up with hearty, complex or highly seasoned dishes. It's certainly the perfect apéritif wine. All California sparklers are of good quality so it seems to be a matter of house style as to what is preferred. Names to remember are Domaine Chandon, Domaine Carneros, Gloria Ferrer, Laetitia, Mumm-Cuvée Napa, Mirassou, Pacific Echo, Roederer Estates, Schramsberg, Iron Horse and J. In Virginia, the winemaker at Oasis learned his trade at California's Domaine Carneros and his sparklers are outstanding.

Vidal Blanc

A cousin to Seyval Blanc, this French hybrid is becoming increasingly popular on the East Coast for its fresh and fruity characteristics. Normally vinified dry or just off-dry, the wine is similar in style and an alternative to Sauvignon Blanc or Muscadet; it is equally as reasonably priced. When harvest conditions permit, some wineries also produce a late-harvest, sweet dessert wine from this varietal. In this part of the country, look for Fiore in Maryland, and Linden and Gray Ghost in Virginia.

Viognier

The most acclaimed white wine grape from France's Rhône Valley, Viognier is a highly aromatic varietal, with a flavor profile that could include peach, apricot, nectarine, lichee, musk and flower blossom. The heady perfume of this varietal is one of its trademarks, although its flavors are sometimes problematic in matching with food. However, it does well with lobster, crab and moderately flavored fish. Use it as an apéritif as an alternative to Chardonnay. The "Rhône Rangers" in California have done an excellent job promoting this varietal. From this part of the country, Horton in Virginia is a world-class producer of Viognier as well as other Rhône-style varietals.

Food & Wine Pairings

Rule One: Drink red wine with meat, and white wine with fish and poultry. Rule Two: Forget about Rule One and marry any food with any wine you wish; when it comes to personal preferences, there are no rights and wrongs. Based on our experience, the following matches of widely available dishes and cuisines with the wines of North America are worthy of special consideration. One caveat: Sauces can change everything, so ask the chef or a server for a flavor forecast.

Appetizers & First Courses

Antipasto
Pinot Gris, (Dry) Chenin Blanc, Sauvignon Blanc, Pinot Blanc, Gamay Beaujolais, Barbera

Asparagus
Sauvignon (Fumé) Blanc, (Dry) Riesling, Vidal Blanc

Carpaccio (beef)
Barbera, Cabernet Rosé, Rhône Blends

Carpaccio (tuna)
Sauvignon (Fumé) Blanc, Vin Gris

Caviar
Brut Sparkling Wine

Clams (raw or casino)
Sauvignon (Fumé) Blanc, Brut Sparkling Wine, (Dry) Chenin Blanc, Pinot Blanc, Seyval Blanc

Cold Meats
Vin Gris, Riesling, Gamay Beaujolais, Barbera, Seyval Blanc, (Dry) Vignoles, Chambourcin Rosé

Crudités
Pinot Blanc, Chenin Blanc, Chardonnay, Gamay Beaujolais

Foie Gras
Brut Sparkling Wine, Late-Harvest Riesling, Sauvignon Blanc, or Gewürztraminer, Muscat, Pinot Noir

Niçoise Salad
Sauvignon (Fumé) Blanc

Nuts and/or Olives
Brut Sparkling Wine

Oysters (raw)
Sauvignon (Fumé) Blanc, Brut Sparkling Wine, Pinot Gris, Chardonnay, (Dry) Riesling, Pinot Blanc, Chenin Blanc

Pasta Salad
Sémillon, Sauvignon (Fumé) Blanc, (Dry) Chenin Blanc, (Dry) Riesling

Pasta with cream sauce
Chardonnay, Pinot Blanc

Pasta with shellfish
Sauvignon (Fumé) Blanc, Chardonnay

Pasta with tomato sauce
Barbera, Sangiovese, Zinfandel, Rhône Blends

Pasta with vegetables
Pinot Blanc, Dry Riesling, Sauvignon Blanc, Viognier, Gamay Beaujolais, Barbera

Pâtés
Gewürztraminer, Seyval Blanc, Gamay Beaujolais, Riesling, Brut Sparkling Wine, Cabernet Franc, Vin Gris

Prosciutto and Melon
Pinot Blanc, Riesling, Late Harvest Riesling or Gewürztra-miner, Muscat

Quiche
Riesling, Chenin Blanc, Chardonnay, Viognier, Gamay Beaujolais

Scallops
Sauvignon (Fumé) Blanc, Chardonnay, Brut Sparkling Wine, Pinot Noir, Sémillon

Smoked Fish (trout, herring)
Riesling, Gewürztraminer, Pinot Blanc, Brut Sparkling Wine

Soups
Usually none, or (Solera) Sherry

Fish & Shellfish

Crab
Sauvignon (Fumé) Blanc, Brut Sparkling Wine, Chardonnay

Lobster
Brut Sparkling Wine, Chardonnay

Mussels
Chenin Blanc, Pinot Blanc, Pinot Gris, Sauvignon (Fumé) Blanc

Red Snapper
Chardonnay, Sauvignon (Fumé) Blanc

Salmon
Pinot Noir, Sauvignon Blanc, Pinot Gris, Sémillon, Vin Gris

Salmon Tartare
Brut Sparkling Wine, Pinot Gris

Sashimi, Sushi
Brut Sparkling Wine, Semi-Dry Riesling

Scallops, Oysters, Clams
See appetizers

Shrimp
Pinot Blanc, Chenin Blanc, Sauvignon (Fumé) Blanc, Chardonnay, Colombard, Vidal Blanc

Striped Bass
Chardonnay, Pinot Blanc, Viognier, (Dry) Vignoles

Swordfish
Sauvignon (Fumé) Blanc, Brut Sparkling Wine, Vin Gris, Pinot Noir

Tuna
Sauvignon (Fumé) Blanc, Pinot Noir, Merlot, Vin Gris, Chardonnay

Other White Fish
Chardonnay, Viognier, Dry Riesling, Semillon

Meat & Poultry

Chicken
Chardonnay, Vin Gris, Riesling, Merlot, Gamay Beaujolais, Chenin Blanc, Pinot Noir, (Lighter) Cabernet Sauvignon

Chicken Salad
Riesling, Chenin Blanc, Gewürztraminer, Pinot Blanc

Chicken (Smoked)
Vin Gris, Pinot Noir, Zinfandel

Duck
Pinot Noir, Merlot, Rosé Sparkling Wine, Cabernet Sauvignon, Zinfandel

Frankfurter
Riesling, (Chilled) Gamay Beaujolais

Ham
Vin Gris, Gamay Beaujolais, Merlot

Hamburger
Cabernet Sauvignon, Gamay, Syrah, Chancellor, Barbera, Zinfandel, Rhône Blends

Lamb (grilled, broiled)
Meritage, Cabernet Sauvignon, Merlot, Pinot Noir, Maréchal Foch, Chancellor, Zinfandel

Pheasant
Pinot Noir, Syrah

Quail
Pinot Noir

Rabbit
Riesling, Pinot Noir, Barbera, Merlot, Zinfandel

Sausage
Riesling, Brut or Rosé Sparkling Wine, Barbera, Gamay Beaujolais, Norton or Cynthiana, Syrah, Zinfandel

Steak (grilled, broiled)
Cabernet Sauvignon, Merlot, Rhône Blends, Zinfandel, Meritage, Norton or Cynthiana, Brut Sparkling Wine

Turkey
Zinfandel, Merlot, Chardonnay, Gamay Beaujolais

Veal
Chardonnay, Barbera, Merlot, Cynthiana

Venison
Syrah, Rhône Blends, Petite Sirah, Zinfandel, Pinot Noir, Norton, Chancellor, Cabernet Sauvignon

Other main courses

Couscous
Cabernet Franc, Merlot, Petite Sirah, Rosé Sparkling Wine, Syrah, Vin Gris

Curry, Fish or Chicken
Riesling, (Chilled) Gamay Beaujolais, Sauvignon (Fumé) Blanc, Zinfandel

Moussaka
Merlot, Sangiovese, Barbera, Zinfandel

Pizza
Barbera, Zinfandel, Sangiovese, Brut or Rosé Sparkling Wine, Cabernet Rosé

Spicy Chinese
Dry (and off-dry) Riesling, Pinot Gris, Pinot Blanc, Brut or Rosé Sparkling Wine, Merlot

Spicy Mexican
Dry (and off-dry) Riesling, Vin Gris, Chenin Blanc, (Chilled) Gamay Beaujolais

Thai
Chenin Blanc, Pinot Blanc, Riesling, Gewürztraminer, Brut or Rosé Sparkling Wine

Cheeses

Goat
Soft: Brut or Rosé Sparkling Wine, Sauvignon (Fumé) Blanc, Cabernet Sauvignon, Merlot, Pinot Noir
Hard: Pinot Noir, Merlot, Syrah, Cabernet Sauvignon
Cow & Sheep
Medium: Pinot Noir, Petite Sirah
Hard: Cabernet Sauvignon, Petite Sirah, Zinfandel, Port Blue, Late-Harvest Riesling, Chenin Blanc, Gewürztraminer, Muscat, Zinfandel

Desserts

Apple Pie, Tart & Baked
Late-Harvest Riesling, Various Ice Wines, Muscat, Demi-sec Sparkling Wines, Blueberry Wine
Berries
Brut Sparkling Wines, Demi-sec Sparkling Wines, Late-Harvest Riesling, Muscat, Zinfandel
Chocolate
Late-Harvest Riesling, Raspberry Wine, Black Muscat, Cabernet Sauvignon
Cakes
Demi-sec Sparkling Wines, Late-Harvest Riesling, Muscat, Various Ice Wines
Creams, Custards, Puddings
Demi-sec Sparkling Wines, Late-Harvest Riesling, Muscat, Various Ice Wines
Fresh Fruit
Late-Harvest Chenin Blanc, Riesling, Gewürztraminer, Muscat
Ice Creams, Sorbets
Usually none, perhaps fruit wine or fruit liqueurs
Nuts
Port, Brut Sparkling Wine, Angelica
Tiramisu
Angelica

Food & Wine Events

Dates vary with the year. For more up-to-date information on food and wine events in Washington, DC, Virginia, Maryland and elsewhere, visit the events calendar on www.gayot.com.

JANUARY

- **Celebration of Wine & Food at Williamsburg**, Williamsburg, VA. Taste pairings of foods prepared by regional chefs with wines from Virginia and around the world. Late January. Information: 757-229-0999.

FEBRUARY

- **Chesapeake Bay Wine Classic Grand Tasting**, Virginia Beach, VA. Don't miss the Chesapeake Bay's fine wine, educational seminars, fabulous food and silent auction. Early February. Information: 757-422-4688, www.cbwc.org.
- **Fairfax Chocolate Lover's Festival**, Fairfax, VA. Held annually in the city of Fairfax, the event is a chocolate lover's smorgasbord. Demonstrations, tastings and dinners are held throughout the city. Early February. Information: 703-385-7855.
- **George Washington's Birthday Party**, Oakgrove, VA. Celebrate the father of our country's birthday with live music and a visit from George himself at Ingleside Winery. Enjoy samples of cherry pie paired with wine. Tours, tastings, wine and special gifts. Late February. Information: 804-224-8687.

MARCH

- **Celebration at Opera House Gourmet**, Manassas, VA. This annual tasting of international and Virginia wineries also features gourmet foods, coffees, breads and chocolates. Early March. Information: 703-330-9636.

APRIL

- **Food & Wine Spectacular at the Homestead**, Hot Springs, VA. Nationally known chefs and wine experts gather with their best offerings. A grand finale dinner highlights the weekend. Early April. Information: 540-839-7917.
- **The National Cherry Blossom Festival**, Washington, DC. The festival annually commemorates the 1912 gift to the city of Washington of 3,000 cherry trees from Mayor Yukio Ozaki of Tokyo to enhance the growing friendship between the United States and Japan. Visitors can shop in the festival marketplace of Japanese groceries, foods, candy and clothing. Watch for seminars and receptions from master sushi chefs. Early April. Information: 202-547-1500, www.gwjapan.com/cherry.
- **Taste of the Nation**, Washington, DC. This is the largest nationwide culinary benefit supporting anti-hunger and anti-poverty efforts. Top chefs contribute to the benefit, which is hosted by Share our Strength (SOS) on behalf of local charities. Late April. Information: 703-218-6500, www.strength.org/see/taste/about_taste.htm.

MAY

- **Asparagus Festival at Tarara,** Leesburg, VA. At this Annual celebration of the Tarara asparagus, chefs prepare meals using the spring harvest. Early May. Information: 703-771-7100, www.tarara.com.

- **Montpelier Wine Festival**, Montpelier, VA. Held on the grounds of President James Madison's home, this festival lets guests explore the historic grounds, taste Virginia wines, and enjoy live entertainment, arts and crafts. Picnic baskets and kites are welcome. Early May. Information: 540-672-6495.

- **Mount Vernon's Wine Tasting Festival & Sunset Tour**, Mount Vernon, VA. Celebrate the history of wine on the east lawn of George Washington's Mount Vernon home overlooking the Potomac. Sample wines and learn about the successes and failures of our founding father's wine endeavors. House tours include a visit to the cellar vaults where Washington stashed his wines. Early May. Information: 703-780-2000.

- **National ZooFari,** Washington, DC. This food event benefiting the Washington National Zoo has been an annual tradition for more than 15 years. It's considered by many to be the best food event of the year, and the recent addition of wine tasting provides a new dimension. The opportunity to sample gourmet fare from 100 of Washington's finest restaurants brings many ZooFari attendees back year after year. Mid-May. Information: 202-673-4613, www.fonz.org/events/zoofari.htm.

JUNE

- **Vintage Virginia**, Great Meadow, The Plains, VA. The Virginia Wineries Association sponsors Virginia's largest festival with 50 wineries pouring wines. It features seminars and wine and food pairing demos by noted chefs, musical entertainment, and food. Early June. Information: 410-267-7020, www.vintagevirginia.com.

- **Capital Pride Festival,** Washington, DC. Concerts, a parade and a street fair with more than 300 crafts, food and other vendors are showcased, a celebration by the area's gay, lesbian, bisexual and transgender residents. Mid June. Information: 202-661-7026.

- **Taste of the Town**, Reston, VA. The restaurants of Reston prepare their specialties for this event in Reston Town Center. Mid to Late June. Information: 703-912-4105.

- **Mid-Atlantic Wine Festival,** Annapolis, MD. Join the fun with music, arts and crafts, wine tastings and regional cuisine. Late June. Information: 410-280-3306.

- **National Capital Barbecue Battle**, Washington, DC. Here, in the shadow of the Capitol, tens of thousands of people watch barbecue teams and restaurants from around the country compete to win cash and prizes and a chance to represent the Mid-Atlantic United States at the Barbecue World Championship. Late June. Information: 301-858-7800.

- **Smithsonian Folklife Festival**, Washington, DC. Visitors are invited to join evening events such as concerts, dances featuring traditional music, and other special community celebrations. Festival visitors may purchase traditional lunches, snacks, and dinners from themed food sites on the National Mall. Late June. Information: 202-357-2700, www.folklife.si.edu/festival2000info.htm.

JULY

- **Latin American Festival,** Washington, DC. One the largest Latin American festivals on the East Coast, this gathering celebrates the food, music and art of the Hispanic community. Late July. Information: 202-319-1300.

AUGUST

- **Virginia Wine Festival,** Great Meadow, The Plains, VA. See Virginia in a day with wines from 45 wineries. Attend wine appreciation seminars and cooking demos by chefs. Awards are given recognizing the best wines of Virginia. Mid to Late August. Information: 800-520-9670, www.showsinc.com.
- **Fine Art of Cuisine,** Tysons Corner, VA. Annual celebration of the "finer things in life" features gourmet food, fine wine and a salute to the arts. The event recognizes honorees who represent the highest level of excellence in the food world. Past recipients include Jean-Louis Palladin (Napa, Las Vegas), Thomas Keller (French Laundry, Napa Valley), and Daniel Mirassou (Mirassou Winery). Late August. Information: 703-917-6505.

SEPTEMBER

- **The National Hard Crab Derby & Fair**, Crisfield, MD. Colorful parades, beauty pageants, boat races, arts and craft exhibits, crab picking contest, swim meet, a carnival, games and lots of great food contribute to the event. Since 1963, the fair has hosted a Crab Cooking Contest. Early September. Information: 410-968-2500, www.crisfield.org/crabderby.html.
- **Washington Irish Festival,** Gaithersburg, MD. The festival features the finest traditional musicians, dancers and artists and foods from Ireland, Irish-America and related communities. Early September. Information: 301-565-0654, www.ncta.net/irish.html.
- **The Adams Morgan Community Festival**, Washington, DC. The is the oldest continuously running street festival in the nation's capital, reflecting the community spirit and pride of this internationally known neighborhood since 1977. Mid September. Information: 202-234-4240, www.adamsmorganday.org.
- **Maryland Wine Festival,** Westminster, MD. Ten Maryland wineries, 50 craft vendors, and more than 30 food vendors along with wine seminars and continuous live entertainment have made this a popular celebration of the state's wine industry. Mid September. Information: 800-654-4645.
- **Northern Neck Seafood Extravaganza**, Oakgrove, VA. Come and enjoy the seafood specialties from the Chesapeake Bay region. Live music, wine tasting and tours. Includes souvenir glass. Mid-September. Information: 804-224-8687.
- **Takoma Park Folk Festival**, Takoma Park, MD. Since 1978, the Takoma Park Folk Festival has been a music and dance community affair, organized by volunteers from the Takoma Park area. Vendors sell food that represents several ethnic cuisines and provides a myriad of options for the entire family. Mid September. Information: 301-589-3717, www.tpff.org/index.htm.

OCTOBER

- **Taste of Bethesda**, Bethesda, MD. This street festival features food from Bethesda's multicultural restaurants.

Early October. Information: 301-215-6660, www.bethes-da.org/events/tasteofbethesda.asp.

- **Taste of DC**, Washington, DC. The East Coast's largest outdoor food and music festival is one of Washington, DC's, most highly anticipated annual events. It celebrates the rich international culture and energy of the nation's capital. More than a million residents and visitors from around the world attend annually. Early October. Information: 202-724-4093, www.washington.org.
- **Fredericksburg Annual Wine Festival**, Fredericksburg, VA. At the Virginia Renaissance Faire Grounds, guests enjoy wines, food, crafts and live music. Mid-October. Information: 888-669-1579.
- **Garlic Festival**, Rebec, VA. Virginia-grown garlic and Virginia wines star here. Meet the Garlic King and Queen, and enjoy the garlic cook-off, music, arts and crafts and seminars. Mid-October. Information: 804-946-5168.
- **Shenandoah Valley Hot Air Balloon & Wine Festival**, Millwood, VA. Held at historic Long Branch, the event features hot air balloons, wine tastings, local foods and tours of the mansion. Late October. Information: 540-837-1856, www.historiclongbranch.com.

NOVEMBER

- **Annual Reedville Oyster Roast**, Reedville, VA. Feast on all the oysters you can eat, roasted or raw, as well as bean soup, clam chowder and hot dogs on the lawn at the Reedville Fishermen's Museum. Also music and line dancing. Early November. Information: 804-453-6529.
- **Lake Anna Winery Open House**, Spotsylvania, VA. Taste foods paired with Lake Anna Winery's award-winning wines. Also tours, tastings and souvenir glass. November 10, 2001. Information: 800-678-4748.
- **Bizarre Bazaar's Christmas Collection**, Richmond, VA. Enjoy a Christmas gift show with Christmas decorations and holiday foods, new gift lines, gourmet food and more. Late November-Early December. Information: 804-673-7015.

DECEMBER

- **100 Miles of Lights,** Richmond, Williamsburg, Newport News, Hampton, Portsmouth and Norfolk and Virginia Beach. Drive-through and walk-through light shows in Newport News, Norfolk, Richmond and Virginia Beach, enjoy the world-famous Grand Illumination in Colonial Williamsburg and see a lighted boat parade in Hampton or Portsmouth. Great shopping and dining are available as well. There will be events and entertainments in all of the cities mentioned above. Call for details. Entire month of December to early January. Information: 800-769-5912.
- **James River Plantation Candlight Carol Tour & Dinner**, Williamsburg, VA. The festive James River Plantation holiday tour and dinner begins at Piney Grove with appetizers, continues at North Bend with the entrée course and finishes at Edgewood for dessert. This event may be arranged on other dates for groups. Late December. Information: 804-829-6684.

WATER SAVVY

Knowing Your Bottled Water

Last year Americans spent $4.8 billion on bottled water, a 10 percent increase over the previous year. A few years ago, there were only a small number of choices for bottled water, but consumers today find more than 900 brands in the marketplace. The deteriorating taste and quality of tap water—and the fear of the contaminants it may contain—have made bottled water not just a choice for some people but a necessity. Drinking more water also goes along with the health-conscious craze today. The demand for bottled water is so high that even Pepsi has come out with Aquafina and Coca-Cola with Dasani to capture some of the market.

Not All Water Is Created Equal

To make an informed choice about which of the various types of bottled waters is for you, scrutinize the labels. European bottled mineral waters come from springs, which are simply underground water sources that flow naturally to the surface. Waters labeled "spring water" must come from a spring source. Federal labeling standards in the United States, which came into force in May 1996, now require that bottlers disclose on the label where the water originated. Purified water is a different story—it's usually produced by distillation, de-ionization or reverse osmosis. This water can originate from either the tap or from ground water. Often labeled "purified" or "drinking water," this processed water often has minerals added to it to give it taste. If the water is produced by vaporization and condensation, it may be labeled "distilled water".

Healthy Water

In Europe, bottlers tout the reputed healthful properties of good water. Almost every European bottled water is "bottled at the source," which means that it comes from a spring where people have gone for hundreds of years to "take the waters" in curative spa treatments. Spas like Vittel and Contrexeville have medical programs designed to address specific ailments. Most spa treatments involve consuming more than 80 ounces of water a day, which is said to remove toxins from the body and to be effective in the treatment of obesity. In Europe, these bottled waters with their mineral contents listed on the label are sold not only in supermarkets but also in pharmacies. Doctors even prescribe certain mineral waters for specific ailments.

In the United States, however, bottled water is marketed with an emphasis on taste, its contribution to fitness regimens and, in some cases, its trendiness. The U.S. Food and Drug Administration does not recognize any therapeutic values of bottled water because the existing medical research does not conform to FDA guidelines. However, the therapeutic value of certain bottled waters is becoming a subject of discussion in American scientific and medical circles.

Bubbly Water

The taste of carbonated water is effected by its level of carbonation—the more carbon-dioxide gas present, the more acidic the water's taste. This sensation, sometimes described by tasters as "bracing," "sharp" and "spritzy," can be positive or negative, depending upon which minerals are in the water. Certain minerals bind the carbonation into the water. Seltzers tend to lose their carbonation quickly because of the lack of minerals. In bottled-water tastings, the more highly mineralized carbonated waters have scored best. To help you become bottled-water savvy, here's a brief primer about popular brands usually available in major restaurants.

The Major Brands

Acqua Panna

For centuries, Italians have fondly referred to Acqua Panna as "baby's water," raising their children from infancy on this clear, crisp water because of its lightness, high quality and purity—appropriate for even a newborn's delicate digestive system. The source is located 3,700 feet high in the serene Tuscan Apennines of Northern Italy. Known for centuries to nobleman, hunters, shepherds and farmers for its remarkable purity and freshness, Acqua Panna Natural Spring Water comes from a pristine source, located on a vast, unspoiled natural reserve 25 miles north of Florence. Legend has it the ancient Romans built the only road stretching from Northern to Southern Italy through Scarperia—and past the source—to provide well-deserved refreshment to weary travelers. It is said that even Amerigo Vespucci sipped from the Panna source.

Arrowhead Mountain Spring Water

Rainfall and snowmelt percolating through soil and metamorphic rock give rise to four springs in California's San Bernardino Mountains. The water was first bottled in 1894 and by 1905 was being transported on "water trains" to consumers in San Bernardino and Los Angeles. Today Arrowhead Mountain Spring Water is transported from the source for bottling in Southern and Northern California and Arizona. The water is micron filtered (to remove particles of sediment), ozonized, passed under ultraviolet light and lightly mineralized (between 100 and 200 ppm of total dissolved solids).

Calistoga

Nestled at the north end of Napa Valley, Calistoga is a spa-resort town where a geyser second in size only to Yellowstone's Old Faithful shoots from the ground, and people have been coming to "take the waters"—in pools and mud-baths—since before the turn of the last century. Of the town's three commercially bottled waters, Calistoga comes from water which emerges from the ground at 212 degrees Fahrenheit and is then cooled to 39 degrees Fahrenheit for bottling. The hydrogen-sulfide aroma is removed from the water at the bottling plant by filtering it through sand. The finished water is then ozonated and carbonated. Calistoga also bottles a noncarbonated water from a Napa County spring.

Crystal Geyser

Located along the High Sierra mountain range in the town of Olancha, California, is the source of Crystal Geyser natural alpine spring water. Mount Whitney and other towering peaks of the High Sierra are a section of the Sierra Nevadas, which are approximately 270 miles long. Glacial waters have seeped over eons through cracks in the granite rocks in this range, the source of alpine spring water. Snow-melt and rain on Olancha Peak, 12,123 feet, filters through multiple geologic strata and the water surfaces at 78 degrees and is bottled at the source, 4,000 feet above sea level.

Evian

This famous non-sparkling European water comes from Source Cachat in France, where the water emerges from a tunnel in the mountain at 52.88 degrees Fahrenheit. The source is fed from the melted snow and rain that filters through glacial sand from the Vinzier Plateau over a period of 15 years. The glacial sand is surrounded by clay, which protects the water from pollution. The water is bottled at a nearby bottling plant, which is highly automated and exceptionally hygienic.

Fiji Natural Artesian Water

The origin of Fiji Natural Artesian Water is rainfall. It is bottled at the source, taken from an aquifer beneath volcanic highlands on the main island of Viti Levu in Fiji. Fiji Natural Artesian Water was first packaged by the company's founder, David Gilmore, to provide to guests at his exclusive Wakaya Club on Wakaya, a 2,200-acre island in the Fiji Republic. The product was launched in Florida and Los Angeles at the end of 1997 in a distinctive, square-shaped bottle, with dramatic graphics. It is said to have a smooth "mouth feel" due to its high silica content.

Hawaiian Springs Natural Water

It begins as rain and snow falling through the cleanest air on earth, to the slopes of Mauna Loa Volcano on the Big Island of Hawaii, thousands of miles from the nearest continent. Mauna Loa is the largest mountain in the world in land mass. This pristine water filters through thousands of feet of lava rock and forms an underground water flow where it is captured at the source in Kea'au (Puna District) on Mauna Loa's slopes. Early Hawaiians always had a reason behind the names they selected for places. Kea'au, District of Puna, means "clear, pure spring water." Every day over one billion gallons of this unusually pure water flows underground toward the ocean to repeat its never ending cycle.

Perrier

The beginning of the Perrier water dates back more than 100 million years to the Cretaceous Period, when limestone deposits began to form faults and fissures that captured water deep within the earth below what is now Vergèze, France. Hannibal's Carthaginian army is said to have paused by the spring, Les Bouillens, in 218 B.C. Remains in the area suggest that the Romans also refreshed themselves in the waters of Perrier, which have a bit of natural carbonation. When it is bottled, extra fizz is created by adding filtered carbon monoxide gas captured at a nearby natural source.

Poland Spring

The history of Poland Spring, Maine, dates back to 1793, when the area around the spring was first settled and the Ricker family opened a small inn. Soon afterward Joseph Ricker lay dying, and to ease his fever someone fetched water from the spring. The story is that Ricker drank it and lived another 52 years to tell the tale! In 1845, Hiram Ricker began to bottle the water and, in 1893, Poland Spring was awarded the Medal of

Excellence at the World's Columbian Exposition in Chicago. Today, Poland Spring comes both still and sparkling.

San Pellegrino

The spring of San Pellegrino is sequestered in the mountains north of Milan, Italy, and was first made famous by quenching the thirst of Leonardo da Vinci. Today the Fonte Termale, an opulent marbled drinking hall is a monument to the glamour of "taking the waters." San Pellegrino's sources are three deep springs, which emerge from the ground at 69.8 degrees Fahrenheit. The waters come from an aquifer 1,300 feet below the surface, where limestone and volcanic rocks impart unique minerals and trace elements. Among its several bottled waters, San Pellegrino also bottles and imports to the United States.

Solé

The Fonte Solé Spring is located in the foothills of the Lombardy region of the Italian Alps and has been revered for its health-giving waters since Roman times. In the Middle Ages, the source was controlled by a monastery when both plague and pestilence threatened the population. A belief grew up that those who drank from the spring would be. Today, the water is recognized as being low in sodium. The University of Pavia has declared it as being microbiologically pure. Solé is packaged in green glass bottles, both noncarbonated and lightly carbonated.

Trinity

The source of Trinity is a place called Paradise, Idaho, located on the edge of the vast Idaho wilderness in the foothills of the Trinity Mountains. A source of exceptional purity, the Trinity springs flow through crystal-lined passageways over 2.2 miles below the planet's surface within the massive granite Idaho Batholith. Emerging from this deep, protected, pristine source at a temperature of 138 degrees Fahrenheit, Trinity is pure enough to be bottled in its natural state without disinfectants. In keeping with the recognized traditions and wisdom of European spring stewardship.

Vittel

This still mineral water comes from three springs in the small town of Vittel, protected within a 5,000-acre forest in the Vosges Mountains in Northeastern France. Vittel comes from an immense underground aquifer where rock strata and sandstone charge the water with calcium, magnesium and sulphates. The spring surfaces at 11.1 degrees Celsius, and its waters are renowned for its stimulating effects on the kidneys, gall bladder and liver.

Volvic

Volvic is bottled exclusively at its unique source in France and available in more than 60 countries. The basin supplying the Volvic spring source is located in the Regional Park of the Old Auvergne Volcanoes, a volcanic region that has been dormant for 10,000 years. The name Volvic refers to the town as well as a type of gray volcanic rock. The Clairvic Spring was discovered in 1927. In 1965, the French Ministry of Health authorized the bottling of Volvic water. Volvic emerges year-round from its protected source at the constant temperature of 8.8 Celsius.

This guide has been prepared by Arthur von Wiesenberger, author of four books on bottled water, a water master at the annual International Water Tasting Competition in Berkeley Springs, W. VA, and the founder of www.BottledWaterWeb.com, the definitive bottled water Web site and www.BottledWaterBoutique.com, the Internet's first on-line water purveyor

Restaurant Indexes

RESTAURANTS BY AREAS   290

RESTAURANTS BY CUISINES   298

RESTAURANTS BY FEATURES   304

RESTAURANTS BY AREAS

WASHINGTON, DC

ADAMS MORGAN

Caravan Grill	12/20
Cashion's Eat Place	14/20
The Diner	12/20
Grill from Ipanema	12/20
I Matti	13/20
Julia's Empanadas	QB
Lauriol Plaza	13/20
Mama Ayesha's	12/20
Meskerem Ethiopian	12/20
Mixtec	12/20
Perry's	13/20

AMERICAN UNIVERSITY

Wagshal's Delicatessen	QB

BROOKLAND

Bamboo Joint Café	13/20

CAPITOL HILL

Anatolia Turkish Café	12/20
Barolo Ristorante	13/20
Bistro Bis	13/20
B. Smith's	13/20
Bullfeathers of Capitol Hill	QB
CapitHawk 'n' Dove	QB
Il Radicchio	12/20
La Colline	15/20
The Monocle	12/20
Two Quail	13/20
The White Tiger	12/20

CHEVY CHASE

American City Diner of Washington	QB
The Cheesecake Factory	13/20

CHINATOWN

Burma Restaurant	12/20
Capital Q	QB
China Boy	QB
Coco Loco	12/20
Fadó Irish Pub	12/20
Full Kee Restaurant	12/20
Hunan Chinatown	13/20
Marrakesh	13/20
Rupperts	14/20
Szechuan Gallery Restaurant	12/20

CLEVELAND PARK

Aranella Grill	14/20
Ardeo	14/20
Cactus Cantina	13/20
Café Deluxe	13/20
Café Ole	13/20
Lavandou Restaurant	13/20
Palena	15/20
Spices	13/20
The Vigorelli	14/20
Yanÿu	16/20

COLUMBIA HEIGHTS

Florida Avenue Grill	12/20

DOWNTOWN

Austin Grill	13/20
Bangkok One	11/20
Bobby Van's Steakhouse	13/20
Bombay Club	14/20
Bombay Palace	13/20
Brasserie Les Halles	13/20
Bread Line	QB
Burrito Brothers	QB
Butterfield 9	14/20
Café Asia	12/20
Café Atlántico	14/20
Café Soleil	12/20
California Pizza Kitchen	QB
The Capital Grille	13/20
The Caucus Room	15/20
CF Folks	13/20
Christopher Marks	13/20
Corduroy	14/20
Corner Bakery	QB
DC Coast	14/20
District ChopHouse & Brewery	12/20
Donna's	QB
Equinox	15/20
ESPN Zone	QB
Famous Luigi's	12/20
Galileo	17/20
Georgia Brown's	13/20
Gérard's Place	16/20
Gordon Biersch Brewery Restaurant	12/20
Iron Gate Inn Restaurant	13/20
Jaleo	14/20
Kaz Sushi Bistro	14/20

Lafayette	14/20
Le Jardin	14/20
Legal Sea Foods	13/20
Luigino	12/20
M & S Grill	12/20
McCormick & Schmick's	13/20
Malaysia Kopitiam	12/20
The Mark	13/20
Mr. K's	13/20
Morrison-Clark Restaurant	13/20
Morton's of Chicago	14/20
Nick & Stef's Steakhouse	13/20
The Oceanaire Seafood Room	14/20
Old Ebbitt Grill	13/20
Olives	13/20
Oodles Noodles	QB
Osteria Goldoni	14/20
The Oval Room	13/20
Palomino	13/20
The Prime Rib	13/20
Primi Piatti Ristorante	14/20
Red Sage	14/20
Red Tomato	14/20
Reeves Restaurant & Bakery	QB
701 Pennsylvania Avenue Restaurant & Bar	14/20
Sholl's Colonial Cafeteria	12/20
Smith & Wollensky	14/20
Star of Siam	12/20
Sticks & Bowls	QB
Taberna del Alabardero	14/20
Teatro Goldoni	14/20
TenPenh	15/20
Timothy Dean Restaurant & Bar	16/20
Vidalia	14/20
The Well-Dressed Burrito	QB
The Willard Room	12/20

DUPONT CIRCLE

Al Tiramisu	13/20
Bacchus	13/20
Bistrot du Coin	13/20
Bua Thai	11/20
Café Citron	11/20
Café Midi Cuisine	12/20
City Lights of China	12/20
Etrusco Trattoria	14/20
Firehook Bakery & Coffee House	QB
Gabriel	15/20
I Ricchi	14/20
Jockey Club	11/20
Johnny's Half Shell	13/20

Levante's	12/20
Luna Grill & Diner	QB
Nora	15/20
Obelisk	15/20
Palm	13/20
Pan-Asian Restaurant	QB
Pesce	14/20
Pizzeria Paradiso	QB
Ruth's Chris Steak House	14/20
Sala Thai	12/20
Sam & Harry's	13/20
Sesto Senso	13/20
Tabard Inn	14/20
Teaism	QB
Thaiphoon	12/20
Vivo! Ristorante	12/20
Xando	QB
Zorba's Café	12/20

FOGGY BOTTOM

The Burro	QB
Kinkead's	15/20
Lindy's Bon Appétit	QB
Roof Terrace Restaurant	12/20
Zuki Moon	13/20

FRIENDSHIP HEIGHTS

Bambulé	13/20
Chadwicks	QB
Heller's Bakery	QB
Matisse Café Restaurant	14/20

GEORGETOWN

Aditi	13/20
Amma Indian Vegetarian Kitchen	QB
Basil Thai Restaurant	13/20
Bistro Français	13/20
Bistro Med	11/20
Bistrot Lepic	14/20
Booeymongers	QB
Busara	12/20
Café La Ruche	11/20
Café Milano	13/20
Ching Ching Cha, a Chinese Tea House	QB
Clyde's of Georgetown	13/20
Confucius Café	12/20
Daily Grill	12/20
Einstein Bros Bagels	QB
Entotto	14/20
Fast Fettoosh	QB
Georgetown Bagelry	QB
Houston's	12/20
Hunan Peking	12/20
J Paul's	QB
Japan Inn Restaurant	13/20
Johnny Rockets	QB

La Chaumière	13/20
Mendocino Grille	
& Wine Bar	12/20
Mes Amis Restaurant	13/20
Michel Richard	
Citronelle	19/20
Miss Saigon	11/20
Moby Dick House	
of Kabob	QB
Neyla	14/20
Old Glory All-American	
Bar-B-Que	QB
Paolo's	12/20
Peacock Café	13/20
Philadelphia	
Cheesesteak Factory	QB
Prospect Pizza	
& Pastries	QB
San Marzano	12/20
Sea Catch Restaurant	
& Raw Bar	14/20
Seasons	14/20
Sen5es Bakery	
& Restaurant	13/20
Sequoia	10/20
1789 Restaurant	16/20
Tahoga	13/20
The Tombs	12/20
Tony & Joe's Seafood	12/20
Wrap Works	QB
Zed's Ethiopian	
Restaurant	12/20

GLOVER PARK

Faccia Luna Trattoria	12/20
Heritage India	15/20
Old Europe	12/20
Rockland's Barbeque	
& Grilling Company	QB
Saveur Restaurant	14/20
Sushi-Ko	15/20

NATIONAL ZOO

Mrs. Simpson's	13/20

SPRING VALLEY

Chicken Out Rotisserie	QB

TENLEYTOWN

a.k.a. Friscos	QB
Hibachi Brothers	
Japanese Restaurant	QB
Krupin's	QB

U ST. CORRIDOR

Ben's Chili Bowl	QB
The Islander Caribbean	
Restaurant & Bar	14/20

UDC

Ledo Pizza	QB

UPTOWN

Politics & Prose	QB
Thai Room	12/20

WATERFRONT

Hogate's	12/20
Phillips Flagship Seafood	
Restaurant	12/20
Zanzibar on the	
Waterfront	11/20

WESLEY HEIGHTS

Chef Geoff's	12/20

WEST END

Asia Nora	15/20
The Bistro	13/20
Blackie's	15/20
Bread & Chocolate	QB
Café on M	13/20
Marcel's	16/20
Meiwah	12/20
Melrose	14/20
Shula's Steak House	13/20
West 24	14/20

WEST GEORGETOWN

Makoto Restaurant	16/20

WOODLEY PARK

Lebanese Taverna	12/20
New Heights	14/20
Petits Plats	13/20
Thai Town	12/20

VIRGINIA

ALEXANDRIA

Alexandria Pastry Shop	
& Café	QB
Ann MeMe's Bakery	
& Cafe	QB
Blue Point Grill	13/20
Bread & Chocolate	QB
Bruscato's	QB
Café Monti	12/20
Dixie Pig	QB
Elysium	13/20
Firehook Bakery	
& Coffee House	QB
Flatbreads Food Shop	QB
Four Seasons	QB
Krispy Kreme	
Doughnuts	QB
La Bergerie	14/20
Le Gaulois	13/20
Maggie Moo's Ice Cream	
& Treatery	QB
Mandarin Inn	12/20
Mediterranean Bakery	QB
Panera Bakery & Café	QB

Pat Troy's Restaurant & Pub	12/20
Po Siam Thai Restaurant	11/20
Potowmack Landing Restaurant	12/20
Ramparts	QB
Ristorante Geranio	14/20
Santa Fe East	13/20
South Austin Grill	13/20
Stella's	12/20
Taqueria Poblano	QB
Thai Old Town	11/20
Union Street Public House	12/20

ANNANDALE
Shiney's	QB
Silverado	11/20

ARLINGTON
A Taste of Casablanca	13/20
Aegean Taverna Restaurant	12/20
Alpine Restaurant	12/20
Atami	QB
Atilla's	QB
Best Buns Bread Co.	QB
Bob & Edith's Diner	QB
Bonsai	QB
Café Asia	12/20
Café Parisien Express	12/20
Capitol City Brewing Co.	QB
Caribbean Grill	QB
Carlyle Grand Café	13/20
Chevys Fresh Mex	QB
Costa Verde Restaurant	11/20
Crisp & Juicy	QB
El Pollo Rey	QB
El Pollo Rico	QB
Faccia Luna Trattoria	12/20
FlatTop Grill	13/20
Food Factory	12/20
Ghin Na Rhee Restaurant	11/20
Hamburger Hamlet	12/20
Heidelberg Bakery	QB
Hope Key	13/20
Hunan Number One	12/20
Il Radicchio	12/20
The Italian Store	QB
Johnny Rockets	QB
La Côte d'Or Café	14/20
Layalina	11/20
Lazy Sundae	QB
Lebanese Taverna	12/20
Lebanese Taverna Market	QB
Little Viet Garden	12/20
Lost Dog Café	QB
Luna Park Grille	QB

Matuba	13/20
Mayan Grill & Bar	12/20
Memphis Bar-B-Q	QB
Metro 29 Diner	QB
Mexicali Blues	12/20
Mezza 9	13/20
Mr. Hibachi	QB
Nam-Viet Pho 79	12/20
Pasha Café	13/20
Pica Deli Gourmet	QB
Queen Bee	12/20
Rhodeside Grill	13/20
Rincome Thai Cuisine	12/20
Rockland's Barbeque & Grilling Company	QB
Ruth's Chris Steak House	14/20
Sala Thai	11/20
Sawatdee Thai Restaurant	12/20
Supee's Kitchen	11/20
Sushi-Zen Japanese Restaurant	12/20
Tandoori Kabob House	QB
Thai Noy Restaurant	12/20
T.H.A.I. in Shirlington	12/20
Thai Square Restaurant	13/20
Toro Tapas & Grill	12/20
Vietnam 75 Noodle Restaurant	QB
Village Bistro	12/20

CENTREVILLE
Copeland's of New Orleans	12/20
Payne's	QB

CHANTILLY
Bo Dean's Pit B.B.Q.	QB
Milwaukee Frozen Custard	QB
Picante! The Real Taco	QB
Thai Basil	14/20

CLIFTON
Rosemary's Thyme Bistro	12/20

FAIRFAX
Baja Fresh Mexican Grill	QB
Blue Iguana	13/20
Bombay Bistro	14/20
Don Pablo's, The Real Enchilada	12/20
Hermitage Inn	14/20
Pars Famous House of Kabob	12/20
P. J. Skidoo's, The American Way	12/20

Red Hot & Blue QB
Sakoontra Thai
  Restaurant 12/20
Silver Diner QB
Star Thai Cuisine 12/20
29 Diner QB
Yum Yum
  Ice Cream Café QB

FALLS CHURCH
Argia's 13/20
Bay Lo QB
Bread & Kabob QB
Bubba's Bar-B-Q QB
Café Rose 12/20
Celebrity Delly QB
Duangrat's 13/20
Flavors Soul Food 13/20
Fortune of Seven
  Corners 13/20
Galaxy Restaurant 11/20
Haandi 12/20
Huong Que (Four Sisters
  Restaurant) 12/20
Huong Viet 11/20
Kim Son Restaurant QB
Little Saigon Vietnamese
  Restaurant 12/20
Malibu Grill 12/20
Mark's Duck House 12/20
Maxim Palace 12/20
Myanmar Restaurant 13/20
Nayeb Kabob
  Restaurant 12/20
Neisha Thai Cuisine 12/20
Old Hickory Grille QB
Panjshir 11/20
Peking Gourmet Inn 13/20
Peking Village 12/20
Pho 75 QB
Pho Tay Ho QB
Rio Bravo 12/20
Saigon House Vietnamese
  Restaurant 10/20
Samadi Sweets Café QB
Sign of the Whale 12/20
Sweetwater Tavern QB
Viet Royale 12/20

GREAT FALLS
Kabob Place Café
  & Bakery QB
L'Auberge Chez
  François 14/20
Le Relais Restaurant
  & Bar à Vin 14/20
The Old Brogue, an
  Irish Pub QB
The Serbian Crown
  Restaurant 12/20

HAMILTON
Planet Wayside 13/20

HERNDON
A Taste of the World 12/20
The Bagel Café QB
Bamyan Restaurant 13/20
Barbeque Country
  Jamboree QB
Chao Pra Ya 12/20
Charcoal Kebab QB
China King QB
El Sabor Latino QB
Euro Bistro 11/20
Fuddruckers QB
Hama Sushi & Grill
  Japanese Restaurant 12/20
Hard Times Café QB
The Ice House Café 12/20
Minerva Indian
  Cuisine 12/20
Outback Steakhouse 11/20
Pollos Inka QB
Thai Luang 12/20
Tortilla Factory 12/20
Zeffirelli 12/20

LEESBURG
Bella Luna 11/20
Casa Gonzalez 11/20
Eiffel Tower Café 12/20
Knossos QB
Lansdowne Grille 14/20
Ledo Pizza QB
Lightfoot 14/20
Tuscarora Mill 13/20

MANASSAS
Ben's Whole Hog
  Barbecue QB
Carmello's & Little
  Portugal 12/20
Chez Marc 15/20
Mike's Diner & Lounge QB
Okra's Louisiana
  Bistro 12/20
Pho Gourmet QB

MCLEAN
Busara 12/20
Café Taj 13/20
California Pizza Kitchen QB
The Capital Grille 13/20
Chesapeake Bagel
  Bakery QB
Chicken Out Rotisserie QB
Corkie's Grill 12/20
Corner Bakery QB
Fleming's Prime Steakhouse
  & Wine Bar QB
The Greek Taverna 12/20
J. Gilbert's Wood-Fired
  Steaks 13/20

J. R.'s Stockyards Inn   12/20
Kazan Restaurant   12/20
Le Petit Mistral   12/20
Legal Sea Foods   13/20
Luciano Italian Restaurant
  & Pizzeria   12/20
Maestro   14/20
Maggiano's Little Italy   13/20
Mirage Restaurant   12/20
Miyagi   QB
Moby Dick House
  of Kabob   QB
The NM Café
  at Neiman Marcus   13/20
Palm   13/20
P.F. Chang's
  China Bistro   13/20
Pulcinella Ristorante   13/20
Ristorante Il Borgo   14/20
Tachibana   14/20
Taste of Saigon   11/20
Three Pigs Barbecue   QB
Wok & Roll Chinese Café   QB

MIDDLEBURG

Black Coffee Bistro   14/20
Upper Crust Bakery   QB

OAKTON

Old Peking
  Restaurant   11/20
Très Joli   QB

RESTON

Big Bowl   14/20
Café Montmartre   12/20
The Cincinnati Café   12/20
Einstein Bros Bagels   QB
Fortune of Reston Chinese
  Seafood Restaurant   12/20
Jasmine Café   13/20
Lake Anne Coffee House   QB
Lakeside Inn   12/20
la Madeleine French
  Bakery & Café   QB
Lee's Ice Cream & Deli   QB
McCormick
  & Schmick's   13/20
Marie's Restaurant   12/20
Market Street
  Bar & Grill   13/20
Paolo's   12/20
Philadelphia Mike's   QB
Primo Italiano   QB
Rio Grande Café   13/20
Ristorante Il Cigno   12/20
Romano's
  Macaroni Grill   12/20
Saint Basil Brick
  Oven Grill   13/20
Simply Grill   QB
Wrap Works   QB

ROSSLYN

China Garden   12/20
Tom Sarris' Orleans
  House   12/20

SPRINGFIELD

Manila Café   12/20
Mike's American Grill   13/20
Papa Petrone's   QB

STERLING

Emilio's Brick Oven Pizza QB
Pacific   12/20

VIENNA

Amphora Restaurant   QB
Anita's Mexican Food   QB
Bistro 123   14/20
Bombay Tandoor   14/20
Cenan's Bakery   QB
Clyde's of Tysons   13/20
eciti Café & Bar   14/20
Hog's Breath   QB
Konami Japanese
  Restaurant   12/20
La Provence   14/20
Le Canard   11/20
Morton's of Chicago   14/20
Nizam's   11/20
The Oriental Regency   13/20
Paya Thai   11/20
Phillips Seafood Grill   12/20
Primi Piatti Ristorante   14/20
Ristorante Bonaroti   12/20
Sahara Grill   11/20
Sam & Harry's   13/20
Shamshiry   12/20
Sunflower Vegetarian
  Restaurant   QB
Tara Thai   13/20
Thai Pilin   11/20
That's Amore   12/20
The Vienna Inn   QB
The White Tiger   11/20
Yama Japanese
  Restaurant   12/20

W. SPRINGFIELD

Austin Grill   13/20

WASHINGTON

The Inn at Little
  Washington   19/20

WOODBRIDGE

Dixie Bones   QB

MARYLAND

ADELPHI

Caribbean Delight   QB

BELTSVILLE

El Mexicano — QB
Gringada Mexican
  Restaurant — 11/20

BETHESDA

Andalucia — 13/20
The Andaman
  Restaurant & Bar — 12/20
Austin Grill — 13/20
Bacchus — 13/20
Bangkok Garden — 14/20
Black's Bar
  & Kitchen — 14/20
Bread & Chocolate — QB
Café Deluxe — 13/20
Café Europa — 12/20
California Pizza Kitchen — QB
California Tortilla — QB
Centro Italian Grill — 13/20
Cesco Trattoria — 14/20
Chipotle Mexican Grill — QB
Corner Bakery — QB
Cottonwood Café — 12/20
Delhi Dhaba — 12/20
Fairmont Bar & Dining — 13/20
Gifford's Ice Cream
  Company — QB
Grapeseed — 13/20
Green Papaya — 13/20
Haandi — 12/20
Hamburger Hamlet — 12/20
Hofberg's Deli — QB
Houston's — 12/20
Jean-Michel
  Restaurant — 12/20
Levante's — 12/20
Louisiana Express — 12/20
Matuba — 13/20
Moby Dick House
  of Kabob — QB
Nam's of Bethesda — 13/20
Oodles Noodles — QB
The Original Pancake
  House — QB
Outback Steakhouse — 11/20
Pastry Designs — QB
Persimmon, An American
  Bistro — 14/20
Red Tomato Café — QB
Rio Grande Café — 13/20
Rock Bottom Brewery — QB
Ruth's Chris Steak
  House — 14/20
Shanghai Café — 12/20
South Beach Café — 13/20
Sushi Sushi — QB
Sweet Basil — 13/20
Tako Grill — 13/20
Tara Thai — 13/20
Tastee Diner — QB
Tel-Aviv Café — 13/20
Thai Leela — 11/20
Thyme Square — 11/20
West End Grill — 12/20
Willie & Reed's — QB
Wok Inn — 12/20

BROOKEVILLE

The Inn at Brookeville
  Farms — 14/20

BURTONSVILLE

Old Hickory Grille — QB
Seibel's Restaurant — 12/20

CHEVY CHASE

Clyde's of Chevy
  Chase — 13/20

CLINTON

Texas Ribs & BBQ — QB

COLLEGE PARK

Mandalay Restaurant
  & Café — 13/20
Taco Fiesta — QB

DICKERSON

Comus Inn — 12/20

GAITHERSBURG

Acajutla — 12/20
Chevys Fresh Mex — QB
Einstein Bros Bagels — QB
House of Chinese
  Delights — 12/20
Hunan Palace — 12/20
Il Forno Pizzeria — QB
India Bistro — 12/20
Madras Palace — 12/20
Mi Peru Restaurante — 12/20
New Fortune Chinese
  Seafood Restaurant — 12/20
The Nibbler — 12/20
Old Siam Restaurant — 11/20
Roy's Place — QB
Star Diner — QB
Summit Station Restaurant
  & Brewery — 12/20

GERMANTOWN

Café Mileto — 12/20
Caspian Café — 13/20

GLEN ECHO

Inn at Glen Echo — 13/20

HYATTSVILLE

Caribbean Palace — QB
Pho 99 Restaurant — QB
Pho 75 — QB
Pollo Casero — QB

Tiffin, The Indian
  Kitchen   13/20
Udupi Palace   13/20
Woodlands   QB

LAUREL
Don Pablo's, The Real
  Enchilada   12/20
Red Hot & Blue   QB

NORTH BETHESDA
The Cheesecake
  Factory   13/20

OXON HILL
Levi's Restaurant
  & Carry-out   QB

POOLESVILLE
Meadow Lark Inn   12/20

POTOMAC
Café Roval   13/20
Chicken Out Rotisserie   QB
Fortune Garden   QB
Old Angler's Inn   14/20

ROCKVILLE
A & J Restaurant   QB
Addie's   14/20
Asia Café   QB
Baja Fresh Mexican Grill   QB
Bamboo Buffet   QB
Bombay Bistro   14/20
The Broadway Diner
  Restaurant   QB
Caribbean Feast Restaurant
  & Catering   QB
Charlie's Open
  Pit Barbecue   QB
China Canteen   12/20
Copeland's of New
  Orleans   12/20
Crisp & Juicy   QB
Cuban Corner   13/20
Eastern Empire
  Buffet-Restaurant   QB
atZi's Market & Bakery   QB
uddruckers   QB
Green Field
  Churrascaria   11/20
Hard Times Café   QB
Il Pinito Trattoria   12/20
oe's Noodle House   12/20
The Kabob House   QB
atz's Kosher
  Supermarket   QB
ohr Brothers   QB
ebanese Taverna Café   QB
Mamma Lucia   12/20
Mediterranean House
  of Kabob   QB

Momo Taro Sushi   QB
Mykonos Grill   12/20
O'Brien's Pit Barbecue   QB
Peking Eastern
  House Restaurant   QB
Pho 95   QB
Pinto & Mazzilli   12/20
Saigon Gourmet   12/20
Sam Woo   13/20
Seven Seas   12/20
Silver Diner   QB
Taipei Tokyo Café   QB
Taipei Tokyo Café #2   12/20
Temari Japanese Café   12/20
That's Amore   12/20
Timpano Italian
  Chophouse   13/20
The Vegetable Garden   QB
Wurzburg Haus
  Restaurant   13/20
Yuan Fu Vegetarian   QB

SILVER SPRING
Bombay Gaylord   11/20
Caribbean Café   QB
Crisfield Seafood
  Restaurant   13/20
El Aguila   12/20
Kefa Café   QB
Negril   QB
Oriental East   12/20
Parkway Deli
  & Restaurant   QB
Thai Spice Café   QB
Thanh Thanh   13/20
York Castle Tropical
  Ice Cream   QB

TAKOMA PARK
Mark's Kitchen   12/20
Pho New Saigon Vietnamese
  Restaurant Seafood
  & Grill   12/20

URBANA
Turning Point Inn   13/20

WHEATON
Asian Foods   QB
The Chicken Place   QB
China Chef   12/20
Full Key Restaurant   12/20
Good Fortune   12/20
Hollywood East Café   13/20
Ledo Pizza   QB
Los Chorros
  Restaurant   12/20
Ruan Thai   14/20
Sabang   13/20
Suporn's Thai
  Restaurant   13/20

RESTAURANTS BY CUISINES

AFGHAN
Bamyan Restaurant 13/20 (VA)
Mirage Restaurant 12/20 (VA)
Panjshir 11/20 (VA)

AMERICAN
The Bistro 13/20 (DC)
Black Coffee Bistro 14/20 (VA)
Blackie's 15/20 (DC)
Butterfield 9 14/20 (DC)
Café Deluxe 13/20 (DC, MD)
Carlyle Grand Café 13/20 (VA)
The Caucus Room 15/20 (DC)
CF Folks 13/20 (DC)
The Cheesecake
   Factory 13/20 (DC, MD)
Chef Geoff's 12/20 (DC)
Christopher Marks 13/20 (DC)
The Cincinnati
   Café 12/20 (VA)
Comus Inn 12/20 (MD)
Corduroy 14/20 (DC)
Corkie's Grill 12/20 (VA)
Daily Grill 12/20 (DC)
DC Coast 14/20 (DC)
The Diner 12/20 (DC)
eciti Café & Bar 14/20 (VA)
Elysium 13/20 (VA)
Fairmont Bar
   & Dining 13/20 (MD)
Grapeseed 13/20 (MD)
Hamburger
   Hamlet 12/20 (VA, MD)
Hermitage Inn 14/20 (VA)
Houston's 12/20 (DC, MD)
The Ice House
   Café 12/20 (VA)
Inn at Glen Echo 13/20 (MD)
J. Gilbert's Wood-Fired
   Steaks 13/20 (VA)
Lafayette 14/20 (DC)
Lakeside Inn 12/20 (VA)
M & S Grill 12/20 (DC)
Meadow Lark Inn 12/20 (MD)
Mendocino Grille
   & Wine Bar 12/20 (DC)
Mike's American
   Grill 13/20 (VA)
The Monocle 12/20 (DC)
Mrs. Simpson's 13/20 (DC)
The NM Café at
   Neiman Marcus 13/20 (VA)
Old Ebbitt Grill 13/20 (DC)
P. J. Skidoo's, The American
   Way 12/20 (VA)
Peacock Café 13/20 (DC)
Planet Wayside 13/20 (VA)
Rhodeside Grill 13/20 (VA)
Roof Terrace
   Restaurant 12/20 (DC)
Seibel's Restaurant 12/20 (MD)
Sequoia 10/20 (DC)
701 Pennsylvania Avenue
   Restaurant & Bar 14/20 (DC)
1789 Restaurant 16/20 (DC)
Sholl's Colonial
   Cafeteria 12/20 (DC)
Sign of the Whale 12/20 (VA)
Tabard Inn 14/20 (DC)
Thyme Square 11/20 (MD)
Tom Sarris' Orleans
   House 12/20 (VA)
The Tombs 12/20 (DC)
Turning Point Inn 13/20 (MD)
Two Quail 13/20 (DC)
Union Street Public
   House 12/20 (VA)
West 24 14/20 (DC)
The Willard Room 12/20 (DC)

AMERICAN/ASIAN
Mark's Kitchen 12/20 (MD)

AMERICAN/CUBAN
South Beach Café 13/20 (MD)

AMERICAN/ITALIAN
Palena 15/20 (DC)
Village Bistro 12/20 (VA)
West End Grill 12/20 (MD)

AMERICAN/MEDITERRANEAN/FRENCH
Café Roval 13/20 (MD)

ASIAN/LATIN AMERICAN
A Taste of the World 12/20 (VA)

BRAZILIAN
Green Field
   Churrascaria 11/20 (MD)
Grill from Ipanema 12/20 (DC)
Malibu Grill 12/20 (VA)

BRAZILIAN/LATIN AMERICAN

Coco Loco   12/20 (DC)

BREWERY

District ChopHouse
  & Brewery   12/20 (DC)
Gordon Biersch Brewery
  Restaurant   12/20 (DC)

BURMESE

Burma Restaurant 12/20 (DC)
Mandalay Restaurant
  & Café   13/20 (MD)
Myanmar Restaurant 13/20 (VA)

CARIBBEAN

The Islander Caribbean
  Restaurant & Bar 14/20 (DC)

CARIBBEAN/AMERICAN/ CONTINENTAL

Zanzibar on the
  Waterfront   11/20 (DC)

CHINESE

China Canteen   12/20 (MD)
China Chef   12/20 (MD)
China Garden   12/20 (VA)
City Lights of China 12/20 (DC)
Confucius Café   12/20 (DC)
Fortune of Reston Chinese
  Seafood Restaurant 12/20 (VA)
Fortune of Seven
  Corners   13/20 (VA)
Full Kee Restaurant 12/20 (DC)
Full Key Restaurant 12/20 (MD)
Good Fortune   12/20 (MD)
Hollywood East
  Café   13/20 MD
Hope Key   13/20 (VA)
House of Chinese
  Delights   12/20 (MD)
Hunan Chinatown 13/20 (DC)
Hunan Number
  One   12/20 (VA)
Hunan Palace   12/20 (MD)
Hunan Peking   12/20 (DC)
Maxim Palace   12/20 (VA)
Meiwah   12/20 (DC)
Mr. K's   13/20 (DC)
New Fortune Chinese Seafood
  Restaurant   12/20 (MD)
Old Peking
  Restaurant   11/20 (VA)
Oriental East   12/20 (MD)
The Oriental
  Regency   13/20 (VA)
Peking Gourmet
  Inn   13/20 (VA)
Peking Village   12/20 (VA)
Shanghai Café   12/20 (MD)

Szechuan Gallery
  Restaurant   12/20 (DC)

CHINESE/AMERICAN

P.F. Chang's China
  Bistro   12/20 (VA)

CHINESE/ASIAN/FUSION

Yanÿu   16/20 (DC)

CHINESE/JAPANESE

Seven Seas   12/20 (MD)
Taipei Tokyo
  Café #2   12/20 (MD)

CHINESE/KOREAN

Joe's Noodle House 12/20 (MD)

CHINESE/MALAYSIAN

Mandarin Inn   12/20 (VA)

CHINESE/VIETNAMESE

Mark's Duck House 12/20 (VA)

CONTEMPORARY

Addie's   14/20 (MD)
Ardeo   14/20 (DC)
Black's Bar
  & Kitchen   14/20 (MD)
Blue Iguana   13/20 (VA)
Café on M   13/20 (DC)
Cashion's Eat Place 14/20 (DC)
Clyde's of Chevy
  Chase   13/20 (MD)
Clyde's of
  Georgetown   13/20 (DC)
Clyde's of Tysons   13/20 (VA)
Equinox   15/20 (DC)
The Inn at Brookeville
  Farms   14/20 (MD)
The Inn at Little
  Washington   19/20 (VA)
Jasmine Café   13/20 (VA)
Lansdowne Grille   14/20 (VA)
Lightfoot   14/20 (VA)
The Mark   13/20 (DC)
Market Street Bar
  & Grill   13/20 (VA)
Melrose   14/20 (DC)
Morrison-Clark
  Restaurant   13/20 (DC)
New Heights   14/20 (DC)
Nora   15/20 (DC)
Old Angler's Inn   14/20 (MD)
Olives   13/20 (DC)
The Oval Room   13/20 (DC)
Perry's   13/20 (DC)
Persimmon, An
  American Bistro 14/20 (MD)
Rupperts   14/20 (DC)
Saint Basil Brick
  Oven Grill   13/20 (VA)
Seasons   14/20 (DC)

Stella's	12/20 (VA)	Saveur Restaurant	14/20 (DC)
Tahoga	13/20 (DC)	Sen5es Bakery	
Tuscarora Mill	13/20 (VA)	& Restaurant	13/20 (DC)

CONTINENTAL
Marcel's 16/20 (DC)

CUBAN
Cuban Corner 13/20 (MD)

DIM SUM
Hunan Number One 12/20 (VA)
Mark's Duck House 12/20 (VA)
Oriental East 12/20 (MD)

EGYPTIAN/MIDDLE EASTERN
Pasha Café 13/20 (VA)

ETHIOPIAN
Entotto 14/20 (DC)
Meskerem Ethiopian 12/20 (DC)
Zed's Ethiopian Restaurant 12/20 (DC)

FRENCH
Bistro Bis 13/20 (DC)
Bistro Français 13/20 (DC)
Bistro 123 14/20 (VA)
Bistrot du Coin 13/20 (DC)
Bistrot Lepic 14/20 (DC)
Brasserie Les Halles 13/20 (DC)
Café La Ruche 11/20 (DC)
Café Montmartre 12/20 (VA)
Café Parisien Express 12/20 (VA)
Chez Marc 15/20 (VA)
Eiffel Tower Café 12/20 (VA)
Gérard's Place 16/20 (DC)
Jean-Michel Restaurant 12/20 (MD)
La Bergerie 14/20 (VA)
La Chaumière 13/20 (DC)
La Colline 15/20 (DC)
La Côte d'Or Café 14/20 (VA)
La Provence 14/20 (VA)
L'Auberge Chez François 14/20 (VA)
Lavandou Restaurant 13/20 (DC)
Le Canard 11/20 (VA)
Le Gaulois 13/20 (VA)
Le Jardin 14/20 (DC)
Le Petit Mistral 12/20 (VA)
Le Relais Restaurant & Bar à Vin 14/20 (VA)
Mes Amis Restaurant 13/20 (DC)
Michel Richard Citronelle 19/20 (DC)
Petits Plats 13/20 (DC)

FRENCH/MEDITERRANEAN
Café Midi Cuisine 12/20 (DC)
Café Soleil 12/20 (DC)
Matisse Café Restaurant 14/20 (DC)

FUSION
Jockey Club 11/20 (DC)

GERMAN
Old Europe 12/20 (DC)
Wurzburg Haus Restaurant 13/20 (MD)

GERMAN/ITALIAN/ASIAN
Euro Bistro 11/20 (VA)

GREEK
Aegean Taverna Restaurant 12/20 (VA)
The Greek Taverna 12/20 (VA)
Mykonos Grill 12/20 (MD)
Zorba's Café 12/20 (DC)

INDIAN
Aditi 13/20 (DC)
Bombay Bistro 14/20 (VA, MD)
Bombay Club 14/20 (DC)
Bombay Gaylord 11/20 (MD)
Bombay Palace 13/20 (DC)
Bombay Tandoor 14/20 (VA)
Café Taj 13/20 (VA)
Delhi Dhaba 12/20 (MD)
Haandi 12/20 (VA, MD)
Heritage India 15/20 (DC)
India Bistro 12/20 (MD)
Madras Palace 12/20 (MD)
Minerva Indian Cuisine 12/20 (VA)
Tiffin, The Indian Kitchen 13/20 (MD)
Udupi Palace 13/20 (MD)
The White Tiger 12/20 (DC)
The White Tiger 11/20 (VA)

INDONESIAN
Sabang 13/20 (MD)

IRISH
Fadó Irish Pub 12/20 (DC)

IRISH/AMERICAN
Pat Troy's Restaurant & Pub 12/20 (VA)

ITALIAN
Al Tiramisu 13/20 (DC)
Alpine Restaurant 12/20 (VA)
Aranella Grill 14/20 (DC)

Argia's 13/20 (VA)
Barolo Ristorante 13/20 (DC)
Bella Luna 11/20 (VA)
Café Europa 12/20 (MD)
Café Milano 13/20 (DC)
Café Mileto 12/20 (MD)
Centro Italian Grill 13/20 (MD)
Cesco Trattoria 14/20 (MD)
Etrusco Trattoria 14/20 (DC)
Faccia Luna
  Trattoria 12/20 (DC, VA)
Famous Luigi's 12/20 (DC)
Galileo 17/20 (DC)
I Matti 13/20 (DC)
I Ricchi 14/20 (DC)
Il Pinito Trattoria 12/20 (DC)
Il Radicchio 12/20 (DC, VA)
Luciano Italian Restaurant
  & Pizzeria 12/20 (VA)
Luigino 12/20 (DC)
Maestro 14/20 (VA)
Maggiano's
  Little Italy 13/20 (VA)
Mamma Lucia 12/20 (MD)
Obelisk 15/20 (DC)
Osteria Goldoni 14/20 (DC)
Paolo's 12/20 (DC, VA)
Pinto & Mazzilli 12/20 (MD)
Primi Piatti
  Ristorante 14/20 (DC, VA)
Pulcinella Ristorante 13/20 (VA)
Red Tomato 14/20 (DC)
Ristorante Bonaroti 12/20 (VA)
Ristorante Geranio 14/20 (VA)
Ristorante Il Borgo 14/20 (VA)
Ristorante Il Cigno 12/20 (VA)
Romano's
  Macaroni Grill 12/20 (VA)
San Marzano 12/20 (DC)
Sesto Senso 13/20 (DC)
Teatro Goldoni 14/20 (DC)
That's Amore 12/20 (VA, MD)
Timpano Italian
  Chophouse 13/20 (MD)
The Vigorelli 14/20 (DC)
Vivo! Ristorante 12/20 (DC)
Zeffirelli 12/20 (VA)

ITALIAN/AUSTRIAN
Café Monti 12/20 (VA)

ITALIAN/PORTUGUESE
Carmello's & Little
  Portugal 12/20 (VA)

JAMAICAN
Bamboo Joint Café 13/20 (DC)

JAPANESE
Hama Sushi & Grill Japanese
  Restaurant 12/20 (VA)
Japan Inn
  Restaurant 13/20 (DC)

Kaz Sushi Bistro 14/20 (DC)
Konami Japanese
  Restaurant 12/20 (VA)
Makoto Restaurant 16/20 (DC)
Matuba 13/20 (VA, MD)
Sushi-Ko 15/20 (DC)
Sushi-Zen Japanese
  Restaurant 12/20 (VA)
Tachibana 14/20 (VA)
Tako Grill 13/20 (MD)
Temari Japanese
  Café 12/20 (MD)
Yama Japanese
  Restaurant 12/20 (VA)

JAPANESE/AMERICAN
Zuki Moon 13/20 (DC)

KOREAN/JAPANESE
Sam Woo 13/20 (MD)

LATIN AMERICAN
Café Atlántico 14/20 (DC)
Rio Bravo 12/20 (VA)

LATIN AMERICAN/CARIBBEAN
Café Citron 11/20 (DC)
Lauriol Plaza 13/20 (DC)

LEBANESE
Bacchus 13/20 (DC, MD)
Lebanese
  Taverna 12/20 (DC, VA)
Sahara Grill 11/20 (VA)

MALAYSIAN
Malaysia Kopitiam 12/20 (DC)

MEDITERRANEAN
Bambulé 13/20 (DC)
Bistro Med 11/20 (DC)
Café Ole 13/20 (DC)
Iron Gate Inn
  Restaurant 13/20 (DC)
Mezza 9 13/20 (VA)
Neyla 14/20 (DC)
Palomino 13/20 (DC)
Rosemary's Thyme
  Bistro 12/20 (VA)
Tel-Aviv Café 13/20 (MD)

MEDITERRANEAN/AMERICAN
Marie's Restaurant 12/20 (VA)

MEXICAN/SALVADORAN
Acajutla 12/20 (MD)
Los Chorros
  Restaurant 12/20 (MD)
Mexicali Blues 12/20 (VA)

MEXICAN/TEX-MEX
Gringada Mexican
  Restaurant 11/20 (M'

MIDDLE EASTERN
Layalina 11/20 (VA)
Mama Ayesha's 12/20 (DC)

MIDDLE EASTERN/TURKISH
Levante's 12/20 (DC, MD)

MOROCCAN
A Taste of
  Casablanca 13/20 (VA)
Marrakesh 13/20 (DC)

PACIFIC RIM/ASIAN
Pacific 12/20 (VA)

PAKISTANI/INDIAN
Food Factory 12/20 (VA)

PAN-ASIAN
Asia Nora 15/20 (DC)
Big Bowl 14/20 (VA)
Café Asia 12/20 (DC, VA)
FlatTop Grill 13/20 (VA)
Spices 13/20 (DC)
TenPenh 15/20 (DC)
Wok Inn 12/20 (MD)

PERSIAN
Café Rose 12/20 (VA)
Caravan Grill 12/20 (DC)
Caspian Café 13/20 (MD)
Nayeb Kabob
  Restaurant 12/20 (VA)
Pars Famous House
  of Kabob 12/20 (VA)
Shamshiry 12/20 (VA)

PERUVIAN
Costa Verde
  Restaurant 11/20 (VA)
Mi Peru
  Restaurante 12/20 (MD)
The Nibbler 12/20 (MD)

PHILIPPINE
Manila Café 12/20 (VA)

RUSSIAN/FRENCH
The Serbian Crown
  Restaurant 12/20 (VA)

SEAFOOD
Blue Point Grill 13/20 (VA)
Crisfield Seafood
  Restaurant 13/20 (MD)
Hogate's 12/20 (DC)
Johnny's Half
  Shell 13/20 (DC)
Kinkead's 15/20 (DC)
Legal Sea Foods 13/20 (DC, VA)
McCormick
  & Schmick's 13/20 (DC, VA)
New Fortune Chinese Seafood
  Restaurant 12/20 (MD)

The Oceanaire Seafood
  Room 14/20 (DC)
Pesce 14/20 (DC)
Phillips Flagship Seafood
  Restaurant 12/20 (DC)
Phillips Seafood
  Grill 12/20 (VA)
Potowmack Landing
  Restaurant 12/20 (VA)
Sea Catch Restaurant
  & Raw Bar 14/20 (DC)
Tony & Joe's Seafood 12/20 (DC)

SOUTHERN
B. Smith's 13/20 (DC)
Copeland's of New
  Orleans 12/20 (VA, MD)
Flavors Soul Food 13/20 (VA)
Florida Avenue
  Grill 12/20 (DC)
Georgia Brown's 13/20 (DC)
Louisiana Express 12/20 (MD)
Okra's Louisiana
  Bistro 12/20 (VA)
Summit Station Restaurant
  & Brewery 12/20 (MD)
Timothy Dean
  Restaurant & Bar 16/20 (DC)
Vidalia 14/20 (DC)

SOUTHWESTERN
Cottonwood Café 12/20 (MD)
Red Sage 14/20 (DC)
Santa Fe East 13/20 (VA)
Silverado 11/20 (VA)
Tortilla Factory 12/20 (VA)

SPANISH
Andalucia 13/20 (MD)
Jaleo 14/20 (DC)
Taberna del
  Alabardero 14/20 (DC)
Toro Tapas & Grill 12/20 (VA)

SPANISH/LATIN AMERICAN
Gabriel 15/20 (DC)

STEAKHOUSE
Bobby Van's
  Steakhouse 13/20 (DC)
The Capital
  Grille 13/20 (DC, VA)
Fleming's Prime Steakhouse
  & Wine Bar 12/20 (VA)
J. R.'s Stockyards
  Inn 12/20 (VA)
Morton's
  of Chicago 14/20 (DC, VA)
Nick & Stef's
  Steakhouse 13/20 (DC)
Outback
  Steakhouse 11/20 (VA, MD)
Palm 13/20 (DC, VA)

The Prime Rib   13/20 (DC)
Ruth's Chris Steak
    House 14/20 (DC, VA, MD)
Sam & Harry's13/20 (DC, VA)
Shula's Steak
    House   13/20 (DC)
Smith & Wollensky14/20 (DC)
Timpano Italian
    Chophouse   13/20 (MD)

SUSHI

Hama Sushi & Grill Japanese
    Restaurant   12/20 (VA)
Kaz Sushi Bistro   14/20 (DC)
Matuba   13/20 (VA, MD)
Sushi-Zen Japanese
    Restaurant   12/20 (VA)
Tachibana   14/20 (VA)

TAPAS

Café Ole   13/20 (DC)
Toro Tapas & Grill 12/20 (VA)

TEX-MEX

Austin Grill 13/20 (DC,VA,MD)
Cactus Cantina   13/20 (DC)
Casa Gonzalez   11/20 (VA)
Don Pablo's, The Real
    Enchilada   12/20 (VA, MD)
Rio Grande
    Café   13/20 (VA, MD)
South Austin Grill 13/20 (VA)

TEX-MEX/MEXICAN

Mixtec   12/20 (DC)

TEX-MEX/SALVADORAN

El Aguila   12/20 (MD)
Mayan Grill & Bar 12/20 (VA)

THAI

The Andaman Restaurant
    & Bar   12/20 (MD)
Bangkok Garden 14/20 (MD)
Bangkok One   11/20 (DC)
Basil Thai
    Restaurant   13/20 (DC)
Bua Thai   11/20 (DC)
Busara   12/20 (DC, VA)
Chao Pra Ya   12/20 (VA)
Duangrat's   13/20 (VA)
Ghin Na Rhee
    Restaurant   11/20 (VA)
Neisha Thai Cuisine12/20 (VA)
Old Siam
    Restaurant   11/20 (MD)
Paya Thai   11/20 (VA)
Po Siam Thai
    Restaurant   11/20 (VA)
Rincome Thai
    Cuisine   12/20 (VA)
Ruan Thai   14/20 (MD)

Sakoontra Thai
    Restaurant   12/20 (VA)
Sala Thai   12/20 (DC)
Sala Thai   11/20 (VA)
Sawatdee Thai
    Restaurant   12/20 (VA)
Star of Siam   12/20 (DC)
Star Thai Cuisine 12/20 (VA)
Supee's Kitchen   11/20 (VA)
Suporn's Thai
    Restaurant   13/20 (MD)
Sweet Basil   13/20 (MD)
Tara Thai   13/20 (VA, MD)
Thai Basil   14/20 (VA)
Thai Leela   11/20 (VA)
Thai Luang   12/20 (VA)
Thai Noy
    Restaurant   12/20 (VA)
Thai Old Town   11/20 (VA)
Thai Pilin   11/20 (VA)
Thai Room   12/20 (DC)
T.H.A.I. in
    Shirlington   12/20 (VA)
Thai Square
    Restaurant   13/20 (VA)
Thai Town   12/20 (DC)
Thaiphoon   12/20 (DC)

TURKISH

Anatolia
    Turkish Café   12/20 (DC)
Kazan Restaurant 12/20 (VA)
Nizam's   11/20 (VA)

VEGETARIAN

Madras Palace   12/20 (MD)
Udupi Palace   13/20 (MD)

VIETNAMESE

Galaxy Restaurant 11/20 (VA)
Green Papaya   13/20 (MD)
Huong Que (Four Sisters
    Restaurant)   12/20 (VA)
Huong Viet   11/20 (VA)
Little Saigon Vietnamese
    Restaurant   12/20 (VA)
Little Viet Garden 12/20 (VA)
Miss Saigon   11/20 (DC)
Nam's
    of Bethesda   13/20 (MD)
Nam-Viet Pho 79 12/20 (VA)
Pho New Saigon Vietnamese
    Restaurant Seafood
    & Grill   12/20 (MD)
Queen Bee   12/20 (VA)
Saigon Gourmet 12/20 (MD)
Saigon House Vietnamese
    Restaurant   10/20 (VA)
Taste of Saigon   11/20 (VA)
Thanh Thanh   13/20 (MD)
Viet Royale   12/20 (VA)

RESTAURANTS BY FEATURES

We've included only the best in each category.

BREAKFAST	304		OPEN LATE	306
BRUNCH	304		OPEN 24 HOURS	306
BUSINESS DINING	304		OUTDOOR DINING	306
CHEF'S TABLES	305		PLACES TO MEET FOR A DRINK	307
HOTEL DINING ROOMS	305		ROMANTIC	307
KID-FRIENDLY	305		VIEW	308
LIGHT & HEALTHY DINING	306		GREAT WINE LIST	308
LIVE MUSIC/ ENTERTAINMENT	306			

BREAKFAST

The Bistro	13/20 (DC)
Café Parisien Express	12/20 (VA)
Clyde's of Tysons	13/20 (VA)
Corkie's Grill	12/20 (VA)
Elysium	13/20 (VA)
Florida Avenue Grill	12/20 (DC)
Gabriel	15/20 (DC)
Jockey Club	11/20 (DC)
La Colline	15/20 (DC)
Melrose	14/20 (DC)
Morrison-Clark Restaurant	13/20 (DC)
Old Ebbitt Grill	13/20 (DC)
The Original Pancake House	QB (MD)
Reeves Restaurant & Bakery	QB (DC)
Seasons	14/20 (DC)
Seibel's Restaurant	12/20 (MD)
Sholl's Colonial Cafeteria	12/20 (DC)
Tabard Inn	14/20 (DC)
Timothy Dean Restaurant & Bar	16/20 (DC)
The Willard Room	12/20 (DC)

BRUNCH

Ardeo	14/20 (DC)
Austin Grill	13/20 (DC, VA, MD)
B. Smith's	13/20 (DC)
Bistro Français	13/20 (DC)
Black Coffee Bistro	14/20 (VA)
Blue Iguana	13/20 (VA)
Bombay Club	14/20 (DC)
Cactus Cantina	13/20 (DC)
Café Deluxe	13/20 (DC, MD)
Café Mileto	12/20 (MD)
Carlyle Grand Café	13/20 (VA)
Cashion's Eat Place	14/20 (DC)
Chef Geoff's	12/20 (DC)
Clyde's of Tysons	13/20 (VA)
Comus Inn	12/20 (MD)
Copeland's of New Orleans	12/20 (VA, MD)
Cottonwood Café	12/20 (MD)
Georgia Brown's	13/20 (DC)
Grill from Ipanema	12/20 (DC)
Lauriol Plaza	13/20 (DC)
Le Relais Restaurant & Bar à Vin	14/20 (VA)
Market Street Bar & Grill	13/20 (VA)
Rhodeside Grill	13/20 (VA)
Saveur Restaurant	14/20 (DC)
Sequoia	10/20 (DC)
Stella's	12/20 (VA)
Tabard Inn	14/20 (DC)
Timpano Italian Chophouse	13/20 (MD)
Turning Point Inn	13/20 (MD)
Two Quail	13/20 (DC)

BUSINESS DINING

Barolo Ristorante	13/20 (DC)
Butterfield 9	14/20 (DC)
Café Atlántico	14/20 (DC)
The Capital Grille	13/20 (DC, VA)

The Caucus Room 15/20 (DC)
Christopher Marks 13/20 (DC)
District ChopHouse
& Brewery 12/20 (DC)
eciti Café & Bar 14/20 (VA)
Equinox 15/20 (DC)
Galileo 17/20 (DC)
Kinkead's 15/20 (DC)
La Colline 15/20 (DC)
Lafayette 14/20 (DC)
The Mark 13/20 (DC)
Market Street Bar
& Grill 13/20 (VA)
Mezza 9 13/20 (VA)
Michel Richard
Citronelle 19/20 (DC)
The Monocle 12/20 (DC)
Morton's
of Chicago 14/20 (DC, VA)
Nora 15/20 (DC)
The Oceanaire
Seafood Room 14/20 (DC)
Old Ebbitt Grill 13/20 (DC)
Osteria Goldoni 14/20 (DC)
The Oval Room 13/20 (DC)
Palm 13/20 (VA)
Palomino 13/20 (DC)
Primi Piatti
Ristorante 14/20 (DC, VA)
Sam & Harry's 13/20 (DC, VA)
701 Pennsylvania Avenue
Restaurant & Bar 14/20 (DC)
1789 Restaurant 16/20 (DC)
Smith & Wollensky 14/20 (DC)
Timothy Dean Restaurant
& Bar 16/20 (DC)
Two Quail 13/20 (DC)
West 24 14/20 (DC)
The Willard
Room 12/20 (DC)

CHEF'S TABLES
Galileo 17/20 (DC)
Maestro 14/20 (VA)
Matisse Café
Restaurant 14/20 (DC)
Michel Richard
Citronelle 19/20 (DC)
Roof Terrace
Restaurant 12/20 (DC)
Teatro Goldoni 14/20 (DC)

HOTEL DINING ROOMS

Cherry Blossom TraveLodge
Rincome Thai Cuisine 12/20 (VA)
Four Points Hotel
Corduroy 14/20 (DC)
Four Seasons Hotel
Seasons 14/20 (DC)

George Washington University Inn
Zuki Moon 13/20 (DC)
The Georgetown Inn
Daily Grill 12/20 (DC)
Hay-Adams Hotel
Lafayette 14/20 (DC)
Hotel George
Bistro Bis 13/20 (DC)
Hyatt Arlington
Mezza 9 13/20 (VA)
Hyatt Regency
Market Street Bar
& Grill 13/20 (VA)
Lansdowne Resort
Lansdowne Grille 14/20 (VA)
Latham Hotel
Michel Richard
Citronelle 19/20 (DC)
The Monarch Hotel
The Bistro 13/20 (DC)
Morrison House Hotel
Elysium 13/20 (VA)
Morrison-Clark Inn
Morrison-Clark
Restaurant 13/20 (DC)
Park Hyatt Washington
Melrose 14/20 (DC)
*Radisson-Barcelo
Washington Hotel*
Gabriel 15/20 (DC)
The Ritz-Carlton, Tysons Corner
Maestro 14/20 (VA)
St. Gregory Hotel
Donna's QB (DC)
St. Regis Washington
Timothy Dean Restaurant
& Bar 16/20 (DC)
Stratford Motor Lodge
Café Rose 12/20 (VA)
Tabard Inn
Tabard Inn 14/20 (DC)
The Westin Fairfax
Jockey Club 11/20 (DC)
Westin Grand Hotel
Café on M 13/20 (DC)
*Willard Inter-Continental
Washington*
The Willard Room 12/20 (DC)
Wyndham City Center Hotel
Shula's Steak
House 13/20 (DC)

KID-FRIENDLY
Bamboo Buffet QB (MD)
Bistrot du Coin 13/20 (DC)
Blue Iguana 13/20 (VA)
Brasserie Les Halles 13/20 (DC)
Bubba's Bar-B-Q QB (VA)
The Burro QB (DC)
Cactus Cantina 13/20 (DC)

Café Deluxe   13/20 (MD)
Café Roval   13/20 (MD)
California Pizza
  Kitchen   QB (DC, VA, MD)
Carlyle Grand Café 13/20 (VA)
Casa Gonzalez   11/20 (VA)
The Cheesecake
  Factory   13/20 (DC, MD)
Chevys Fresh
  Mex   QB (VA, MD)
Chipotle Mexican
  Grill   QB (MD)
The Cincinnati Café 12/20 (VA)
The Diner   12/20 (DC)
ESPN Zone   QB (DC)
Fleming's Prime Steakhouse
  & Wine Bar   12/20 (VA)
Fuddruckers   QB (VA, MD)
Giffords Ice Cream
  Company   QB (MD)
Hamburger
  Hamlet   12/20 (VA, MD)
Hard Times Café QB (VA, MD)
Jasmine Café   13/20 (VA)
Krupin's   QB (DC)
Ledo Pizza   QB (VA, MD)
Lost Dog Café   QB (VA)
Luciano Italian Restaurant
  & Pizzeria   12/20 (VA)
Metro 29 Diner   QB (VA)
Mike's American
  Grill   13/20 (VA)
Old Ebbitt Grill   13/20 (DC)
The Original Pancake
  House   QB (MD)
Temari Japanese
  Café   12/20 (MD)
Tortilla Factory   12/20 (VA)

LIGHT & HEALTHY DINING

Amma Indian Vegetarian
  Kitchen   QB (DC)
Madras Palace   12/20 (MD)
Mark's Kitchen   12/20 (MD)
Seasons   14/20 (DC)
Seibel's
  Restaurant   12/20 (MD)
Silver Diner   QB (VA, MD)
Sunflower Vegetarian
  Restaurant   QB (VA)
Thyme Square   11/20 (MD)
The Vegetable
  Garden   QB (MD)
Udupi Palace   13/20 (MD)
Woodlands   QB (MD)

LIVE MUSIC/ENTERTAINMENT

Aegean Taverna
  Restaurant   12/20 (VA)

Alpine Restaurant12/20 (VA)
Coco Loco   12/20 (DC)
eciti Café & Bar   14/20 (VA)
ESPN Zone   QB (DC)
The Ice House
  Café   12/20 (VA)
Inn at Glen Echo 13/20 (MD)
The Islander Caribbean
  Restaurant & Bar 14/20 (DC)
Marrakesh   13/20 (DC)
Pat Troy's Restaurant
  & Pub   12/20 (VA)
Pulcinella
  Ristorante   13/20 (VA)

OPEN LATE

American City Diner
  of Washington   QB (DC)
Amphora RestaurantQB (VA)
Bistro Français   13/20 (DC)
Bistrot du Coin   13/20 (DC)
Bob & Edith's   QB (VA)
Brasserie
  Les Halles   13/20 (DC)
eciti Café & Bar   14/20 (VA)
Clyde's
  of Georgetown 13/20 (DC)
Coco Loco   12/20 (DC)
The Old Brogue, an
  Irish Pub   QB (VA)
Old Glory All-American
  Bar-B-Que   QB (DC)
Paolo's   12/20 (DC, VA)
Pat Troy's Restaurant
  & Pub   12/20 (VA)
Rock Bottom
  Brewery   QB (MD)
Smith & Wollensky 14/20 (DC)

OPEN 24 HOURS

Amphora Restaurant QB (VA)
The Diner   12/20 (DC)
Krispy Kreme
  Doughnuts   QB (VA)
Mike's Diner
  & Lounge   QB (VA)
Tastee Diner   QB (MD)
29 Diner   QB (VA)

OUTDOOR DINING

Addie's   14/20 (MD)
Aranella Grill   14/20 (DC)
Brasserie Les Halles13/20 (DC)
Bua Thai   11/20 (DC)
Cactus Cantina   13/20 (DC)

Café Ole	13/20	(DC)
Cashion's Eat Place	14/20	(DC)
CF Folks	13/20	(DC)
Chef Geoff's	12/20	(DC)
Clyde's of Tysons	13/20	(VA)
Delhi Dhaba	12/20	(MD)
FlatTop Grill	13/20	(VA)
Hermitage Inn	14/20	(VA)
Iron Gate Inn		
Restaurant	13/20	(DC)
The Italian Store	QB	(VA)
Jasmine Café	13/20	(DC)
Lauriol Plaza	13/20	(DC)
Levante's	12/20	(DC)
Little Viet Garden	12/20	(VA)
Marcel's	16/20	(DC)
Melrose	14/20	(DC)
Neyla	14/20	(DC)
Old Angler's Inn	14/20	(MD)
Perry's	13/20	(DC)
Ristorante Il Cigno	12/20	(VA)
Sea Catch Restaurant		
& Raw Bar	14/20	(DC)
Sequoia	10/20	(DC)
Stella's	12/20	(VA)
Tabard Inn	14/20	(DC)
Tel-Aviv Café	13/20	(MD)
Tony & Joe's		
Seafood	12/20	(DC)
Zorba's Café	12/20	(DC)

PLACES TO MEET FOR A DRINK

The Andaman Restaurant		
& Bar	12/20	(MD)
Ardeo	14/20	(DC)
Austin		
Grill	13/20	(DC, VA, MD)
B. Smith's	13/20	(DC)
The Bistro	13/20	(DC)
Bistro Français	13/20	(DC)
Bistrot du Coin	13/20	(DC)
Black's Bar		
& Kitchen	14/20	(MD)
Blackie's	15/20	(DC)
Blue Iguana	13/20	(VA)
Bobby Van's		
Steakhouse	13/20	(DC)
Bombay Tandoor	14/20	(VA)
Bullfeathers of		
Capitol Hill	QB	(DC)
Butterfield 9	14/20	(DC)
Cactus Cantina	13/20	(DC)
Café Asia	12/20	(VA)
Café Atlántico	14/20	(DC)
Café Roval	13/20	(MD)
The Capital		
Grille	13/20	(DC, VA)
Capitol City		
Brewing Co.	QB	(VA)
The Caucus Room	15/20	(DC)
Centro Italian Grill	13/20	(MD)

Chadwicks	QB	(DC)
Christopher Marks	13/20	(DC)
Clyde's of		
Georgetown	13/20	(DC)
Coco Loco	12/20	(DC)
DC Coast	14/20	(DC)
District ChopHouse		
& Brewery	12/20	(DC)
eciti Café & Bar	14/20	(VA)
ESPN Zone	QB	(DC)
Fairmont Bar		
& Dining	13/20	(MD)
Gabriel	15/20	(DC)
Grapeseed	13/20	(MD)
Grill from Ipanema	12/20	(DC)
Hawk 'n' Dove	QB	(DC)
Inn at Glen Echo	13/20	(MD)
J Paul's	QB	(DC)
Johnny's Half Shell	13/20	(DC)
Lauriol Plaza	13/20	(DC)
Marcel's	16/20	(DC)
Mendocino Grille		
& Wine Bar	12/20	(DC)
The Old Brogue, an		
Irish Pub	QB	(VA)
Old Ebbitt Grill	13/20	(DC)
Palm	13/20	(DC, VA)
Palomino	13/20	(DC)
Peacock Café	13/20	(DC)
Rock Bottom Brewery	QB	(MD)
Sea Catch Restaurant		
& Raw Bar	14/20	(DC)
South Austin Grill	13/20	(VA)
Tony & Joe's		
Seafood	12/20	(DC)
Union Street Public		
House	12/20	(VA)
West 24	14/20	(DC)
Willie & Reed's	QB	(MD)

ROMANTIC SETTING

Al Tiramisu	13/20	(DC)
Alpine Restaurant	12/20	(VA)
Andalucia	13/20	(MD)
Bistro 123	14/20	(VA)
Black Coffee Bistro	14/20	(VA)
Bombay Tandoor	14/20	(VA)
Butterfield 9	14/20	(DC)
Chez Marc	15/20	(VA)
Ching Ching Cha, a Chinese		
Tea House	QB	(DC)
Clyde's of Tysons	13/20	(VA)
Elysium	13/20	(VA)
Etrusco Trattoria	14/20	(DC)
Heritage India	15/20	(DC)
Hermitage Inn	14/20	(VA)
Inn at Glen Echo	13/20	(MD)
Inn at Little		
Washington	19/20	(VA)
Iron Gate Inn		
Restaurant	13/20	(DC)
Jasmine Café	13/20	(VA)

Lafayette 14/20 (DC)
Lansdowne Grille 14/20 (VA)
L'Auberge Chez
   François 14/20 (VA)
Lightfoot 14/20 (VA)
Maestro 14/20 (VA)
Marrakesh 13/20 (DC)
Matisse Café
   Restaurant 14/20 (DC)
Melrose 13/20 (DC)
Mes Amis Restaurant 13/20 (DC)
Michel Richard
   Citronelle 19/20 (DC)
Morrison-Clark
   Restaurant 13/20 (DC)
Neyla 14/20 (DC)
Nora 15/20 (DC)
Old Angler's Inn 14/20 (MD)
Osteria Goldoni 14/20 (DC)
Palena 15/20 (DC)
Ristorante Il Borgo 14/20 (VA)
Rupperts 14/20 (DC)
Sea Catch Restaurant
   & Raw Bar 14/20 (DC)
Seasons 14/20 (DC)
Sen5es Bakery
   & Restaurant 13/20 (DC)
The Serbian Crown
   Restaurant 12/20 (VA)
1789 Restaurant 16/20 (DC)
Taberna del
   Alabardero 14/20 (DC)
Teatro Goldoni 14/20 (DC)
TenPenh 15/20 (DC)
Timothy Dean Restaurant
   & Bar 16/20 (DC)
Turning Point Inn 13/20 (MD)
Tuscarora Mill 13/20 (VA)
Two Quail 13/20 (DC)
Vidalia 14/20 (DC)
Yanÿu 16/20 (DC)

Paolo's 12/20 (VA)
Perry's 13/20 (DC)
Phillips Flagship Seafood
   Restaurant 12/20 (DC)
Potowmack
   Landing 12/20 (VA)
Sea Catch Restaurant
   & Raw Bar 14/20 (DC)
Sequoia 10/20 (DC)
Tony & Joe's
   Seafood 12/20 (DC)
Turning Point Inn 13/20 (MD)

GREAT WINE LIST

Al Tiramisu 13/20 (DC)
Ardeo 14/20 (DC)
Barolo Ristorante 13/20 (DC)
Bistro Bis 13/20 (DC)
Bistro 123 14/20 (VA)
Bobby Van's
   Steakhouse 13/20 (DC)
Butterfield 9 14/20 (DC)
The Capital
   Grille 13/20 (DC, VA)
The Caucus Room 15/20 (DC)
Cesco Trattoria 14/20 (MD)
DC Coast 14/20 (DC)
eciti Café & Bar 14/20 (VA)
Equinox 15/20 (DC)
Etrusco Trattoria 14/20 (DC)
Galileo 17/20 (DC)
Gérard's Place 16/20 (DC)
Grapeseed 13/20 (MD)
I Matti 13/20 (DC)
I Ricchi 14/20 (DC)
The Inn at Brookeville
   Farms 14/20 (MD)
The Inn at Little
   Washington 19/20 (VA)
Lafayette 14/20 (DC)
Lansdowne Grille 14/20 (VA)
L'Auberge Chez
   François 14/20 (VA)
Le Relais Restaurant
   & Bar à Vin 14/20 (VA)
Lightfoot 14/20 (VA)
Matisse Café
   Restaurant 14/20 (DC)
Melrose 14/20 (DC)
Michel Richard
   Citronelle 19/20 (DC)
Nora 15/20 (DC)
Old Angler's Inn 14/20 (MD)
Osteria Goldoni 14/20 (DC)
Persimmon, An
   American Bistro 14/20 (MD)
Seasons 14/20 (DC)
1789 Restaurant 16/20 (DC)
Taberna del
   Alabardero 14/20 (DC)
Vidalia 14/20 (DC)

VIEW

Aegean Taverna
   Restaurant 12/20 (VA)
Aranella Grill 14/20 (DC)
Black Coffee Bistro 14/20 (VA)
Café Montmartre 12/20 (VA)
Café Ole 13/20 (DC)
Comus Inn 12/20 (MD)
Hermitage Inn 14/20 (VA)
Hogate's 12/20 (DC)
The Inn at Brookeville
   Farms 14/20 (MD)
Inn at Glen Echo 13/20 (MD)
The Inn at Little
   Washington 19/20 (VA)
Jasmine Café 13/20 (VA)
Lafayette 14/20 (DC)
Lakeside Inn 12/20 (VA)
Lansdowne Grille 14/20 (VA)
Maestro 14/20 (VA)
Marie's Restaurant 12/20 (VA)
Old Angler's Inn 14/20 (MD)

Index

A

Acajutla, 204
ACQUA PANNA, 286
Adams Morgan Community
    Festival, The, 293
Addie's, 204
Addisu Gebeya, 97
Aditi, 18
Aegean Taverna Restaurant, 107
Afton Mountain Vineyards, 267
A & J Restaurant, 244
a.k.a. Friscos, 89
ake Anne Coffee House, 163
A. Litteri, 98
Al Tiramisu, 18
Alexandria Pastry Shop
    & Café, 165
Alpine Restaurant, 107
American Center Office Park
    RESTAURANT, 144
American City Diner
    of Washington, 81
Americana Market, 195, 259
Amma Indian Vegetarian
    Kitchen, 90
Amphora Restaurant, 179
Anatolia Turkish Café, 18
Andalucia, 204
Andaman Restaurant
    & Bar, The, 205
Anita's, 180
Ann MeMe's Bakery
    & Café, 175
Annual Reedville Oyster
    Roast, 294
Apsara Oriental Gourmet
    Market, 192
Aranella Grill, 19
Ardeo, 19
Argia's, 107
ARROWHEAD MOUNTAIN
    SPRING WATER, 286
Arrowine, 200
Asia Café, 244
Asia Nora, 19
Asian Foods, 252, 257
Asparagus Festival
    at Tarara, 281
Atami, 178
A Taste of Casablanca, 106
A Taste of the World, 106
Atilla's, 182
Austin Grill, 20, 107, 205

B

Autumn Hill Vineyards Blue
    Ridge Winery, 267

Bacchus, 21, 206
Bagel Café, The, 174
Baja Fresh Mexican Grill, 248, 181
Bamboo Buffet, 245
Bamboo Joint Café, 21
Bambulé, 21
Bamyan Restaurant, 108
Bangkok Garden, 206
Bangkok One, 22
Barbeque Country
    Jamboree, 167
BARBERA, 272
Barboursville Vineyards, 267
Barolo Ristorante, 22
Basignani Winery, 269
Basil Thai Restaurant, 22
Bay Lo, 184
Bell Wine Shoppe, 102
Bella Luna, 108
Ben's Chili Bowl, 81
Ben's Whole Hog Barbecue, 167
Best Buns Bread Co., 165
Big Bowl, 108
Bistro, The, 23
Bistro Bis, 23
Bistro Français, 23
Bistro Med, 24
Bistro 123, 109
Bistrot du Coin, 24
Bistrot Lepic, 24
Bizarre Bazaar's Christmas
    Collection, 294
Black's Bar & Kitchen, 206
Black Coffee Bistro, 109
Blackie's, 25
Blue Iguana, 109
Blue Point Grill, 110
Blue Ridge Winery, 267
Bo Dean's Pit B.B.Q., 168
Bob & Edith's Diner, 172
Bobby Van's Steakhouse, 25
Bombay Bistro, 110, 207
Bombay Club, 25
Bombay Gaylord, 207
Bombay Palace, 26
Bombay Tandoor, 110
Bonaroti (Ristorante), 148
Bonsai, 179
Booeymongers, 81
Boordy Vineyards, 269

Bostetter's Wine & Gourmet, 201
Bowers Fancy Dairy Products, 96
Bradley Food & Beverage, 263
Brasserie Les Halles, 26
Brazilian Market, 259
Bread & Chocolate, 84, 165, 238
Bread & Kabob, 182
Bread Line, 85
Breaux Vineyards, 268
Broadway Diner
  Restaurant, The, 235
Bruscato's, 177
B. Smith's, 20
Bua Thai, 26
Bubba's Bar-B-Q, 168
Bullfeathers of Capitol Hill, 82
Burma Restaurant, 27
Burnley Vineyards, 267
Burrito Brothers, 91
Burro, The, 91
Busara, 27, 110
Butterfield 9, 27

C

CABERNET FRANC, 272
CABERNET SAUVIGNON, 272
Cactus Cantina, 28
Café Asia, 28, 111
Café Atlántico, 28
Café Citron, 29
Café Deluxe, 29, 207
Café Europa, 208
Café La Ruche, 29
Café on M, 30
Café Midi Cuisine, 30
Café Milano, 30
Café Mileto, 208
Café Monti, 111
Café Montmartre, 111
Café Ole, 31
Café Parisien Express, 111
Café Rose, 112
Café Roval, 208
Café Soleil, 31
Café Taj, 112
California Pizza
  Kitchen, 93, 188, 254
California Tortilla, 249
CALISTOGA, 286
Calvert Woodley, 102
Cameron's Seafood Market, 261
Cannon's Seafood, 99, 197
Capital Grille, The, 31, 112
Capital Pride Festival, 282
Capital Q, 86
Capitol City Brewing Co., 171
Caravan Grill, 32
Caribbean Café, 242
Caribbean Delight, 243
Caribbean Feast Restaurant
  & Catering, 243
Caribbean Grill, 176
Caribbean Market, 260
Caribbean Palace, 243
Carlyle Grand Café, 113

Carmello's & Little Portugal, 113
Casa Gonzalez, 113
Casa Pena, 98
Cashion's Eat Place, 32
Caspian Café, 209
CATAWBA, 272
Catoctin Vineyards, 269
Caucus Room, The, 32
Ceciles Finewine.com, 201
Celebration at Opera House
  Gourmet, 281
Celebration of Wine & Food
  at Williamsburg, 281
Celebrity Delly, 174
Cenan's Bakery, 165, 190
Centro Italian Grill, 209
Cesco Trattoria, 209
CF Folks, 33
Chadwicks, 82
CHAMBOURCIN, 272
Chantilly Park, 156
Chao Pra Ya, 114
Charcoal Kebab, 175
CHARDONNAY, 274
Charlie's Open Pit
  Barbecue, 238
Château Morrisette Winery, 268
Cheesecake Factory,
  The, 33, 210
Chef Geoff's, 33
Chermont Winery, 267
Cherry Blossom TraveLodge
  RESTAURANT, 147
Chesapeake Bagel Bakery, 174
Chesapeake Bay Wine Classic
  Grand Tasting, 281
Chevy Chase Wine & Spirits, 103
Chevys Fresh Mex, 181, 249
Chez Marc, 114
Chicken Out
  Rotisserie, 82, 162, 235
Chicken Place, The, 252
China Boy, 90
China Canteen, 210
China Chef, 210
China Garden, 114
Ching Ching Cha, a Chinese
  Tea House, 88
Chipotle Mexican Grill, 249
Chocolate Chocolate, 95
Christopher Marks, 34
Chrysalis Vineyards, 268
Cincinnati Café, The, 115
City Lights of China, 34
Classic Wines
  of Great Falls, 201
Clyde's of Chevy Chase, 210
Clyde's of Georgetown, 34
Clyde's of Tysons, 115
Coco Loco, 35
Comus Inn, 211
CONCORD, 272
Confucius Café, 35
Congressional Plaza
  RESTAURANTS, 248, 251

Congressional Plaza SHOP, 259
Cooper Vineyards, 267
Copeland's
  of New Orleans, 115, 211
Corduroy, 35
Corkie's Grill, 116
Corner Bakery, 85, 166, 238
Costa Verde Restaurant, 116
Cottonwood Café, 212
Courtyard by Marriott
  RESTAURANTS, 41, 119
Creative Cakes, 256
Crisfield Seafood
  Restaurant, 212
Crisp & Juicy, 168, 239
CRYSTAL GEYSER, 286
Cuban Corner, 212

D

Da Hua Market, 97
Daily Grill, 36
Daily Planet, 201
Dana Bazaar, 259
Daruma, 258
DC Coast, 36
De Fluri's Fine Chocolates, 192
Dean & DeLuca, 99
Dean, Timothy, 75
Deer Meadow Vineyard, 268
Delhi Dhaba, 212
Diner, The, 36
District ChopHouse
  & Brewery, 37
Dixie Bones, 168
Dixie Pig, 169
Dominion Wine Cellars, 267
Don Pablo's, The Real
  Enchilada, 116, 213
Dong y China Herbs, 193
Donna's, 87
Donna, Roberto, 40
DRESS CODE, 9
Duangrat's, 117
- Oriental Food Mart, 193
Dye's Vineyards, 268

E

Eastern Empire
  Buffet-Restaurant, 245
eatZi's Market
  & Bakery, 235, 261
eciti Café & Bar, 117
Eden Supermarket, 193
Eiffel Tower Café, 117
Einstein Bros Bagels, 89, 175, 241
Eko Food Market, 257
El Mexicano, 250
El Pollo Rey, 169
El Pollo Rico, 169
El Sabor Latino, 181
Elk Run Vineyards, 269
Elysium, 118
Emilio's Brick Oven Pizza, 188
Entotto, 37
Equinox, 37
ESPN Zone, 82

Etrusco Trattoria, 38
Euro Bistro, 118
European Market, 260
EVIAN, 287

F

Faccia Luna Trattoria, 38, 118
Fadó Irish Pub, 38
Fairmont Bar & Dining, 213
Fairfax Chocolate Lover's
  Festival, 281
Famous Luigi's, 39
Farfelu Vineyard, 268
Farmers Markets, 98, 197, 260
Fast Fettoosh, 92
Federal Plaza
  RESTAURANT, 220
Fern Street Gourmet, 202
FIJI NATURAL ARTESIAN
  WATER, 287
Fine Art of Cuisine, 293
Fiore Winery, 269
Firehook Bakery & Coffee
  House, 85, 95, 166
Flatbreads Food Shop, 162
FlatTop Grill, 119
Flavors Soul Food, 119
Fleming's Prime Steakhouse
  & Wine Bar, 119
Florida Avenue Grill, 39
FOOD
- EVENTS, 281
- TIPS, 281
- & WINE PAIRINGS, 277
Food Factory, 120
Food & Wine Spectacular
  at the Homestead, 281
Fortune Garden, 251
Fortune of Reston Chinese
  Seafood Restaurant, 120
Fortune of Seven Corners, 120
Four Points Hotel
  RESTAURANT, 35
Four Seasons, 172
Four Seasons Hotel
  RESTAURANT, 68
Fredericksburg Annual Wine
  Festival, 294
Fresh Fields, 100, 198, 262
Friscos (a.k.a.), 89
Fuddruckers, 162, 236
Full Kee Restaurant, 39
Full Key Restaurant, 214

G

Gabriel, 39
Galaxy Restaurant, 121
Galileo, 40
Garlic Festival, 294
George Washington's
  Birthday Party, 281
George Washington
  University Inn
  RESTAURANT, 80
Georgetown Bagelry, 89
Georgetown Inn, The
  RESTAURANT, 36

Georgetown Square
  Wine Shop, 264
Georgia Brown's, 40
Gérard Pangaud, 41
Gérard's Place, 41
German Deli, 98
German Gourmet, 195
Geranio (Ristorante), 148
GEWURZTRAMINER, 274
Ghin Na Rhee Restaurant, 121
Giant Gourmet Someplace
  Special, 192, 198
Gifford's Ice Cream
  Company, 254
Good Fortune, 214
Gordon Biersch Brewery
  Restaurant, 41
Grace's Pastries, 190
Grape Finds, 103
Grapeseed, 214
Gray Ghost Vineyards, 268
Grayhaven Winery, 267
Great Harvest Bread Co., 190, 256
Greek Taverna, The, 121
Green Field Churrascaria, 215
Green Papaya, 215
Greenberry's Coffee
  & Tea Company, 192
Grill from Ipanema, 41
Gringada Mexican
  Restaurant, 215
Guilford Ridge Vineyard, 268

H

Haandi, 121, 216
Hall of States, 47
Hama Sushi & Grill Japanese
  Restaurant, 122
Hamburger Hamlet, 122, 216
Han Ah Reum, 193, 258
Hard Times Café, 163, 236
Harris Teeter, 198
Hartwood Winery, 268
HAWAII SPRINGS
  NATURAL WATER, 287
Hawk 'n' Dove, 83
Hay-Adams Hotel, The
  RESTAURANT, 47
Heidelberg Bakery, 166, 190
Heller's Bakery, 86
Heritage India, 42
Hermitage Inn, 122
Hibachi Brothers Japanese
  Restaurant, 91
Hofberg's Deli, 242
Hog's Breath, 169
Hogate's, 42
Hollywood East Café, 216
HoneyBaked Ham
  Company, 261
Hope Key, 123
Horton Cellars Winery, 267
Hotel George
  RESTAURANT, 23
House of Chinese Delights, 217
Houston's, 42, 217
Hunan Chinatown, 43

Hunan Number One, 123
Hunan Palace, 217
Hunan Peking, 43
100 Miles of Lights, 294
Huong Que (Four Sisters
  Restaurant), 123
Huong Viet, 124
Hyatt Arlington
  RESTAURANT, 136
Hyatt Regency Reston
  RESTAURANT, 135
Hyatt Washington (Park)
  RESTAURANT, 53
Hyde Park Plaza
  RESTAURANT, 198

I

Ice House Café, The, 124
Il Forno Pizzeria, 255
Il Borgo (Ristorante), 149
Il Cigno (Ristorante), 149
Il Pinito Trattoria, 217
Il Radicchio, 44, 124
I Matti, 43
India Bistro, 218
Indian Spices & Appliances, 195
Ingleside Plantation
  Vineyards, 267
Inn at Brookeville Farms,
  The, 218
Inn at Glen Echo, 218
Inn at Little Washington,
  The, 125
Inter-Continental
  Washington (Willard)
  RESTAURANT, 79
I Ricchi, 43
Iron Gate Inn Restaurant, 44
Islander Caribbean
  Restaurant & Bar, The, 44
Italian Store, The, 178, 195

J

Jaleo, 45
James River Plantation
  Candlight Carol Tour
  & Dinner, 294
Japan Inn Restaurant, 45
Jasmine Café, 126
Jean-Michel Restaurant, 219
Jefferson Vineyards, 267
Jessie Yan, 79
J. Gilbert's Wood-Fired
  Steaks, 125
J Paul's, 83
Jockey Club, 45
Joe's Noodle House, 219
John F. Kennedy Center for
  the Performing Arts,
  The, RESTAURANT, 66
Johnny's Half Shell, 45
Johnny Rockets, 83, 163
J. R.'s Stockyards Inn, 126
Julia's Empanadas, 93, 100

K

Kabob Place Café & Bakery, 183
Katz's Kosher Supermarket, 242
Kaz Sushi Bistro, 46
Kazan Restaurant, 126
Kefa Café, 241
Kim Son Restaurant, 185
Kinkead's, 46
Kitchen Etc., 200
Knossos, 180
Kohr Brothers, 254
Konami Japanese
   Restaurant, 126
Krispy Kreme Doughnuts, 166
Krupin's, 90

L

La Bergerie, 127
La Chaumière, 46
La Colline, 47
La Côte d'Or Café, 127
La Cuisine, 200
La Provence, 127
Lacoste, Rist, 70
Lafayette, 47
Lake Anna Winery, 267
- Winery Open House, 294
Lakeside Inn, 128
Landwirt Vineyards, 268
Lansdowne Grille, 128
Lansdowne Resort
   RESTAURANT, 128
Latham Hotel, The,
   RESTAURANT, 54
Latin American Festival, 293
L'Auberge Chez François, 129
Lauriol Plaza, 47
Lavandou Restaurant, 48
Lawsons, 100
Layalina, 49
Lazy Sundae, 186
Le Bon Pain, 256
Le Canard, 129
Le Gaulois, 129
Le Jardin, 48
Le Petit Mistral, 130
Le Relais Restaurant
   & Bar à Vin, 130
Lebanese Taverna, 48, 130
- Café, 251
- Market, 183, 196
Ledo Pizza, 94, 188, 255
Lee's Ice Cream & Deli, 187
Legal Sea Foods, 49, 130
Les Délices d'Isabelle, 96
Levante's, 49, 219
Levi's Restaurant
   & Carry-out, 239
Lightfoot, 131
Linden Vineyards, 268
Lindy's Bon Appétit, 84
Linganore Winecellars, 269
Litteri (A.), 98
Little Saigon Vietnamese
   Restaurant, 131

Little Viet Garden, 131
Loew Vineyards, 269
Los Chorros Restaurant, 220
Lost Dog Café, 189
Lotte, 194
Loudoun Valley
   Vineyards, 268
Louisiana Express, 220
Luciano Italian Restaurant
   & Pizzeria, 132
Luigino, 49
Luna Grill & Diner, 84
Luna Park Grille, 163

M

Mabuhay Oriental Store
   & Bakery, 194
MacArthur Beverages, 103
McCormick
   & Schmick's, 50, 132
Madras Palace, 246
Maestro, 132
Maggiano's Little Italy, 133
Maggie Moo's Ice Cream
   & Treatery, 187
Magruder's Grocery, 101, 262
Makoto Restaurant, 50
Malaysia Kopitiam, 51
Malibu Grill, 133
Mama Ayesha's, 51
Mama Lavash, 191
Mamma Lucia, 220
Mandalay Restaurant
   & Café, 221
Mandarin Inn, 133
Manila Café, 134
Marcel's, 51
Marie's Restaurant, 134
Mark's Duck House, 134
Mark's Kitchen, 221
Mark, The, 52
Market Street Bar & Grill, 135
Marketplace Kitchen
   & Coffee, 200
Markette, The, 101
Marrakesh, 52
Marriott (Courtyard by)
   RESTAURANTS, 41, 119
Marvelous Market, 95
Maryland Wine Festival, 293
Matisse Café Restaurant, 52
Matuba, 135, 221
Maxim Palace, 135
Maxim, 258
Mayan Grill & Bar, 136
MCI Center RESTAURANT, 58
Meadow Lark Inn, 222
Mediterranean
   Bakery, 180, 191, 196
Mediterranean House
   of Kabob, 251
Meiwah, 53
Melrose, 53
Memphis Bar-B-Q, 170
Mendocino Grille
   & Wine Bar, 53

Meredyth Vineyards, 268
Merkato Market, 97
MERLOT, 273
Mes Amis Restaurant, 54
Meskerem Ethiopian, 54
Metro 29 Diner, 172
Mexicali Blues, 136
Mezza 9, 136
Mi Peru Restaurante, 222
Michel Richard Citronelle, 54
Mid-Atlantic Wine
    Festival, 282
Mike's American Grill, 136
Mike's Diner & Lounge, 173
Milwaukee Frozen Custard, 187
Minerva Indian Cuisine, 137
Mirage Restaurant, 137
Miss Saigon, 55
Mr. Hibachi, 179
Mr. K's, 55
Misty Mountain Vineyards, 267
Mixtec, 56
Miyagi, 179
Moby Dick House of
    Kabob, 92, 183, 251
Mom's Apple Pie, 191
Momo Taro Sushi, 247
Monarch Hotel, The
    RESTAURANT, 23
Monocle on Capitol
    Hill, The, 56
Montdomaine Cellars, 267
Montpelier Wine Festival, 282
Morrison House Hotel
    RESTAURANT, 118
Morrison-Clark
    Restaurant, The, 57
Morton's of Chicago, 57, 137
Mount Vernon's Wine
    Tasting Festival & Sunset
    Tour, 282
Mountain Cove Vineyards, 267
Mrs. Simpson's, 56
M & S Grill, 50
MUSCADINE, 273, 275
Myanmar Restaurant, 138
Mykonos Grill, 222

Naked Mountain Vineyard, 268
Nam's of Bethesda, 223
Nam-Viet Pho 79, 138
Nathan's, 57
National Capital Barbecue
    Battle, 282
National Cherry Blossom
    Festival, 281
National Hard Crab Derby
    & Fair, The, 293
National ZooFari, 282
Nayeb Kabob Restaurant, 138
Negril, 244
Neisha Thai Cuisine, 139
New Fortune Chinese
    Seafood Restaurant, 223
New Heights, 58

Neyla, 58
NIAGARA, 275
Nibbler, The, 223
Nick & Stef's Steakhouse, 58
Nizam's, 139
NM Café at Neiman
    Marcus, The, 139
Nora, 59
North Mountain Vineyard
    & Winery, 268
Northern Neck Seafood
    Extravaganza, 293
NORTON, 273

O

Oakencroft Vineyard
    & Winery, 267
Oasis Winery, 268
Obelisk, 59
O'Brien's Pit Barbecue, 239
Oceanaire Seafood
    Room, The, 60
O'Connell, Patrick, 125
Okra's Louisiana Bistro, 140
Old Angler's Inn, 224
Old Brogue, an Irish
    Pub, The, 171
Old Ebbitt Grill, 60
Old Europe, 60
Old Glory All-American
    Bar-B-Que, 86
Old Hickory Grille, 170, 240
Old Peking Restaurant, 140
Old Siam Restaurant, 224
Olives, 61
Oodles Noodles, 92, 252
Oriental East, 224
Oriental Regency, The, 140
Original Pancake
    House, The, 236
Osteria Goldoni, 61
Outback Steakhouse, 140, 224
Oval Room, The, 61

P

Pacific, 141
Palena, 62
Palm, 62, 141
Palomino, 62
Pan-Asian Restaurant, 93
Panera Bakery & Café, 167
Pangaud, Gérard, 41
Panjshir, 141
Paolo's, 63, 142
Papa Petrone's, 189
Park Hyatt Washington
    RESTAURANT, 53
Parkway Deli & Restaurant, 242
Pars Famous House
    of Kabob, 142
Pasha Café, 142
Pastry Designs, 238, 256
Pat Troy's Restaurant
    & Pub, 143
Pâtisserie Poupon, 96
Patrick O'Connell, 125

Paul's (J), 83
Paya Thai, 143
Payne's, 173
Peacock Café, 63
Peking Eastern House
  Restaurant, 245
Peking Gourmet Inn, 143
Peking Village, 144
Pentagon Center
  RESTAURANT, 181
Pentagon City Mall
  RESTAURANT, 163
PERRIER, 288
Perry's, 64
Persimmon, An
  American Bistro, 225
Pesce, 64
Petits Plats, 64
P.F. Chang's China Bistro, 144
Philadelphia Cheesesteak
  Factory, 84
Philadelphia Mike's, 164
Phillips Flagship Seafood
  Restaurant, 65
Phillips Seafood Grill, 144
Pho Gourmet, 185
Pho New Saigon Vietnamese
  Restaurant Seafood & Grill, 225
Pho 95, 253
Pho 99 Restaurant, 253
Pho 75, 185, 253
Pho Tay Ho, 186
P. J. Skidoo's, The American
  Way, 144
Pica Deli Gourmet, 178
Picante! The Real Taco, 182
Pie Gourmet, 191
Piedmont Vineyard
  & Winery, 268
PINOT GRIGIO, 275
PINOT NOIR, 273
Pinto & Mazzilli, 225
Pizzeria Paradiso, 94
Planet Wayside, 145
Po Siam Thai Restaurant, 145
POLAND SPRING, 287
Politics & Prose, 88
Pollo Casero, 250
Pollos Inka, 184
Potowmack Landing, 145
PRICING SYSTEM, 8
Prime Rib, The, 65
Primi Piatti Ristorante, 65, 146
Primo Italiano, 178
Prince Michel Vineyards, 267
Prospect Pizza & Pastries, 94
Pruitt's Seafood, 99
Pulcinella Ristorante, 146

Q

Quartermaine Coffee
  Roasters, 257
Queen Bee, 146

R

Radisson-Barcelo Washington
  Hotel RESTAURANT, 39
Ramparts, 164

Rapidan River Vineyards, 267
RATING SYSTEM, 7
Rebec Vineyards, 267
Red Hot & Blue, 170, 240
Red Sage, 65
Red Tomato, 66
Red Tomato Café, 247
Reeves Restaurant & Bakery, 86
Rhodeside Grill, 147
Richard, Michel, 54
Rick's Wine & Gourmet, 202
RIESLING, 275
Rincome Thai Cuisine, 147
Rio Bravo, 147
Rio Grande Café, 147, 226
Rist Lacoste, 70
Ristorante Bonaroti, 148
Ristorante Geranio, 148
Ristorante Il Borgo, 149
Ristorante Il Cigno, 149
Ritchie Center
  RESTAURANTS, 225, 253
Ritz-Carlton, Tysons Corner,
  The RESTAURANT, 132
Robert Wiedmaier, 51
Roberto Donna, 40
Rock Bottom Brewery, 240
Rockbridge Vineyard, 267
Rockland's Barbeque
  & Grilling Company, 87, 170
Rodman's Gourmet
  Foods, 103, 264
Romano's Macaroni Grill, 149
Ronald Reagan International
  Trade Center
  RESTAURANT, 62
Ronald Reagan National
  Airport RESTAURANT, 145
Rose Bower Vineyard
  & Winery, 267
Rose River Vineyards
  & Trout Farm, 267
Rosemary's Thyme Bistro, 149
Roy's Place, 236
Ruan Thai, 226
Ruppert's, 66
Russian Gourmet, 196
Ruth's Chris
  Steak House, 67, 150, 226

S

Sabang, 227
Sahara Grill, 150
Saigon Gourmet, 227
Saigon House Vietnamese
  Restaurant, 150
Saigon Supermarket, 194
Saint Basil Brick Oven Grill, 151
St. Gregory Hotel
  RESTAURANT, 87
St. Regis Washington
  RESTAURANT, 75
Sakoontra Thai Restaurant, 151
Sala Thai, 67, 151
Sam & Harry's, 67, 152
Sam Woo, 227

Samadi Sweets Café, 184
San Marzano, 67
SAN PELLIGRINO, 288
Santa Fe East, 152
SAUVIGNON BLANC, 275
Saveur Restaurant, 68
Sawatdee Thai Restaurant, 152
Schneider's of Capitol Hill, 103
Sea Catch Restaurant
   & Raw Bar, 68
Seasons, 68
Seibel's Restaurant, 227
Sen5es Bakery
   & Restaurant, 69
Sequoia, 69
Serbian Crown
   Restaurant, The, 153
Sesto Senso, 69, 701, 70
Seven Seas, 228
1789 Restaurant, 70
SEYVAL BLANC, 275
Shadwell-Windham Winery, 268
Shalom Kosher, 259
Shamshiry, 153
Shanghai Café, 228
Sharp Rock Vineyards, 268
Shenandoah Valley Hot Air
   Balloon & Wine Festival, 294
Shenandoah Vineyards, 268
Shiney's, 177
Sholl's Colonial Cafeteria, 70
Shula's Steak House, 71
Sign of the Whale, 153
Silesia Wine Cellar, 264
Silver Diner, 173, 237
Silverado, 154
Simply Grill, 184
Smith's (B.), 20
Smith & Wollensky, 71
Smithsonian Folklife
   Festival, 282
SMOKING RESTAURANTS, 10
SOLÉ, 288
South Austin Grill, 154
South Beach Café, 228
SPA, 288
SPARKLING WINES, 276
Spices, 71
Spotted Tavern Winery
   & Dodd Bros. Cider Mill, 268
Springfield Butcher, 198
Star Diner, 237
Star of Siam, 72
Star Thai Cuisine, 154
Stella's, 155
Sticks & Bowls, 93
Stonewall Vineyards
   & Winery, 267
Stratford Motor Lodge
   RESTAURANT, 112
Sudhir Seth, 42
Sukhothai Oriental Market, 194
Summit Station Restaurant

& Brewery, 229
Sunflower Vegetarian
   Restaurant, 186
Supee's Kitchen, 155
Suporn's Thai Restaurant, 229
Sushi-Ko, 72
Sushi Sushi, 248
Sushi-Zen Japanese
   Restaurant, 155
Sutton Place
   Gourmet, 101, 199, 262, 264
Sutton Plaza RESTAURANT, 33
Swedenburg Estate
   Vineyard, 268
Sweet Basil, 229
Sweetwater Tavern, 172
SYRAH, 274
Szechuan Gallery
   Restaurant, 72

T

Tabard Inn RESTAURANT, 73
Taberna del Alabardero, 73
Tachibana, 155
Taco Fiesta, 250
Tahoga, 73
Taipei Tokyo Café, 248
- # 2, 230
Tako Grill, 230
Takoma Park Folk Festival, 293
Tandoori Kabob House, 177
Taqueria Poblano, 182
Tara Thai, 156, 230
Tarara Vineyards
   & Winery, 268
Taste of Bethesda, 293
Taste of DC, 294
Taste of the Nation, 281
Taste of Saigon, 156
Taste of the Town, 282
Tastee Diner, 237
Teaism, 88, 96
Teatro Goldoni, 74
Tel-Aviv Café, 230
Temari Japanese Café, 231
TenPenh, 74
Texas Ribs & BBQ, 240
Thai Basil, 156
Thai Leela, 231
Thai Luang, 157
Thai Market Oriental
   Grocery & Carryout, 258
Thai Noy Restaurant, 157
Thai Old Town, 157
Thai Pilin, 157
Thai Room, 74
T.H.A.I. in Shirlington, 158
Thai Spice Café, 253
Thai Square Restaurant, 158
Thai Town, 75
Thaiphoon, 75
Thanh Thanh, 231
That's Amore, 158, 232
Three Pigs Barbecue, 171
Thyme Square, 232
Tiffin, The Indian Kitchen, 232

Timothy Dean Restaurant
& Bar, 75
Timpano Italian
Chophouse, 233
TIPPING, 10
Tom Sarris' Orleans House, 159
Tomahawk Mill Winery, 268
Tombs, The, 76
Tony & Joe's Seafood, 76
Toro Tapas & Grill, 159
Tortilla Factory, 159
Total Beverage, 202
Totier Creek Vineyard
& Winery, 267
Trader Joe's, 199, 263
TraveLodge (Cherry
Blossom) RESTAURANT, 147
Très Joli, 176, 199
TRINITY, 289
Turning Point Inn, 233
Tuscarora Mill, 159
29 Diner, 173
Two Quail, 76

U

Udupi Palace, 233
Union Street Public House, 160
Upper Crust Bakery, 167

V

Vace Delicatessen, 263
Vegetable Garden, The, 246
VIDAL BLANC, 276
Vidalia, 77
Vienna Inn, The, 164
Viet Royale, 160
Vietnam 75 Noodle
Restaurant, 186
Vigorelli, The, 77
Village Bistro, 160
Vintage Virginia, 282
VIOGNIER, 276
Virginia Wine Festival, 293
VITTEL, 289
Vivo! Ristorante, 77
VOLVIC, 286

W

Wagshal's Delicatessen, 90, 102
Washington Harbour Complex
RESTAURANTS, 69, 76
Washington Irish Festival, 293
Washington Monarch Hotel,
The RESTAURANT, 23
Washington Park Gourmet, 102
WATER SAVVY, 285
Well-Dressed Burrito, The, 91
West End Grill, 234
West 24, 78
Westin Fairfax Hotel,
The RESTAURANT, 45
Westin Grand Hotel,
The RESTAURANT, 30
Wheaton Center

RESTAURANT, 231
Wheaton Manor
- RESTAURANTS, 214, 252
- SHOPS, 257, 259
White Flint Station Center
RESTAURANTS, 246, 251
White Hall Vineyards, 267
White Tiger, The, 78, 161
Wiedmaier, Robert, 51
Willard Inter-Continental
Washington RESTAURANT, 79
Willard Room, The, 79
Williams-Sonoma, 200
Williamsburg Winery, 267
Willie & Reed's, 241
Willowcroft Farm
Vineyards, 268
Windy River Winery, 267
WINE
- EVENTS, 281
- GLOSSARY OF GRAPES, 272
- GLOSSARY OF TASTING
TERMS, 271
- PAIRINGS, 277
- SAVVY, 266
- TOURING, 266
- VINTAGE CHART, 270
Wine Seller, The, 202
Wintergreen Vineyards
& Winery, 267
Wok Inn, 234
Wok & Roll Chinese Café, 176
Woodhall Vineyards, 269
Woodlands, 247
Woodmont Station
RESTAURANT, 244
Wrap Works, 87, 164
Wurzburg Haus Restaurant, 234
Wyndham City Center Hotel
RESTAURANT, 71

X

Xando, 88

Y

Yama Japanese Restaurant, 161
Yan, Jessie, 79
Yanyu, 79
Yekta Deli Imported
Grocery, 260
York Castle Tropical
Ice Cream, 254
Yuan Fu Vegetarian, 246
Yum Yum Ice Cream Café, 188

Z

Zanzibar on the
Waterfront, 79
Zed's Ethiopian Restaurant, 80
Zeffirelli, 161
ZINFANDEL, 274
Zorba's Café, 80
Zuki Moon, 80

ABOUT GAYOT

Gayot/GaultMillau travel and restaurant guidebooks have provided readers with a map to the good life for over 40 years, setting standards for accuracy, frankness and wit in their reviews. *The Best of* series gives travelers comprehensive information on restaurants, hotels, shopping, nightlife, sports and leisure in such popular destinations as London, Paris, New York City, Los Angeles/Southern California, Chicago, New Orleans, Hawaii and more. Guidebooks in the Gayot *Restaurants* series cater to food-lovers, offering insightful reviews and ratings of dining establishments and an extensive selection of the area's gourmet food and wine shops. Our *Restaurants* series covers the scene in New York, Los Angeles, San Francisco and other U.S. cities.

ON THE INTERNET

Gayot provides the latest up-to-date information on food, wine and travel at its web site, **GAYOT.com.** Food connoisseurs can surf the site for all kinds of culinary recommendations, from new cookbooks and products to food and wine events worldwide. Through Gayot's partnership with America Online's local interface, Digital City, the dining scene all across the United States is at your fingertips, presenting the latest restaurant news and reviews from New York to San Francisco, Chicago to New Orleans and points between. At **GAYOT.com**, wine fanciers can find tasting notes and information about boutique wineries worldwide. Travelers can tap into our experts' reviews about the Top Ten hotels in major destinations from London to Hawaii and can journey with us to such exotic destinations as Bora Bora and the Amazon.

Visit **GAYOT.com** or **America Online Keyword: GAYOT** for your ticket to essential food, wine and travel information.

SPECIAL SALES

Gayot guidebooks are available at discounts for bulk purchases, direct sales or premiums. They make a great gift that will put your name in front of important clients over and over again—and at a small cost.

- Orders over 1,000 can be customized with your logo on the cover at no extra charge.

Call our toll-free number for information and orders:

1 (800) 532-3781

Or e-mail us at gayots@aol.com

GAYOT